Prairie Spirit

Prairie Spirit:
Perspectives on the Heritage of the United Church of Canada in the West

DENNIS L. BUTCHER

CATHERINE MACDONALD

MARGARET E. MCPHERSON

RAYMOND R. SMITH

A. MCKIBBIN WATTS

Editors

THE UNIVERSITY OF MANITOBA PRESS

© The University of Manitoba Press 1985

Printed in Canada

Canadian Cataloguing in Publication Data

Main entry under title:
Prairie spirit

ISBN 0-88755-614-0

1. United Church of Canada – History –
Addresses, essays, lectures.   2. Prairie
Provinces – Church history – Addresses,
essays, lectures.   I. Butcher, Dennis L.
(Dennis Lloyd), 1948–
BX9881.P73 1985   287′.92′09712   C85-091123-0

Contents

Foreword
by The Right Rev. Robert F. Smith

One of the benefits of such brief notoriety as I am experiencing these days is the plethora of reminders of my history which arrive in the daily post. Pictures of my parents when they were "courting" accompany letters from their childhood friends. A distant cousin encloses a refined edition of the family tree that tells me of my links with Ushers and Kilkerrys, and of high drama, a century and a half ago in County Cork, when the Catholic stable boy eloped with the Protestant squire's young daughter. A Manitoba minister encloses a photostat of my wife's great-great-grandfather's strong handwriting on a page from the baptismal register of the Methodist Church where he was minister a century ago.

We are richer for our archives. Blessed by the news of those who have gone before us, whose genes swim in our cells and whose foibles are engrained in our psyches, we need to remember that we too have a responsibility to pass the archive along.

I commend the Archives Committee of the Conference of Manitoba and Northwestern Ontario for this imaginative approach to the task of remembering and I pray, as the apostle Paul said, that "since we are surrounded by so great a cloud of witnesses, we may also lay aside every weight and sin which clings so closely, and run with patience the race that is set before us, looking to Jesus, the pioneer and perfecter of our faith who, for the joy that was set before him, endured the cross, despising the shame, and is seated at the right hand of the throne of God."

The Right Rev. Robert F. Smith
Moderator
United Church of Canada

Foreword
by The Rev. Robert P. Hamlin

A parent is normally surprised and always proud when one of the offspring does more than is expected. The Archives Committee is a child of our conference and, if we are not surprised, we are certainly proud of what they have done in our name: a substantial book on *our* story!

Few of us have much of a hold on most of the elements in that story. As one who has had close contact for many years with the Grace Church Fund, I have known something about one of the churches that was once important in Winnipeg and which, through the fund, still affects us. Many other events, people and churches from the past likely affect us still, although most of us are unaware of them. This book will allow us to be more aware.

I congratulate the Publication Sub-Committee of the Archives Committee on a job well done, and on behalf of the conference thank them and all the contributors for putting us in touch with the people and events in our past which will enable us to move into the future more conscious of our heritage.

The Rev. Robert P. Hamlin
President
Conference of Manitoba and Northwestern Ontario

Preface

The book that you hold in your hands began as an idea during the summer of 1981. It was an idea that came to the Archives Committee of the Conference of Manitoba and Northwestern Ontario, and was prompted by the sixtieth anniversary of the United Church of Canada's formation to be celebrated in 1985. The committee felt the anniversary could be the occasion for the publishing of a book on the history of the United Church and its founding denominations in Manitoba and the West. The purpose of the book, beyond the celebrative one, would be to encourage the writing and reading of Manitoba and western Canadian church history, and to make known the resources of the Conference Archives located at the University of Winnipeg Library. Accordingly, a sub-committee was formed to bring the idea to fruition. Here it is.

Some of the articles contained in the book have been written by professional historians; others have been done by those who would describe themselves as amateur historians; still others have been written by people who fall somewhere between those two categories. With this variety we have aimed to reach a middle ground stylistically; we've tried to produce sound, well-researched but readable articles that can appeal to historians as well as to members of the general public. And even though this is a celebrative volume, we hope it is also an honest one. Our intention has been to present a true account of some aspects of our history on the prairies.

The collection has been organized chronologically into three identifiable eras: the early period, the developmental or extension period, and the church union period. Within the major articles we have attempted to be faithful to the three traditions which make up our heritage as a united church: Methodist, Presbyterian and Congregational. Most articles bring to light new material or interpretations hitherto unpublished.

The story begins with Gerald Hutchinson's account of the arrival of the first Methodist missionaries, Evans, Mason, Rundle and Barnley, to the area of Rupert's Land, and of the foundation which they laid that continues strong in our native communities to this day. John Badertscher interprets that story from the point of view of other major institutions in the West: the Hudson's Bay Company and the Anglican and Roman Catholic Churches. Our Presbyterian heritage in the West originates with John Black, pioneer missionary to the Red River settlement, as told by James Marnoch.

Articles about the developmental period begin with Catherine Macdonald's contribution on Presbyterian Church extension under James Robertson; they continue with Benjamin Smillie's work about the Woodsworths, father and son, contrasting their different but major influences on the Methodist Church of their time. The story of the Congregationalists in Manitoba is told here for the very first time by Clark Saunders. In an article by Margaret McPherson, the place of the Presbyterian Women's Missionary Society in the development of feminism is highlighted. Gordon Harland, in his article on John Mark King, points to the strong intellectual heritage with which Manitoba College and the Church was blessed in these formative years. In an article on the Presbyterian Women's Missionary Society's school-homes for Ruthenian children, Michael Owen explores the Church's attempt to assimilate and "Canadianize" non–Anglo-Saxon immigrants. Carol Hancock tells of the relationship between Nellie McClung, one of the West's most ardent early feminists, and our church. The place of "social gospel" in the heritage of the United Church is explored in Richard Allen's article on Salem Bland, Canada's pre-eminent exponent of this movement. The Labor Church, a unique manifestation of the social gospel in Manitoba and its strong ties with Methodism, is discussed by Vera Fast.

Gerald Friesen looks at the central role that J.H. Riddell, Principal of Wesley College, had in the life of the Church in the pre- and post-union periods. The hitherto untold story of the place of the United Church and its antecedents in providing medical services in Manitoba is the subject of Raymond Smith's chapter. Keith Clifford concludes the section of major articles with his research on the role of the founding denominations in the West on the church union movement.

The short articles which appear after the section of major articles present very briefly the stories of six of our congregations, a sampling of the kaleidoscope which makes up our church in this conference. A photo essay by Donald Ross, which appears at the beginning of the book, illustrates some aspects of the architectural heritage of our church. In the appendix section, we have included a select bibliographic listing of the resources for research on the United Church in Manitoba and northwestern Ontario: Neil Semple lists the holdings in the national United Church Archives in Toronto; and Catherine Macdonald lists those in the conference's own archives, which are housed at the University of Winnipeg Library.

If we have passed over many aspects of the story it is not because we consider them unimportant. The themes covered herein have been determined largely through the process of identifying people willing to contribute to the book. Thus there are important areas that are not touched and which we hope will soon be taken up by others. A few examples are the deaconess order, inner city missions, native residential schools, and the effect on the Church of the Depression and the world wars.

There are many people to whom we are indebted. Our contributors have been willing to spend hours of work on their articles without any remuneration. The Conference of Manitoba and Northwestern Ontario Executive trusted us enough to agree to be "publisher and banker" of a project that was at that point still only an idea. We have received grants from the G.B. King Trust Fund of the national United Church Archives, from the Book Publishing Fund of the Division of Communications of the United Church of Canada, from the Mrs. James A. Richardson Foundation, and from the Department of Culture, Heritage and Recreation of the Province of Manitoba. Without this support the book would not have been possible. A number of professional historians have willingly served as referees for all our major articles. Adena Franz, our editorial assistant, has carried out the day-to-day work of the Committee in the final stages with remarkable effectiveness. Our stylistic editor, Carol Dahlstrom, has done exceptional editorial work on the whole book. Our relationship with the University of Manitoba Press has been ably facilitated by its director, Patricia Dowdall, who encouraged us throughout the preparation and production of the book.

We hope that all our readers will enjoy and benefit from our sixtieth anniversary publication. Having unearthed parts of our story which have hitherto gone untold, we trust that others will be stimulated to continue the task as we seek to understand the heritage which is ours.

Publication Sub-Committee:
Dennis L. Butcher, Chair
Catherine Macdonald
Margaret E. McPherson
Raymond R. Smith
A. McKibbin Watts

Prairie Spirit

A guided tour of church architecture in the Conference of Manitoba and Northwestern Ontario: A photo essay

Donald Ross

United Church people tend to take the buildings in which they worship for granted. We love the familiar eccentricities of our own local church, likely because we have given donations and held bake sales to get the church carpeted or have the ceiling painted. But we seldom reflect on the beauty or lack of it in our neighbouring churches. We do not think about whether there is a United Church architectural style or whether there is something special about the spaces we create for worship. Do the buildings we erect say something about our identity as a community of faith? This guided tour is intended to be a preliminary exploration of this question using buildings in our own region, past and present. These buildings are not necessarily the most beautiful of our built heritage, but they are representative of styles we have embraced over the last century. Nor is this survey exhaustive. It is intended to stimulate the visual appetite, not satisfy it, and the questions it raises are more important than the questions it answers.

St. Stephen's-Broadway Church, Winnipeg, built 1907. This is the original Broadway Methodist Church, Winnipeg, dressed for Christmas. Note the communion rail with offering plates. The pulpit antependium, with its three Greek crosses, is rather more sophisticated than was typical of the period. (Photo courtesy of St. Stephen's-Broadway United Church.)

St. Stephen's-Broadway Church, Winnipeg, built 1907. In a remarkably successful renovation of the chancel in 1952, the choir was divided into two sections facing each other, the communion table was positioned at the rear of the apse, the centre window above it was enlarged and all three filled with stained glass. Most photographs of this fine interior were destroyed in the fire which deprived Winnipeg of one of its most impressive church buildings in 1968. (Photo courtesy of St. Stephen's-Broadway United Church.)

St. Stephen's-Broadway Church, Winnipeg, built 1970. The interior of the new St. Stephen's Broadway Church, constructed following the fire which destroyed the former building on the same site in 1968. Designed as a multi-purpose facility with moveable partitions, the seating in one part is stationary, while the seating in the other area is moveable. The entire structure is characterized by the imaginative use of wood, metal, glass, stone and textiles. (Photo courtesy of St. Stephen's-Broadway United Church.)

St. Paul's Church, Boissevain, Manitoba, built 1893. An attractive building built of locally quarried stone, St. Paul's, Boissevain, with its worship center placed in one corner and its pews radiating diagonally across the floor to the main entrance in the opposite corner, is constructed according to the "Akron plan" much favoured in the period. First Church, Brandon (now demolished), with its overflow–Sunday School wing was a perfect realization of the Akron ideal. (Photo courtesy of Adena Franz/United Church Archives, Winnipeg.)

St. Andrew's Church, Elgin Ave., Winnipeg, built 1895. The dramatic fire of 1968 took from the people of St. Andrew's Elgin, Winnipeg, their home of seventy-five years and gave them the impetus to build, in 1975, St. Andrew's Place. The old church housed one of the early organs of the city – a fine Casavant instrument purchased in 1903 and powered by water until 1949 when the action was electrified. (Photo courtesy of Western Canada Pictorial Index.)

St. Andrew's Place, Winnipeg, built 1975. St. Andrew's Place, Winnipeg. The congregation of St. Andrews's Elgin shares this building with apartment dwellers and business tenants, and for worship makes use of a multi-purpose room, located on the main floor, which is visible from the street. (Photo courtesy of Adena Franz/United Church Archives, Winnipeg.)

Regent's Park Church, Winnipeg, built 1958. Regent's Park, Winnipeg, is a church clearly built to provide space for liturgical worship. Note the spacious chancel and the sedilia for the elders at Communion. (Photo courtesy of Adena Franz/United Church Archives, Winnipeg.)

Regent's Park Church, Winnipeg, built 1958. Uncommon in United Churches, the choir and organ of Regent's Park, Winnipeg, are located in the west gallery. (Photo courtesy of Adena Franz/United Church Archives, Winnipeg.)

Young Church, Winnipeg, built 1911. Spacious and blessed with excellent acoustics, Young Church, Winnipeg, has for years accommodated concerts, festivals, conferences and great gatherings. The openness of the interior space and the careful avoidance of "mystery" are typical of church buildings of its age, style and tradition. Visual interest is offered by the polychromed ceiling and the powerful sweep of the arches. The total effect of the building is to be experienced only in the gallery in the midst of a crowd. (Photo courtesy of Greg McCullough/United Church Archives, Winnipeg.)

Crescent–Fort Rouge Church, Winnipeg, built 1911. With the exception of the recently acquired communion table, the furnishings and structure of this Methodist tabernacle in Romanesque style remain today virtually the way they were when the building was erected in 1911 and this photograph was taken. The arches above the gallery are particularly fine, and the organ, a splendid Casavant of 1913, is voiced along nineteenth-century French lines – rare in a prairie church. (Photo courtesy of Crescent–Fort Rouge United Church.)

Stella Mission (All Peoples' United Church), Winnipeg, built 1909. Simple, with liturgical furnishings nicely scaled to the apse-like worship area, Stella's design deserves attention by other congregations considering building or remodelling. (Photo courtesy of Adena Franz/ United Church Archives, Winnipeg.)

Rosedale Church, Winnipeg, built 1957. Long and narrow, a "processional" church of the style popular in the 1950s, Rosedale was originally designed to accommodate a divided choir in the chancel. The choir has since been moved to face the congregation and the communion table has been brought forward – a return to a setting with which United Church congregations appear to be more comfortable. (Photo courtesy of Adena Franz/United Church Archives, Winnipeg.)

James Evans Memorial Church (Rossville), Norway House, Manitoba, built 1932. The first Methodist mission in the Canadian Northwest was established at Norway House in 1840. This church stands as a tribute to the first chairman of the Norway House District of the Wesleyan Church, the Rev. James Evans. James Evans perfected a system of Cree syllabics – a flexible method of writing which allowed the Scriptures to be rendered into nearly all the regional tongues from Hudson Bay to the Mackenzie River. Evans died in England in 1846; his remains were brought, after World War II, to the church in Norway House which bears his name. (Photo courtesy of United Church Archives, Winnipeg.)

Westminster Church, Winnipeg, built 1912. Westminster Church, with its broad stone stairs, its walls and towers crowding the corner and dominating the landscape, splendidly typifies the faith and human values of its time and place. No longer is there the confidence that the world and its systems can be explained and dealt with in as straightforward a fashion as the exterior of this building suggests. The outside of Westminster says "cathedral"; the interior, however, says "auditorium" – a conflict integral to virtually all buildings of the uniting churches of the period. While this conflict is disturbing, it does leave open the possibility that all is not in fact settled, and that security is not to be sought in things made with hands. These church buildings thus, paradoxically, manage to bring under judgement the kind of idolatry they encourage. Westminster has a treasure in its organ – a four-manual, uncompromisingly romantic Casavant which is one of the finest of its type anywhere. (Photo courtesy of Adena Franz/United Church Archives, Winnipeg.)

Crestview Church, Winnipeg, built 1979. All the furnishings in this multi-purpose building are moveable, and the modular platform can be relocated or removed altogether. The cantilevered ceiling, the stained glass behind the font and the pipe organ in the rear of the room contribute colour and interest to a simple and functional worship space. (Photo courtesy of Adena Franz/United Church Archives, Winnipeg.)

Trinity Church, Thunder Bay, Ontario, built 1905. The communion table was given new prominence when Trinity's platform was redesigned. The divided choir faces the congregation and represents a not uncommon compromise. The furnishings are richly carved and the total effect is very pleasing. (Photo courtesy of Janet Buckley/United Church Archives, Winnipeg.)

Westworth Church, Winnipeg, built 1959. Quite likely the finest of the A-frame church buildings so popular twenty or thirty years ago, Westworth possesses an enviable lightness and a quality of repose rare in United Churches; nothing is crowded, overdone or in the way. The glass in the east window, the work of Winnipeg artist and sculptor Leo Mol, depicts the Last Supper. A non-scriptural, but not inappropriate, lamb appears on the table in this window. The fine glass in the south-aisle chapel, also by Mol, should be noted especially by those interested in church history. (Photo courtesy of Adena Franz/United Church Archives, Winnipeg.)

Island Lake Church (Garden Hill), Island Lake, Manitoba, built 1977. The most recent of the native churches in the north, this building was constructed following its predecessor's destruction by fire. This new church represents a return to architectural values which are more traditional than those characteristic of the older building it replaced. (Photo courtesy of Conference of Manitoba and Northwestern Ontario/United Church Archives, Winnipeg.)

Grace Church, Winnipeg, built 1883. Nothing about the exterior of this building, built in 1883 and demolished in 1957, indicates the purpose for which it was built and used; it housed, however, the parent congregation of English prairie Methodism and the first classes of Wesley College. In this photograph, the pioneer Presbyterian congregation in Winnipeg, Knox Church, can be seen around the corner in one of its earlier incarnations. (Photo courtesy of St. Stephen's-Broadway United Church.)

Grace Church, Winnipeg, built 1883 (closed 1955). The front of Grace Church, with its wide pulpit platform and its choir situated almost at gallery level, is a classic example of an urban Methodist church of the late nineteenth century. Characteristic also is the attractive pierced-wood screen around the pulpit and the intentional elimination of explicit symbols throughout the auditorium. A scriptural proclamation such as that above the organ was virtually manda-tory then: all things, in a church of the Word, must submit to a text. (Photo courtesy of United Church Archives, Winnipeg.)

Knox Church, Winnipeg, built 1917. The fourth of the Knox Church buildings, this elegant Gothic structure was completed, at a cost of $350,000, in 1917. Best viewed from Central Park across the street, Knox invests the changing human scene before it with a sense of permanence. Due to structural defects, the pinnacles surmounting the main towers have been removed – an unfortunate necessity which seriously mars the effect of the building. (Photo courtesy of United Church Archives, Winnipeg.)

Little Britain Church, Little Britain, Manitoba, built 1874. Established in 1852, Little Britain is the oldest United Church of Presbyterian origin in the Canadian West. This stone building, dedicated in 1874 and still in regular use, was built facing the Red River since the river was an important means of access then. The cemetery in which the church is set records the toll taken by whooping cough, typhoid, diphtheria, consumption, pneumonia and freezing. That so many children and young wives were among the victims is a sad surprise. (Photo courtesy of Adena Franz/United Church Archives, Winnipeg.)

Carman Church, Carman, Manitoba, built 1907. Often overlooked details are among the finer features of many church buildings, as this window in Carman Church, with its chastity of design and graceful tracery, indicates. (Photo courtesy of Carman United Church.)

Dauphin Plains Church, Dauphin Plains, Manitoba, built 1910. The fir ceiling of the Dauphin Plains church gave an unpretentious frame structure unexpected richness. (Photo courtesy of Donald Ross.)

British Methodists and the Hudson's Bay Company, 1840–1854

Gerald Hutchinson

In January 1840 the Hudson's Bay Company (the Company) and the British Wesleyan Missionary Society (the Society) entered into an unusual partnership. They agreed that "the Mission shall appoint three of their Missionaries to proceed to the Company's Territories . . . [one at Moose Factory, one near Norway House, and third on the Saskatchewan River]. The salaries . . . to be paid by the Society, the conveying, . . . Board and lodging in the country paid by the Company."[1] This cooperative venture survived the conflicting expectations of the Society and the Company, as well as the normal tensions between fur trader and missionary, to leave a significant and enduring legacy to western Canada.

The full story of the British Wesleyan Mission within the Hudson's Bay territory has yet to be told. Until recently the major documents have not been available and, as a result, legends have developed around the mission and its most controversial figure, Superintendent James Evans. Three books have been written about Evans and in each he is presented as the victim of a vicious conspiracy by the Company and by his missionary assistant, the Rev. William Mason.[2]

The true story is less dramatic but more interesting. In this article I present a fresh appraisal of the mission and of the controversy surrounding the career of James Evans.

WHY THEN (1840)?
AND WHY THEM (THE BRITISH METHODISTS)?

By the 1840s, the European and Métis population of the West was increasing rapidly, creating a growing need for religious, educational and medical services. American settlers and their missionaries were also beginning to move north into the territory of the Hudson's Bay Company. Although the Company had repeatedly refused the requests of the Roman Catholic Church to send missionaries through its lands, in 1838 it made an exception for Fathers Blanchet and Demers. The Company conveyed them through its territory enroute to Oregon giving them missionary privileges at the posts en route, possibly hoping to counter the influence of the Americans.

The Roman Catholics were eager to send missionaries into the Northwest where more and more of the French and Catholic Métis of Red River were beginning to settle. However, the governor of the Hudson's Bay Company, George Simpson, was concerned about the strong influence the missionaries might have on people in the Company's territory as well as the tensions between French and English. He continued to refuse the Catholic Church's requests for expansion.[3]

The Roman Catholic Church was not the only church wanting to expand to the west and north of the Red River Settlement. The Church of England was well established in the colony and wanted to expand, but the bequest designated to support the expansion was disputed, and the funds were held in chancery for ten years, delaying the Church's plans.

The Methodists of Upper Canada were also interested in serving the West. In 1838, two ministers, the Rev. James Evans and the Rev. Thomas Hurlburt, made an exploratory trip along the north shore of Lake Superior and into Company territory. They met with George Simpson to request that they be allowed to open a mission, then returned east to await his decision.

When George Simpson decided to open the territory to missionaries, he looked not to the local churches of Red River, nor to the churches of Upper Canada, but to England. He came to an agreement with the secretary of the British Wesleyan Missionary Society, Dr. Robert Alder, who was a close personal friend, that the Company would support three missionaries chosen by the Society. Although their friendship probably made it easier to reach such an agreement, it also led to a sense of uneasiness in the Society about the terms of the agreement. As the Wesleyan Society reported, "This was the first Canadian Governor to show an open mind toward Methodist work and to deal courteously with its representatives. His friendship with Dr. Alder went so far as to cause misgivings in Alder's own church."[4]

The agreement reached by Simpson and Alder was to place three missionaries in widely separated forts on the Saskatchewan River, on Hudson Bay and at Norway House. If the missionary were single, he would have a room in the fort and take his meals at the mess table. If he were married, the Company was to provide a separate house. Three young men were quickly chosen by the

Society for this assignment: George Barnley, William Mason and Robert Rundle. They were ordained in London on 8 March 1840; they preached at a special service in Liverpool on 15 March and the following day they embarked for Montreal, via New York.

In the meantime, authorities of the Methodist Conference were having some misgivings about sending three young missionaries to isolated posts with no supervision. In April 1840, the Rev. Joseph Stinson, Toronto-based secretary of the Society, summoned the Rev. James Evans, who had tried to convince Governor Simpson two years earlier to open his territory to missions, and assigned him to the mission party as superintendent. Evans was well qualified for the position and an obvious choice, the only surprise being the late and hasty summons. Born in England, Evans had taught school in Lower Canada, was married and had one child before being ordained in 1833. He served at Rice Lake, the Credit Mission and the St. Clair Mission. He was deeply involved in working with the native people, learning their languages and fostering the printing of hymns and texts in their languages. Before moving to the West, he chose two men to assist him: Peter Jacobs, a native preacher, and Henry Steinhauer, a native teacher.

The appointment of Evans changed the original plan and led to some difficulties. First, travel arrangements were bungled. Evans was instructed to meet the three British missionaries in Montreal by 2 May, in time to travel west with the Company's spring brigade. But the brigade expected to meet Evans at Sault Ste. Marie.[5] Taking advantage of an early spring breakup, the brigade left Montreal on April 23. Evans arrived the next day, and so had to make his own way to Norway House at extra cost and with a two-month delay. Second, the mission party was now expanded from three to eight with the addition of Mr. and Mrs. Evans and daughter Clarissa, Peter Jacobs and Henry Steinhauer. Third, the placement of the additional missionaries complicated the schedule. Mason was now assigned to Lac la Pluie but when he arrived with the spring brigade, he was surprised to find Jacobs and Steinhauer already there.

Fourth, and of deepest significance, the mission now had a superintendent. Instead of having three young men widely dispersed under Company supervision, the responsibility of the mission was vested in James Evans, a potential rival to the authority of Simpson.

Nevertheless, by October 1840, Rundle was at Fort Edmonton, Barnley at Moose Factory, Mason and Steinhauer at Lac la Pluie, Evans and Jacobs at Norway House. The British Wesleyan Mission within Hudson's Bay territory had begun.

THE EARLY YEARS OF THE MISSION

James Evans was thirty-nine years old and at the peak of his career as he entered Norway House in July 1840. He had had experience at sea, in business and in teaching. He had been ordained for seven years, serving in various Indian missions in Upper Canada. He had demonstrated his linguistic genius in translating and printing in the Ojibwa language. Working with others, he had developed a syllabic alphabet for Ojibwa. Although this alphabet was rejected by the British and Foreign Bible Society, it no doubt served as the base for the Cree syllabic he created within months of his arrival in Norway House. His enthusiasm, dedication and wide-ranging interest won the initial admiration of Donald Ross, chief factor at Norway House.

For the first two years, the Evans family lived in the fort, and from there developed the mission at Rossville, the native community a few miles north. The mission developed quickly and impressively. The Cree syllabic spread steadily over the entire region. Evans seemed tireless in his extensive travels to understand and serve his immense district. One of his first priorities was to translate the Bible into Cree. John Sinclair, a local leader educated in English and Cree, and Henry Steinhauer, who had received a classical education, proved to be invaluable assistants. The publication process, however, was slow and tedious. Type was prepared and shipped from England, but the press required to print the book was delayed for five years.

William Mason, who had originally gone to Lac la Pluie with Henry Steinhauer, joined Evans at the Rossville Mission and gradually became skilled in the use of the syllabic and in the expanding program of printing. In time, the Rossville Mission Press became a highly successful venture of far-reaching influence.

The other two missionaries from England had much less contact with their superintendent. George Barnley had met Evans only briefly in Lachine before he went to Moose Factory, arriving just before his twenty-third birthday. He was well received by the Company officials at Rupert's House and Fort George on the East Coast, at Fort Albany on the West Coast, and Abitibi to the south. He developed an ambitious "plan for educating," and devised an alphabet based on Byron's stenography before finally adopting the syllabic form that Evans had created soon after his arrival in Norway House. He returned to England in 1844 to be married, and then went back to Moose Factory with his bride. Mrs. Barnley shared with enthusiasm in the school and the visiting of homes but complications soon developed which entirely frustrated the mission. Her first pregnancy and miscarriage left her weakened and an invalid. The separate house promised for the married missionary was not yet built, and the close confines of the fort became intolerable. Barnley could not undertake the extended trips to other forts as he had done while he was single. Hostilities between Chief Factor Robert Miles and Barnley made further work impossible, so the missionaries returned to England in 1847 and released their bitter complaints to the press.

However, there were positive and permanent effects of Barnley's seven years' work. Foundations had been laid for Christian communities, his comprehensive "plan for educating" had been introduced, and many individuals had been influenced by his work. Seventy years later, the Venerable Archdeacon of Saskatchewan John A. MacKay said, "I think of George Barnley as my spiritual father."[6]

Robert Rundle was twenty-nine years old on his arrival at Norway House where he had the great advantage of two months under the genial and encouraging influence of Chief Factor Ross, and a few weeks with Evans. The Indian communities gave him a friendly welcome and a surprisingly ready response. He gained two insights of major importance to his future work: "July 21, 1840. . . . What a contrast between my feelings now and on my first undertaking the journey to this wilderness. Then the thought of an Indian was almost accompanied by terror and dread. But now my chief delight is to be with them."[7] And he learned that when he "went to them," visited them on their own terms in their own settlement, they responded warmly.

The mission was firmly established by 7 September when he left with the Fall Brigade for the long trip to Fort Edmonton. Chief Factor John Rowand, a Roman Catholic, was not much pleased at having a minister in the fort, but received him kindly.

In November 1841, Evans visited Fort Edmonton where he enlisted the assistance of Chief Trader J.E. Harriott in translating the Cree, and where he taught Rundle the newly created Cree syllabic. Learning the Cree language was a slow and difficult process for Rundle, but the amazing Cree syllabic, which simply expressed Cree sound in symbolic form, could be learned in hours. He now had an invaluable tool for communication. Texts, hymns and prayers translated into Cree, written in syllabic form, could be readily copied into "Sunday books." An interested Indian could learn the syllabic quickly and read the Sunday books to his entire camp in their own language.

Rundle was surprised, and his work profoundly affected by the unexpected arrival of Father Thibeault in June 1842. Governor Simpson and Rowand were both out of the country when Thibeault was sent in without consent or support of the Company. (The Company continued to refuse transportation and accommodation to the Roman Catholic priests even after the agreement with the Methodists had been made.) After a period of painful adjustment, Rundle found substantial areas of support amongst the natives south of Edmonton and eventually developed a degree of friendly association with the priests. The pattern of Methodist and Roman Catholic missions continued for thirty-five years before the arrival of Anglican or Presbyterian missionaries.

Rundle's promised furlough was cancelled in 1844, and again in 1845, and in 1846, he travelled as far as Fort Carlton before learning that Evans had gone to England and that he must stay on. By 1847 he had the approval for a mission site and had given up the thought of going to England. But in 1848 he broke his arm in a fall from a horse, and he went to England for assistance. His hopes of returning to the Company territories were frustrated by the decision of the British Wesleyans to transfer the missions to the Canada Conference of the Methodist Church.

In 1858 Captain Palliser led a scientific expedition through the West, and was so impressed by the influence of Rundle on the Indian communities that he named the now famous Mount Rundle in the Banff townsite after him. His name and memory are now preserved in the names of churches, schools and parks, and in the Memorial Rundle's Mission at Pigeon Lake, Alberta.

THE RECALL OF JAMES EVANS

Norway House and Rossville were the nerve centres for both the Company and the mission. Tensions experienced elsewhere assumed critical proportions here as Superintendent Evans met with Chief Factor Ross every day, and confronted Governor Simpson in his annual visit and report. Furthermore the majority of the Mission party was located in or near Norway House – Evans and Mason, Jacobs and Steinhauer, and the local leaders, Thomas Hassall, John Sinclair and Ben Sinclair.

This tension between the Company and the Mission eventually led to Evans' recall to England in June 1846. The circumstances of the recall were greatly worsened, however, by charges of sexual misconduct made against Evans for which he was tried and acquitted in February 1846. William Mason presided over the trial.

Canadian Methodists were deeply distressed by the surprising events of 1846. They knew of the dedication and competence of Evans from his work in Upper Canada. They learned with pride of the developments at Rossville although they had scanty communication with the mission. They were shocked by the scandalous rumours and by his sudden removal to England, and by his death in November 1846. They had no access to Company records, and the British Methodists refused to share their information, so the Canadians were left guessing. Dr. Ephraim Evans, brother of the late James, summed up their understanding, and provided the clue which eventually led to severe distortions of the story. He wrote in 1865: "As regards the difficulty into which you allude that 'It has been hinted that he fell into disgrace &c', you have been misinformed in supposing that the HB Co. were prominent if at all connected with the attempt to blast his reputation. At least I have no evidence of that. . . . I have reason to believe that the attempt to injure his moral character was made by an assistant [William Mason] to the mission, who soon after left our work, and became a Puseyite ultra."[8]

The correspondence now available reveals a much different story. The Company did continue to support the mission, and to write congratulatory reports. But behind the scenes, the extensive private correspondence between Ross and Simpson reveals the growing concerns and increasing hostility of the Company officials, especially towards Evans.[9] Simpson felt that Evans's zeal went far beyond religious matters to the point of interference in Company policy. The simple policy of board and lodging being provided by the Company became an intolerable grievance at Norway House where six to eight people had unlimited claim on the strictly monitored supply of imported food. The Wesleyan opposition to Sunday travelling was a continuing source of tension, in spite of the numerous attempts to reduce it. By 1845 the matter had become critical and explosive. The Indians were caught between their loyalty to Ross who employed them, and Evans who instructed them. After a lengthy involved dispute, Ross was unable to get a crew to take him to the meeting of the Company Council in the Red River Settlement. Evans had also begun to challenge their monopoly in supplying goods by dealing with the free traders. The Company was infuriated by the reports that Evans had advised the Indian hunters that they were entitled to give furs to their relatives if they wished, and even to sell outside the Company. Evans denied issuing any such advice, and in turn, sent them "a decided remonstrance against the course you have adopted in trying to coerce the people of our Charge into disobedience of the Divine Law." Evans added that if the Company refused to employ native Christians, "we shall find them employment at the Society's expense."[10]

On 16 June 1845, Simpson wrote to Dr. Alder, the secretary of the Wesleyan Missionary Society:

I am deeply pained to see that the Rev'd Mr. Evans has in public and in private, in writing and in conversation, represented us not only to our people but also to the Indians as unfriendly to the very establishment for which we have so spontaneously made so many sacrifices. . . . I have observed his proceeding with growing solicitude and dissatisfaction, hoping that experience might temper his zeal with discretion, but I have just now received a letter of so insidious a tendency as to render further forbearance incompatible with my official obligations. In a word . . . recall Mr. Evans.[11]

Needless to say, Evans knew nothing of such a development. it is worth noting also that this decision was made before there was any hint of sexual impropriety, and that Mason was not at all involved except that, as Simpson reported to Ross, "Mason would have a rap over the knuckles for siding with him."[12]

The request was made in June 1845 and received in London in the fall. Alder wrote to the Rev. Dr. Matthew Richey in Montreal who conferred privately with Governor Simpson, and then replied to London. Alder then wrote to Evans on 31 March 1846 requesting him to come to London for talks on the mission. Evans received it with amazement in June 1846, and left almost immediately. He had not the slightest hint that the Company had requested his recall.

In the meanwhile a second major disturbance, quite unrelated to the decision on removal, was developing in Rossville and Norway House. Evans had been responsible for a tragic shooting accident in 1844 in which his assistant and native teacher, Thomas Hassall, was killed. Shock, grief and a sense of responsibility lay heavily on Evans so that, as reported by Letitia Hargrave, "Mr. Evans is in bad health, a chronic affection [sic] of the kidneys. I see no change in him but Hargrave says he is quite broken down. The Norway House people are aspersing his character & say that since the accident he has become deranged & that his conduct is immoral."[13]

The rumours developed into formal charges against him in February 1846, so Evans requested a church trial under the Methodist Discipline. Since Mason was the only ordained Methodist available, he would have to conduct the trial; it was a very difficult assignment for a young man to try his own superintendent, especially on such a personal matter. The young and inexperienced Henry Steinhauer was required to spend day after day during the trial writing, interpreting and translating. Mason rendered his verdicts – not guilty – on each of the three charges of fornication, but added, "I think you have acted imprudently and unbecoming the high and responsible office you hold in the Church of God."[14]

For a few days after the trial it seemed that the matter had been handled to everyone's satisfaction, but then uncontrollable disputes developed over contradictory statements and over the handling of the documents. From a 1980s perspective, these seem of minor importance since the removal of Evans had already been determined on other grounds. The documents of the trial had been sent to London, so Evans was delighted with the invitation received in June 1846 to return to London. Following the trial (from which the Hudson's Bay officials had been excluded) Simpson and Ross pursued charges against Evans, sending their reports to the secretaries of the British Wesleyan Mission Society.

The secretaries conducted their private enquiries with Evans in the light of the whole array of documents then before them. Before they had reached their conclusion, and while fresh documents were still being prepared, Evans died suddenly of heart attack, on 23 November 1846. The secretaries then wrote their conclusions to Simpson:

> Not guilty of the charges. . . . It was to us a cause of deep regret to learn as we did from himself as well as from Mr. Mason that it was his practice to treat the Indian girls connected with the Mission and under his roof at Rossville with the same kindness and familiarity as he treated his daughter Clara [Clarissa].
>
> We could not do otherwise than consider such conduct, however benevolent the motive from which it proceeded, as unseemly and improper in itself, more especially in a person occupying the position in which Mr. Evans stood in the country, and was almost sure to lead to evil surmisings on the part of others -- to excite suspicions as to his intentions -- to injure his reputation, and to lessen that esteem in which it is so desirable a Christian minister should be held by the people under his care. This view of the case was faithfully and forcibly pointed out to Mr. Evans before his departure from London, and he saw, and acknowledged its propriety.[15]

With the death of Evans the case was closed, the documents were buried in a private file, and the Canadian documents were buried in a private file, and the Canadian Methodists were left to draw their own conclusions.

THE LATER YEARS OF THE MISSION

William Mason was now left in charge of the Rossville Mission and, in effect, was responsible for all Methodist work in the Company territories. The Company insisted, however, that no superintendent be placed at Rossville. Instead, the Rev. Dr. Matthew Richey of Montreal was named superintendent so that Simpson could consult with him there.

Ephraim Evans had been quite mistaken in writing that Mason had "soon after left our work." He continued as a faithful Methodist for eight years, acted as superintendent, built up the Rossville Mission Press, and with the assistance of his Cree-speaking wife and of Henry Steinhauer, pressed on with translating, editing and printing Scriptures. He regularly sent long and detailed reports to "the revered and honored fathers" of the Wesleyan Society.

The work at Rossville was becoming more isolated and lonely. Evans had returned to England in 1846, Barnley in 1847 and Rundle in 1848. Steinhauer was sent to open the mission at Oxford Lake in 1850. The British Wesleyans were preparing to relinquish the missions in the Company territories to the Canada Conference of the Wesleyan Methodist Church and gave them scant attention. But in the meantime, the Anglican Church had secured their funds and regained their initiative in Rupert's Land. Clergymen John Smithurst and James Hunter became Mason's friendly neighbours. They learned from him and others the Cree syllabic, and Mason was able to do some printing for them. When Bishop David Anderson arrived in 1849 in Red River he too befriended Mason. When it was proposed that the Hudson's Bay missions be transferred to the Canada Conference of the Methodist Church, Mason and the Bishop each urged that the missions should instead be placed under the Church of England since it was now organized in strength in the same region. But Methodists decisions had already been made.

It seemed natural then, that Mason, who had no connections with the Canada Conference but did have strong continuing ties with England, should give the Wesleyan secretaries six months' notice of his decision to "Return to the Church in which I was baptized, and to which I am indebted for the first dawn of spiritual light on my dark soul. . . . I am not insensible to the obligations under which I am laid to you & to Methodism for the many blessings I have enjoyed during connection with you, a deep and abiding sense of which I shall retain while memory lasts."[16]

The resignation of Mason in July 1854 marked the end of the British Wesleyan Missionary Society work in the Hudson's Bay territories since it coincided with the transfer of these missions to the Canada Conference. Mason was accepted into the Anglican Church and stationed at York Factory.

THE FIRST BIBLE TO BE PRINTED IN THE CREE SYLLABIC

Before Evans left Upper Canada for Norway House he had urged the British and Foreign Bible Society to coordinate the efforts of the various demonstrations in preparing a Bible in the native language that would serve all the denominations who participated in its preparation. Bishop Anderson of Rupert's Land later wrote that "one of his objects in visiting England in 1856 was to propose to the Bible Society the production of a Cree Bible for the use of the CMS and the Canadian Wesleyan Missionary Society."[17]

Unfortunately, neither intention was fulfilled. The first Bible to be printed in the Cree syllabics, the New Testament in 1859, and the entire Bible in 1861 bore only one name as translator – William Mason, Minister. The Canadian Methodists were openly resentful at this historical injustice, and many of their successors in the United Church of Canada still feel the need for a more balanced statement. T.C.B. Boon, the fair-minded Anglican historian, said, "How this happened is now inexplainable."[18]

Methodist Mason had learned the Cree syllabic from its inventor, James Evans, had used the translations of Sinclair and Steinhauer and, with his wife Sophia, had spent years in the Methodist program of preparing scriptures and worship materials for printing. After Evans departure in 1846, Mason became responsible for the Rossville Mission Press and its impressive achievements.[19] The Gospel of John had been printed in its entirety, as were many other portions of Scripture, and publication of the whole Bible awaited only the final revisions. Anglican Mason and his wife completed the final revisions in their four years at York Factory before presenting the final texts to the British and Foreign Bible Society for printing.

The worth of the years of work devoted by William and Sophia Mason in preparing the Bible for publication in Cree cannot be underestimated. The dispute seems to arise in regarding Mason an Anglican, as he was at the time of printing, and obscuring the long years of Mason as Methodist. It seems probable, from a 1980s perspective, that Mason, in identifying himself simply as "minister," may have intended the recognition of both Anglican and Methodist administrations but that the enthusiasm of his new colleagues created the distortion. In any case, as the dispute developed in the face of Methodist criticism, Mason wrote from his retirement home in England on 30 December 1886: "In the translation of the Bible into the Cree language, I was assisted by Henry Steinhauer and John Sinclair who were at the time school master and interpreter at the Rossville Station where I was minister, and by other Indians. The final revision was the joint work of myself and my wife. I never claimed to be the inventor of the Cree syllabary, that honour belongs to the Rev. James Evans."[20]

Two features of the 1850s no doubt contributed to the claim of Anglican achievement. The name of James Evans did not at that time receive the acclaim it would awaken in later decades. The intense hostilities with the Company in 1845 produced marked resentment toward him, as is clearly shown in Company correspondence. The shocking church trial in Rossville in 1846 was widely known, and its effects were widely felt throughout the whole region. Evans's sudden death in England seemed like a life gone down under a heavy cloud, a life better forgotten. Naturally, the work associated with him was obscured until much later, when the Canadian Methodists forced a fresh assessment.

At the same time, the tide had turned for the Anglicans. After the frustrating years while their expansion funds were being held in chancery in England, and while the Methodists occupied the field so vigorously with Company support, they now had their funds and fresh inspiration. The Rev. James Hunter began his long and resourceful ministry in 1844. His sound education in English at first led him to reject the Cree syllabic because it interfered with what he thought was a more desirable education in English. His wife died in 1847, and a year later he married Jean Ross, the eldest daughter of Chief Factor Donald Ross of Norway House. Jean Ross had lived all her life in a Cree-speaking community, had studied for eight years with the Wesleyans, and was skilled in the use of the syllabics. The effectiveness of the syllabic writing amongst the native communities had convinced Hunter of its usefulness, so the new husband-and-wife team devoted their years and considerable talents to translation and education in the native language.

Bishop Anderson had also rejected the syllabic option but by 1853 also became a promoter of its use.[21] Consequently, in 1854, Mason joined a rising tide of Anglican interest and work in translating and teaching the use of the Cree syllabics. It seemed to be an Anglican story. T.C.B. Boon, in his summary of the Anglican Church, discusses this tradition. As though Rossville and its printing press had never been, Boon wrote:

It was from York Factory that James and Jean Hunter set out to get the first translation of Scriptures, hymns and prayers in the Cree language printed, and William and Sophia Mason sailed with the text of the first Bible in Cree Syllabics.[22]

Their tombstones (James and Jean Hunter). . . bears the inscription: "By their joint labours they gave the Bible and the Prayer Book in their native tongues to the Cree Indians of Northwest America."[23]

The anger of Canadian Methodists was predictable, and it is easy to understand how they came to believe that Evans was the victim of a vicious conspiracy by the Company and by his missionary assistant, William Mason.

A more balanced account shows Evans as a man of genius and dedication, who should be recognized as the creator of the Cree syllabic. At the same time, however, through poor judgment in his relations with the young girls living in his house he created some of his own problems. William Mason was a man of more limited abilities, but he was a faithful Methodist who did his best in a very difficult situation and deserves more grateful recognition. The Hudson's Bay Company did not withdraw support from the mission, nor conspire to destroy it, but it was very critical of Evans and requested his removal on grounds of interference in Company affairs.

THE LASTING EFFECT OF THE WESLEYAN MISSIONS

The major questions of effect on the native peoples, on the western territories and on the historical development of the West must await the work of

Henry Bird Steinhauer (Photo courtesy of Glenbow Archives, Calgary, Alberta.)

historians competent to make such judgments. The present writer can only report as a churchman who has become acquainted in some detail with the missions themselves, identifying those aspects which seem most prominent.

Protestant communities of native people
The British missionaries provided the initiatives and traditions of native church work which are still visible in the congregations of the United Church such as in the Keewatin Presbytery of the Manitoba Conference, and on the reserves within the Alberta Conference. The work in Saskatchewan is not so easily traced since there was no centre in Saskatchewan as dominant as Norway House and Fort Edmonton had been.

The strength and significance of native people in the Methodist tradition may be appreciated in the careers of some of their leaders, one of the most prominent being the Rev. Henry Bird Steinhauer. This remarkable man is still emerging in historical perspective as his life and work comes under continuing scrutiny. He was the only person to experience all three phases of Methodist growth – twelve years in the missions and schools of Upper Canada, fourteen years in or near Norway House with the British Wesleyans, and thirty years in Alberta under the Canada Conference. His particular talents and piety were recognized early in mission schools leading to extensive education in Cazenovia College, New York, and in the Upper Canada Academy at Coburg.

When Evans was appointed as superintendent of the Hudson's Bay missions, he selected Henry Steinhauer as a native teacher. Steinhauer was twenty-three years of age, had a few years' experience of teaching in mission schools, and was well equipped with the use of five languages – Cree, Ojibwa, English, Greek and Hebrew. Both Evans and Mason reported through the years on the great usefulness of Steinhauer's classical education in the huge tasks of translating at Rossville. He served as well as school teacher and lay preacher.

As the Canada Conference assumed responsibility for the western missions in 1854, they invited Steinhauer to share a speaking tour in England, then presented him for ordination at the meeting of the Canada Conference in London, Upper Canada, in 1855. Steinhauer and the Rev. Thomas Woolsey became the first appointments of the Canada Conference in the Alberta region to resume the work initiated by Rundle. Mason had sent Ben Sinclair from Norway House to assist Rundle at the Pigeon Lake Mission and later to open a mission at Lac la Biche. In 1855 Steinhauer joined his old friend Sinclair at Lac la Biche, then changed the location to Whitefish Lake where the two developed their native Christian community for thirty years. They died on the same weekend and were buried in a common grave.

Henry Steinhauer represents the capacity of native people to absorb and use classical education, to shape and develop communities under native leadership and to produce leaders for communities under changing conditions.

The invention and use of the Cree syllabic
The new Cree syllabic was first used for the propagation of Methodist teaching and worship and steadily developed into broader areas of commerce and correspondence. As it became an accepted form of native communication, it was adopted and used by other churches and institutions working with native people, including both Indian and Inuit languages.

After the Cree syllabic had been in use for more than a century, Professor Wallace Chafe, University of California, Berkeley, wrote: "The most workable of [several Indian writing systems devised by missionaries] . . . was the Cree Syllabary invented by James Evans around 1840."[24]

Realization of a new concept of Canada
When the Methodist Conference of Upper Canada sent Evans and Hurlburt to probe the north shore of Lake Superior and into the West of the Hudson's Bay territories, a new stage in the evolution of Canada was under way. In the Red River Settlement, the Roman Catholic missionaries had come from Lower Canada and the Protestants had come by direct appointment from England. Evans's trip was the first probe of the Protestants of Upper Canada into the western territories. The intention seemed frustrated when the Company invited the British Wesleyans to initiate the missions but, by 1847, the British had begun negotiations to transfer responsibility to the Canada Conference.

This transfer was a bold new idea for Canada, but its time had come. For more than a century, Hudson's Bay territory had been linked to Britain by direct shipping through Hudson Bay. Canadian politicians were beginning to assert the rights of Canada to annex the western territories, in spite of the obvious barriers. Hence, when the British Wesleyan Missionary Society proposed to transfer their missions to the Canada Conference, they touched a live political issue. The Church of England was comfortable in the traditional pattern linking the western territories to Britain through Hudson Bay as the Hudson's Bay Company had done for so long. But the Canadian Methodists were stirring with a vision of a new Canada. They wanted not only to assume responsibility for the western territories, but to bring under a single administration the work of Methodists in the eastern Maritime provinces, in Upper and Lower Canada, the western prairies, and across the mountains to the Pacific Coast.

By June 1854, the Methodist Conference meeting in Belleville recorded the stirring achievement in "taking over the Hudson's Bay Missions and the incorporation of the Eastern District. We have now before us the whole of that large section of North America extending from the Atlantic to the Pacific and from the St. Lawrence to the Arctic Ocean."[25]

British efforts to provide missions in the Company territories did not last long and must have been a disappointment to each of the sponsoring bodies as tension and tragedy combined to thwart their high intentions. But they could neither foresee nor appreciate what is now, in the 1980s, apparent, that a significant and enduring work was accomplished by them in the life of the Canadian nation.

As others saw us

John Badertscher

In the spring of 1840, with the blessing and financial support of both the Wesleyan Missionary Society of London [wms] and of the Hudson's Bay Company (the Company), the first Methodist missionaries arrived in what today is Western Canada. The territory was then known as Rupert's Land, and was by Royal Charter the virtual possession of the Hudson's Bay Company. The party consisted of three distinct groups of people. There were three young, single British missionaries – George Barnley, William Mason and Robert Rundle. A second group consisted of the two native teachers, both Mississaugas from Upper Canada, fruits of the vigorous Methodist mission to Amerindians there. One, George Bird Steinhauer, was young and single, although he eventually married and remained in Western Canada, providing through his descendants generations of church leaders and a lieutenant-governor of Alberta. The other Mississauga, Peter Jacobs, was married. He came accompanied by his family and by a reputation for the seduction of young women.

The third group in the missionary party was the appointed superintendent, James Evans, his wife Mary and his teen-aged daughter Clarissa. The Evanses were only in their mid-thirties, but were already seasoned and respected veterans of several missionary postings among the Algonquian Indian communities of Upper Canada. All three had shown considerable facility in the Ojibwa language.

This missionary party was eventually scattered across a territory comparable in size to Europe. Barnley was stationed in Moose Factory, a Company post just south of James Bay. Rundle was sent to the far West, even to the eastern slopes of the Rocky Mountains, where a picturesque peak would eventually bear his name. Mason and Steinhauer were posted at Rainy Lake among the Ojibwa, a group whose ability to resist missionary efforts is nearly unmatched.[1] Peter Jacobs, at first left under the watchful eye of the Evans family, exchanged places with Mason and Steinhauer after a frustrating year. Mason and Steinhauer then joined the Evanses at Norway House, designated as the administrative centre of the mission, even as it was the centre of the Northern Department of the Company's operations. From this centre, James Evans would travel across this vast territory, supervising his missionaries and locating new openings for the Gospel to be preached.

This ambitious undertaking did not happen in a vacuum. The Company, well into the second century of its presence in the territory, had seen fit two decades earlier to permit and even encourage the entry of Roman Catholic and Anglican missionaries on a permanent basis. The coming of the Methodists and their work was viewed in differing ways by the clergy of these denominations. One also finds that the Methodists were viewed differentially by various employees of the Company, from Governor George Simpson and the influential chief factors to their wives and lower-echelon Company personnel. These very Company employees were of course often lay people of the Anglican, Presbyterian or Roman Catholic communions.

In this article, we shall be looking at the Methodists through the eyes of these varied people. We shall find much evidence of the "bad old days" of bitter denominational rivalry, but also some features of the coming ecumenical spirit. We shall see, in the response of the Company personnel toward the mission, the familiar clash of secular with religious values, the unlovely effect of social status on human relationships, and the disrupting struggle for power and profit. We shall have to confront once again the fact that it is only in the midst of the secular world and its struggles that the reign of God is to be sought.

Finally, remembering that this was primarily a mission to Amerindians, we shall try to see the Methodists through their eyes. Facing the silence or ambiguity of the records, we will be reminded that too often Euramericans have not cared enough how their presence was perceived by the very people they ostensibly came to serve. But we will also be telling the story of a mission which set a new standard in taking seriously both the leadership and the language of Amerindians. We shall see, as a result, the increased vulnerability of this mission to misunderstanding and conflict. Even so, it is worth remembering that this Methodist mission led to the founding of the first Methodist (hence United Church) congregations in western Canada, some of which have continued to this day.

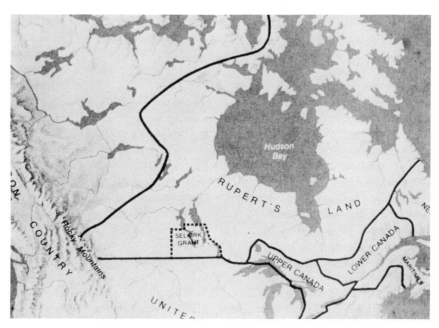

Map of Rupert's Land (Photo courtesy of Western Canada Pictorial Index.)

THE ROMAN CATHOLICS

In searching for the view of Methodist missionaries held by Roman Catholics, we encounter eloquent, if mute, testimony to Canada's "two solitudes," borne by the relative silence of the records on the Roman Catholic view of the Methodist mission to Rupert's Land. Many of the most likely sources of information, such as some archives of the Diocese of St. Boniface, have been lost in fires over the years. However, even when this factor is taken into account, there is a striking silence in the Roman Catholic records on the matter of the Methodists. Several reasons for this silence can be adduced.

First of all, Franco-Canadian Roman Catholics have been guarded in what they said in English about the English, and about their religion. The tenuous compromise which enabled Roman Catholics to continue to flourish under a Protestant monarch dictated this prudence. We may assume that the most trenchant Roman Catholic evaluations of Protestants were not published, at least not where Anglophones would be likely to read them. Secondly, nineteenth-century Roman Catholics were not given to making fine distinctions between Protestant groups. It is not easy to tell whether comments about "Protestants" are meant to apply only to a particular group the writer has in mind and, if so, which group that might be.

Finally, we must recognize that having to deal with the "Anglo-Protestant fact" did not shake the confidence of our Catholic sources in their view of themselves as the embodiment of the ultimately legitimate form of Christian civilization. We cannot fail to note in both Protestant and Catholic writers of the time a naive arrogance which saw the other as aberrant, and therefore not needing to be taken seriously. Part of the silence of the records reflects that sense of superiority.

Two old sayings help us deal with this silence. One is that actions, while being often highly ambiguous, still "speak louder than words." We may then look at what the Roman Catholics did in response to the Methodist presence. As we do, we will be able to see beyond the negative evaluation which can be presumed with certainty, for "imitation is the sincerest form of flattery." We will see that, despite viewing the Methodist mission as a threat to the spiritual well-being of the inhabitants of Rupert's Land, the Roman Catholics were impressed enough by the Methodist initiative to copy it in their own way.

The permanent presence of Roman Catholic clergy in Rupert's Land began in 1818 with the arrival of the soon-to-be Bishop Joseph Norbert Provencher and others. Despite having the mission to the Amerindians at the top of their mandate, very little was accomplished in converting the Indians for two decades. Georges-Antoine Belcourt, a secular priest who arrived in

1831, was the first missionary west of the Great Lakes to master any of the Amerindian languages. He founded a Saulteaux settlement, Baie St. Paul, on the Assiniboine River in 1833, but by 1836 had received only five communicants. During these years, he found himself in frequent conflict with Provencher, and so returned discouraged to Quebec in 1838. By the next year, the impending arrival of the Methodists had helped to reverse this casual approach.

The Methodist mission would not have arrived when it did had it not been for the initiative of the Hudson's Bay Company. The first steps had already been taken by the spring of 1839. At that time, a meeting took place at Ft. William, a Company post on Lake Superior, between Sir George Simpson and James Evans. Evans, representing the already-successful Indian mission of the Methodists in Upper Canada, was conducting a missionary probe. Simpson was resident Governor of the Hudson's Bay Company in Rupert's Land. It is clear from Evans's account of this meeting that Simpson was already assessing the feasibility of a Methodist mission in "his" territory.[2] The numerous Catholic employees of the Company could not have been unaware of the significance of this meeting, and word of it could hardly have failed to reach the ears of the Catholic hierarchy.

Soon after this meeting, Provencher choked down his personal distaste for Belcourt, his only successful Amerindian missionary, and secured Belcourt's return to Rupert's Land. Upon his return, Belcourt did not confine his attention to the prairie settlement of Baie St. Paul, but began a series of journeys north to Lake Manitoba and east to the Winnipeg River watershed, establishing mission stations by the symbolic planting of crosses as he went. Jean Baptiste Thibault, another secular priest showing aptitude for Amerindian missions, was also given an expanded area of work. In 1842 Thibault was sent, against the wishes of the Company, to the western prairies and foothills country, there to contest for Amerindian loyalties with the Methodist Rundle. In this contest he was relatively successful, and in his zeal we can see a clear reflection of the sense of rivalry which prevailed.

In the summer of 1842, Thibault and Rundle were in Fort Edmonton at the same time. Rundle recorded on 22 June that "the Priest had made almost a dead sweep excepting the English [employees of the Company]." On 27 June, Rundle lamented: "The Priest was telling them yesterday that neither the Gov. [Simpson] nor the Queen had any right to send [missionaries] here, [that] the power belonged to the Pope!"[3]

But the Roman Catholic response looked well beyond the intermittent ministries of secular priests on loan from Quebec bishops. With the news of the Methodist advent in his ears, Provencher began a search for a time-honoured remedy for such challenges, the resources of religious orders. By 1841, Bishop Ignace Bourget of Montreal was in Europe, beating the monastic bushes for Provencher's cause. The Jesuits, stalwarts of the earlier Amerindian missions in Canada, proved unavailable. However, on a visit to the Bishop of Marseilles, seeds were planted which bore fruit four years later. The Oblates of Mary Immaculate, an order of missionaries to the poor founded by the same bishop in 1816, were persuaded to take up the challenge. As Catholic historian Adrien G. Morice remarks, justifying this shift of attention from the urban poor to the Amerindians, "who was poorer than [Provencher's] own Indians, half-breeds, or even whites?"[4] The first Oblates, who were to provide episcopal leadership for the formative period of western Canada, arrived in August 1845, when the first stage of the Methodist mission was nearly at an end. They were preceded by one year by the first Grey Nuns, a female order whose mandate to aid the urban poor was, like the Oblates, stretched to include Rupert's Land, and who were no less important in building the Church in the West than the Oblates were.

Meanwhile, Thibault's flanking strategy brought him by 1844 into contact with the Dene or Athapaskans, the Amerindians of the northwestern part of Rupert's Land. Seeing in the Dene a field ripe for missionary harvest, and hearing that the Methodists were planning to establish a mission among them, Thibault fired off messages to Provencher calling urgently for help.[5] Two years later, the Oblates were on the scene in the person of future Bishop Alexandre Taché, soon followed by many others.

The Oblate mission to Rupert's Land, then, was in considerable part a response to the Methodist mission, as well as to the Anglican expansion which was beginning at the same time. Joseph E. Champagne, writing on the methods of the Oblate mission, testifies to the matter: "Four principal factors determined the decision on the placement of a mission: its strategic importance, the number of Indians in the area, their disposition towards missionaries, and economic conditions in the area."[6] Concerning "strategic importance" he says:

The primary concern of the missionaries was to occupy the territory, to reach as many Indians as quickly as possible. Above all, it was important to precede Protestantism, and to form a nucleus of Christians before Protestant propaganda could make its influence felt. Where the Protestants became established first it became extremely difficult, not to say impossible, to convert the Indians. When it was impossible to precede the [Protestant] minister, every opportunity was taken at least to follow him closely, and to offset his influence by founding a Catholic mission nearby the Protestant one. Otherwise, an entire band would have been stolen away (echappaient) from the faith for many generations.[7]

The seriousness with which the Roman Catholics took the Methodist mession is shown not only in this competitive strategy, but also in positive ways, most notably in the use of the syllabic alphabet which Evans and the Methodists developed for the Cree, but which the Oblates enthusiastically adopted for writing the Dene Languages.

Finally, it must be noted that contact between the two groups was not exclusively negative and competitive, although this was definitely the rule. One exception was the relationship which developed in the autumn and winter of 1845–46 between Robert Rundle and Pierre Jean de Smet, a Jesuit from the United States who fell in with Rundle while travelling in the foothills on an inter-tribal peacemaking expedition. Rundle records: "I found him very agreeable and we parted with each other when we left on very friendly terms. He did not interfere with my Indians at all, though he had an opportunity of doing so."[8] Rundle's journal records on several occasions, "up late at night with Mr. Du Smet [sic]." The relationship was even strong enough to bear the risk of the discussion of controversial subjects.[9] But such relationships, we must note, were the rare exception. In general, the Roman Catholics saw the Methodists as dangerous rivals, to be countered when possible and imitated when necessary.

THE ANGLICANS

The Anglican missionaries to Rupert's Land, operating under the guidance of the evangelically oriented Church Missionary Society, (CMS), tended to regard the Methodists as allies rather than as rivals. Having said this, we can go on to recognize that other sentiments were often expressed under the pressure of circumstances.

When the Wesleyans arrived, William Cockran had been labouring for over a decade at the work of building an agricultural-missionary settlement for the group of Cree and Saulteaux who had come together under the leadership of Chief Peguis. This settlement, the present-day parish of St. Peter Dynevor, was on the east bank of the Red River below Lower Fort Garry. Although he was encouraged by the arrival in 1839 of help, in the person of John Smithurst, the work had been slow and frustrating. Cockran had often been near total exhaustion, both physically and spiritually. In such times of distress, Cockran sometimes exhibited a paranoid attitude, especially towards the Hudson's Bay Company. Since the Wesleyans arrived at the invitation and with the support of the Company, it is not surprising that Cockran saw them as tools of a Company plot to undo his mission. Thus he wrote in 1840 to the CMS: "They have imported five this season from Canada. [He seems unaware that it was a British mission.] Mark the Doctrine of the Wesleyans. *We will not civilise one family. Rupert's Land* is *destined* by *God* to *remain forever* in a *state of barbarism.* We shall only preach the gospel to the Indian, to comfort him when he is travelling through the Wood. This is very charitable indeed. They propose that the Body of the Indian shall be made over as a legacy for the Fur Trader, and his soul make an offering to God. You have lost the cordial support of the Hon. Company by attempting to save both."[10]

Smithurst, writing to the CMS by the same packet, shared Cockran's scepticism about the Methodist work, but not Cockran's animosity. Smithurst noted the unrealistically large territory given to this small group of missionaries, and he saw the Methodists, not as doctrinally in error, but as being, like the Anglicans, under the constraint of Company policy. Having spoken with Evans and Mason, Smithurst recorded this analysis of the parties involved: "The present Enlightened state of England renders it impossible for the Hudson's Bay Co. longer to keep Missionaries out of their Territory. Hence the plan of getting men who, *as they think*, will be creatures of their own, and spend all their time travelling about the immense districts assigned them, without being able to adopt those measures by which alone the Indian can be permanently benefited." However, continued Smithurst, "I apprehend the Wesleyan Missionaries are men not long to be amused by travelling through the solitude of America without the means of doing any real good to the Indian." Smithurst then makes reference to the fact that the Methodists of Canada had recently made a successful intervention with the Foreign Office to prevent the enactment of Sir Francis Bond-Head's scheme to resettle the Indians of Upper Canada onto Manitoulin Island. He concluded: "Governor Simpson does not know the Wesleyans as well as I do or he would not have put himself into their hands. He has unconsciously given a deathblow to that system of iniquity by which thousands of immortal souls have been sacrificed at the shrine of Mammon. But be it so I hearily rejoice at it, I congratulate our Wesleyan brethren and bid them God speed. I trust we shall soon go hand in hand making common cause against the enemy.[11] In their reply the CMS Secretaries noted Smithurst's analysis, and cautiously expressed their agreement.[12] When, a year and a half later, the Wesleyans were still itinerating and had not adopted the Anglican strategy of agricultural settlements, Smithurst attributed it to the fact that they were so financially dependent upon the Company. "You cannot serve God and mammon,"[13] he quoted. These views were typical of the range of judgements expressed by Anglican clergy about the Methodists.

Later in 1840, Smithurst met Peter Jacobs for the first time and judged him to be "an intelligent and pious man."[14] Jacobs was invited to deliver the sermon at evening worship, and astonished Smithurst by preaching "in Indian." This event marked the opening of a set of issues on which the Anglicans were alternatively critical of and followers of Methodist practice. Cockran, and Smithurst after him, were committed to Anglicizing the Amerindians, and even convinced themselves that the Amerindians preferred it so.[15] Following this policy, even the first Amerindian cathechists preached and taught in English to those who shared with them Cree as an original language. Bishop David Anderson, arriving in 1849 to take charge of the diocese, noted positively the Methodist contributions to evangelizing the Indians. But he went on to say that the Methodists "have, very unfortunately as far as I can see, adopted the invention of the late Mr. Evans. . . . A few of the Indians can read by means of these syllabic characters; but if they had only been taught to read their own language in our letters, it would have been one step towards the acquisition of the English tongue."[16]

This rejection of the use of native languages and the syllabic alphabet was, however, already being challenged in the CMS. Henry Venn had just begun his remarkable career as secretary, espousing the goal of a church indigenous in language, culture and leadership. His policy would be pursued most vigorously in Rupert's Land by John Horden, first a missionary to Moose Factory (by that time abandoned by the Wesleyans) and later bishop. Beginning with Horden's example, Anglican language policy became a continuation of the Methodist approach. As early as 1853, Horden wrote, in an official organ of the CMS: "If we can supply these Cree hunters with a teacher, who shall accompany them in all their wanderings, and place the arts of reading and writing in their own tongue within their reach, by a phonography in accordance with its peculiar genius, we shall be accomplishing an object which, with the Divine blessing, may redound still more to the Red Man's best welfare."[17]

Not surprisingly, the Methodists were held in highest esteem by the indigenous Anglican clergy. Henry Budd was the first of these to be appointed to his own station (the Pas) as catechist, and later was the first to be ordained. He and Evans thought highly of each other, and on one of Evans's journeys through the area Evans baptized Budd's son.[18] George Barnley was perhaps the least effective member of the Methodist team but, nearly 20 years after his departure from Moose Factory, John McKay, a Métis who had been born there and was then priest of that parish, remembered Barnley as his first instructor in the faith with what seemed to a Methodist visitor as "much emotion."[19]

Most of the principal Anglican missionaries were not, however, quite so kindly disposed to the Methodists. Cockran, Smithurst and others continued to think the Methodist travels a waste of time, and to be wary of Methodist visits to Anglican locations as possible occasions for proselytizing. When tensions between the Methodists and the Company developed in the mid 1840s, a subdued sense of glee emerged, as this comment in a letter from Smithurst to the CMS shows: "It is I repeat very annoying to see all [these restrictions upon us] when we consider that the Methodists are taken about the country free of expense. If I mistake not however things will take a turn ere long. The Company already finds the Methodists a thorn in their side of which they would be glad to rid themselves."[20] To the Anglicans' great credit, it must be noted that in 1846, when Evans was recalled to England in the midst of a sex scandal which must have dominated the gossip of Rupert's Land, not a word of the scandal found its way into the extant letters or journals of the Anglican missionaries.

Perhaps the most eloquent tribute paid by an Anglican missionary to the Methodists is found in the journal of John Smithurst in 1848, when the Methodist mission was clearly on the wane. It is an ironic tribute, insofar as in it Smithurst contradicts much of his earlier critique, and distances himself from Cockran's policies, which he had previously supported fully. He wrote:

In the afternoon I visited the Wesleyan Missionary Station near Norway House and was much pleased with the same. In some respects the Wesleyans have managed the Indians better than we do. They have given them less temporal assistance and thereby taught the people to depend more upon themselves. It has always been Mr. Cockran's error to concern himself too much with the temporal wants of his people as if civilisation was a primary and evangelisation a secondary object. I have always viewed things as quite the reverse of this. Most of my difficulties at the Indian Settlement have arisen from the people not realising all the dreams held out to them as to the advantages of civilisation. As regards myself I never held out any golden expectations as an inducement to Indians to alter their mode of life. I simply told them I came to teach the word of God and their own temporal affairs was a concern of their own. Such has ever been the Wesleyan system. Acting on such principles the missionary and his people never come into collision. They are ready to assist him and do not expect him to be always assisting them. As a proof of this I would remark that the Indians at the Norway House station have put a neat and substantial fence around their burial ground without any expense or trouble to their minister. My people will do no such thing.[21]

THE HUDSON'S BAY COMPANY

The Methodists in Rupert's Land were cautiously grateful for whatever recognition and friendship they received from the Anglicans, and took the hostility and competition of the Roman Catholics for granted. The opinion of themselves they were most concerned about was that of the Hudson's Bay Company, the "powers that be" in Rupert's Land. Well they might be concerned, for the mission depended upon the sufferance and support of the Hudson's Bay Company for food, shelter and transportation. We need to look carefully at the Company's evaluation of the mission and the missionaries, for a superficial glance tends to confirm Smithurst's prophecy that the Company would turn on the Methodists whenever they showed any independence. After all, Evans was recalled upon the intervention of Governor George Simpson, and the mission went into sharp decline thereafter. But the facts are, as usual, more complex.

As we have already seen, the evidence indicates that the initiative for the sending of Methodist missionaries to Rupert's Land came from the Company. The minutes of the WMS record that the action was taken, after considerable debate about whether an entirely new territory ought to be opened when the present missions could hardly be sustained, "according to the proposal made by the Company through their offices."[22] At the next meeting it was reported that, in response to this decision, the Company had given the WMS £100 towards the missionary salaries. Resolutions of thanks are passed to the Company, and to its Governor Sir George Simpson, "as an expression of the high regard which is entertained for him by the Committee."[23]

What was behind this sudden interest and investment? The Company had, as we have seen, already secured the presence of and given financial support to two agencies. Their interest in these had been to help legitimize the Red River Settlement, to build Canadian support for its merger with the North West Company, and to defend itself against charges of exploitation made by humanitarian agencies in England, notably the Aborigines Protection Society.[24] Also, there is reason to believe that, at least among some directors of the Company, there was genuine concern to support and extend the work of the CMS. But why, after two decades of missionary presence, did the Company seek out this "third force"?

The reasons are contained in a letter from George Simpson to Donald Ross, written as soon as Simpson had received word of the Wesleyans' positive response.[25] Simpson credits Ross with the idea, although we may speculate that it emerged from a conversation between Simpson and Ross following Simpson's 1839 meeting with James Evans. Ross, the chief factor at Norway House and senior field officer of the Company's Northern Department, was concerned that the ablest young Indian and Métis men were being drawn to the Red River Settlement by the lure of education offered there by the missionaries. As a result, traplines were not as vigorously cultivated and personnel for transportation were harder to secure. The two key elements in Company productivity were in jeopardy.

The answer, it seemed to Ross and Simpson, was to provide in the northern areas the possibility of missionary instruction. It was thought undesirable to encourage the expansion of Roman Catholic work, for their loyalty was suspect and their potential for independent action was great. The Anglicans seemed committed to agricultural settlements, and Cockran had already challenged the Company's authority on several occasions. So Donald Ross had seen the need, and so Governor Simpson had seen – in the person of James Evans – the possibility.

Evans would have impressed Simpson favourably on several counts. First of all Evans, like Simpson, was an intrepid traveller, unafraid of wilderness danger and undaunted by the hardships of life in the bush. Second, Evans's experience on the Precambrian Shield had already convinced him that unlike the Indians of Upper Canada, some of whom had become successful farmers, the Indians of the north "can never become farmers, they must hunt forever."[26] That judgement would have been especially welcome to Simpson's ears.

Finally, while it is doubtful that Simpson was very familiar with the internal dynamics of Methodism, he would surely have been aware of the political situation in Canada which saw a group of Methodists with British ties on one side, and a group of Methodists with American ties on the other. Simpson would have been impressed to learn that James Evans's brother and close friend Ephriam was a leader on the pro-British side. This helps explain why Evans, a Canadian, ended up as superintendent of a British mission.

And so the Company, and especially its leaders, gladly received the Methodists, and especially their leader. Ross shared initially his superior's good impression of Evans. In a December 1840 report to the Northern Department he wrote: "The Rev'd Mr. Evans who has been indefatigable in his labour has had much success in the conversion of the natives. . . . I am quite satisfied that they are in a fair way of becoming more useful and industrious than heretofore."[27] By the following spring he wrote to Simpson: "The Wesleyan Mission established here . . . has [also] been . . . useful I trust as regards the members of the Establishment who now enjoy a blessing hitherto unknown in the wilderness. The more we know of Mr. Evans the more we admire the good qualities of the man and the powerful talents of the Preacher."[28]

This positive evaluation was shared at other Company forts where Evans called. John Rowand, the Roman Catholic layman in charge at Edmonton, was impressed with Evans' ability to move through the countryside and to communicate with the Amerindians.[29] About Robert Rundle, the missionary assigned to that western area, George Simpson reported: "From what I have heard of him, [Rundle] possesses more zeal than judgment, [but] he is nevertheless well spoken of and much liked by Mr. Rowand and the different other

Gentlemen in the District."[30] Letitia Hargrave, wife of the head of York Factory, reported her pleasure at the prospect of Evans's regular visits and ministry, although her envy of the superior social life of those in the Anglican parishes of the Red River Colony led her to say that the Methodists were satisfactory "for want of others."[31]

This is not to say that everything was perfect between missionaries and Company personnel. George Barnley at Moose Factory and William Mason at Lac la Pluie had quarrels with the factors whose limited quarters and supplies they shared over the long winters. But these personal problems do not seem to have called the mission itself into question. In fact, Donald Ross saw the possibility of such problems at Norway House within a few days of the arrival of the Evans family. Ross wrote to Simpson: "Our modes of living would in most cases be disagreeable and unsuitable to the tastes and disposition of the missionaries; nor can the means we have to provide by the present arrangement in the way of Board, Lodgings and various other matters, be ever sufficiently defined to as to prevent disputes eavils and misunderstandings."[32] Ross's recommendation was to construct housing and other buildings for the mission in the Indian village (on Playgreen Island, two miles from Norway House, which came to be called Rossville after the factor), and to give the mission a line of credit at the Company store. These recommendations were implemented as soon as possible, in about two years, with the full agreement of the missionaries. There is evidence that by then there had been enough difficulty between the two families (especially between the two women who, unlike their husbands, had to deal with each other every day) to give rise to rumours that the missionaries had been expelled from the fort.[33] However, the rumours may have been made worse by the fact that by 1843 there was a more serious kind of trouble brewing between Company and mission, especially Evans.

That trouble focused on the matter of working on the Lord's Day. More particularly, Evans had noted early in his tenure that "trippers" – those employed to paddle and portage the Company boats – were required to travel, and thus to work, every day until their destination was reached. Evans discussed the matter with Simpson in 1841, and was told simply that it was necessary. During much of the following year, Simpson was himself absent from Rupert's Land. Upon his return, he learned that Evans had persuaded a few factors to try Sabbath observance on their trips, and that their travel time had actually decreased. Simpson, no doubt furious at this challenge to his authority, nevertheless was gently ironic in his reprimand. He argued that idleness was at least as bad as Sabbath violation, and then elaborated his view that it was a necessary evil, concluding that "the practice in question as a general rule, seems to fall within the allowed exceptions both of necessity and mercy in a country where the summer is so short, the navigation so disjointed, the living so precarious and the winter so severe."[34]

Evans had the bad judgement to reply to this argumentatively and rather self-righteously, denying that he had ever preached publicly against Sunday travel, but saying that he intended to continue to maintain "the supremacy of God's law."[35] Simpson received this reply along with a confidential note from Donald Ross, both the contents and tone of which indicate that Evans had lost Ross's personal support. Ross reported that Evans had received Simpson's directive with animosity, and that Evans was a power-seeker, "grasping."[36]

Obviously there had been a drastic change, but Ross's letter still contained expressions of support for the mission, even while criticizing Evans personally. Strangely, Evans seems to have failed to realize that he was in trouble with Ross. If he had, the wound might well have been healed. Instead, matters went from bad to worse.

Evans's health began to decline and his emotional stability appears to have been affected by it. In 1844, Evans accidentally shot and killed Thomas Hassal, the Chipewyan teacher who had been working most closely with him. The accident threw Evans into an understandably deep depression. At about the same time, a packet from England was lost at sea. The packet contained a letter of encouragement and words of caution from Robert Alder, secretary of the WMS. It was a letter Evans needed badly to receive.

In 1844, Sir George Simpson made a trip to London, in the course of which he visited Robert Alder. He impressed Alder as a man committed to the support of Christian missions. Simpson wrote to Ross from London, assuring him that henceforth the Company would have the support of the WMS in any conflict with their missionary agents.[37] This set the stage for the decisive confrontation which took place in 1845.

It is impossible to tell from the records just how or why the matter began, or who was at fault. Evans sent a private letter to Ross, with the transcript of a conversation Evans and Steinhauer had had with three of their Cree parishioners, alleging that Ross had threatened to blacklist them from employment by and trade with the Company if they refused to work as "trippers," and thus break the Sabbath.[38]

Ross replied with two letters, one official and one private. In the official letter, Ross replied that "the Statements of the Indians are very far from being correct, and your remarks, which appear to be founded on these Statements, must necessarily be erroneous also. . . . As regards the matter in other respects, authorities to which you and I must yield obedience will have to decide for the future." In the private letter, he declared that he has always tried to be on good terms with his neighbours, and to keep his personal feelings out of his official duties. He reassured Evans of his continuing good will toward the mission and the Indians, but then informed him that he (Evans) would have to make the next trip to the Red River on his own, no longer depending upon Company transport.[39] Evans chose to reply with a threat to employ any workers blacklisted by the Company, paying them with mission funds.[40] All must have known it to be an empty threat. Finally, Ross wrote to Simpson, giving his account of the affair, interpreting it as a power play by Evans, with the Indians caught innocently in the middle. In a private addendum to this correspondence, Ross suggested that Evans was involved in the current plotting to bring free trade in furs to Rupert's Land.[41]

This would, of course, be the accusation best calculated to arouse the governor's wrath. Incredibly, Evans himself gave it unwitting support. He wrote his annual report to Simpson and the Northern Department, full of expressions of gratitude to the Company and to Ross in particular, but containing the suggestion that his native parishioners be allowed to contribute to the mission by donating "a few skins."[42] Could Evans not have known that the Company regarded any exchange of furs to which it was not a direct party as a violation of its charter? The letter proved to be "the last straw." Simpson immediately wrote to the Company in London, asking them to secure Evans's recall: "Since the very commencement of his residence in this country, that Gentleman has to a great extent mistaken his position, habitually and systematically, exhibiting an assumption of superiority, which however harmless at first soon gave uneasiness, as the probable source of more serious usurpations."[43] At the same time, Simpson wrote to Alder, asking him "to exert [his] influence . . . to carry into effect a measure which, to speak candidly, can alone assure a steady progress of the original plans of the Wesleyan Missionary Society and the Hudson's Bay Company. Nothing but our trade can bear the expense of diffusing the Blessings of Christianity and civilization through this inhospitable land and, if Mr. Evans had wished to obstruct and defeat the noble enterprise to which he had dedicated himself, he could not have adopted a more efficacious course than that of embarrassing the trade in question by impracticable principles and unwarranted pretensions."[44] This correspondence fairly summarizes both the final verdict of the Company on Evans, and its continuing if ambivalent commitment to the Methodist mission.

However, our account cannot end here. To their credit, Alder and the WMS did not simply cave in to Simpson's demands. The matter was treated circumspectly, never finding its way into WMS minutes. Finally, Evans and his wife (his daughter had left Rupert's Land in 1844) were given a furlough, and Evans was asked to come to England for consultations and a speaking tour.

The letter reached Evans in early June 1846. By this time, a scandal, which had broken out in Rossville the preceding February involving charges of sexual immorality against Evans, was reaching its final stages.[45] Although the situation was handled internally by the mission, it took place under the watchful eye of Donald Ross. After Evans's departure, Ross and Simpson conducted their own inquiry which, unlike the internal one, predictably found Evans guilty. This data was forwarded by Simpson to Alder, indicating that Simpson wanted to make certain that Evans's departure was permanent.

The issue, for Simpson and Ross, was clearly insubordination. The matters of Sunday travel and even free trade were secondary. Something in the Methodist approach to the mission "gave uneasiness" to the Company. One other incident will show that it was not simply a matter of Evans's personality, or of his domestic situation. In March 1844 – not long before his accidental death – Thomas Hassal had been dispatched by the mission to journey to Churchill, where he was to contact some of the Chipewyans to whom he was related, a journey which was aborted at York Factory when no Company transport was available. In his journal, he records the following encounter en route with George Gladman, the Company man in charge at Oxford House:

[The issue of Sunday travel having arisen,] he said the Indians at his place knew very well of these things and that he did not want me to preach to the Indians at his place that the Missionaries [had] nothing at all to do with the Company. I told him again I . . . should be very sorry to interfere with . . . their worldly affairs but that did [not] hinder any Christian to declare the Truth of God's Word. Then [he] got in a rage and said that he did not want me to preach to him about these [things] as he knew of [them] better [than] I did. I told [him] that God did not Look at the Knowledge of [the] thing, if the deed did not go with the Knowledge. He replied I tell you again I don't want you to preach to me here. I replied I did not intend to preach if I saw him so obstinate as to go against his conscience.[46]

Whatever the accuracy of this recollection of a heated conversation was, it is clear that Company officials were not accustomed to being spoken to in this way by Amerindians.

Nevertheless, Company support for the mission did continue after Evans's departure,[47] and the Company managed finally to accommodate itself to the Methodist use of Amerindian leadership. For example, by 1850 the Company had agreed to provide shelter for a mission at Oxford House, and the first man in charge was Henry Steinhauer.[48] The Company had, however, learned its lesson in dealing with the Methodists, a lesson which Sir George Simpson expressed in these words written to Donald Ross:

Now that Evans is off, we must not allow his successor, whoever he may be, to play the Bishop at Norway House, where you alone must be prophet, priest and king--Mason merely acting under your advice. By having him in your hands, he may be useful to the trade and may, unquestionably, better carry out the views of the Society than by acting on his own judgement and discretion, in which I have little confidence: and you must endeavor to render the mission as little burdensome as possible.[49]

THE AMERINDIANS

It is conventional wisdom to lament the effect that Christian missions have had on aboriginal people all over the world. Indeed, there is reason for such a lament. Disease, defeat, demoralization, drunkenness – these effects and others like them follow in the wake of European civilization wherever it has touched people who lack the military and economic techniques necessary to resist.[50]

When we look at the Methodist mission in Rupert's Land, such an interpretation is also possible. But, once again, it is far too simple. The way the Amerindians, particularly the Cree, viewed the Methodist mission ranged from outright hostility to sullen tolerance to practical curiosity to enthusiastic acceptance.

In documenting this range of views, it is necessary to be even more cautious than it is in dealing with the other groups we have examined. The fundamental reason for this caution is that we have almost no documents from the Amerindians themselves, except from those who most fully accepted Euramerican culture. Consequently, we must infer Amerindian views of the Methodists mostly from Euramerican documentation of the behaviour which reflected those views.

One common response to the missionaries in this first decade of their presence was that of passive resistance on the part of the Indians. This view would have manifested itself as a polite but silent watching and listening. Repeatedly, the missionary journals record that a group of Indians attended a service at which they sat and listened. Fortunately for the morale of the missionaries, they were able to interpret this response as acceptance. By European norms, sitting and listening was the way to join in worship. For the Amerindians, this was not the case. To sit and listen to a visitor was the least that one could do. But to make no response was a fairly clear expression of at least temporary rejection. It must have seemed to the Amerindians that the missionaries were expecting and even inviting such rejection when they did not sit silently and wait at the end of their presentations.

Sometimes the missionaries did get a verbal response which expressed resistance. Mason recorded this from Lac la Pluie, among the Ojibwa: "The River Chief with several Indians arrive for their Winter supplies. I conversed with them a considerable time, and persuaded them to attend the meeting which in the evening we held. After reading and expounding of the Scriptures and Prayer, its chief said it was no wonder we knew everything and they nothing, for we had nothing to do but to look and read the book. Yet he manifested no desire to learn, nor did he at all wish to become acquainted with the principles of Christianity."[51] The irony dripping from the chief's response comes through in Mason's account, even though he missed it himself. An Ojibwa elder, knowing that religious knowledge comes through personal experiences, would have been amused by the bookishness of the youthful missionary.

Resistance could also be expressed as an assertion of the difference between two ways of life. Rundle reported: "Went also to another tent, saw an old man, etc., but he spoke against the religion of the Bible. He appeared to be Pharisaical; 'I want to go where my friends are gone,' he said."[52] What Rundle seems to mean by "Pharisaical" is confidence in one's own religion, culture and way of life. The straightforwardness of this man's rejection may very well have been a back-handed compliment to Rundle, a recognition of his own unvarnished and honest approach.

Outright resistance, however, was not the characteristic Amerindian way. Much more typical was a desire to learn, to borrow and to adapt from whatever sources were available. If one could deal advantageously with the Company, so might it be with the missionaries. These Europeans were obviously a formidable lot; why not accept from them whatever one could use? Amerindians had religious practitioners from whom a variety of benefits – such as health, wisdom, power – could be gained. One could expect similar benefits from these European shamans. Thus Rundle tells of a Cree coming to visit him at Ft. Edmonton, hoping to have his vision restored. "I believe he was much disappointed on finding that I had only to do with the blindness of the mind."[53] Another poignant example comes from Evans's journal at a time when he was travelling on the prairies:

During the day I was introduced to the Principal Chief of all the Crees. He is a rather genteel looking [sic] and at present an invalid having been wounded last summer in an affray with the Slave Indians. The ball entering on his right side just above his hip and passing along his back remains still in his left shoulder.

I gave him a brief outline of the leading Truths of Christianity. He assented to their suitableness to the wants and ignorance of himself and his people. He appeared very serious while I assured him that this was the only remedy which could be applied to remove the miseries of his day, and to save them from sin and eternal pain. He sat mute for some time evidently in deep thought, then remarked "I believe all this. Last summer I was as I have always been hunted by my enemies, and when driven from place to place with my people, going not whither to flee, I lifted up my eyes and hands alone to the Great Spirit. I said 'Great Spirit I live in this way because I am an Indian, because I live in darkness. O send me help and give me a little rest and peace before I die.'[54]

One must admire Evans's willingness to wait and listen, but one must also wonder what happened after this, and whether the chief felt that his expectations had been fulfilled. Evans's journal gives no indication, which leads us to believe that not much happened.

For some Amerindians, the appearance of missionaries and their efforts at conversion signaled a new stage in interaction between Euramerican and Amerindian people. For well over a century, the traders had been offering a limited involvement with their culture, through its material artifacts and some more-or-less permanent marriages. Now the missionaries seemed to be offering an opening into this new way of life at its spiritual centre, an opportunity for fuller integration. To some, the Wesleyans seemed to express this with special clarity. They were willing to come north, visiting both Company fort and Indian camp. They included in their numbers some Amerindians who were themselves almost fully integrated. (Steinhauer, for example, had spent much of his youth under the tutelage of Methodist missionaries, eventually going on to receive a degree from Victoria College, the Methodist institution of higher learning in Upper Canada.) But most important, they came to teach literacy, that mysterious technique which appeared to be at the centre of European power. And the Methodists not only taught literacy in English but, thanks to Evans's invention of the syllabic alphabet, in Amerindian languages as well.

It was this perception of the Methodists as friendly gatekeepers that accounts for what an unbiased observer would have to say was their remarkable success, especially among the Cree and the Assiniboine. Methodist congregations and "classes" were established from Island Lake, Manitoba, to Morley, Alberta. These would continue a Methodist ministry in the native languages without (and sometimes in spite of) the presence of a missionary.

Of course, one could say that the conversions were often superficial. People continued, after becoming Methodist, to live very much as they had before, to the unjustified dismay of missionaries who failed to reflect very deeply on the history of Christianity in their own land.[55] But to an amazing degree, numbers of Amerindians seem genuinely to have embraced the Wesleyan piety of their evangelists. The following report of Evans to his brother is not unrepresentative:

I have cause of unspeakable gratitude to Almighty God for his continued mercy to my dear family and myself. And for the favourable reception I have met with in every place. Nor can I feel otherwise than deeply humbled under a sense of my unworthiness when informing you that God has deigned to crown my feeble efforts to benefit the Indians with gratifying success. We have now [after a year and one-half] on the Baptismal Register connected with Norway House Station one hundred and seventy three souls – Our Classes at Norway House are lively and devoted without fanaticism or undue excitement. God has done his own work: To him be the glory.[56]

It is significant that this was written to Ephriam Evans, and not to the source of funding in London, for it was in correspondence to Ephriam that James Evans most readily poured out his disappointments and failures.

Lest one think this only a Euramerican interpretation, we should consider how these words from the Chipewyan Thomas Hassal's journal seem to express the very spirit of Wesleyan piety:

Just along side our Campment I remember a little House still standing up where I remained about a fortnight 14 years ago. . . . my faithfulness to God was very weak, while remembering the time I lived in that house a Prayerless man indeferent [sic] to God and my soul. I could not suppress my feeling. I drop'd my axe took my snow shoes and went away to a hammock of wood and poured out my soul before God who dispis'd not the sighing of a contrite spirit and him that trembled at his word. . . . I felt encouraged as if God had answer'd my cry. I went back to my hut greatly refresh'd blessed be to His Holy Name for his enexhaustable fulness. . . . I endeavoured to Proclaim to my two Companions the glad tidings of salvation purchased for perishing sinners. After having comited [sic] myself to the care of God I went to rest.[57]

The invention of the syllabic alphabet enabled the Cree, and later other groups, to respond religiously in a way that was neither simple acceptance nor rejection. One of the great advantages of Evans's alphabet was that it could be taught by one person to another without the intervention of a European teacher or alphabet. It put literacy education in the hands of Amerindians. Precisely because this literacy was seen to be a source of power, it was religiously valuable. Out of this power, the religious traditions of the Cree, and reports of what the missionaries of various sorts were doing came an indigenous religious movement which caused consternation among missionaries and Company personnel alike, and was suppressed with the help of some Cree.[58]

Finally, we must note that those Amerindians who adopted the missionaries as role models were able to internalize the Methodist ethos so thoroughly as to use it as a criterion of judgement upon even the missionaries themselves. The tragedy which concluded Evans's work in Rupert's Land illustrates this well.

Without going into detail, Evans was accused of adultery by a young married woman, and of "taking liberties" with other, even younger, women who lived in his house. In a chaotic "trial," conducted by Mason, Evans was found not guilty as charged, but guilty of "indiscretion." Most of the witnesses changed their stories at least once during the trial or soon after, and some of them died in an epidemic the following winter, so that attempts to find out "what really happened" are futile. But one can offer at least some reconstruction of the situation.[59]

The code of sexual conduct for Methodist missionaries was strict, to say the least. Alder's instructions to Barnley were typical: "Keep at the utmost distance from all trifling and levity in your intercourse with young persons – more especially with females. Take no liberties with them. Converse with them very sparingly and only for religious purposes; even then do not converse with them alone. Be above suspicion."[60] There was concern about the single young men being sent to Rupert's Land, but not about Evans, who was accompanied by his family. The marriage seems from all indications to have been a good one. The correspondence of Mary and James with each other is affectionate and joyful. Evans was also close to his daughter, Clarissa, and often playful with her. But Clarissa grew up and left her parents (with their blessings), and James Evans was becoming destabilized by constant pressure, by "bush" living and failing health.

Naturally, there were young people in the Evans's house. There they received board and education in return for domestic services. Mostly they were superivsed by Mary Evans. But to James and Mary, these children were their family, not domestic servants. And James Evans played with his children. In the traditional culture of the Cree of Norway House, however, the pattern suggested by Alder's instructions was more the norm for relations between older and younger, and between the sexes, than was the pattern Evans demonstrated in his playfulness. This discrepancy, added to the concern for personal morality institutionalized in Methodist class meeting, laid a trap for Evans. The trap was sprung by a woman who had lived in Evans's home, whose moral conduct he had often corrected, and whose unhappy marriage he had personally arranged.

What the case shows us is the Wesleyan moral code run amok, becoming the tool of vindictive self-righteousness, undermining the spiritual health of a whole community. Such cases are, of course, not unknown elsewhere. Even in distorted forms, the Amerindian perceptions of Methodism are faithful to their Euramerican models.

We have seen the Methodist mission to Rupert's Land as others saw it. Our investigation was conducted in the hope that some readers, to the extent that they can identify themselves with these pioneers of the faith, and affirm the ties that bind us to them, might also see themselves in these reflections. May such self-knowledge as can be gained from these reflections: ". . . frae monie a blunder free us / 'An foolish notion."[61]

John Black

James D. Marnoch

When the Rev. John Black arrived at the Red River settlement in 1851, he came not as an evangelist to begin slowly winning converts to a new faith, but to an isolated group of Presbyterians who had been waiting almost forty years for a minister.

THE LONG SEARCH

The story begins in the late-eighteenth century with that sorry chapter of Scottish history called the Highland Clearances. Landowners in the Highlands systematically and often cruelly expelled tenants from their homes and small farms in order to convert the land to sheep farming. In the early years of the nineteenth century the Earl of Selkirk became a director of the Hudson's Bay Company and he purchased a large tract of land surrounding the junction of the Red and Assiniboine Rivers for the purpose of establishing a settlement for the victims of the Clearances. Between 1812 and 1815 they arrived at York Factory on Hudson Bay and travelled via the Nelson River and Lake Winnipeg to Red River.

They were not welcome. The Hudson's Bay Company, their official hosts, and the rival North West Company, felt that the fur trade would be adversely affected by the settlement. The settlers suffered greatly from lack of preparation for their arrival, from natural disasters and especially from the schemes of the North West Company to prevent them from settling.

In 1817 Lord Selkirk himself came from Upper Canada when the morale in the Settlement was at a low ebb. He encouraged the people by setting apart land for a church and school and repeating the promise he had made to them at Helmsdale in Sutherlandshire that he would send them a clergyman of their

John Black (Photo courtesy of Western Canada Pictorial Index.)

own persuasion. The next year he sent two Roman Catholic priests to minister to the French-speaking settlers. They were the pioneers of what became the diocese of St. Boniface. Following Lord Selkirk's death in 1820, his executors and the Hudson's Bay Company arranged for a minister for Red River, the Rev. John West, "a good and suitable man."[1] But he belonged to the Church of England, and the Presbyterians complained that there were not twenty individuals in the whole colony belonging to the Church of England.[2] By the time he arrived, a church and a school had already been built, and West began to preach and teach. The Presbyterians faithfully attended the Anglican services. Thus began the work which over the years developed into the Anglican Diocese of Rupert's Land.

Beginning in 1822 the settlers appealed repeatedly to Lord Selkirk's executors, to the Hudson's Bay Company and to the Presbyterian Church in Scotland for their promised minister, but with no result. In 1835, 110 Scottish settlers moved to the United States, followed by other families two years later, "solely because they had neither minister nor church of their own."[3]

Finally, in 1846, an appeal was sent to the three-year-old Free Church of Scotland. Dr. John Bonar of Glasgow, chairman of the Free Church's Colonial Committee, responded by appealing to ministers in Scotland, and then to ministers in Canada. Among those to whom he wrote in Canada was John Black. Black wrote to his brother on 11 January 1849 from Montreal that he "had a letter from Mr. Bonar, Convenor of the Colonial Committee, about the difficulty in finding a minister."[4]

Bonar referred the matter to his relative and former Glasgow colleague, Dr. Robert Burns, minister of Knox Church, Toronto, an energetic mission-minded leader of the Free Church in Canada. Burns became chairman of the Committee on Mission to Red River. Soon, Sir George Simpson, governor of the Hudson's Bay Company, stationed at Lachine, was asked for his support, both by the settlers at Red River and by the Rev. William Rintoul of Montreal. Chief Factor Ballenden of Red River directed encouraging words of his own to Burns when he passed through Toronto.[5]

The search was now very active and by 8 May 1851, Burns could write to Ballenden at Lachine: "I believe a missionary of approved character will be free to go by the Caravan from St. Anthony's Falls about the beginning of July. Sorry he could not be ready to go with you as you offered."[6]

Meanwhile, at Red River, the Presbyterians with new hope, were actively preparing for the arrival of their minister. They carried on difficult negotiations with the first Bishop of Rupert's Land, which finally resulted in a settlement of the Presbyterians' rights in the original church at Red River. The church then became the Anglican Church of St. John. The Hudson's Bay

Company made a grant of land to the Presbyterians at Frog Plain, about three miles down the Red River from St. John's Church. The Presbyterians lived on narrow river lots in between these two properties. They soon built a manse and a school on their new land, assuming that the manse could be used for services until a church could be built.

The finalization of Burns's plan to have a missionary leave about the beginning of July is recorded in two letters which he wrote to Montreal in the last days of June 1851. The first was to the secretary of the French Canadian Missionary Society asking for the services of John Black, "whom we have fixed on as a fit person to make an exploratory visit to the [Red River] settlement. . . . We know Mr. Black's peculiar qualifications. I gave the pledge as chairman of the Committee and Mr. Ballenden will be entitled to hold me good for it personally. . . . If necessary I am ready to resign my charge here and throw myself on the far west, for I am clear that our Church is called to do some good work in those regions." The second letter went to John Black, calling him to a most important duty, and "on the manner in which you shall discharge it will depend, under God, the position which we as a Church may be called to occupy in regard to the progress of Christ's kingdom in these western regions. . . . Your object being exploratory, keep note of all. . . . Come up as soon as you can."[7]

THE MAKING OF A MINISTER

On 8 January 1818, a few months after Lord Selkirk's visit to Red River, John Black was born, the eldest son of William and Margaret Black, shepherd farmers of Eskdale in the Scottish Border country. The Border shepherd people were great readers who undertook to master the deepest books and often turned their hand to poetry. In writing poetry, they followed the example of James Hogg, the Ettrick Shepherd, whose popular poems had been published and were widely read in Scotland. Theologians, philosophers and novelists flourished in the area. Names such as Thomas Boston, Edward Irving, Thomas Carlyle and Sir Walter Scott were well known. It is not surprising that John Black had a thirst for knowledge, especially of the Bible.

John began his education at the Gair School, located at the corner of his home farm. He was fortunate in that his teachers taught everything from the alphabet to Latin and Greek authors. John loved learning new languages as well as studying English literature, and despite frequent absences from school in order to help his father on the farm, he added French to his studies in his adolescence. His study of French profoundly affected the later course of his life.

When he was about twenty, Black was called upon to act as teacher in his old school during a vacancy. Although he was retiring and bashful by nature, he did well as a teacher and later taught in a village in Cumberlandshire. In his late teens, John and a group of young friends had made public profession of their faith in Christ. He thought much of preparing for the ministry, but he hesitated; he wanted to be sure that providence was leading him. Once clear about his duty, he would let nothing stop him from fulfilling it.

When Black was twenty-three, there came a great change in his life. His parents were in financial difficulty on the farm. His father had relatives in New York State, and in 1841, using borrowed money, the family, including four sons and four daughters, left their homeland and settled at Bovina Center in the Catskill Mountains of New York State, which was a dairy farming region. After helping the family settle, Black taught school again, which provided the means for continuing his own studies, for he had now determined to become a minister. Soon he and two of his cousins were studying at an academy in Delhi, the county town, under an accomplished teacher, the Rev. Daniel Shepherd. The school had an excellent reputation for academic excellence and John had a distinguished record there.

By 1844, John Black was ready to study theology; the question was, where? John and his family were members of the Associate Church at Bovina Center. Black was happy there as a member, but that denomination required its ministers to subscribe to the Scottish Convenants of 1638 and 1643, when great numbers of people had pledged to oppose prelacy and keep the Church of Scotland pure. Black could not convince himself that it was necessary, two hundred years later, in America, to sign these noble documents. He decided to look elsewhere. Princeton College was a likely choice. However, at the time, the question of slavery was very much alive in the United States. Since Princeton was the seminary of the Old School Presbyterian Church whose teachings were not in accord with Black's abolitionist sympathies, he could not attend Princeton in good conscience. During this time of indecision for Black, the Rev. James George, a minister of the Church of Scotland in Upper Canada, came to visit his parents on a farm near the Black home. George interviewed Black and urged him to go to Queen's College in Kingston, where he was an examiner.

In the previous year in Scotland (1843), the Disruption in the Church of Scotland occurred, which led to the founding of the Free Church. The issue was a protest against the "intrusion" of hereditary patrons who could choose and place ministers in congregations. The Free Church people insisted upon the right of congregations to call their own ministers. George expressed the hope that the Church of Scotland in Canada would not divide, but when the synod in Canada met in 1844, disruption did take place. This posed a problem for Black's theological education: his sympathies were with the new Free Church but the sympathies of Queen's College remained with "the Kirk." He wrote to the Rev. Mark Y. Stark at Dundas, Upper Canada. Stark had been moderator of the synod and had chosen the Free Church side. Black was informed of a meeting in Toronto which would decide about a Free Church college. He attended this meeting and thus was part of the first class of what became Knox College. The College opened on 5 November 1844 in the home of Professor Henry Esson. The Rev. Andrew King from Scotland taught theology while Esson taught arts. That first year, fourteen students took classes around a large table and used Professor Esson's personal library as well as books loaned by other ministers.

Black was a good student, winning several bursaries and prizes. The small group of students and professors formed a company of friends, a group which Black cherished through the years. After his second academic year, he plunged into the student missionary experience at the communities of Brock, Uxbridge, Reach and Scott which were new settlements of British people, not far from Toronto. He served two of these communities on one Sunday and the remaining two on the next Sunday; as well he held mid-week prayer meetings and other preaching services when he could.

In the third year (1846–47), the students showed their missionary zeal by forming the Knox College Missionary Society. They worked in city missions and helped to support a foreign missionary of the Scottish Free Church. John Black shared the desire of the group to reach and rescue the perishing. During the school year, the Rev. Mr. Doudiet, a Swiss Protestant who worked with the French Canadian Missionary Society in Montreal, spoke to the Knox students and succeeded in inspiring in them a concern to help him in his effort to evangelize French-speaking Catholics. Black's knowledge of French made him the best choice among the students to spend the next summer at the Society's school at Pointe aux Trembles, near Montreal. After he completed his Knox College course, Black decided to postpone ordination and join the staff of the French Canadian Missionary Society. He soon became their secretary and served them for three years. But he was frustrated in this work because of the calls upon him to supply vacant Free Church pulpits in the Lower Province. In his letters to his brother James, who had entered Knox College during John's last year, he refers to Quebec, Côte St. Church in Montreal and the Chateauguay area south of Montreal, as some of the places where he preached. In January 1849 he wrote that he could "not get at French," and added, "I must wait till providence opens a way to get out if the Association should be dissatisfied, and my own mind be a little discontented."[8]

"Waiting till providence opens a way" was characteristic of John Black. He spoke often in this way in later years. He had his own desires about the course of his life and ministry, but was never able to push himself forward. He very consciously waited to be led by providence.

At the end of May 1851, he told his brother that he had resigned as secretary of the French Canadian Missionary Society, and informed him that "the people of North Georgetown are going ahead with a call for me – without my leave. I am not resolved what I shall do. It is one of the most desirable in the Lower Province [there being] . . . considerable French population in the region of it, and this ought to weigh something with me. . . . I think I shall in all probability accept their invitation. With faithful labour and God's blessing that field may be mostly won to our Church, and what is better, we may hope many souls won to Christ. What shall I do? I pray that I may be directed aright."[9]

A month later Black received Robert Burns's call to Red River. After much consideration of it, he declined to go. He was still wrestling with the Georgetown decision, and was also concerned about leaving his parents for such a considerable time, since they were now alone. In mid-July he wrote his brother, "I still continue here and in connection with the mission, but for how long I shall do so I do not know. I must give an answer yea or nay to the North Georgetown people on Tuesday next."[10]

When Burns received Black's refusal, he approached other ministers, but without success, and then renewed his appeal to Black. John now heard the call that he must answer, and it was the one that shaped the rest of his life.

On 31 July 1851 Black wrote to his brother from Toronto, "You will no doubt be surprised to learn that I am so far on my way to the Red River. I am to be ordained to-night, and go on tomorrow at 7:30. I have been forced into it against my will. It is a very important mission, yet I leave one important also. What grieves me much is that I go without seeing friends – yourself and the family at home. Nobody else would go, and so I am called on to go. I shall not be able to return before next spring."[11]

John Black had come to Canada without knowing anyone there, but soon became part of a warm group of friends. Now the call of duty led him away from them all, to a distant place where once more he would be alone. But at last he was an ordained minister of the Gospel, and was being sent on his first mission with a deep sense of being especially called to it. His ordination took place in Knox Church, Toronto, with his classmate, James Nisbet, preaching the sermon.

The journey which brought John Black and the Red River Presbyterians together was a long and arduous one. In the first two weeks he travelled from

Buffalo to Detroit by steamer, then by train to Elgin, by stagecoach to
Galena, Illinois, on the Mississippi River, then by riverboat up the great river
to St. Anthony's Falls (near St. Paul). On 15 August, he wrote to his brother
that "the Red River people had left before my arrival, but the Governor of
Minnesota starts on Monday, and I go with him and his party. This brings me
to within 60 miles of my station. It is costly."[12] The arrival date of 15 August
was a month and a half later than the date which Robert Burns had hoped for.
A party of people from Red River had made the long journey to meet the
missionary at St. Anthony's Falls, but, the season advancing and a long road
by Red River carts ahead of them, they had left for home on 1 August, the day
that Black left Toronto. Fortunately, Governor Ramsay of Minnesota Territory was about to travel with a military escort to Pembina, at the extreme
northwest corner of the territory, to sign a treaty with the Chippewa Indians.
Black was welcome to travel with the party and journalist J.W. Bond was also
included. They had to provide their own ponies and camping outfits. The
party of about fifty people reached Pembina three and a half weeks after
Black's arrival at St. Anthony's Falls. It was a hard journey: they had to build
corduroy roads of poles, they had to cross swamps, suffer mosquitoes, hunt
meat, replace cart axles and gather dried buffalo manure to serve as fuel for
their fires because of the lack of wood on the prairie. On Sunday, 14 September, Black conducted what was probably his first service as an ordained
minister at the governor's house at Pembina for about fifteen people.

On Wednesday, 17 September, Black and Bond, who had become good
companions on the journey, set out with two Métis boatmen to travel by
canoe to the Red River settlement, a distance of about 180 miles (now about
sixty miles by road). On Friday afternoon, 19 September 1851, the party
arrived at St. Boniface, across the Red River from the mouth of the Assiniboine River and in sight of Fort Garry. There they were welcomed at the home
of M. Narcisse Marion, to whom they had been referred by relatives at
Pembina. After a short rest they were taken about a mile down the river to
Colony Gardens, the home of Alexander Ross.

THE EXPLORATORY VISIT

Alexander Ross was sixty-nine when he welcomed the minister whom he had
persistently sought for over a quarter of a century. He had come to Canada as
a young soldier from his home at Nairn in the north of Scotland. In 1803,
when his regiment was disbanded, he settled for a few years in Glengarry,
Upper Canada, where he taught school. In 1810 he sailed from New York
around Cape Horn to the mouth of the Columbia River where he worked for

the Pacific Fur Company. Later he served the North West Company in the British Columbia interior, where he married the daughter of the chief of the Okanagan Indians, whom he called Sally. In 1825, after the amalgamation of the North West Company and the Hudson's Bay Company, he retired from the Company's service and was given a grant of land at Red River, as well as a pension. He became a farmer, a free trader and sheriff of the Settlement. He wrote of his experiences in British Columbia and of life in the Red River area. His family was large and he was very conscious of the fact that they were "halfbreeds." He loved his Indian wife and gave her every attention and respect. His children were as well educated as he could manage and he urged them to be dependable and helpful citizens. They, along with the other families, took part in the life of the original church at Red River with its Anglican clergy, but they also maintained family worship and the teaching of the Shorter Catechism the standard teaching tool in Presbyterianism. Ross was the one who led the long campaign to secure a minister, and it was he who negotiated the settlement with the Bishop, and also the grant of land at Frog Plain. As he met John Black and introduced him to his family, he must have rejoiced that the long night was over and looked forward to the new day that was about to dawn for them.

On his first Sunday, Black attended worship at St. John's Church, and met many members of his future congregation. During the next week he met many others. Their houses sat on narrow strips of land and were fairly close to one another on each side of the Red River, north from St. John's Church to beyond Frog Plain, the site of the awaiting manse. This area had been named the Parish of Kildonan by Lord Selkirk in 1817, after the home parish of many of the Selkirk settlers in Sutherlandshire in the north of Scotland. On Sunday, 28 September 1851, about three hundred people gathered at the Frog Plain manse for the first service by a Presbyterian minister in all the vast territory west of Lake Superior. In the next few weeks the missionary received forty-five people into membership in the Presbyterian Church; they, in turn, elected six elders by ballot, five of whom agreed to serve. They were ordained on 7 December and on the following Saturday a preparatory service was held, when communion tokens were given to the members to signify their readiness to receive communion. Black wrote of the sacramental service of 14 December 1851: "It was to all of us a solemn day, being the first time in which, according to our simple and scriptural form, that blessed ordinance was ever dispensed here. It was also the first time for the pastor who administered; the first time for the elders who served; and the first for not a few who sat at the table – among others, two old men – the one 87 and the other 99 years of age; and all this in addition to its own intrinsic solemnity."[13]

The Kildonan Presbyterians were at long last a congregation, and, even though winter was fast approaching, they began preparations for building their church. It was to be a stone building patterned after the old Church of Kildonan in Sutherlandshire, Scotland. They quarried stone at Stony Mountain, a few miles west of Frog Plain, and carried it to the site on ox-drawn sleds. They prepared lime and brought timbers from St. Peters, north of Selkirk, and from Bird's Hill, east of the Red River; all was ready for building in the spring.

John Black had found a congregation of theologically minded people who were familiar with the Shorter Catechism. His sermons and services were shaped by his awareness of their expectations. They coincided with his own early experiences. Kildonan Church would be a Scottish parish church, with settled minister, manse and school.

Black received a warm welcome from the people of Red River. He could see the potential of this eager group but could not forget that his visit was only exploratory. Even though he and the congregation thought alike on theological matters, he was not convinced that he was the best man to meet their needs; for one thing, he knew they would have liked a minister who "had the Gaelic." He decided he would return east in the spring and report before settling the matter.

THE 1852 RED RIVER FLOOD

The spring of 1852 saw one of the devastating floods which occurs periodically on the Red River. It was the worst one in twenty-six years. Many people could remember the flood of 1826 and knew what they must do, but Black had never seen anything like it. He wrote of the inexorable rise of the water until "houses, barns, byres, stacks of wheat, etc., were floating thick and fast . . . from 3,000 to 4,000 people have been driven from their homes."[14] They fled to the higher land of Little Stony Mountain on the west and of Bird's Hill on the east. The minister went to Stony Mountain and, on the first Sunday, preached to the people in the open. Later in the day he crossed the nine-mile-wide lake to the people at Bird's Hill where he held another service. That day's text was, "All things work together for good to them that love God; to them who are the called according to his purpose" (Romans 8:28).

The experience of the flood created a bond which drew minister and people together in mutual regard. It was June before the waters receded and the people could return to their destroyed homes. There was much rebuilding to be done. Crops were sown late. Construction of the church could not be started. The lime had disappeared; the timbers were washed away and had to be recovered. Black did not feel free to leave. On 11 August 1852, Adam Thom, recorder of Rupert's Land, laid the cornerstone of the church (in which was placed a sealed bottle containing names and details about place and time), and construction of the church began.

It was not until the summer of 1853 that Black took the long journey back to Toronto to report and to try to resolve the problem of whether he, or someone more suitable, should become the permanent minister of Kildonan Church.

RETURN TO RED RIVER

John Black was not the only one concerned with the question of whether or not he should return to Red River. The congregation wanted to keep him; Burns wanted him to stay; and he had sufficiently impressed the Hudson's Bay Company that on 16 September 1853, Sir George Simpson felt it important to send an encouraging letter to Alexander Ross: "I wrote to Burns stating my desire to secure Mr. Black's return, which I was certain would prove exceedingly gratifying to the Presbyterian Community at Red River, and adding as a substantial proof of the Company's feeling of regard for that gentleman, that in the event of his re-appointment to Red River I would undertake to add the sum of 50 [pounds] . . . to his stipend from the Company."[15]

On that same day, 16 September 1853, James Ross, who was the young son of Alexander and a student at the University of Toronto, wrote happily to his father, "Mr. Black, your beloved pastor, will leave Toronto, if all be well, on Tuesday next, the 20th inst. He is deeply regretted by all here, and leaves amid the sighs, good wishes and prayers of hundreds – may I not say thousands. He has been down to see his parents and friends in New York and bade them all farewell. I am sure you will be very happy to see him back. He has collected upwards of 130 [£] for the Red River Church."[16]

By 4 November, however, the good news had not yet reached Red River. That day William Ross, the oldest son of Alexander, wrote to his brother in Toronto. He described the progress on the church building, "but sadly do we want him who would give fresh courage and energy to all our undertaking. . . . Tell old Dr. Burns he has broke [sic] his pledge. . . . He has not only deprived us of our minister, but also his salary which was guaranteed by the HBC to Rev. John Black and to no other."[17]

Black's second journey, this one so late in the season, took eight weeks. Black arrived at the Ross home at night on 15 November 1853, after walking the last forty miles. It had been a harrowing physical experience, hampered by the rapidly forming ice on the Red Lake River in Minnesota, but helped greatly by the hospitality and kindness of Presbyterian missionaries to the Indians at Red Lake.

There was great joy at Red River on his return, especially in the Ross home. However, he was still ambivalent about his position at Kildonan, and in a long letter to his father describing the journey, he concluded, "I had many thoughts of turning back, but still felt that I should not be satisfied in my own mind . . . 'til I should try by all possible ways of accomplishing my purpose. This journey has been very appreciated, . . . people here had given up hopes of my return. . . . whether the Canadian Church will allow me to stay here or not, I do not yet know. I am probably willing to return if they find someone to supply this place."[18]

THE PASTORAL TIE

In spite of his own uncertainty about his adequacy, Black began his work in Kildonan with a rush of activity. To no one's surprise in the Ross home, but with a ripple of excitement in the parish, John Black became engaged to marry Henrietta Ross, the tall, attractive daughter of Alexander and Sally Ross. Henrietta had been well educated at Red River, and was a popular member of Kildonan Church. They were married on 21 December 1853 at Colony Gardens, by the veteran Anglican missionary, William Cochran. The opening and dedication of Kildonan Church occurred two weeks later, on 5 January 1854. Then, during the next week, after it had been partitioned, the newlyweds moved into the manse. At last all the elements for the life and work of the Presbyterian parish were in place; the solid stone church was built, the parish school was operating and the minister was settled in the manse. The pastoral tie between John Black and Kildonan Church, which really began in early 1854, was to last for twenty-eight years.

For the congregation, the long search for a minister was most happily ended. And the pastor, after all his struggles and wrestlings of the spirit, felt that he was now located where providence had led him. Despite occasional frustrations, John Black and the Kildonan people developed a warm bond of love and respect for one another. Many surprising changes came to the Presbyterian Church in the West in those years, and the isolated settlement changed out of all recognition over the years, but much of the shape and style of both Church and settlement were built on the foundation so well and truly laid.

THE PREACHER

John Black, in Geneva gown and moccasins, conducted two services each Sunday, one in the morning and the other in the afternoon, with Sunday school in between. Knowing the people's love for Gaelic, he learned to read a chapter or give a prayer in their native tongue, but he always preached in English. And it was the sermons which most impressed his listeners. As early as September 1852, William Ross wrote a remarkable letter to his young brother James in which he referred to a sermon preached on the Sunday following the funeral of a leading man in the congregation. The text had been from Revelation 21:4: "And God shall wipe away all tears from their eyes." William wrote: "Truly it was a soul cheering, life-moulding, and soul-elevating discourse, and his exhortation to the bereaved so vivid, affectionate, joyful and hopeful, and so impressive – it was such a sermon as I never heard the equal in my life – and more, I hope it has *done good*. Mr. Black is a man who truly applies the acquirements of a vigorous and well-trained understanding to explain and enforce the great topics of Gospel truth, and he makes this application . . . in the most attractive form of whatever knowledge such a mind . . . can obtain to the great end of the Christian ministry . . . and surely a minister cannot be too much in earnest to proclaim the great and glorious doctrines of revealed truth, and life eternal; surely they deserve and demand the mightiest energies of the noblest intellects – oh, what a difference when I come out at the Frog Plain, – and when I used to come out of the Upper Church." William went on to compare the atmosphere of the two types of service, and the effect of the two ministers, and concluded: "As to Mr. Black's preaching, I can safely appeal to all the intelligent and unprejudiced minds of Red River, and not be afraid of the results."[19]

William Ross was an English-speaking half-breed, educated at Red River. The letter reveals something of that education, but also something of the results of the years of home teaching in the Bible and the Shorter Catechism. It shows the expectations that he and no doubt others had of a minister, and how Black, devoting his energies, through systematic study, met those expectations year after year. John Black's preaching became the standard for his congregation of sermon tasters. This remained so even in later years when they had opportunities to hear other ministers. His preaching was spoken of with nostalgia long after he had died.

THE PASTOR AND HIS CONGREGATION

Black was not only evangelical in preaching; he was also evangelical at heart. The people accepted him heartily but he was frustrated at what he called their stagnant state. He longed to find evidence of awakening spiritual life, but he found it all too seldom. He certainly did not think highly of his own ministry. In a letter to James Ross in Toronto in 1855, Black speaks of his congregation: "but not many tokens of spiritual life. I beseech you do not speak again of my success here (as you do in your last to your father) it seems like mocking."[20] It was years before he could feel satisfied that the people were being well served by him. He longed for a minister to visit, so that they would hear a different voice, or at least that the Church would send a pastoral letter which he could read to them. He envied his brother's experience of a community "revival" with "showers of blessing" for many. In the spring of 1877 he wrote to his brother, "In church matters I think there is a little brightening upon this province, tho' it is but small yet. We have had a few evangelistic meetings, both here and in town and have been a good deal encouraged. We are only sorry we did not begin earlier."[21] Yet, when faced, as early as 1854, with the possibility that the Church might actually recall him to Upper Canada, he had to say, "Many things draw me homewards, yet I am well here, and the people most kind and agreeable, and we have become attached to one another exceedingly."[22]

In John Black's later years, as the waves of settlers moved out across the prairies, some Kildonan people followed them. As new congregations were established and grew, Kildonan was weakened. A letter which he wrote in 1878 expressed Black's distress at this condition: "Were religion and congregational life lively otherwise it would largely compensate for these difficulties but when everything is going backward, nothing advancing, it is hard to keep up heart and interest."[23]

THE PASTOR AND THE LARGER COMMUNITY

The community at Red River included not only the Kildonan parish of Scottish settlers, but also, to the north, the Image Plain, or Middlechurch Settlement, of retired Hudson's Bay Company servants and their families; to the south was the small community of merchants who are remembered in Winnipeg street names such as Ross, McDermot, Logan and Bannatyne; and beyond these was the Hudson's Bay Company's establishment of Fort Garry at the junction of the rivers; there was also the small community around Point Douglas and south, which grew to become the City of Winnipeg. Across the Red and Assiniboine Rivers were the French-speaking Métis and other French-speaking people. St. James, Headingley and St. Francois-Xavier were located west along the Assiniboine. St. Andrew's and the Indian settlement at St. Peter's were north along the Red River.

As the Red River community grew larger and more diverse, John Black continued his quiet and effective work. A local branch of the British and Foreign Bible Society had already been established by the time Black arrived. It had its beginning at York Factory when the Rev. John West arrived from England in 1820. West had taken a collection from the fur traders gathered there, and with it formed one of the earliest overseas branches of the Bible Society. It continued to thrive at Red River and John Black shared in its work.

Black also founded a temperance league whose members took a pledge of abstinence from alcohol. He was consistently vocal against the drunkenness which was all too common throughout his thirty-year ministry. He also raised his protests against the widespread use of foul language. When grasshopper plagues on the prairie caused serious food shortages, Black became, on at least two occasions, an active member of the Relief Committee.

In inter-church relations, Black sought to foster cooperation. He attended St. John's, the Upper Church, on his first Sunday in Red River. At the time, feelings were running high because the Anglicans were about to lose three hundred or more people to the Presbyterian congregation. The Anglican Bishop had refused Ross's request to have Black preach at a Presbyterian service in the afternoon of that first Sunday. But Black sought to heal rather than to harm. One of the earliest acts of the Presbyterian congregation was in 1851 to send shipments of wheat to the Anglican missionaries at Fairford and the Pas (who were well known to them) in gratitude for all the services given them by the Anglican clergy for over thirty years. For years, Black, the Presbyterian, and the Anglican clergy maintained a regular service in the fort. They presided by rotation.

John Black believed firmly that a minister should not take part in political matters. Therefore, he took no part in the increasing pressure against the Hudson's Bay Company's trade monopoly nor did he participate in the later campaign against the Company's government.

In 1857, the Red River community was "qui vive for union with Canada."[24] Black was not sure how union would improve the Settlement, but he felt that it would help to relieve the isolation of Kildonan Church, and might stimulate a Presbyterian mission to the Indians. In 1869, when the Government of Canada agreed with the Hudson's Bay Company to transfer their territories in the Northwest, there was an almost total lack of government. The movement under Louis Riel attempted to fill the need.

In response to Riel's invitation to the English-speaking parishes to send delegates to a conference in October 1869, the Kildonan and St. John's people sent James Ross. He was instructed to express regret for the seizure of Fort Garry and the barricading of the road; to press for the admittance of

Lieutenant-Governor McDougall to the colony; and if this was not possible, to propose that the Hudson's Bay Company's Council of Assiniboia carry on the government until it could be replaced by an authorized government.[25] Subsequently, James Ross became chief justice in Riel's provisional government, an act which earned him the disapproval of some of his Kildonan neighbours. When the "Canadian" party under Dr. John Christian Schultz gathered at Kildonan for an attack on the provisional government, Black and other clergy successfully urged them to disperse.

The Province of Manitoba was formed out of the struggle, but the Red River community was never to be the same. In 1872 John Black was distressed. He wrote to his brother: "There is very little that is satisfactory – The herd of miserable, selfish political parties keeping the country in a turmoil and dividing our once content and happy people. I do not know how much longer I can stand it."[26]

HOME AND FAMILY

In a very real sense, John Black's marriage to Henrietta Ross gave him the close relations with a large family which he so much missed in his separation from his own family. The Ross family happily, and perhaps proudly, made him one of their own; but they always continued to refer to him as Mr. Black.

In 1856, while Black was making plans to take his family to Upper Canada the next summer, both William Ross, the eldest son, and Alexander, the respected father, died. James, the second son, was at the University of Toronto. James Ross and John Black were executors of the estate, but with James away, Black became the effective head of the family. He considered this new situation to be the work of providence. He wrote: "As . . . providence has twice sent me here contrary to my own expectations, and now prevents me leaving in the same way, it looks as if it may be I have to stay here, and if it is clearly God's will, so be it."[27] He had a real love and sense of responsibility for them, but his new responsibilities entailed a great deal of work and constant correspondence. Jemina and Sandy, the youngest of Alexander Ross's children, as well as some of the Ross grandchildren stayed at the manse often and for extended periods in order to go to school at Kildonan and to study with Black.

John and Henrietta were much in love and were very happy. Altogether they had nine children, but they lost three little boys: Robert Burns in 1863, of a choking accident when he was just a few months old; seven-year-old Sandy, their third child, the victim of an epidemic, on the day after Christmas, 1865; and, their baby, Donald McLellan, in January, 1866. The three little boys were buried beside each other in the Kildonan churchyard.

The surviving children were William Ross, Sarah Margaret, James, Henry, Annie and Henrietta. William and Henry became lawyers and lived in Morden, Manitoba where William was registrar of land titles, and Henry was in private practice. Henry was well known as a leader of a large nondenominational men's Bible class in Morden. Sarah Margaret married Mr. Francis, a Winnipeg businessman, and they lived latterly at Headingley. Black was able to take his wife and children to meet his family and friends in the East on only one occasion. The visit took place in 1859 and they left Red River on the Anson Northrup, the first steamship to arrive at Fort Garry.

The manse family was desolated by the death of the beloved wife and mother, Henrietta, on 21 March 1873 after just over nineteen years of marriage. She lies buried at the Kildonan Churchyard beside their three little boys. Black was in the midst of the busy expansionist years of the Presbytery, and it was difficult for him to look after the home and family. It 1875 he married Laurenda Bannatyne, a sister of the merchant, A.G.B. Bannatyne, and she became the source of much contentment to Black and his children.

EDUCATION IN THE KILDONAN PARISH

The school was a valued institution in the life of a Scottish parish, and Kildonan was no exception. When Black arrived in 1851, he found a school already in operation at Frog Plain, whose teacher was Alexander Matheson. The new minister entered enthusiastically into the life of the school. He encouraged its members in every way. He wanted it to become the best school at Red River. In 1864, James Nisbet, Black's classmate at Knox College who had come in 1862 to assist Black at Kildonan, supervised the building of a stone school to replace the original log structure. A Sunday school was soon functioning as well and Black always led a large Bible class.

During his first stay at Kildonan, Black had encouraged and prepared three young men for higher education: Alexander Matheson, Donald Fraser and James Ross. When Black returned to Toronto in 1853, they accompanied him. These were the first fruits of Black's ministry and teaching. Matheson graduated from Knox College; Fraser had to return home because of illness after completing his course there, and he died shortly after. Ross became a journalist with the *Hamilton Spectator,* then the *Globe* in Toronto, and also served as an editor of the Red River *Nor'Wester.*

A new development in Black's educational work came in 1854 when, as he wrote to James Ross, "the Bishop [who was the head of St. John's College] now refuses to take any more scholars from among the Presbyterians, whether male or female and the consequence will be that we must as soon as possible establish some sort of school of our own."[28] In anticipation of this, Black began to teach some of the older pupils in Latin, French and other subjects. He continued this practice for years, always hoping and planning for the day when a Presbyterian College could become a reality.

PRESBYTERIAN WORK EXPANDS BEYOND RED RIVER

Black's ministrations did not end at the stone church in Kildonan. Presbyterian families to the north, south and west of Frog Plain also claimed his attention. By 1862, Black was holding services at four preaching points: Kildonan, Little Britain, Upper Fort Garry and Headingley. In the same year, the Rev. James Nisbet, an old college friend of Black's, was sent out to assist at Red River. Nisbet's arrival meant that the four preaching points could be given services on a more regular basis. The Rev. Alexander Matheson, a native of Kildonan who had earlier taught school there, replaced Nisbet when Nisbet and a party of Kildonan people left to form the Indian mission at Prince Albert in 1866.

A great deal of credit for the successful establishment of the Prince Albert Mission must go to Black. His frequent pleas for a missionary to the natives on the plain kept the matter before the Foreign Missions Committee in Toronto. When he made the return journey to Red River in 1853 across northern Minnesota, Black had been deeply impressed by the work of American Presbyterian missionaries to the Indians and by the "industrial school" method they were using. He shared this passionate interest with Alexander Ross who, during the winter of 1853–54 was writing his book on the history of the Red River Colony. Because Black was staying in Ross's house, the two men would have ample opportunity to discuss their common interest in evangelizing the Indians. When Ross's book was published, it featured a detailed plan for an Indian mission that plainly showed Black's influence and that of the American Presbyterian missions.[29] The mission that Nisbet founded at Prince Albert was based on this plan. There was to be a heavy emphasis on traditional evangelism but there would also be a school and a model farm to teach agricultural skills to the men and housekeeping skills to the women. It was hoped that this approach would encourage the Indians to settle and become independent of the hunt. Here they would begin to learn how to cope with the changes the coming of the whites would bring.

THE PRESBYTERY OF MANITOBA

In 1868 the Rev. William Fletcher took charge of preaching points in the Portage la Prairie area; and in 1869 the Rev. John McNabb came to Little

Britain. Change was in the air, and in 1870, after Manitoba became a province of Canada, the General Assembly of the Canada Presbyterian Church created the Presbytery of Manitoba, with Black, Fletcher, McNabb and James Nisbet as ministers, with representative elders Polson, Sutherland and Gunn. Black's sermon, as moderator of the new presbytery, was on the text, "Therefore, seeing we have this ministry, as we have received mercy, we faint not" (2 Corinthians 4:1). Black's response to the new era was not faint. For the next twelve years he threw himself into church extension with as much enthusiasm as did the younger ministers. A valuable addition to the presbytery was the Rev. George Bryce, who in 1871, was sent to found Manitoba College and to assist in home missions work. The Kildonan people built a college beside their manse and school; but the college was moved to Winnipeg in 1874. Black lived long enough to see a new chapter of Presbyterian history in the West begin with the appointment in 1881 of the Rev. James Robertson as superintendent of missions.

THE MISSIONARY CALLED AND HONOURED

During his long years as minister of Kildonan, Black was a "foreign missionary." That is, he had not been formally "called" and inducted as minister to the congregation according to the rules of Presbyterian policy. The congregation first called him to be their minister before he left for Toronto in 1853. Since he was not settled in his mind and spirit about returning, he could not accept the call. In 1859 they called him again. He was about to take his family to the East, and the Rev. Mr. McTavish would come to Kildonan to relieve him. Black decided to accept the call on his return when McTavish could induct him, but on their respective return journeys they passed each other. Black was therefore still a missionary.

In 1872 Black received his third call to Kildonan, at a regular Presbytery meeting. He accepted this one, and with the acceptance, knew that finally he had put behind him his thoughts of a scholarly ministry in the East. He and Kildonan were tied to one another for his lifetime.

By 1881 Black was tired and ill. The various exertions between 1870 and 1880 had taken their toll. He was given leave and he made a journey to his old home, to relatives and friends, seeking some improvement, but while the visit was refreshing, the improvement was only temporary.

In 1875, the several Presbyterian bodies in Canada had combined to form the Presbyterian Church in Canada, and the surging new West was becoming one of its great challenges. The General Assembly of 1881 met in Kingston while Black was in the East. He attended and found that no fewer than ten presbyteries had nominated him as moderator. But this honour came too late for Black; his poor health forced him to decline.

THE SEVERING OF THE TIE

Black returned home to Kildonan, not to the manse where he had brought Henrietta, but to the deserted College building between the manse and the Nisbet school. He had bought it in 1878, along with a quarter acre of church land for a home for Laurenda and his young children after he was gone. In September 1881 he celebrated with his people the thirtieth anniversary of his arrival. He had come resentfully and with self-depreciation, at the call of the Church, to end their isolation at the expense of his own. On the foundation of their faithfulness he had led them in building a lighthouse on the prairies. The light attracted other lights to shine around them: James Nisbet had come to the Indians and a valiant company followed him; George Bryce had come to the College and his colleagues had begun to arrive; James Robertson had gone to follow the new settlers wherever they would go. John Black could pass on the torch.

On 11 February 1882, at age sixty-four and after several months of incapacitation, Black died. The Kildonan folk laid him beside Henrietta and the three boys in Kildonan churchyard. At the service in the church, the Rev. Thomas Hart, classics professor at Manitoba College, said, "The all Wise Disposer of events seemed to say that our friend's work on earth was done, and called for him from labour and trial here, to the rest that remains for the just."[30]

James Robertson and Presbyterian Church extension in Manitoba and the North West, 1866–1902

Catherine Macdonald

GAINING A FOOTHOLD

Following the 1869–70 Riel Rebellion, the Canadian Presbyterian Churches became more and more confident of the potential of the West for agricultural settlement. Full of nationalistic enthusiasm imbibed from the pages of newspapers like George Brown's *Globe*, Presbyterians prepared to take part in the winning of the West for Canada and for Christ. These two missions – the national and the spiritual – seemed inextricably bound together in the minds of mid-Victorian Canadian churchmen and churchwomen. In the struggle to establish churches on the plains after 1870, Canadian Presbyterians felt that they could not evangelize without Canadianizing, nor could they Canadianize without evangelizing. They took for granted the fact that Canada was a unitary English-speaking state based on British parliamentary and judicial traditions which looked to Britain for a sense of identity and kinship. Their need to reinforce this vision of Canada came to influence decision making about church extension as much as did the desire to spread the gospel message and to provide western communities with the spiritual and social services of the Church.

During the period between 1866 and 1902, Presbyterians found themselves dealing not only with the practical problems of raising buildings and finding missionaries, but also with evangelizing groups outside their dominant Anglo-Saxon constituency: natives, French Canadians, Mormons, Icelanders and Chinese to name a few. The urgency of molding these people into good Canadians as well as good Presbyterians introduced additional complications into the evangelical process. Ministering to such a diverse clientele, Presbyterians found that, rather than compete with other Protestant denominations and duplicate their services, practicality dictated cooperation and the raising of a common Protestant front in the face of contentious issues like the "Manitoba school question."[1] How the Church accomplished this many-sided mission and, in so doing, how it worked out relationships with other churches in the region had crucial implications both for the subsequent history of the Church and for the society in whose welfare the Church was so earnestly concerned.

By 1901, the Presbyterian Church had cause for satisfaction. Numerically the third largest denomination in eastern Canada in 1871, the Presbyterian Church in Canada had become the largest Protestant body in western Canada and was gaining on the Methodists in the national tally.[2] In order to reach that point, the Church had shown a surprising ability to adapt its traditional ways of doing things. The awesome energy and persuasive personality of James Robertson, as first superintendent of home missions, ensured that the administration of church extension was kept simple and direct. Due in large part to his efforts, the Church was able to establish a solid presence in a region with sparse population, separated by vast distances, whose ability to raise buildings and support ministers was limited by the high cost of living and scarcity of cash.

Prior to 1866, the efforts of the Presbyterian Church in Canada in the West had centred on the ministry of the Rev. John Black. Black's isolation at Red River ended with the arrival of the Rev. James Nisbet in 1863. Though Black certainly had use for an assistant in the expanding Red River parish, Nisbet had come west on the understanding that the Foreign Missions Committee would begin a mission to the Indians, and that he would be the first missionary. Although the Roman Catholic, Anglican and Wesleyan Methodist Churches had already initiated missions to the Indians of the region, the Presbyterians had been unable to find either a willing missionary or money to fund such a project.

Finally, in 1866, Nisbet left Red River with Hugh McKay, a Metis who was fluent in Cree, to found an Indian mission at Prince Albert. Evidence of an increasing interest in the West on the part of the Canada Presbyterian Church,[3] the Prince Albert Mission was to be the central hub of a system of regional Indian missions. These missions were to be run on the industrial school model – an idea used with some success by the Presbyterian Churches in the United States. It was a measure of the geographic naiveté of Robert Burns, convenor of the Foreign Missions Committee, that he envisioned Prince Albert as the mid-point between the existing Presbyterian missions in the West – one at Red River and two others at Nanaimo and New Westminster, British Columbia. Nevertheless, the location of the mission was carefully planned to fit in with the existing missions of the other denominations. "The regions spoken of," said Burns, "combined the advantages of being easily accessible from Red River; within reach of the Mines, and of experienced Missionaries of the Episcopalian and Wesleyan bodies, whose connection and cooperation would be of material consequence, and yet sufficiently isolated, as not in the least to interfere with their Departments."[4]

It is not unlikely that Church leaders were looking ahead to the time when settlers would begin to head west from Ontario. The American westward trek, which had begun three decades earlier, had been bloodied by Indian wars. The image of Indians in the Canadian mind had been formed from accounts of the Battles of Bull Run and Wounded Knee. Presbyterians sincerely wanted to bring Christ to the natives and to prepare them for the changes that would soon be at hand. However, the pacification of the tribes that would be the desirable by-product of Christian outreach cannot have been far from the minds of Burns and his contemporaries. As the Rev. George Bryce later said, "It is only now by persistent and unwearied efforts that we can hope to conquer the Indians by the arts of peace, and by inducing him to take the hoe in place of the tomahawk, to meet nature's obstacles."[5]

The founding of the Prince Albert Mission also underscored a fundamental cleavage in Presbyterian thinking between what constituted "home" missions and what constituted "foreign" missions. Even after the transfer of the North West to Canada, Indian missions continued to be administered under the Foreign Missions Committee, as were the later missions to the Ruthenian, Chinese and Japanese in Canada. The distinction was therefore not geographic, but linguistic and cultural. The world was divided, effectively, into Anglo-Saxons and non-Anglo-Saxons. It was an acknowledgement that, in practical terms, ministering to the pagans in Korea presented the same problems as ministering to the pagans in western Canada.

The home missions front was less culturally complicated than the foreign mission front was, but presented formidable practical problems. The decade following the 1869–70 Riel Rebellion brought many changes to the West. In late 1870, the small group of Presbyterian missionaries centred at Red River was authorized to form the Presbytery of Manitoba and the North West. Black had been joined by the Revs. William Fletcher and John McNabb. In 1871 the Rev. George Bryce was sent to found a Presbyterian college at Red River and to throw his formidable energies into the growing home missions work of the new presbytery. The founding of the presbytery meant that administration in the region could be carried on much more efficiently without the necessity of consulting the Home and Foreign Missions Committees in Toronto over every minute point.[6] This autonomy was further enhanced when, in 1875, the Presbytery of Manitoba and the North West was granted synodical powers.[7] In this way the General Assembly, which was the highest court of the Church, was able to give the presbytery more power in relation to disbursement of home missions grants and other financial matters than would normally be the case.

The Church's growth was slow and difficult during this period. Mission stations covered large areas and served many preaching points. For instance, in 1880, the Rev. James Farquharson's station at Rock Lake included Cartwright, Pilot Mound, Carman, Miami, Baldur and Snowflake. Presbyterian ministers could have been forgiven for thinking that they had unwittingly joined the ranks of the itinerant Methodists. Problems with weather and transportation meant that mission fields staffed during the summer had to be abandoned during the winter months. The completion of the rail link between St. Paul and St. Boniface in 1879 speeded up the rate of incoming settlers, but travel within Manitoba was still a matter of cart trails and mud in summer, sleighs and bitter cold in winter. As the Canadian Pacific Railway (CPR) inched through the Precambrian Shield toward Winnipeg, the Rev. Daniel McKerracher conducted a lonely ministry to the railway navvies from his headquarters at Prince Arthur's Landing, now Thunder Bay.

Winnipeg soon established itself as the centre of population. The presbytery accepted the fact and moved Manitoba College, over Black's objections, from Kildonan to a house on Main Street. In its first years, the College was little more than a glorified high school. The two professors, Bryce and the Rev. Thomas Hart, were required to do their share of home missions work in addition to keeping a full teaching and administrative schedule. Bryce saw the urgency of providing theological training at the College, but the General Assembly refused to allow it.

The administrative aspects of church extension – organizing new congregations, pressing the General Assembly for more missionaries, providing services for vacant and fledgling congregations – pressed the presbytery members to the limits of their time and energies. It was clear that more men were required for the work. The Assembly Home Missions Committee, which oversaw all domestic missions, was far away in Toronto. Its long-time convenor, the Rev. William Cochrane, kept tight hold of the purse strings. His policy was caution; a mission would have to prove a significant measure of financial stability before he would allow a missionary to be sent. Those on the spot, especially Bryce and James Robertson, chafed against the conservative policy of Cochrane. They viewed church extension as nothing less than a race in which the first person on the ground would gain the advantage. The Presbytery Home Missions Committee report to the Assembly in 1880 urged more concerted action, more money and more missionaries. It recommended that a missionary should appear in the field as soon as some families had gathered in the area; here the missionary should hold prayer and praise at a central point for any who would come.[8]

Adopting such a policy would mean that the committee's budget would have to provide the missionary's salary for an indefinite period until the congregation gathered enough income to become self-supporting; the significance of the situation was not lost on the convenor. Since homesteading families were notably cash-poor, it could easily be years before the committee was freed of the multiplying financial burden. Cochrane declined to implement the recommendations.

THE ROBERTSON ERA

The forthright voice of James Robertson speaks clearly in the 1880 Report of the Presbytery of Manitoba and the North West to the General Assembly. Abrupt in manner and inelegant in appearance, Robertson dominated the period between 1880 and 1902. Though it is unfashionable to give more weight to individuals than to impersonal forces in historical analysis, much credit for the success of the Presbyterian effort in the West must go to Robertson. He showed an almost frightening degree of stamina and attention to detail in performing his duties as superintendent of missions, and the trim bureaucratic structure that allowed churches and manses to be raised with amazing despatch in new locales was largely his brainchild.

Robertson was born in Scotland in 1839 and educated at the University of Toronto, Princeton Seminary and Union Theological Seminary. He was acquainted with the methods of church and mission extension of the American Presbyterian Churches and this was to stand him in good stead.[9] In 1868 he spent a period of time working in a Settlement House in a slum neighbourhood of New York. He wanted to return to Canada, however, and decided to accept a call to Norwich, Ontario, in 1869. Here he laboured diligently: too diligently, perhaps – at the end of five years he had to take a six-month leave to rest and regain his health. A mood of restlessness led him to volunteer for a short term of missionary duty in the clear air of the North West, where the climate was said to have great curative powers. He was to supply the pulpit of Knox Church in Winnipeg, but when he arrived, the position was occupied by a Church of Scotland missionary. Seeing a potentially divisive situation at hand, Robertson wisely informed the Presbytery Home Missions Committee that he would tour the outlying missions and fill in where needed. This tour brought the problems of church extension clearly into focus for him. His description of the usual venues for church services during this period, contained in a much later report to the General Assembly, is worth quoting at length:

Religious services were therefore conducted in country districts almost wholly in settler's houses. These were frequently small, and so low of roof sometimes as to make it difficult for an ordinary man to stand erect. Granaries, stables and stable lofts were sometimes resorted to, but the sounds and sights and smells occasionally marred the effect of the service. . . . The C.P.R. Company generously put their station houses at our disposal, and in several cases their offer was accepted. The arrival of trains, however, during the time of service – a frequent occurrence – interefered seriously with the effect produced by the preaching of the truth. In some instances the only available places were billiard rooms, bar rooms, or the dining rooms of hotels. People who were accustomed to frequent such places on other days for other purposes scarcely cared to attend religious services there on the sabbath. They were anxious not to mix things.[10]

The next year, 1875, Robertson was called to Knox in Winnipeg, and he soon became the powerhouse behind home missions in the presbytery. His ability, ambition and stamina quickly made him the leader of the "progressive" faction of younger ministers in the presbytery. This group, which included Bryce, threw itself into the political and social development of the province as members of the Protestant school board, founders of the provincial university, members of the new Historical and Scientific Society and, more often than not, supporters of the Liberal Party. In 1880 Robertson was appointed to the Assembly Home Missions Committee where he was able to press his views directly to Cochrane. He felt that the Church needed a man whose sole job was to travel to new areas, assemble congregations, oversee the creation of mission stations, and carry the heavy administrative load of arranging for missionaries to supply new stations. The rest of the presbytery, overworked and stretched too thinly, welcomed the idea. When, at the Assembly of 1881, the position was approved, Robertson was already the prime candidate.

The creation of the office of superintendent of home missions was significant in a number of respects. Traditionally, power and authority had been vested in the corporate bodies of the Church: ministers and elders gathered into presbyteries, synods, and finally, the General Assembly. Robertson's appointment maintained the tendency of the Church to create a bureaucracy to take over the executive functions that could no longer be handled by the Church courts. Mindful of the dangers of this, the Assembly established guidelines which were intended to control the power of the superintendent. Robertson's prime duty was to conduct the general "supervision and furtherance of the entire mission work of our Church in Manitoba and the North-West,"[11] which meant that he was responsible for visiting all mission stations, and supplemented congregations, organizing new stations and moderating in financial matters between the stations and the Home Missions Committee.

The guidelines were somewhat vague, however, on the point of Robertson's accountability. Was he subject to the control of the presbytery or the Assembly Home Missions Committee? There had already been some friction between the two bodies. The presbytery was fearful that the superintendency would minimize the influence of presbytery in mission decision making within the region. The guidelines represented a compromise between the two authorities. Robertson was to report to and consult with the presbytery and was a member of the committee. Although he would personally pay out grants to the stations, no money could be drawn by him without the consent of Cochrane. However, Robertson's personal connection with the presbytery and his efforts to take presbytery's wishes into account tended to minimize the friction.

That there was widespread support for the office of superintendent was indicative of the willingness of Presbyterian church members to change traditional ways of doing things to meet what was clearly felt to be the urgent challenge of establishing the Church in the West. Yet, among more conservative Presbyterians, there was a slight undercurrent of fear that a new prelacy was being introduced into this least hierarchical of churches. A slanderous letter, signed by "a Blue Presbyterian," was published in the *Toronto Daily Mail* in 1883 which accused Robertson of ignorance, incompetence and of assuming the powers of a bishop. The letter also contained allegations about his private life; he was accused of being the kind of man who, "unbishoplike, lives part from his wife and family with his wife's friends, while he boards like a boss Walker at Winnipeg's Queen's, which grand hotel is the land bourse of the North-West, where speculators from everywhere congregate and gamble in 'Manitoba dirt.' "[12]

The letter was mischievous in intent and the editors quickly issued an apology to forestall legal action. It showed clearly, however, that there was some opposition to Robertson and his methods and some feeling that he had too much power.

This power was increased with the founding of the Church and Manse Building Fund, the sole purpose of which was to grant and lend money to new congregations. Robertson had seen similar funds in action in the United States. Here was a way, he felt, of solving the problem of cash-poor settlers with no place to worship. The Church could be not only quickly on the spot but also highly visible.

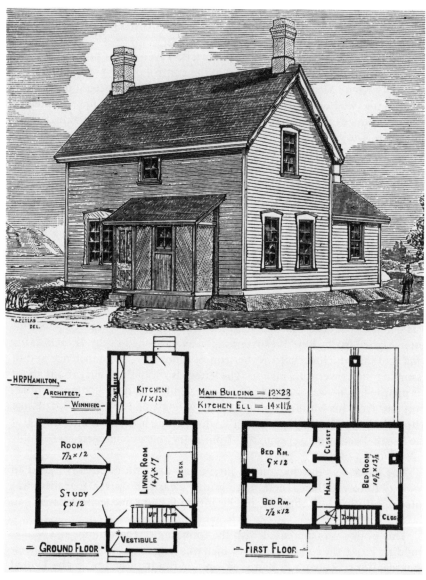

Design for combined church and manse, Presbyterian Church and Manse Building Fund Committee, 1886. (Photo courtesy of United Church Archives.)

The plan, as adopted by the Assembly of 1882, was for the Building Fund to be capitalized at $100,000, raised by subscription and bequests, the canvassing to be undertaken both in Canada and in Britain. The fund was to be disbursed by a board consisting of the convenor of the Assembly Home Missions Committee (Western Section), the superintendent and six other members to be appointed annually by the Assembly. As if to underline the Church's intention to be closer to the scene of the action, the board was to meet quarterly in Winnipeg.

All applications to the Building Fund were to be made through the presbytery and with the recommendation of the presbytery but the board was to be the final judge of the merits of the application. Grants were not to exceed one-fifth of the total cost of the building and loans were not to exceed fifty percent. No loans or grants were to be made without the congregation obtaining a valid deed to the property in the form approved by the board. Loans were made at five percent per annum – a favourable rate compared to the six percent offered by banks and commercial lenders. Typical of the first loans made by the board was the $800 loan made to the Nelson congregation in December 1882 for the building of a manse. The board requested security either in the form of personal bonds from the trustees or as a mortgage on the property, the amount to be repaid in two annual instalments with interest at five percent.[13]

In 1883 the Building Fund became incorporated in order "to receive property in trust for congregations that exist or may yet be formed, in places where it may be difficult for some time to secure a resident board of trustees."[14] This allowed Robertson to scout out attractive parcels of land in new townsites. When he was assured that a site would be serviced by the railway, he would buy the land, which would be held in trust by the fund until such time as a congregation could be formed. To assess whether Robertson's land dealings crossed the thin line between prudent investment and speculation is beyond the scope of this paper. Suffice it to say, however, that the intent behind these land purchases was to secure property at reasonable prices in order to facilitate the building of places of worship.

Robertson did everything he could to reduce construction costs. He arranged for standard contractor's plans of simple frame buildings to be drawn up and made available to congregations. Through the board of the Building Fund, he arranged for lumber to be made available at below-market prices and persuaded the CPR to transport it at half the ordinary freight rate.

Combined with the Augmentation Fund, a fund which paid the portion of a missionary's salary that the local church was unable to pay, the Church and Manse Building Fund allowed congregations to worship in proper surroundings and have the services of a minister while the community was still at a formative stage. During the first four years of the Building Fund, seventy-five churches and manses were built in Manitoba and the North West, compared with fifteen buildings in the previous eight years.[15] Unfortunately, the board had overestimated the ability of local churches to pay back the loans in the two or three large annual payments required. Many accounts went into arrears with the Building Fund between 1882 and 1896 as the Prairie economy endured a series of depressions punctuated by pallid rallies. The original capitalization had to be augmented with yearly increases. What was originally intended to be a short-time fund-raising effort continued on, with altered terms of reference to match the new conditions of the twentieth century, right up to the time of church union.

In carrying out his varied duties as superintendent, Robertson seems almost to have taken up residence on a CPR train. Day or night, he could often be found waiting for his train at a railway siding, perhaps seated on his carpet-bag, passing the time by writing letter after letter to Cochrane in Toronto, Bryce in Winnipeg or the Rev. J.C. Herdman in Calgary, among many others. The letters might be about pulpit supply in Kamsack, a new application to the Building Fund, the disgraceful state of religion on Indian reserves, improvement of the Protestant schools, or the complaints of new missionaries faced with the deprivations of remote missions. When the train steamed up to the siding, the conductor would help him stow his bag on board and Robertson would find an unoccupied seat and settle in for a few hours' sleep under his coat until his next stop. At the end of the line, he would rent or borrow a horse and buckboard to drive to the outskirts of the line of settlement.

It is hard not to make a hero out of Robertson, and C.W. Gordon did not resist the temptation when he came to write *The Life of James Robertson* in 1908.[16] The popular image of Robertson perpetuated by his book minimized the abrasive, stubborn side of Robertson's personality and emphasized the sacrifices he and his family made for the Church. Much sentiment was wrung from the lonely vigil of Mrs. Robertson as she waited for her husband to make his occasional visits to her home in Toronto. He allowed himself to spend only one Christmas with his family during his twenty-one years as superintendent.

Robertson was a profoundly restless person. He could not stay in one place for long – not in college, not in the pastorate at Norwich, not even in the bustling village of Winnipeg. He was happiest when on the move. The life he chose was lonely and full of physical deprivations but the letters he wrote are full of unforced zest. Whether joking to his wife about the peccadillos of a fellow minister or sharing a few choice bits of gossip with his friend the Rev. Andrew Baird, the writer of these letters was no martyr.[17]

Nor could he understand why the missionaries under his supervision could not measure up to the standard he set for himself. Recruiting them in the first place was difficult. People in the East were less confident of the rosy future of the North West than were the western boosters. A Knox College student contemplating a missionary career wrote to Andrew Baird at Fort Edmonton in 1885: "The conduct of many missionaries is hard to explain. Many of them tell us wonderful tales of what they have done and indulge in wild imagination regarding the future, but then they are so anxious to make way for someone else."[18]

During the 1880s and early 1890s it was easy to build churches but hard to fill pulpits. Many ministers came for a few years and then returned, consciences salved, to the relative comforts of the East. Others came and gave their best effort only to suffer complete breakdowns in health. According to Robertson, the bookish men succumbed early; he once said that missionaries should learn "less Latin and more horse."[19] The farm-bred boys were better suited to missionary life on the prairies. Blessed with an ox-like constitution nurtured on a farm in Perth county, Baird built the first Presbyterian Church at Fort Edmonton in 1882, doing much of the hauling and carpentry himself. Ministers needed practical skills as much as they did clerical skills in order to survive. It took the economic boom of the later 1890s and the establishment of Manitoba College as a local training centre for western missionaries to increase the number of ministers willing to make a career of ministry in the West.

PROTESTANTS CLOSE RANKS

When a Presbyterian missionary arrived in a new settlement, he would often find that a Methodist missionary was not far away. Their relationship was usually civil, often cordial. Sometimes a subtle competitive spirit arose, but more often than not both were content to hold service in the area and minister to whomever would come. Often arrangements were made that were satisfactory to both parties. For instance, in Birtle during the early 1880s, the Methodist and Presbyterian missionaries held services on alternate Sundays in the school house, the same congregation attending both services.[20] The two denominations were still very conscious of their differences, but they realized that, in relation to the task of church extension and to other churches, they had a great deal in common.

One of these common bonds was a belief that Canada was a British country and that its future depended on the upbuilding of a unified English-speaking society in which diversity would be tolerated, but only within strict limits. It was in defence of this belief and against the forces perceived to be threatening it that Methodists, Presbyterians and most other Protestant denominations closed ranks together.

The late nineteenth century was a time of palpable tension between Protestant and Catholic in Canada. By tying French-Canadian survival to a strong Catholic Church, the Roman Catholic hierarchy had regained the position of leadership that it had lost during Lower Canada's brief fling with liberal ideas in the 1830s.[21] Following the first Vatican Council in 1870, at which papal infallibility was declared, Quebec clergy, aided by a considerable immigration of clergy from Europe, increasingly embraced ultramontane ideas. Pious the Ninth, in his syllabus of errors, emphatically rejected the separation of church and state and other liberal ideals that had come to be the cornerstone of the reform church social outlook. With growing anger, Canadian Protestants watched what they regarded as unwarranted interference by Roman Catholic clergy in the affairs of the Canadian state. In justification of the French-Canadian mission work of the Canada Presbyterian Church, Robert Burns had said, "Nowhere is Papal devotion more ardent, or priestly tyranny more grinding, or the servitude of the masses more abject, than in Lower Canada. The Protesant element is being sedulously weeded out. The chains are being rivetted on the soil and on society."[22] One could imagine the unease with which Protestants of every stripe regarded the population statistics of the new Province of Manitoba in 1871. French-Canadian and French-speaking Metis taken together, almost all Catholic, were the most numerous section of the population.

Following the 1869–70 Riel Rebellion, the young Presbytery of Manitoba felt some urgency about obtaining at least one missionary who spoke French to work in the predominantly French-speaking parishes south of Winnipeg. A motion was passed by the presbytery in March 1872 "to recommend the Home Missions Committee to send a Missionary to this province as soon as possible, able to preach in the French and English languages. There being no protestant minister at Pembina in which place and vicinity there are a few Presbyterian families and others who it is believed would readily follow us if the means of grace could be supplied to them, it is most desirable that that field should be occupied by us without delay."[23]

This is not the language of frontal assault on Catholicism, to be sure. But the phrase "those who it is readily believed would follow us" must surely be a coy reference to French-speaking Catholics of the district. Presbyterians had devoted considerable effort to "French evangelization" in Quebec during the previous decade, erecting a school at Pointes aux Trembles and creating a board of French evangelization to oversee the work. In spite of this effort, outright converts were few. Getting converts was important in Manitoba too, but the main strategy for Manitoba appeared to be to establish a Protestant presence to prevent the Catholics having an overwhelming numerical influence.

In any case, a bilingual missionary did not materialize. By 1876, when the Rev. John Scott arrived in Emerson, it was already clear that the rate of immigration from Ontario would reduce the much-feared influence of French-speaking Catholics. There was never again any talk of a French evangelizing mission in Manitoba; there would be no western Pointes aux Trembles.

If Presbyterian fears of Catholic domination of the non-Indian population were allayed by the demographic shift, they were exacerbated on the Indian missions front. Following the negotiation of the treaties throughout the 1870s, the Indian bands began to settle on reserves, making the Indians easier to evangelize. As a result, the pace of competition for Indian converts was stepped up considerably. Presbyterians resolved to intensify their efforts in their sphere of influence, that is, the newly settled reserves of the southern plains. They continued to cooperate with the other Protestant denominations in sharing the "territory." When a band of Sioux from the Dakotas took refuge near Birtle, the presbytery looked into sending a missionary to them. Upon receiving word from the bishop of Rupert's Land that an Anglican mission was in the late planning stages, the presbytery abandoned its own plan. (In the end, the Anglican initiative fell through and a Presbyterian mission to the Sioux was begun.)

When one looks beyond the united front presented to the world by the Protestant denominations, however, their relationships, one to another, were not so straightforward. By and large, the cooperative strategy and the tacit agreement not to "poach on each other's preserves" prevailed. But there were some tensions. The Anglicans retained the air of an established church. Presbyterians rankled at the order of precedence in the new province by which only the bishop of Rupert's Land and the archbishop of St. Boniface were invited to ceremonial occasions at Government House. This and the distaste of Presbyterians for the episcopal system of church government tended to make Anglicans and Presbyterians aloof from one another.

Although the educational standard of the Methodist clergy was, by this time, similar to their own, Presbyterians persisted in regarding themselves as the more literate church. This condescension gave rise to a number of small disputes related to the public school system in which the clergy of both churches were heavily involved as trustees, school board members and inspectors. In 1884, for example, when the Winnipeg School Board was reviewing new textbooks prior to choosing a series, Robertson wrote to Professor Thomas Hart to persuade Hart to emphasize the value of the Royal Readers and minimize the Gage series which the Methodists supported.[24] In spite of such petty squabbles, in 1902 when plans for union began to intensify, the two churches could look back on an era of substantial cooperation on the larger issues.

Only occasionally did the Presbyterian Church break the unwritten law of non-interference with another Protestant denomination. When interference did occur, there was usually a political reason. When George Bryce founded a mission to the Icelandic community in north Winnipeg in 1883, the Icelandic Lutheran Church was outraged.[25] The Lutherans had only recently been able to build and staff their own church in the neighbourhood. Where had the Presbyterians been when Icelanders were pining for the consolations of religion? As the Lutherans suspected, Bryce was more worried about the social separatism of the Icelanders than he was about the possibility of their falling away from God. They were setting up their own schools, retaining their language and, what was worse, some were flaunting radical political opinions. In the end, the mission failed because the Icelanders supported their own church and because Superintendent Robertson did not support the idea. He was no more in favour of ethnic enclaves than Bryce was, but he balked at interfering so openly with another denomination.

The appearance of Mormons (Latter Day Saints) in southern Alberta severely tried the tolerance of Presbyterians. Although the main-line denominations did not regard Mormonism as even Christian, Presbyterian opposition to the Latter Day Saints was not, in the end, based on doctrinal difference, but on the matter of the social separatism of the Mormon colony. Still Robertson was torn because, in all other respects, the Mormons made excellent settlers. As he said in a report to the Home Missions Committee in 1893, "the importance of doing something for the spiritual welfare of these people will be apparent when we take into account the rapid natural increase which is a characteristic of Mormon communities, their industry, thrift and steady increase in wealth, and the influence unfavourable to evangelical religion which such a powerful organization must exert on the general public, morally, socially and politically."[26] The Canadian state required unity, not pluralism; large unassimilated groups dissenting culturally from the British vision of Canadian society presented too many problems for the young nation to handle. At least this was the view of the majority of people in western Canada, and the Presbyterian Church identified totally with it. Enforcing unity was regarded as the concern of the Church just as much as it was the concern of the state.

The large numbers of Presbyterians recorded in the 1901 census signalled that the formative period of church extension in the West was drawing to a close. On the evidence of numbers of worshippers and buildings raised, the Church had been successful in its outreach on the home missions front. The success of the foreign mission effort was harder to assess. The sense of unease behind Presbyterian outreach to natives, Roman Catholics, Mormons and Icelanders betrayed a fear that these groups would undermine the stability of Canadian society and, by extension, undermine the secure place of the Presbyterian Church, along with other Protestant churches, close to the locus of power in that society. The Anglo-Canadian social and political views of Presbyterians became so interwoven with their Christian evangelism that the distinction between the two was lost. Social gospel critics, who became more vocal after 1902, would accuse the Church of valuing middle-class respectability more than the prophetic vision of Christ. The Church's close identification of its own interests with those of the Canadian nation impaired its ability to recognize those occasions when justice demanded that the Church stand with the weak against the powerful.

But however compromised the Church was by its worldliness, however paternalistic its outreach to "foreign" people seems to modern eyes, Presbyterians sincerely grappled with the world as they saw it, and much that they accomplished in the West deserves praise. Robertson and many others of his generation spent themselves trying to bring the spiritual comforts of the Church to the new society on the plains. Their down-to-earth pragmatism and moral earnestness, for good or ill, left its mark, and allowed denominational pride to be laid aside in favour of cooperation with other Protestant churches. It was the experience of cooperation that allowed serious union talks between the Methodists and Presbyterians to begin in 1902. Robertson's death in the same year, of diabetes and exhaustion, seemed to symbolize that one period in the history of the Church was ending, and another, no less challenging and confusing, was on the horizon.

The Woodsworths:
James and J.S. – father and son

Benjamin Smillie

How could two men, father and son, be at the same time very different yet very similar? Both Woodsworths had the same first name, James, although the son was frequently called J.S. (To avoid confusion, James will be the name used to refer to the father and J.S. to the son throughout this article.) Both men had an important effect on the history of western Canada. Both had six children and both are recorded by their families as ideal fathers. They were very fond of each other.

James, the father, is described by S.D. Chown, general secretary of the Methodist Church, as a man with "the prophet's vision of the possibilities of this continent-wide Dominion of Canada, and of the organising strategy by which her riches will, with increasing lavishness, be distributed for the benefit of the whole world."[1] J.S., the son, is described by the Canadian historian, Kenneth McNaught, as a man whose "greatest achievement was his constant battle against the demands of institutional conformity."[2] The father, a man of enormous endurance, has been described as the prophet of missionary expansion; the son, better known than the father, could be described as the prophet of the "Great Refusal."[3]

JAMES, THE FATHER:
THE PROPHET OF MISSIONARY EXPANSION

Courage is one of the most striking qualities characteristic of James. Yet this quality is difficult to capture because of his modesty, also characteristic of him. In 1888, he was appointed superintendent of Methodist Missions for Manitoba and the Canadian Northwest. Two years later, he was on tour, doing "Indian work" for his church on Lake Winnipeg. His diary for 19 July, written while his party rested after travelling in a small sailboat, reads: "Passed Montreal point, then Warren's Landing or the 'Old Fort,' the building had long since either been removed or crumbled into ruins. . . . We are now among the scenes familiar to the Hudson's Bay Company *two hundred years ago.*"[4] The reader of James's saga is jolted from a world of central heating, jet travel and instant communications back to a pioneer day less than a hundred years ago when transportation was similar to that of more than two centuries before. This indomitable man with a "Parish" responsibility for the Methodist Church, had a superintendency which stretched for three thousand miles – from the Lakehead to Vancouver Island – yet transportation and living conditions were as primitive as they had been for centuries before.

Much of the epic quality of his work is understated in James's cryptic writing style. For example, after touring Methodist missions in Alberta with his son, he states simply, "We have just covered 800 miles on this buckboard trip."[5] This unemotional style is again apparent as he describes, while on a walking trip, coming across such discomforts as timber wolves "who fortunately were not hungry";[6] a mosquito-infested farmhouse in the vicinity of Moose Mountain in southern Saskatchewan;[7] sleeping on a "tick" mattress in an unheated shack at twenty below zero in Treherne, southern Manitoba, in the company of a student minister;[8] and a storm on Lake Winnipeg in a small sailboat which brought him and his companions to record their gratitude to God "for [His] care over [them] when exposed to imminent peril."[9] He records a similarly bad experience of a "dirty day" on the Pacific Ocean off the West Coast near the Queen Charlotte Islands with Thomas Crosby, the veteran west-coast missionary.[10]

Occasionally, however, James's reports change from his usual laconic narrative to one which shows his love of adventure and the more humorous side of life. On one such occasion, he describes reaching the end of the rail line at Lethbridge and travelling to Fort MacLeod by stagecoach; he puts the driver (Pollinger, usually referred to as Polly) at centre stage:

"Polly" (driving six horses) was not wanting in a love for adventure. The bottle was never far distant, and when specially hilarious he would sometimes make the descent of the hill much in the same spirit that a boy does that of a tobaggan slide, as if the sense of exhilaration experienced in a rapid descent were the object in view. . . . [Once] we were informed that the ferry was out of commission. Without a moment's hesitation "Polly" turned his horses towards the river. In these swiftly flowing mountain streams the river bottoms are continually changing through the influence of the currents. "Polly" had not forded this river that season, but in he dashed. . . . As if the bottom were well known, the driver plunged into the stream. Soon one wheel mounted a boulder; the coach almost overturned. The water rushed in, we climbed on the seats in order to keep dry. This dangerous emergency was instantly met by "Polly" who dexterously manipulated

James Woodsworth Sr. (Photo courtesy of Western Canada Pictorial Index.)

J.S. Woodsworth (Western Canada Pictorial Index)

his horses. They seemed to be all in a heap in the water, but they soon righted themselves and the coach regained its equalibrium. In a few minutes they were tearing up the other bank with the water escaping from our coach as from a very leaky bucket.[11]

The life of James unfolded over a wide expanse of inhospitable frontiers, and his quiet heroism was that of the early settlers. The hardships and perils he endured leave the reader in awe, asking, "What made it possible for him to survive when younger clergy went back east or gave up?" To answer this question it is important to see that he represented one thread of the biblical prophets' vision – the ability to see into the future in the light of contemporary events.

Writing in 1914 after the three prairie provinces were established, James recorded with excitement the waves of prairie immigrants expanding from 90,000 to 1,400,000 in thirty years.[12] Quoting Lord Dufferin on the governor-general's visit to Winnipeg, he described Canada as a young nation possessing the wealth of half a continent, "the peer of any power on earth." He concluded: "The day of the prophetic utterance is already dawning."[13]

His expectations included another vision of prophetic expansion, that is, the hope of union among the Presbyterian, Methodist and Congregational Churches. In 1914 he wrote, "The time is ripe for such a union. Essentially one in doctrine and discipline, it is difficult to justify existence as distinct organizations in this great land, especially at the present time, when all sources of every kind are necessary to do the work for which these churches are responsible, and which can be much more effectively accomplished by a united body than by each acting independently of the others."[14] To find personnel to meet the needs for the developing western frontier, James constantly quoted the Bible to the Ontario Church and to the potential new recruits amongst the Methodists in Britain. His favourite quote was Paul's call for help in his missionary journeys, "Come over to Macedonia and help us" (Acts 16:9).[15]

J.S., THE SON: THE PROPHET OF PROTEST

While J.S. had his father's passion for travel and could recount with vividness the stories of those he met, he was not the enthusiastic church supporter that his father was. Indeed, this may have been a disappointment to James, who felt that his first son should be "set aside" for the church. Although their paths parted in their reactions to the church, James and J.S. did have similarities, says Grace MacInnis, J.S.'s daughter. In a recent interview she said: "In personal lifestyle, my grandfather and father were very similar; they were incredibly abstemious. My father had only two suits at any time. Neither would drink or smoke. Everything went according to well prepared living."[16] Even on the issue of the church, James, the father, held on to the important principle that J.S. should "be true to [his] own convictions."[17] J.S.'s misgivings about the church are reflected in his letters to the Methodist Church in Manitoba. Twice J.S. resigned his ordination to ministry: first in 1902, two years after ordination, and again in 1907. On each occasion, J.S. was given a more challenging job, but being a Woodsworth may have made it difficult for him to abandon the church. Furthermore, as Grace MacInnis says in her biography of J.S., the Methodist Church proved to be flexible, theologically, if not politically, in its willingness to make room for a theological rebel.[18]

Many accounts of the lives of J.S. and his father, James, show how similar they were in their inexhaustible ability to live, themselves, in the skins of other people. But while they had this common capacity for empathy, the way in which each perceived life was often quite different. For example, on a trip to Britain shortly after his graduation, J.S., like his father, could express with some excitement the privilege of standing in John Wesley's pulpit in City Road Chapel in London.[19] But J.S. saw other sights that never grasped his father's attention. In a letter to his sister Edith, written in 1899 while he was studying at Mansfield College, Oxford, J.S. made a trip to Mansfield House, a settlement house sponsored by the College in the slums of London. J.S. describes the hungry faces of boys wanting to get the soup ladle at the bottom of the bowl to get the meaty soup.[20] In a letter to his mother the next year, J.S. contrasts the magnificence of Edinburgh Castle with the rat-infested squalor of the Cowgate and Canongate, the poorest areas of the city.[21] Back in western Canada, in the farm weekly called *The Grain Growers Guide*, J.S. describes the terrible injustice of the premature death of a baby and the funeral service of a little child. He recalls how the words, "For as much as it has pleased Almighty God – in [God's] wise Providence to take unto [this child]," choked in his throat. "In my heart I said, 'This is not true! I know what had killed the baby, it was bad milk and bad housing.' "[22] On another occasion, in beautiful poetic prose, J.S. writes about the consecration of a child's grave and reflects his love for the prairie:

Headed by the crucifix, the little procession moved slowly from the church to the grave – rough sunburned men, kerchiefed women and little children. The grave – it was only the third in "God's acre" – was marked by a crude wooden cross. The priest read the service and sprinkled the grave, then all knelt in a little group and chanted a hymn. It was a most touching scene – the little grave, the reverent spirit of the kneeling group, the subdued grief of the parents. . . . The wind stirred the long prairie grasses, a meadow-lark's note rang across the fields and the Western sun bathed the whole in a golden glow. It was the hour when the mystery of the prairie cast its spell. . . . All heads were bowed low to receive the blessing. The great, rude tree with its crossbeam had been planted in the prairie soil. Death and Life were both there! Their spirits subdued, their faith strengthened, the little company departed quietly in the stillness of the evening.[23]

While James, the father, does not have the keen insight of J.S. into the political implications of poverty, nevertheless he does see Indians, lonely homesteaders and frightened women with the eye of pastoral compassion. In a tribute written thirteen years after his father's death in 1917, J.S. said: "It is difficult for one who lived so close to Dr. Woodsworth to sketch – much less appraise – his character and work. . . . In the best sense of the word my father was a gentleman. He had a high sense of honor, an unfaltering devotion to duty and a never failing courtesy. A literary purist once tried to convince me that 'kindly' was not an adjective. He had never known my father nor looked into his eyes."[24]

THE EFFECT OF SOCIAL AND ECONOMIC CONDITIONS ON JAMES IN THE PERIOD OF EARLY SETTLEMENT (1890–1917)

It would be misleading to explain the differences between father and son only as a contrast in personality and vocational interests. It is important to show also that the rapidly changing economic conditions in the fifty years between 1890 and 1940, the years which span the working lives of both men, did much to mold their outlooks.

We will first examine the economic conditions in the early frontier days. According to Canadian historian A.R.M. Lower, 1896 was the dramatic year of change in Canada's fortunes.[25] It was certainly a propitious time in the West. Settlement between 1865 and 1896 was predominantly in the United States where industry was flourishing, spurred on by new techniques developed after the Civil War. By 1890, the last boundary state, North Dakota, had been settled. The population in western Canada mushroomed, partly spurred on by the "manifest destiny" expansionism of American Republicanism and partly by the fact that the American frontier was now fully populated. By 1900, Manitoba number one hard wheat had won the reputation of being the best wheat in the world. Bonanza farms sprang up, inspiring the wealthy farmer and real estate speculator to endorse a popular phrase describing the optimism of the times: "If you couldn't boost, you mustn't knock."[26] Between 1901 and 1931, the population in the prairie provinces increased five-fold to 2,345,000. In 1901, Canadian production of wheat was fifty-two million bushels; in 1911, the volume had grown to 208 million bushels on the prairies alone and, by 1928, it had peaked at 544 million bushels from the three prairie provinces.[27] Wheat and flour exports yielded $10.9 million in

1901. In 1929, wheat and flour had become Canada's largest exports, bringing in $495 million.[28] It is this expansion that James, Methodist superintendent, celebrated in his pioneer ministry.

James was born in 1845.[29] His father was a building contractor and an active Wesleyan local preacher who helped to lay the foundation of civic and church life in Toronto. Grace MacInnis, James's granddaughter, says that her father, J.S., had a sword that belonged to his grandfather which the old patriarch had carried in the Rebellion of 1837 when, along with other Toronto Tories, he defended the city against the forces of William Lyon Mackenzie.[30] It was important for Methodists to defend their British connection because their arch enemy, John Strachan, a Presbyterian-turned-Anglican and later a bishop, was a member of the Upper Canada Executive Council which referred to Methodist preachers as "American in origin and sympathies, ignorant persons who had forsaken their proper callings to preach what they neither understood nor cared to learn."[31]

James would qualify as a Methodist who would have received Strachan's scorn. He came from a family with insufficient means to put him through university. His family were immigrants – United Empire Loyalists from the United States – who had lost all their financial resources in their move to Canada. James and his two brothers had to work for their educations. James wanted to become a Methodist minister and did so by taking his theological training under the direction of the district chairman of the Methodist Church in the Toronto area. He was ordained and appointed to a charge at Islington. Here he met and married Esther Josephine Shaver, a devoted Methodist like himself. It was in their Methodist home, Applewood, that their son J.S. was born in 1874. In 1882, James moved his family to Portage la Prairie in Manitoba where the charge was then under the authority of the Toronto Conference of the Methodist Church. James, the young ordained pioneer in the West, points out: "In 1882 the Toronto Conference included all the territory in Canada from the Belleville District on the East to Vancouver Island in the Pacific Ocean on the West."[32]

In 1883, a separate northwest conference of the Methodist Church in Canada was formed. In 1885, James was appointed to the pastorate of Brandon. It was an important historic year in the West because it marked the completion of the Canadian Pacific Railway and the second Riel Rebellion.

James's reaction to the Riel Rebellions illustrates his passion for British stability and "good government." He refers to the "salutary lesson" in British rule learned by "half-breeds and Indians." He adds: "They likewise experienced something of its clemency and righteousness."[33] A similar Anglophone outlook is represented in James's attitude toward immigration. He quotes with approval the headmaster of Upper Canada College in Toronto who felt that one of the great values of thirty-below weather in Canada was that it was "relieving Canada of the negro problem and was keeping out the lazy and improvident white."[34] He speaks with fear of Mormons who were flooding into the United States from central Europe. "Many of these," he says, "have brought with them the elements of a destructive, anti-Christian socialism."[35] It's startling to read these comments by James, whose son was the founder of the first democratic socialist party in Canada. James's comments underscore the shift in the political atmosphere that took place between 1900 and 1920 from frontier optimism to radical political action that culminated in the Winnipeg General Strike of 1919.

In 1905, James moved the headquarters of his home mission office from Brandon to Winnipeg. When the Alberta and Saskatchewan were made separate conferences in 1906, he retained the superintendency of the Methodist Church in Manitoba. Methodism on the frontier kept expanding, along with the growing nation. In his 1911 Annual Report, he illustrates the eloquence of statistics in showing this growth: "In 1902 there were 22,392 members; in 1910, 43,000. In the same year Manitoba Conference had 176 fields, 209 ministers and probationers; Saskatchewan Conference had 227 fields and 217 ministers and probationers. Alberta Conference had 201 fields and 255 ministers and probationers."[36]

J.S., in his tribute to his father, says, "Because of the limited opportunities of frontier ministry in the West, Dr. Woodsworth's intellectual interests may, perhaps, have been limited."[37] But, reading the story of James's superintendency, one must marvel at his organizational capacity. For example, he organized an intricate system of summer student mission fields in the West with the assistance of the Educational Society of the National Methodist Church in Canada in which the local charges were responsible for "board, lodging, railway fare from the field to the college and horse keep."[38] This system has been a model for subsequent student mission fields ever since (except that "horse keep" is now out and "gas mileage" is in). In one sentence, he makes another unheralded comment about ministerial leadership: "As a result of my seven visits, two hundred and eighty men have been brought from the Old Country."[39] Methodism had relied heavily on recruitment of ministers from Britain back to the days of the opening up of the West by the Hudson's Bay Company. The recruitment from Britain became particularly urgent in James's period of superintendency because Methodist churches were mushrooming with the new immigrants; at the same time, they hesitated to recruit from the United States for fear of being stigmatized as American sympathizers.

At the time of his retirement in 1914, James summed up his fifty years in the ministry in one long sentence:

In attempting to execute as far as I might be able, the instructions received from you, and what seemed to be in the best interests of the Church, I have visited once or oftener nearly every circuit and mission to ascertain from personal observation the exact state of affairs, to learn the needs and prospects of each locality and to render assistance as I could to further the interests of the Church in every possible way; to devise methods that would ensure greater efficiency and larger results, and to acquire such information as might be helpful in laying larger and broader plans for the upbuilding of our beloved Zion, and for promoting the cause and spreading the Gospel of our Lord Jesus Christ.[40]

THE EFFECT OF SOCIAL AND ECONOMIC CONDITIONS ON J.S.

In his tribute to his father, J.S. relates one occasion when he had told his father that his own thinking was changing and that it would lead him far from the position his father held. His father replied: "I am afraid I cannot help you much in the newer problems."[41] No one could have conceived, least of all his father who died in 1917, that one of the "newer problems" facing the son would be a docket in a Winnipeg court in 1919 which read, "The King versus J.S. Woodsworth."[42]

Canadian sociologist John Porter suggests that eastern Methodism was responsible for the wealth of Canada after Methodism became established in the Timothy Eatons, the Flavells and the Burtons who lived by the philosophy that thrift and hard work were marks of God's election. Methodism also spawned the radicals of the West, people like J.S. Woodsworth, Salem Bland, William Ivens and A.E. Smith, who emphasized the egalitarian, non-conformist tradition that came to be associated with the social gospel.[43] And, ironically, Methodism in the West also spawned capitalists like J.H. Ashdown, the hardware entrepreneur; Clifford Sifton, the newspaper mogul and Donald Mann, the railway tycoon. It was this group of capitalists whose influence and power were diminished after the Winnipeg General Strike, when radical Methodists were elected to political office. Is it surprising that J.S., along with other Methodist radical ministers, became incensed at the brutality of life in a most primitive "capitalist jungle," a jungle in which oppressive conditions were exacerbated by the hinterland status of the West?

His glimpse of the sordid life in the slums of Britain awakened the consciousness of J.S. Ordained in 1900, he was posted to a little church at Carievale, Assiniboia, where he had served as a student pastor. After a year he became pastor at Keewatin in the Lake of the Woods district, where logging and flour milling were the major industries. He describes the townspeople as "lonely people." Perhaps he was registering his own feelings, because by 1902 he had written his resignation to leave the parish ministry. However, he deferred his decision to leave the parish ministry when he was appointed assistant minister to Grace Church in Winnipeg. He said of the move, "I think I could understand how a man condemned to death would feel if suddenly he was reprieved and a good position offered to him."[44] This may indicate J.S.'s longing to be more intellectually challenged and also his wish to get married and bring his wife to a stimulating city setting.

In 1904 he married a college friend, Lucy Staples, and in 1905 their first child, Winona Grace, was born. Grace (now MacInnis) explains, in a biography of her father, that her name is "a combination from Longfellow's Hiawatha and [Grace Church] where [her parents] had started their work together."[45] Grace Church in Winnipeg had in its membership some of the wealthiest merchants in Winnipeg. This group had heard of the assistant minister's unorthodox theology but was perfectly willing to make allowances for Dr. James Woodsworth's son!

Winnipeg in 1904 was the home of Canada's great wheat barons and J.S. saw the unshared prosperity of these people as a subject for preaching. By the summer of 1906, his sermons at Grace were received with increasing disfavour. One conservative lawyer in the congregation suggested that the junior minister should give "less ill-digested sociology and more simple gospel preaching."[46] In a sermon delivered in 1904, J.S. stated his belief that money not only talks but also rules.[47] In another sermon he spoke about the "costly dresses, magnificent houses, expensive entertainment, as signs of the snobbishness and vulgarity of newly acquired wealth."[48] By the summer of 1906, the theological questions in his mind and the tension he was causing in the congregation, combined with ill health, necessitated that he take a leave of absence from the Church.

After a short interim pastorate at Revelstoke in the Rocky Mountains of British Columbia, Woodsworth again planned to resign from Methodist ministry. His resignation in 1907 was foiled by the offer of the superintendency of All Peoples' Mission in Winnipeg. Both J.S. and his wife, Lucy, expressed their delight over this appointment. In a letter to his friend, Charles Sissons, he explained, "Now I have been appointed to All Peoples' Mission. . . . This suits me better than any other appointment they could have given me." Lucy added this postscript: "James [J.S.] is working very hard. . . . I do think that at last he is in his element."[49]

As superintendent of All Peoples' Mission, J.S. became famous. His work among the immigrants, his establishment of the People's Forum, his organization of the Associated Charities of Winnipeg, his successful agitation for the first juvenile court in Canada in 1907, his organization of the Social Welfare League, plus the writing of two books were all accomplished while he was superintendent of All Peoples' Mission. In an article he wrote during this period for the *Christian Guardian*, he gives advice to ministers which he himself incorporated into his Winnipeg church: "There are some things the church cannot do; there is nothing it may not, through its pastor, inspire."[50]

J.S. found the rescue-mission orientation of All Peoples' Mission too frustrating for the massive needs of a city with a population outstripping its social resources. His increasing awareness of the need for social-political change made him impatient with the church's orientation of short-term solutions. "Justice, not charity" was the watchword of his new orientation. In 1913, he resigned from All Peoples' Mission to become secretary of the Canadian Welfare League. Then, in 1916, the governments of the three prairie provinces invited him to do the same work under government auspices rather than with the aid of private philanthropists. His tenure in the new position of director of the Bureau of Social Research was brief, however: after one year he wrote a letter to the *Manitoba Free Press* protesting the government's National Service Registration Scheme and his employers called for his resignation.[51]

J.S.'s written opposition to the National Service Registration Scheme may be viewed as pacifistic opposition, but it is important to note what some Canadian historians have missed – that his pacifism did not espouse an idealistic type of peace. Rather, his pacifism struck at the mountains of wealth that were being accumulated in the hands of arms dealers. His slogan was Conscript Capital Not Men[52] because he (and others) believed that distributive justice could only be achieved in a peaceable, sharing society. In an article he wrote in 1919, J.S. endorsed the main theme of a British Labour Party platform which called for progressive elimination of control of industry by capitalists through political means. The first means would be confiscation of private capital which would be brought about not by armed takeover, but by heavy taxation on large incomes and great estates. J.S. recommended that small incomes should not be taxed at all and that the largest incomes should be taxed at ninety-five percent. He also recommended a heavy inheritance tax based on the principle, "Naked a man comes into the world and naked he should leave it."[53]

Underlying his philosophy was the assumption that we must have production for use, not for profit. At the time of the Winnipeg General Strike in 1919, an apprentice's wage was ten cents per hour; the average construction worker earned $915 annually when the minimum annual requirement for a family of five was assessed at $1,503.[54]

J.S.'s outlook on justice stood in sharp contrast to his father's Methodism, which held in awe its rich, entrepreneur Church members. In an illustration of earlier Methodism, J.H. Riddell (a contemporary of James Woodsworth and president of Wesley College) describes in his book, *Methodism in the Middle West*,[55] an elderly pioneer minister, J.M. Harrison. When he retired in 1914, Harrison needed to buy furniture for his home. The store he chose in Calgary was owned by prominent Winnipeg Methodist millionaire J.H. Ashdown, to whom Riddell refers as the "merchant prince."[56] Ashdown refused to allow Harrison to pay for his furniture and picked up the bill himself. J.S. saw this outlook by Church leaders towards wealthy Methodists as obsequious and as a way of sanctifying their wealth.

This charity outlook brought J.S. to question an economic system where a woman in a Canadian city was reported by a church deaconess as working from morning to night to make a dozen pair of overalls for a total remuneration of fifty cents. He commends the philanthropic people who helped this woman but then adds, "Why should the welfare of this woman be dependent on the efforts of a few self-sacrificing individuals? . . . The whole wretched story makes our blood boil."[57]

Following his dismissal from the Bureau of Social Research, J.S. put his name before the Stationing Committee of the Methodist Church. He was called for one year as Methodist minister at Gibson's Landing, a coastal fishing village in British Columbia. But again his outspokenness – specifically, his opposition to the war – was met with much Church resistance and criticism. Consequently, in 1918, J.S. resigned from the ministry. He addressed ministers who failed to speak out, and chided them for their spineless behaviour. One minister replied, "One dare not be brave unless he has money."[58] Another had empathetic feelings but stopped short of action, saying, "I have often thought of making public the social conditions which are grinding down my poor people, but you know what the result would be – my usefulness would be gone."[59] Quoting the poet J.R. Lowell, J.S. reminded his fellow ministers that "they are slaves who fear to speak for the fallen and the weak."[60] While in the ministry at Gibson's Landing, J.S. Woodsworth organized a local cooperative which brought him into conflict with a group he called the "local store keeper and a few of his toads."[61] He was dismissed from the Church at Gibson's Landing in 1918.

Following his dismissal, J.S. found work as a stevedore on the Vancouver docks while his family remained in the fishing town where his wife, Lucy, taught school. J.S. referred to this manual work as "a great experience," saying, in an autobiographical pamphlet called *On the Waterfront*, "I thought I knew something about the problems of labor through my long years at All

Peoples' Mission. It was a different thing to stand outside in the rain waiting for a job."[62]

However, it did not take long for J.S. to realize that the hypocrisy he found in the church was also in the labour movement. One day in March 1919 he arrived at the government docks and discovered that a ship he was to work on was loading ammunition destined for Siberia. J.S. discribed his actions in the same pamphlet: "So I quit and by the rules I am prohibited from taking any work for twenty four hours."[63] This novice stevedore was the only dockyard worker out of twelve hundred to engage in a one man strike! In his hard-hitting pamphlet, Woodsworth attacked the stevedores' hypocrisy. While passing a resolution of sympathy with the Russian Revolution, they had justified remaining on the job themselves on the grounds that if they did quit, members of the Seattle local or soldiers would be given their job.[64] J.S. concluded his message to the dockyard workers: "If we are not prepared to stand by them, don't let us pass any more pious resolutions of sympathy with the Bolsheveki. We are accusing the church people of sending guns and Bibles to the heathen, don't let us send guns and resolutions to Siberia. Let us cut out one or the other.[65]

Although it is obvious that J.S. stood a long way from the antisocialist position of his father, what is important to recognise is that J.S. sought to work out a distinctively Canadian socialism from a base in the trade union movement and the agrarian revolt on the prairies. His socialism was informed by his involvement in justice issues in the frontier areas of downtown mission work in Winnipeg. His constant theme, "justice, not charity," reflected his concern to change the structure of society.

After J.S. resigned from ordained ministry, he did not abandon his conversation with the Church, a conversation that needs to be carefully analyzed to assess his relationship to the Church. It is precisely such an analysis that was neglected by Kenneth McNaught, who, in his biography of J.S., asserts that the mainline churches rejected the social gospel while J.S., William Ivens, A.E. Smith and other Methodist radicals were the true representatives of the social gospel outside the church. Perhaps the clearest exposition of J.S.'s own position is reflected in a letter he wrote to a United Church minister who asked whether it is necessary to resign from ordained ministry in order to act on justice issues. "No," said J.S. as he pointed to the influence of his father and Dr. Salem Bland, professor of church history at Wesley College. In reflecting on the theological outlook one should take, J.S. asked the provocative question of whether Erasmus or Luther was right.[66] (Erasmus, the sixteenth-century scholar, was more a Renaissance humanist than a Christian theologian. Luther, also a giant of the sixteenth century, has become the symbol of reformed theology.) Because J.S. finished his life in a Unitarian theological allegiance, it is obvious he chose the route of Erasmus without cutting off dialogue with the more orthodox Protestant theology represented in the churches. In a moving prayer at a memorial service for J.S. in 1942, Rev. Ernest Marshall Howse sums up the ministry of J.S. in a prayer of Thanksgiving for his life: "We thank Thee for his life shining with the natural lustre of truth and sincerity, ennobled with the love that beareth, believeth, hopeth, endureth, and never faileth."[67]

Undoubtedly, many Church people were glad to see J.S. leave the Church. There has always been a jaundiced outlook amongst some Church people, those who perceive it as dangerous for ministers to mix the Bible with politics. Invariably, such ministers are accused of not being spiritual enough and of not taking the Bible seriously enough. The reverse, in fact, is true – they are the ones that see the Word of God as sharper than any two-edged sword (Hebrews 4:12). Is it not ironic that someone would be brought to trial on charges of sedition for quoting the Bible in a "Christian" country like Canada? But this is exactly what happened to J.S. when he quoted the prophet Isaiah in an issue of the *Western Labour News* near the end of the Winnipeg General Strike. Ironically too, part of the charge of seditious libel against J.S. read by the Crown prosecutor included verses from Isaiah 10 and 65:

Woe unto them that decree unrighteous decrees, and that write grievousness which they have prescribed; to turn aside the need[y] from judgment and to take away the right of the poor of my people that widows may be their prey and that they may rob the fatherless (Isaiah 10: 1–2).

And they shall build houses and inhabit them; and they shall plant vineyards, and eat the fruit of them. They shall not build and another inherit; they shall not plant and another eat; for as the day of a tree are the days of my people and mine elect shall long enjoy the work of their hands (Isaiah II.65:21–22).[68]

The events leading up to J.S.'s trial happened rapidly. The flash point was the Winnipeg General Strike. Although the Strike did not start until 15 May 1919, on 1 May the workers in the building trades in Winnipeg struck for increased wages and the right to bargain through the building Trades Council. The next day the metal workers struck to get a nine-hour day and the right to bargain through the Metal Trades Council. By the middle of May, the Strike received strong endorsement from all of the local union membership; they voted fourteen to one in favour of strike action. On the same day, two bodies which gradually polarized the city were organized in Winnipeg. On one side was the Central Strike Committee and on the other side was the Citizens Committee of One Thousand.

On 21 May, sympathetic strikes broke out in Vancouver, Lethbridge, Drumheller, Calgary, Edmonton, Regina, Saskatoon, Medicine Hat, Prince Albert and Brandon. On 6 June, although there had been no violence, the mayor of Winnipeg banned all parades and forbade the congregation of crowds. On 8 June, after quitting his job as a stevedore in Vancouver, J.S. arrived in Winnipeg to find himself in the middle of the Strike. On 12 June, he published a famous letter in which he attempted to speak to all Winnipeg citizens. In this letter he said: "The 'general public' is up in arms. They have suffered inconvenience and loss. Why should innocent non combatants suffer? The general public has not been innocent. It has been guilty of the greatest sin, the sin of indifference." Addressing the business people as his "old Winnipeg friends" who had set up an alliance to stop the Strike, he said that they were not the "hard hearted hypocrites pictured by perfervid orators." In defence of the strikers, J.S. explained that they were not "terrible reds" bent on establishing a soviet on the banks of the Red River in Winnipeg but rather, "they are victims of a social and economic system that must be replaced by a new economic order."[69]

On 10 June, a rally addressed by the popular army padre, Canon F.G. Scott, was broken up by the action of "special deputies" who unwisely and ineptly, tried to disperse a crowd which had gathered downtown. In the early hours of the morning of 16 June, ten prominent strike leaders were arrested, including Rev. William Ivens, editor of the *Western Labour News*. On the same day, J.S. took over as editor of the labour paper. Finally, on 25 June, after the arrest of more labour leaders including J.S. Woodsworth, the Strike collapsed. After serving five days in jail, J.S. was acquitted, on the defence of F.J. Dixon, a colleague in the labour movement, a strike leader and a co-defendant against the charge of sedition.

In 1921, J.S. was elected member of parliament for Winnipeg North-Centre (as a member of the Independent Labour Party) along with William Irvine from Calgary (a Presbyterian-turned-Unitarian minister). J.S. was elected again in 1925 when A.A. Heaps, another strike leader, was elected and Irvine was defeated. J.S. was elected again in the riding of Winnipeg North-Centre in 1925, 1926 and 1930 as an Independent Labour Party Member, and in 1935 and 1940 as leader of the Cooperative Commonwealth Federation (CCF). During his active political career, he remained the person whom Prime Minister Mackenzie King later described as "an ornament to any parliament."[70] Bruce Hutchinson, a well-known Canadian journalist, described J.S. as the "saint in politics."[71]

THE THEOLOGY OF FATHER AND SON

The key to understanding the Methodist emphasis on morality is the understanding of the central role of "righteousness" or "sanctification" in Methodist self-identity. Methodists reacted against the assumption that God's grace left little room for human initiative (a type of Presbyterian Calvinism). A major reason for this was the influence of Jacob Arminius, a Dutch Reformed theologian (1560–1609) who, in the biblical paradox on grace (Philippians 2:12–13), emphasized the importance of "[working] out your own salvation with fear and trembling" but de-emphasized that "God is at work in you both to will and to work for [God's] good pleasure" (Philippians 2:12–13). Arminius's emphasis (and consequently Methodist emphasis) on the centrality of human action for salvation, was reinforced by the Epistle of James: "For as the body apart from the spirit is dead, so faith apart from works is dead" (James 2:26).

Ironically, these influences resulted in two quite different theological outlooks in the lives of James and his son J.S. Central to the theology of both was the process of sanctification in Jesus's call: "You, therefore, must be perfect, as your heavenly Father is perfect" (Matthew 5:48). Sanctification in James's theology was similar to Methodist "holiness" which called for individual moral purity and national individual purity requiring citizens of the nation to keep the moral code.[72] That personal good behaviour was central to James's theology is evident in his account of a trip to the St. Peter's Indian Reserve near Selkirk, Manitoba. Observing the $5 treaty money which was paid out to each person, James, with the rather typical "social Darwinism" attitude of the period (which assumed that the survival of the fittest had brought the Anglo-Saxon to the top), made no comment about the unfairness of the treaty or about the small amount given out, but said only that "It is a time of feasting and dancing. . . . Although this is a time of rejoicing it is a most dissipating time, drinking, dancing and general carousing."[73]

In another incident, James refers to the Indians as "heathen" and "savages,"[74] yet is impressed by their religious purity, an example of which is that they honoured their dead by not touching their belongings after death. After observing native religious practices in Alberta, James concluded: "Whatever anyone may say as to this corrupt form of religion, these people were sincere in their devotion and loyal to the native instincts of the soul, and none can gainsay the benefits of religion coming to men and women who are true to the light which they enjoy."[75]

A similar theme of equating moral purity with national righteousness and progress is reflected in James's discussion of immigrants. Immigrants, he said, should be culled so that only those with intelligence and moral and religious fibre would be brought in. The result would be that Canada would be a nation "whose foundations are laid in righteousness, whose people are the Lord's."[76] James assumed that where there was moral purity there would also be prosperity.

Private moral shortcomings are therefore the sins that James attacked. Emphasizing the importance of "working out your own salvation," in Arminian philosophy, he condemned government hand-outs to Indians. He never questioned the lack of opportunity for a people marginalized in an economic system based on farming, hunting and trapping. Says James: "It seemed to us that with such a liberal allowance from the Government, and opportunities for self-help by farming and hunting, the people ought to be well off. But they are always for 'more, more.' It may be a question whether a too liberal paternalism on the part of both State and Church has not been a mistaken kindness, the effect being to pauperise instead of to produce independence of character."[77]

James showed a sense of humour even as he practised Methodist moralism. On one occasion, when he was travelling by horse-drawn coach through the Rocky Mountains, a young female traveller allayed her fears by smoking and by producing a flask of whiskey to quiet her nerves: "Again she offered to 'treat.' As I persisted in a polite refusal she remarked, 'You must be a very moral man to neither smoke nor drink.' We had not proceeded far before she again called on the driver to stop that she might take another drink. After again refreshing herself she placed the bottle between us on the seat. Before reaching Trail, I discovered that the stopper had come out and that the escaping contents had been largely absorbed by my coat."[78] Reeking of whiskey, James might have worried that his image would be tarnished. In fact he could have been accused in a jocular way of "falling off the wagon." But James, far from being angry that his dignity might have been tarnished, said gently: "How I pitied her! Young, good looking, well dressed, yet apparently thoroughly demoralised and terrified by fears of the dangers of the journey."[79]

James's theological outlook endorsed a Methodism that was moral, practical and dependent on showing the fruits of one's faith. However, it was theologically shallow because it was easily co-opted by the dominant culture and seduced by a doctrine of progress that came to be equated with Protestant nationalistic values that remained condescending to Roman Catholics, immigrants and Indians. For Protestants, success in building the Kingdom of God involved increasing numbers; hence, importance was placed on the number of new Methodist churches mushrooming on the prairies.

Like his father, J.S. endorsed the Methodist Arminian emphasis on works. This similarity is evident in a statement made by Grace MacInnis about her father, J.S.: "He was born into a Canada which believed that the Golden Rule could and should be applied to people's private lives. . . . He showed that it applied in our public life with the same uncompromising logic as in private conduct."[80]

J.S. understood the word *sanctification* as meaning *social sanctification* or *social perfection*. He believed that we are all totally bound in the destiny of one another. He stressed the theme of Paul: "For as in Adam all die even so in Christ shall all be made alive" (I Corinthians 5:22). Out of this theological framework, J.S. saw a common identity of the righteous with the unrighteous,[81] for "there is so much angel in the worst of us."[82] He also used Paul's emphasis on "one body" in seeking unity among potentially factious groups. The farmer, he said, should not imagine he could live without the city dweller. It is like an eye saying to the hand, "I have no need of you" (I Corinthians 12: 14–26).[83]

The liberal theology of J.S. carried the same optimism in human progress as that espoused by his father. For J.S., progress meant the development of a better social and political society rather than of a more religious church-centred society. His assumption was that the secular was becoming more sacred every day. He was confident that in his day, the slums of Winnipeg could be cleaned up in the same way as the swamps of the Panama had been cleared of malaria-carrying mosquitoes.[84]

J.S. was impatient with all theological training that did not have a practical emphasis; hence, he attacked training that crammed students with "scraps of literary criticism and metaphysical theology."[85] He criticized "the need to teach the theological nuance of 'hypostasis' and 'idiotes' when grinding monopolies are crushing the life out of the masses and tuberculosis, bred in wretched tenements, is carrying off its thousands."[86] As well, said J.S., the ten commandments needed the whitewash taken off them. He identified as the modern killer not only the person who swings from the gallows but also the church-going railroad entrepreneur who orders poor rails.[87]

J.S. criticized also the individual moral code of Sabbath observance. His own job on the docks of Vancouver necessitated his working on Sunday. This caused him to reflect on the church-going wealthy employers of Sunday labourers[88] who spoke in the liturgy: "Lord have mercy upon us and incline our hearts to keep this law." Yet these employers kept their plants in operation every day of the week. Dropping a coin into the collection for the poor, J.S. asked, "Whose coin? Do I receive all that I produce? Surely it pays someone to keep me working on Sundays even at time and a half rates. The employer goes home to his wife and family and music and friends and I work on in the rain and out of hearing even of the church bells."[89]

Although J.S. exposed the cant and hypocrisy of his society and used biblical sources to inform both his critique and his prophetic ministry, his Arminian Methodist theology, like that of his father, is shallow. The reason for this is considered by David Summers in his history of the Labor Church in the West. Growing out of the Winnipeg General Strike in 1919, the Labor Church had an attendance so large that it could not be housed in the existing church building. But by 1924, attendance had declined and by 1926, the Labor Church was extinct. Of the leaders of this Church, including J.S., Summers says, "They tried to enjoy the fruits of the Christian ethic without the roots of the Christian faith."[90]

In the formulation of his doctrines, J.S. ignored the historical experience of the Church. He emphasized a "religion of the future" and rejected the "religion of the past." This new religion would be "progressive, dynamic, with no final point of perfection, scientific, practical, and non-speculative."[91] But when he came to elaborate on the religion of the future, he could only express it in metaphors that were more vague than the doctrines he rejected! He described God as "our deepest experience raised maybe to the nth degree."[92] To express the movement from orthodoxy to heterodoxy, he said, "We are emerging from the confines of a stuffy room into the sweet pure air of God's out of doors."[93] His doctrine of creation was "the story of the rocks is considered more credible than Genesis."[94] Such syncretistic pantheism tends to absorb all religious outlooks into the religion of the lowest common denominator. This is evident, for example, in J.S.'s description of a predicament faced by the Labor Church when the Sunday school superintendent was confronted by some parents who wanted "orthodox Christianity" while others wanted "scientific Marxian socialism." Observed J.S., "One man made the happy suggestion, don't you think you could mix them up a bit?"[95]

Oftentimes, J.S. stood on the verge of resigning from the ministry of the Methodist Church on doctrinal issues. His ability to address concrete social issues with the biblical word was impressive. However, when one examines the issues that caused him to lose his faith in the church, one cannot help wondering if he understood the doctrines he was rejecting.

THE LEGACY OF FATHER AND SON

The establishment of a Methodist network of frontier churches in the West is the most obvious contribution of James Woodsworth, the father. This network has been part of the heritage of the United Church of Canada which is spread throughout the West in rural hamlets, service towns, and small and large cities because James Woodsworth and the Church leaders at the turn of the century shared the life of privation and hardship of the early settlers. Like Ezekial among the Babylonian captives, James could say, "I sat where they sat" (Ezekiel 3:15). In the foreword to James's book, S.D. Chown wrote: "It is my sincere hope that young men with the tinge of heroism in their blood may, by the inspiration of this volume, be led to follow the example of such men as James Woodsworth and John McDougall, and may give themselves as builders of the kingdom of heaven in this 'Great West.' "[96]

The theology represented by father and son followed the liberal theological tradition of stressing the moral influence of great leaders. In this tradition, Jesus is the supreme moral example who calls us to take up our cross and follow him – the one who is "the pioneer of our salvation" (Hebrews 12:2). Although this theme of holding up the moral influence of great leaders did inspire young missionaries to great sacrifices on the frontier, it also carried an ideology of growth which was seen by some Methodists in terms of material growth. Consequently in James's theology, the Kingdom of God came to be expressed in commercial terms. As he caught the vision of an expanding church, James quoted Isaiah: "The desert rejoices and blossoms like the rose" (Isaiah 35:1). And then he added, "The thrifty settler amasses wealth, and in turn, if properly educated, becomes a contributor to the great cause of missions, thus passing on, with large interest the blessings which have helped him and his family in their struggles."[97] Missionary expansion is equated by James with material success as a sign of God's favour.

The same type of liberal theology (that is, a theology with a moral influence) is represented in J.S.'s theology as he lived out a high optimism that the secular was becoming more sacred every day. The Progressive Party in Canada (and in fact the ideology of much of left-wing politics in Canada) lived in the confidence that God will reward righteous causes. In J.S. and other leaders of the social gospel, this feeling produced an over-confidence that their party was the most righteous political movement in Canada. What invariably happened with this moralism was that the progressives and the socialists began to eulogize their successes, giving themselves much more credit for their performance than the record could bear. Or, when they found that things were not working out well, they became cynical about all good causes – an accusation which does not apply to J.S.

In the final analysis, the theology of both James and his son, J.S., cannot be judged in terms of its doctrinal accuracy. With a call to action in discipleship, their theology was indeed practical, especially in light of the macabre acts of violence in the world today which are being perpetrated by "orthodox" conservative Christians. What becomes obvious is that we need the prophetic courage of the Woodsworths, particularly J.S. While both men refused to believe that Christian discipleship should be confined to "in-house" spiritual faith, J.S. was a pioneer in questioning the blind obedience to temporal authorities and the assumption that structures which oppressed the poor "were ordained of God" (Romans 13:1).

James Woodsworth and his son, J.S. – two men in different types of prophetic ministry, one opposing the social evils of individuals, the other opposing the structural evils of society – stand as forerunners of contemporary political theology. Dorothea Soëlle (a German political theologian) says that individual in-house religion insults not only the prophets Amos, Jeremiah, Martin Luther King, Dietrich Bonhoeffer and Oscar Romero, but indeed it insults Jesus Christ.[98] The Woodsworths, with their compassion for lonely, victimized people, show that God uses "earthen vessels" like you and me to accomplish the purposes of "making and keeping human life human."[99]

Congregationalism in Manitoba, 1879–1937

J. Clark Saunders

BEGINNINGS

Far and away the smallest of the denominations to enter the United Church in 1925 was the Congregational Union of Canada. As a church, the Congregationalists traced their history to those "non-conformist" or "independent" churches which appeared in England at the time of the Reformation. The hallmarks of the Congregational style in twentieth-century Canada, as in sixteenth-century England, were liberty of conscience, a strange mixture of evangelical zeal and doctrinal eccentricity and a devotion to the principle of congregational independence. The loose polity of the church had created problems of which some Congregationalists were only too well aware. Without a well-developed structure to supervise local churches, some congregations found themselves burdened with "unworthy" or idiosyncratic ministers and became hotbeds of factionalism and intrigue. Congregational polity was also a hindrance as the denomination wrestled with the problem of responding in an organized way to the opportunities presented by a rapidly expanding nation. In the end, the Congregationalists tried to emulate the Presbyterians and Methodists in their missionary efforts in Manitoba and the West. But the initiatives came too late and received too little support for Congregationalism to gain much more than a tentative foothold in a few widely scattered areas.

Manitoba in the 1870s was a rapidly growing young province. The decade saw Winnipeg develop almost overnight from a small, remote village into the bustling gateway to the West. The major Protestant denominations responded quickly to the influx of their co-religionists from overseas and the East, but it was not until 1879 that Congregationalism made its debut in the fledgling city.

The need for mission work in the West had been weighing on the minds of eastern Congregationalists for some years. Beginning in the early 1870s, the Colonial Missionary Society of the Congregational Church of England and Wales (CMS) had been steadily reducing the size of its grants toward the home mission efforts of the Canada Congregational Missionary Society (CCMS). In an effort to work out a new funding arrangement, the great patriarch of Congregationalism in Canada, Dr. Henry Wilkes, visited London in 1875. The result of his discussions with the CMS was a formula by which the CMS undertook to contribute £20 for every £100 raised for home mission purposes in Canada.[1]

The new arrangement came into effect in 1878, and the following year, eastern interest in westward expansion together with requests from Congregationalists resident in Winnipeg led to the founding of First Congregational Church in the young city.

The summer of 1879 saw a rapid succession of events leading to the formation of the new congregation. In June, the Annual Convocation of the Congregational Union of Ontario and Quebec discussed the spiritual needs of eastern Congregationalists who were heading for Manitoba.[2] Debate centred on whether it would be better to try to establish local colonies of Congregationalist settlers from such places as Lanark County or to engage in direct missionary enterprise among people with no Congregational background. The Convocation decided that at least one missionary be sent to Manitoba to assess the situation first-hand.

There was one missionary ready and willing to go. The Rev. William Ewing, a twenty-five-year-old graduate of McGill University and the Congregational College in Montreal, and just recently ordained, had for some time contemplated settling in Manitoba. At that particular moment, however, the CCMS was in straitened circumstances and was unable to support him financially. Nevertheless, Ewing "took the plunge" and set out for the West, hoping that interest expressed by the CMS would soon be translated into specific support.

Ewing arrived in Winnipeg late in June. Two weeks later he was joined by a young colleague – another easterner who was to devote himself for some time to the work of evangelism – the Rev. Robert MacKay. MacKay had been pressed by mutual friends to spend a few weeks doing evangelistic work with Ewing. After his week-long journey (by rail to Sarnia, by steamer to Duluth and eventually by Red River boat to Winnipeg), he found Ewing encouraged by two weeks of visiting and canvassing.

The first Congregationalist service in Winnipeg was conducted in the Temperance Hall on the evening of 13 July 1879. About forty attended. The following Thursday, after visiting most of the Protestant clergy in Winnipeg, Ewing and MacKay conducted an evangelistic meeting in the same hall, a meeting in which the Methodist and Baptist ministers took part. The twentieth of July was a busy Sunday for the Congregationalist leaders. They conducted the first morning service, at which twenty worshippers were present. (Already, it seems, the long-standing Winnipeg Congregationalist tradition of larger attendances in the evening than in the morning was being established.) In the afternoon, MacKay held an open-air service at the immigrant sheds. At 6:00 p.m., he and Ewing took part in a tent meeting on Main Street, attended by two hundred people, some of whom seemed rough, but all of whom were attentive.[3] And an evening service was held once again at the Temperance Hall.

It was a good beginning. For the two missionaries, the irritation of mud and mosquitoes was mitigated by the warm response of both the handful of Congregationalist stalwarts and the rough-and-ready fortune seekers who crowded the little city. As August began, the stage was set for the formation of a Congregational church.

Over the course of that month, a series of meetings was held at the home of one K.F. Lockhart. At these meetings, First Congregational Church was duly constituted with twenty-four charter members, Ewing was formally called as the first minister, and the first assurance of outside financial support was announced. Ewing had heard from Wilkes that the CMS had promised aid at the rate of £100 per year[4] and that George Hague of the Merchants' Bank in Montreal had agreed to serve as treasurer for an eastern group which had also offered to raise funds for Ewing's work.

In the midst of this rapid succession of events surrounding the formation of a church in Winnipeg, Ewing and MacKay managed to undertake a week-long tour of the little "postage-stamp province" of Manitoba. Their journey – by primitive means of transportation – took them to the Stony Mountain Penitentiary, Stonewall, High Bluff and Portage la Prairie. At Portage, they conducted a service near a saloon. Many in the congregation were drunk, but the atmosphere was convivial. Some offered to sing, while others – not surprisingly, perhaps – expressed a willingness to take up the offering.[5]

The missionaries found several Protestant denominations already established in Portage, but nevertheless expressed the opinion that "Congregationalism should make an effort in the same direction."[6]

On their return to Winnipeg, the missionaries held a service at which deacons, trustees and other officers were elected, and the Rev. L.H. Cobb of Minneapolis preached on the virtues of Congregationalism. A few days later a

Sunday school was begun. With the new church well launched, MacKay took his leave. He continued to travel, however, and to encourage support for Congregationalism in the West.

By the end of 1879, Ewing himself was making plans for a fund-raising tour of the East. By the time the tour actually took place in the summer of 1880, arrangements had been made for the Rev. J.B. Silcox, the pastor of the Western Church in Toronto and a relative of Ewing's,[7] to supply the Winnipeg church in Ewing's absence. It soon became clear that Ewing's first interest was in organizing new congregations. On his return to Winnipeg in the fall, he resigned from First Church. The committee in Montreal – now called the Manitoba Mission Committee (MMC) – agreed that he should move on to other work. At the end of the year, he left Winnipeg to travel up the Red River in search of promising sites for new Congregational churches – a journey that eventually took him into North Dakota where he remained for several years.

The two-month summer ministry of J.B. Silcox had impressed the Winnipeg congregation – so much so that he was invited to succeed Ewing. The MMC endorsed the invitation and promised to contribute two-thirds of the Winnipeg church's budget (with money from the CMS of England and from Canadian supporters). Early in 1881, thirty-four-year-old Silcox left the Western Church in Toronto – and several friends who questioned his sanity[8] – for First Church in Winnipeg (later to be Central Congregational Church).

Silcox could not have known it at the time, but he was beginning what was to be virtually a life-long association with Central Congregational Church. He was to serve twice as its pastor and on other occasions as pulpit supply. Having been involved in the church almost from its inception, he was invited to preach at its thirtieth, fortieth and fiftieth anniversaries. The fiftieth anniversary took place in 1932, shortly before both church and minister passed away.

Silcox came from a prominent eastern Congregational family. His grandfather had founded the first Congregational Church in Upper Canada at Frome. J.B. Silcox was born there in 1847. An 1876 graduate of the Congregational College in Montreal, First Church, Winnipeg, was just his second pastorate.

Unlike many of his fellow Congregationalists in the 1880s, Silcox was not preoccupied with Congregational polity. Rather, he had become convinced that the real need was to proclaim the Gospel[9] and that denominationalism was purely secondary.[10] Throughout his first pastorate in Winnipeg, Silcox resisted pressure from the CCMS to start new churches in other parts of the province.[11]

Central Congregational Church and manse, c. 1885. (Photo courtesy of Provincial Archives of Manitoba.)

Certainly J.B., as he was often called, had his hands full in Winnipeg. He came to a church that was still meeting in a hall. Rapid growth in the congregation was attributable mainly to new professions of faith; few who joined the church had a Congregational background. Silcox attributed this partly to the fact that emigration from Britain to western Canada was primarily a lower-class phenomenon brought about be economic pressure in the "old country." British Congregationalism flourished primarily among the middle classes and exported few adherents to Canada.

The immediate task facing Silcox – beyond building up the congregation – was providing it with a permanent home. In this endeavour he and his people were, in the short term at least, beneficiaries of the "boom-bust" cycles that were characteristic of Winnipeg's economy in those early days. A site was bought at the corner of Princess Street and Notre Dame Avenue. It was sold in 1882 at a considerable profit, and a new site was purchased from the Hudson's Bay Company at a much lower price. The new site was at the corner of Hargrave Street and Qu'Appelle Avenue, a location which was then at the edge of the city. Construction of the church building began in the spring of 1882 and was completed in December. The young congregation ended the year with a new building and a financial position so solid and promising that support from the East and from the CMS could be discontinued.

Sadly, the future for First Congregational Church was not as bright as it appeared. The "boom" during which the first site was sold was followed by a "bust." Having fallen on hard times, the man who had bought the first site managed to find a clerical error in the transaction and took the church to court in order to be released from the agreement. The result was a long period of litigation, a period made longer by the death of the first judge in the case and the necessity of beginning over again under a new justice. The judgement, which was finally rendered in 1886, required the church to repay $25,000 already received from the purchaser, and, of course, to forfeit any future income.

The effect of the judgement had the appearance of a calamity for the church. The debt was far beyond the congregation's capacity to pay. And with a $15,000 mortgage on the new building, there seemed to be no alternative but to let the Merchant's Bank take the church for mortgage arrears and dissolve the congregation. Accordingly, Silcox and the trustees resigned and the sheriff sold the church's goods and chattels.

The Congregational Church was now without a home in Winnipeg, and the bank had something of a while elephant on its hands. Silcox saw a mutually advantageous solution to the problem. He managed to raise a $1,400 down payment and bought the church building back on his own responsibility. As "proprietor" of the building, Silcox "loaned" the parlour for a series of meetings early in 1887 at which a new congregation was formed and given the name Central Congregational Church, and Silcox himself was called to be the minister. The new congregation was incorporated by provincial charter, presumably to limit the liability of the trustees.

But the church was not "out of the woods" yet. There was a newly arranged mortgage to be paid and the debts of the old congregation to be settled.[12] Funds were desperately needed. With this need in mind, Silcox, at his own expense, undertook a trip to England where he pleaded the church's case before the CMS. The members' initial coolness turned to appreciation as Silcox recounted the recent events. They paid his way back to Canada, and in January 1888 he was able to tell the congregation that the CMS had purchased from him the lots on which the church and parsonage were built and were now conveying the property to Central Congregational Church as a gift. The church accepted the gift (with an $18,000 mortgage) and helped Silcox recoup his own financial investment by buying chairs, carpeting, seat covers and the like from him. Later in the year, the new congregation finally devised a plan – and canvassed the congregation – to settle at a reduced rate the debts of First Congregational Church.

The year 1888 brought Silcox's departure for a church in California. He left a church that had come through a major crisis but which was well launched on a new beginning. By his own energy and imagination he had been instrumental in saving it, and the congregation was properly grateful.[13]

Silcox's successor was the Rev. Hugh Pedley, another young minister who, like Silcox, had supplied the Winnipeg church during the summer prior to his being called, while his predecessor was away on a fund-raising expedition. Pedley differed from Silcox in that he favoured Congregationalist expansion, and his twelve-year pastorate saw an increase in Congregationalist activity not only in Winnipeg, but in parts of rural Manitoba as well.

Outside of Winnipeg, Congregationalism in Manitoba was very much a "flash-in-the-pan" affair. With the exception of the Brandon Church, which itself had had a chequered career, none of the rural churches survived into the twentieth century.

In the early days, Ewing and MacKay were anxious to scout possible sites for new churches. In 1880, a building site in Rapid City was deeded to the Congregational Church provided a building was erected within a year. But when the Canadian Pacific Railway (CPR) route was established further south, thoughts of a Rapid City church were abandoned. The Pilot Mound area offered more promise. The Pembina Mountain district had been visited in the late 1870s by twin brothers from Ontario, the Rev. John and the Rev. Robert Brown. Both were Congregationalist ministers, but both were also interested in farming. Returning to Lanark County where John had been minister, they persuaded some of their friends to move west with them. John settled at Wood Bay, about five miles north of Pilot Mound, in 1880, and Robert followed him two years later. In addition to their agricultural interests, the two conducted services, first in houses and later in schools, in the surrounding districts. John was soon recognized by eastern authorities as the Congregationalist minister in the area, and Wood Bay and its satellites took on the status of a charge.

Ties with the East were loosened, however, as the Browns failed to report on their work. Finally in 1886, wishing to re-establish an official presence in the area, the ccms sent out a Scottish-born minister, the Rev. John MacKinnon. MacKinnon worked hard and found the Browns ready with friendly support. His congregation managed to build him a parsonage. But the scope for growth was limited. Some of the Congregationalist settlers moved further west, and Pilot Mound itself – where the Presbyterians and Methodists were becoming well-established – surpassed Wood Bay as the leading community in the area.[14] Seeing little future for the denomination in that part of the province, the ccms withdrew support for MacKinnon in 1890.

It is of interest to note, however, that the Brown and MacKinnon families both stayed on at Wood Bay and maintained a kind of independent Congregationalist presence in the little community. MacKinnon continued to live in the former parsonage and took up farming. Although a formal connection with the Congregational Union had lapsed, he went on providing services at the local school on a fairly regular basis until about 1904.

Robert Brown raised a family that included a missionary and several ministers. The most prominent of his sons, the Rev. John L. Brown, took a keen interest in agriculture, education and the Church. After attending the Congregational College in Montreal, he served briefly at the church in Brandon before taking up residence at Snowflake where he conducted worship for the local people. He returned to farm at Wood Bay just as MacKinnon was retiring from preaching, and over the next twenty years, in rotation with Presbyterian and Methodist ministers from Pilot Mound, John L.Brown conducted worship at the Wood Bay school. In 1921 he was elected member of parliament for Lisgar and had a hand in drafting the legislation that brought the United Church of Canada into being.[15]

The kind of independent local arrangement which evolved at Wood Bay ("primitive Congregationalism," one might call it) was an unusual development. It is also worth noting, however, that two English Congregationalist ministers who had retired to the Canadian prairies for their health conducted community worship services at Oberon and MacGregor for a time in the 1880s and 1890s.

After Wood Bay, the next rural area to see some organized Congregationalist activity was Portage la Prairie. Ewing and MacKay had visited the town in 1879. Four years later a Congregationalist minister, the Rev. Charles Duff, passed through Portage and reported that a real opportunity existed there. But it was not until 1887 that a substantial increase in CCMS funds (one Canadian donor had given $2,000 toward work in the West[16]) and the availability of a young missionary named A.W. Gerrie allowed work to proceed.

Gerrie looked over the situation in both Brandon and Portage and decided that Portage offered the brighter prospect. But Silcox, nearing the end of his pastorate in Winnipeg, was characteristically sceptical. Knowing that the group pressing for a Congregational church in Portage consisted mainly of disgruntled Presbyterians and that the offending Presbyterian minister was about to leave, he saw little future for the cause in the town.[17] At first, the work proceeded quickly. A building was erected. But before long Silcox's prediction came true. The last services were held in 1892.

While concentrating his efforts at Portage la Prairie, Gerrie had made frequent trips to Brandon where he met with Congregationalists and conducted some services. A visit in 1888 by the superintendent of the CCMS and the secretary of the CMS, together with a visit to the East by a Congregational layman named Hunt, who was then living in Brandon, prompted more definite action. The next year, an ordinand from the Congregational College, the Rev. H.D. Mason, arrived in Brandon with the promise of a year's financial support from the CMS.

During 1889, the Brandon congregation – soon to be called Calvary – met in an ice rink. By 1891, they had their own building, a modest, wooden structure, distinguished by a rose window. Despite the death of his young wife and the onset of an economic depression, Mason remained in Brandon until 1896. During his pastorate, the congregation grew, the sanctuary was enlarged to seat four hundred, outside financial support was reduced, and a missionary was sent to Africa. Of its membership in the mid-1890s, the majority had no Congregational background.

Mason's departure, however, heralded uncertain times for the church. For a time before he left, Mason had had to sacrifice much of his salary to keep the church afloat. His next two successors[18] stayed only a year or two each, and left a congregation that had become discouraged and rudderless.

The story at Brandon continued to be one of "ups and downs." Nevertheless, it was the only charge outside Winnipeg to survive, as part of the Congregational Union, beyond the turn of the century.

Hugh Pedley, whose attitude toward new churches was quite different from that of Silcox, tried to encourage the rural congregations. During the brief period in which Congregational churches existed simultaneously in Winnipeg, Wood Bay–Pilot Mound, Portage la Prairie and Brandon, he even instituted the rather pretentious sounding Council of Congregational Churches of Manitoba. But the need for such an august body soon faded.

While admitting that the Presbyterian and Methodist Churches were larger and better equipped, Pedley held that "in some respects our system is more suited than any other to the temper of western life. With a theology, 'free, broad and evangelical' and a system of church government democratic in principle, but orderly and practical in method, we ought to command the sympathy of many of the more independent-minded people in this country."[19]

Pedley was partly right. Independence and pragmatism were qualities that Congregationalism shared with the western settlers. But in the event, these qualities were translated into a kind of congregationalism (with a small c) which manifested itself in the two larger Protestant denominations and especially in the local union churches after the turn of the century. In the laissez-faire attitude toward denominationalism that characterized so many westerners, Congregationalism (with a capital C) reaped little benefit from the spirit of the West.

While the 1890s offered little encouragement to Congregationalism in rural Manitoba, the work of church extension in Winnipeg itself showed, for a time at least, more signs of promise. A "pocket" of Central Church members lived in the area around the CPR station and found it difficult to get to the church over a mile away. (This was an age in which streetcars did not run on Sundays.) In 1889, with Pedley's blessing,[20] a group of worshippers began to meet in a local biscuit factory. The following year, Alexander Black – lumberman, sometime alderman, and leading Congregational layman – built a church on Maple Street, south of Higgins Avenue.[21] The CMS sent £150 toward the project.

In its early years, the Maple Street Church flourished on a small scale. However, a number of factors conspired against its survival. Through its short life, the church was served by a rapid succession of brief pastorates interspersed with periods during which pulpit supply had to be arranged. Then there were the physical limits to the congregation's growth: the CPR tracks to the north, the Red River to the east and south, and Central's own territory to the south and west. And finally, by the turn of the century, the area was beginning to change. Immigrants from eastern European ethnic groups were moving in, the church members were moving out, and it was becoming clear that the church could have a future only as a mission. A scheme whereby a position of part-time assistant to Pedley would be created for a part-time minister at Maple Street was aborted by Pedley's resignation in 1900, and shortly afterwards, Central backed out of any form of financial assistance. The congregation's last hope for survival vanished. In 1902, the church was sold to the Methodists' All Peoples' Mission. Proceeds from the sale, amounting to $2,000 were given to Central Church to be held in trust until the money could be used toward the purchase of a site and the building of a new church elsewhere in Winnipeg.

The Pedley years also saw church extension work in the west end of the city. Central established a branch Sunday school on Portland Street (now McGee Street) in about 1894. The following year, however, poor accommodations and the fact that the Rev. Samuel Polson, a renegade Presbyterian, was doing his own mission work in the same area led to a move to seek an arrangement with Polson. The arrangement eventuated in the Congregationalists' work being swallowed up by Polson's at the Beverley Street Mission.[22]

For Central Church itself, Pedley's pastorate had been a time of growth and consolidation. Under his popular preaching, the congregation and its various programs saw steady progress in size and energy. Following Pedley's resignation in 1900, Silcox was invited to return from California. J.B.'s second pastorate was uneventful compared with his first one, and in 1904 he left a healthy and prospering congregation to become minister of another American church, this one in Lansing, Michigan.

THE GOLDEN AGE

What may fairly be called "the golden age" of Congregationalism in Manitoba took place during the decade or so in the middle of Central Church's fifty-seven-year existence. It also corresponded, not surprisingly perhaps, with the pastorate of remarkably able and energetic minister, the Rev. (later Dr.) James L. Gordon.

Gordon was an American who entered the ministry after serving as secretary to the YMCA in Boston. He moved in a few short years from a small church in Saint John, New Brunswick, to Bond Street Congregational Church in Toronto to Central, Winnipeg, where he took up his duties in February, 1905.

Such was the force of his preaching that almost immediately it became apparent that the sanctuary would have to be enlarged to accommodate the commercial travellers and office workers, the people of other churches or no church who swelled the evening congregations. When the building addition was completed a year or so after his arrival, its seating capacity of 2,100 made it the largest church in Winnipeg. In the coming years, the dearth of suitable concert halls in the city made it the venue not only of services and religious meetings, but of concerts and lectures by the likes of Paderewski, Christabel Pankhurst, Helen Keller and Mrs. Booth-Clibborn.

It was not a particularly attractive buiding. Like so many Protestant churches of the day, it was designed as an auditorium, with rows of pews arranged, semi-circular fashion, around a central pulpit and an inconspicuous communion table.

In 1912, a reviewer for the *Manitoba Free Press* described the atmosphere of an evening service. At Central, he wrote, "everything conspires to reflect the busy, unquiet, western world of today, perplexed by problems of faith and conduct and consumed by an insatiable curiosity." Central's style, the reviewer felt, was "better adapted [than that of Holy Trinity, Anglican] to the genius of the people of the new world, who prefer what we may call the 'prophetic' note in worship rather than the 'priestly.' "[23]

The reviewer found that the church was full fifteen minutes before the service was to begin, and by service time, people were standing. (During much of Gordon's ministry, in fact, seats were reserved for the congregation's own pew holders until ten or twenty minutes before the service. Then, at a signal from the head usher, seats were open to those who had been lining up outside.)

The congregation included few who were rich and many who were young. And in the opinion of the *Free Press* reviewer, it was James L. Gordon who drew the crowd. The reviewer speaks of the preacher's "wide human sympathy and breadth of outlook" and of the "catchy" sermon titles that laid him open to criticism from the city's more staid church-goers. Even Gordon's appearance and preaching style drew comment. He wore a grey frock coat and a black bow tie. He had a large head with iron grey hair and a bushy moustache, with "eyes entrenched under heavy brows, a strong nose, full cheeks, and a determined shaven chin. He speaks with a pronounced American accent, and the style of the service generally is American."[24] Gordon read from large square sheets with huge letters "that can be seen from the gallery. . . . His feeling comes in frequent gusts, then we have a perfect whirlwind of vehement oratory, the face becomes red and swollen, and lines appear, the clenched fist is raised above the head, brought down in a sweep and resounds on the desk."

One who, as a girl, often heard Gordon preach, corroborates this description. "Dr. Gordon was a most dynamic preacher," she writes, "using every ounce of his energy, to the point where at the close of his sermon, he struggled into his overcoat and literally collapsed into one of the pulpit chairs, his big white handkerchief much in evidence. At this point someone – usually Ald. McLean came up and announced the closing hymn, but Dr.Gordon was always ready to pronounce the benediction."[25]

The titles of Gordon's sermons, many of which were printed at the expense of his admirers, show him to have been no spurner of controversy.[26] He preached on topics as far-ranging as anti-Semitism and the liquor traffic, the problems of youth and the nature of heaven, international relations and family life. And as if topical subjects on Sunday were not enough, he instituted a Wednesday evening activity in the church parlour called The Question Drawer. There he dealt with questions that had been submitted to him in writing. These were no less far-ranging than his sermon topics: "What would you do if outside relatives interfered in the happiness of your home?" "Why is the black man black?" "Would the people in the north of Ireland be justified in opposing Home Rule by force of arms?" "Do you believe that the size of a man's head has anything to do with the strength of a man's mind?" – a delicate question, one would think, in view of the prodigious dimensions of Gordon's own head. And an even more delicate question: "Why don't you give folks who differ with your 'answers to questions' a chance to answer back on Wednesday evenings?"

There is little doubt that Gordon was something of a showman. But it seems, too, that there was substance behind the showmanship. During his pastorate the membership roughly quadrupled in size, groups and organizations abounded, and the need for church extension in the city was seriously addressed.

When Gordon came to Winnipeg, Central once again stood alone as the only Congregational church. But the growth of the city and of the Church soon led to another venture in mission work. The necessary catalyst for the "forward movement" took the form of a visit to Winnipeg by the secretary of the CCMS, the Rev. W.T. Gunn, in May 1907. A joint meeting of the Board of Deacons and the Board of Managers took place to discuss with Gunn ways and means of extending Congregationalism in Winnipeg and the West in general. It was the feeling of some that the CCMS was too remote from the scene to give effective direction.[27] Gunn suggested that it would be better to have church extension work for western Canada directed from Winnipeg. The CMS and CCMS, he said, would each pay half of a missionary's salary for three years, but the missionary's work should be directed by a western committee.

The meeting was chaired by the president of Central Church, Arthur Wickson. Before the month was out, Wickson had been instrumental in bringing into being the Congregational Church Extension Society of Western Canada (CES) with himself as president. At the time of the society's incorporation two years later, it declared its first object to be "to establish and foster Christian Churches of the Congregational Faith and Order for the maintenance of the public worship of God as revealed in the Holy Scriptures, the enjoyment of Church Ordinances, and the extension of the kingdom of Christ, in its varied religious, benevolent and educational enterprises."[28]

The missionary on whom the burden of this work was to fall was a thirty-one-year-old Englishman, the Rev. Ernest R. Weeks. In 1906, Weeks had come to Canada and travelled across the country, taking particular note of the condition of the Church in the West. On his return to Winnipeg under the auspices of the CES in August 1907, he turned his attention first to the possibilities of church extension in the city.

Both the west and south ends of the city looked promising. In 1899, a few years after the work on Portland Street had been discontinued, a branch Sunday school had been opened at the old Mulvey School House on Boundary Street (now Maryland). The fact that a start had been made there may have tipped the scales in favour of dealing with the west end first.

After a brief organizational period, Weeks conducted the first service of what was then known as the Western Congregational Church at the Arlington Street Roller Skating Rink on 13 October 1907. By the following February, the congregation had grown to fifty, and the CES purchased a lot at Preston Avenue and Home Street near St. James (now Vimy) Park. A year after the first service was held, Gordon preached to a congregation of four hundred at the dedication of St. James Park Congregational Church.

Under Weeks's capable leadership, the Church continued to grow, and organizations of all kinds were inaugurated. But Weeks's job was not to become the long-term pastor of any one congregation. Having set the wheels in motion, he left the Church in order to pursue other projects and was succeeded in 1909 by another young Englishman, the Rev. Edgar Whitehouse.

Whitehouse's successful pastorate was marred by one unhappy period. A group within the Church managed to gain control of the congregation in 1910 and apparently demanded the resignation of some of the church officers. Because the congregation was not yet independent of the CES, Arthur Wickson met with the church council and overruled their action. The CES gave "the organization known as St. James Park Congregational Church" one week to vacate the premises and appointed six of the ten members of a new committee of management to see out the year.

Apparently the conflict did little long-term harm, because the congregation continued to grow. By 1914 the Church was in a position to ask the CES to sell the property in order to build a larger church on a less expensive site somewhere to the west of the existing building.

Weeks, meanwhile, had turned his attention to the Fort Rouge district, south of the Assiniboine River, where a considerable number of Central's members had moved. The Presbyterians and Methodists were already established at Augustine and Fort Rouge Churches respectively, when the CES, under Weeks's direction, entered the field. In 1907, Central Church had used the proceeds from the sale of the Maple Street Church to help purchase property at Helen Street and Jessie Avenue, with a view to a future project. In 1909, Central signed this property over to the CES which, in turn, sold it and used the proceeds to buy three lots at the corner of Aynsley Street (now Arbuthnot) and McMillan Avenue.

As at St. James Park, the availability of funds through the CES enabled a building project to proceed almost at once. Alexander Black, late of the Maple Street Church, took a prominent role in erecting the structure. The building was opened in March 1910, and again it was James L. Gordon who preached the dedicatory sermon.

The new church was given the name Crescent and showed signs of strong, secure growth. By 1912, the congregation was able to buy the building from the CES for $3,000 cash and the assumption of the mortgage. Crescent was thereby given a degree of independence that St. James Park never attained.

Weeks's association with Crescent followed the pattern established at St. James Park. He was absent from the charge for some months in 1911 when he undertook a speaking tour in Britain and did much to acquaint British Congregationalists with mission work in Winnipeg and western Canada. He returned to Crescent briefly, but resigned in 1912 to be succeeded by yet another young pastor, the Rev. J.G. Hindley.

The story of Congregational Church extension and mission work in Winnipeg in this period would not be complete without reference to a project that may have owed less to the CES than it did to the Woman's Missionary Society (WMS) of Central Church.

The WMS had taken an active interest in home and foreign missions for some years. Like other branches of the WMS across the country, it supported work in what are now Angola and Turkey as well as in western Canada. But it was the engaging of a Miss K.D. Young as a part-time secretary and part-time pastoral visitor that provided the resource needed for some serious mission work to be done in Winnipeg.

Young was a middle-aged woman when she began her professional work for Central. In visiting people in hospital and elsewhere she became aware of the needs of recent immigrants to the north end of the city. She took her concerns to the meetings of the wms who, in May 1908, passed a resolution stating "that we (as a society) express our continued appreciation of the work of the [national] Woman's Board, and that, in view of the continual influx of people of all nationalities into the West, we urge the claims of this great Western country as well as those of Africa."[29]

The small but dedicated group of women that made up Central's wms soon showed that they were prepared to do their part in meeting the need. Money was raised to support Young's work in the north end, and in the spring of 1909, a lease was taken on the house at 377 Redwood Avenue. There, aided by volunteers from Central, Young organized a neighbourhood Sunday school, a mothers' group and a girls' club.

The mission work grew at such a pace that space (and heat) in the house on Redwood became inadequate. With help from the ces, a long search for an appropriate site eventually produced fruit in the form of a lot nearby on Aberdeen Avenue just west of Salter Street. The purchase of property and construction of a building demanded greater financial resources than the wms possessed. To their own plethora of fund-raising projects were added a legacy from the Alexander Black family and funds from the ces. Finally, in December 1914, a two-storey building – in appearance much like other mission buildings in the area – was opened by Arthur Wickson, with J.S. Woodsworth on the platform. At Wickson's suggestion, it was named the Pilgrim Institute.

The wms had taken a lead in bringing the Institute into being and in bringing the importance of mission work before the people of Central and the other Winnipeg Congregational churches. They drew other organizations into the work and continued to play a vital role through the years of the Pilgrim Institute's existence. There are signs of condescension and Anglo-Saxon superiority in the wms's recorded statments – not surprising in that period – but what shines through is a sense of concern and kindliness expressed in simple, thoughtful gestures and in an obvious wish to include the people "on the other side of the tracks" in the church family.

Both the wms and the ces took an active interest in mission work beyond the city itself. During the years before World War I, churches were established in several places in the North West Territories (after 1905, Saskatchewan and Alberta), but with the exception of Calgary these were all in remote rural areas that offered little opportunity for growth.

At the Carlton Union Charge (in the Battleford area), the indefatigable Benjamin Ralph presided as minister for a quarter of a century over a collection of frontier churches. Holding a doctorate in law from Trinity College, Dublin, Ralph came to the Northwest in 1904 because of ill health. His health must have taken a dramatic turn for the better, because he launched himself at once into the work of establishing congregations and caring for the material and spiritual needs of his scattered flock. In this work he was assisted for a time by one Nurse Halpenny, whose efforts were of particular interest to the WMS of Central Church. When Ralph died in 1930, he had become a veritable institution and was mourned by a great number of people with whose interests he had identified himself over the years.

Carlton Union was largely the creation of one man among a disparate group of people, few of whom had a Congregational background. Nearby Landis Charge, on the other hand, grew from a core of Congregationalists, many of them Scots, who had moved into the area. While Ernest Weeks, in his capacity as superintendent of the CES, made occasional courtesy calls on Ralph, at Landis he used his own influence (and CES money) to create an unusual facility known as the Landis Institute. Constructed by local Scottish stonemasons, the two-storey building contained a hall for services and community activities on the ground floor and living quarters for a minister on the upper floor. The project was an imaginative response to the social problems of single men in a lonely place and provided a much-needed opportunity for fellowship and recreation in a healthy atmosphere.

During the pre-war period, the Northwest became dotted with a variety of ethnic congregations. A group of Welsh exiles from Patagonia established a church at Glyndwr, in the Saltcoats area, in 1905. This congregation formed fairly close ties with the Congregational Union. The Swedish and so-called Russo-German churches that came north with American immigrants shared Congregational polity and outlook but stopped short of formal association with the Congregational Church.

A turning point in the relationship of the CES with the western fields came with Weeks's resignation as superintendent in 1911. About the same time, Weeks resigned from Crescent Church to become associate pastor at Central. In this new position he succeeded the Rev. D.S. Hamilton who in turn took Weeks's place as superintendent of the CES.

Hamilton had come to Winnipeg from Ontario in 1909. Soon after his arrival he was taken on as associate at Central. Before long, however, he was expressing frustration that his position curtailed what he called "the more important work," that of founding new churches.[30] While still attached to Central, Hamilton became an active member of the CES and, under their auspices, visited the fledgling congregation in Calgary. Soon afterwards, Weeks went to Saskatoon in order to assess the possibilities of a new congregation there. But by the time Weeks resigned as superintendent, the CES was beginning to realize that personnel and money would never be sufficient for them to pursue an aggressive policy in the West. The 1912 shareholders meeting was told that because of the CMS "having practically withdrawn its support" and the CCMS "reducing its gifts," the CES had been unable to enlarge its work outside Winnipeg.[31]

Hamilton's superintendency was virtually stillborn. Late in 1911, he resigned to take up child welfare work for the provincial government, while maintaining an active association with Central. Weeks remained at Central until 1914, when it had become clear that the sort of work to which he felt called was no longer available to him. He left Canada to pursue mission work in other outposts of Empire. And the CES, lacking the services of a superintendent, retreated into a maintenance role.

While disappointed in their hopes of having an effect on the prairie provinces as a whole, the men who animated the CES were encouraged by developments in Winnipeg itself, and not least by the dramatic growth of the Central congregation. In 1910, in anticipation of a day when the church, and especially the Sunday school, would require larger facilities, Arthur Wickson gathered together a group of businessmen to buy a piece of property at Ellice Avenue and Kennedy Street. The church was given a three-year option on the site. By 1911, the site, in the opinion of Wickson and most of his colleagues, had become unsuitable. The group offered to sell the land and to give the church $30,000 from the proceeds of the sale. Accordingly, the church released the group from the option and agreed to hold the funds in trust, pending the selection of an alternate site.

After some debate, the church arranged to buy, for $105,000, a lot on the corner of St. Mary Avenue and Vaughan Street. The deal was closed in January 1913, and a year later the property was half paid for. Gordon arranged a trip for himself and an architect to examine church buildings on the West Coast. Sketches were prepared. But before the work could proceed, in May 1914, Gordon resigned.

When Gordon left the city for Los Angeles in September, he left a situation which, for Congregationalists, was full of promise. Central itself was getting ready to construct a new building. St. James Park was looking for a new site. Crescent was well established and independent of the CES. The Pilgrim Institute was about to open its new facility. And Calvary Church in Brandon, after a somewhat chequered career and a split in the congregation in 1911, was sufficiently strong under the Rev. A.J. McKenzie to be thinking of a new building as well.[32] No one could have anticipated the variety of circumstances that were to turn the promise to disappointment.

DECLINE AND FALL

Gordon's eventual successor at Central was the Rev. W.J. Hindley, a Canadian Congregational minister, brother of the Rev. J.G. Hindley (who until just before then had presided at Crescent) and sometime commission mayor of Spokane, Washington. By the time he arrived in Winnipeg at the end of 1914, Canada was involved in a war that was to have a profound effect on the Congregational churches. For Central, in particular, it meant that money was now in short supply and that construction workers were no longer readily available. The building project had to be postponed.

Unfortunately, Hindley's private life dealt another blow to the church. Initially, he had proved a popular and influential pastor, but in 1916 it was alleged that he had become involved in an extra-marital affair.[33] A series of Church board meetings was hastily convened to discuss the minister's behaviour, and at the end of the year, citing "the very unsettled condition of my own affairs,"[34] Hindley resigned. Once again, J.B. Silcox was recalled for an extended period of pulpit supply.

No sooner had the church come through this upheaval than it had to contend with another problem. It was sued for mortgage arrears on its new site. The suit was settled out of court by a cash payment and the title was returned to the mortgage holder. The congregation's hopes of a new building vanished. And to add insult to injury, financial stringency made it necessary that the church take out a $20,000 mortgage on its existing building. To the people of Central Church, it must have seemed that the good times had departed with James L. Gordon.

The war years were harder on St. James Park Church than on Central. In fact, they proved fatal. In 1915, Edgar Whitehouse resigned to go to a union church in Dryden. As the church looked in vain for a new minister, the people felt discouraged by the enlistment of many of the laity in the armed forces. By 1916, the congregation was still solvent, but there seemed little hope of maintaining the situation. That spring, the CES made the difficult decision of discontinuing services and of closing the Sunday school at the end of the term. In July, the building – which, it had been thought only a few years before, would be sold so that a better Congregational church could be built – was bought by the Christian Church (Church of Christ, Disciples).[35] Some of the proceeds were used by the CES to pay off the mortgage on the Pilgrim Institute.

Wartime stringency played havoc with the Brandon church too. Plans for a new building gradually faded. Regular ministers were difficult to find, and the congregation had to survive between student placements. For a time, an invalided armed forces chaplain restored a semblance of continuity. But after the war it became impossible to call a Congregational minister. After some years of local supply from other denominations, services were discontinued. In 1924, the building and parsonage were sold to the CCMS. Sunday school continued until church union in 1925. Finally, the CCMS sold the building to a Pentecostal group.[36]

For the Pilgrim Institute as well, the war years marked a watershed. In a sense, its opening in December 1914 could not have been more ill-timed. Being a mission, it was heavily dependent on outside financial support, and this kind of support was in short supply. The group that met there for worship was getting smaller rather than larger.

Finally, in 1922, Arthur Wickson and others conducted a survey in the area. The survey showed that most of the people in the district were either Jewish or of another denomination. And while some ethnic groups tended to rent their homes with the idea of moving elsewhere eventually, the Jews were inclined to buy their houses with the intention of staying. The handwriting was on the wall. Feeling that Christian mission work in the north end was being adequately conducted by other denominations, the CES reluctantly sold the building to a Jewish institution, the I.L. Peretz School.[37] With the work of the CES practically at an end, Wickson finally left the city to finish his retirement in Vancouver.

The closing of the Pilgrim Institute in 1922 left Central and Crescent Churches as the only Congregational foundations remaining in Winnipeg – and the only Congregational churches in Manitoba to survive long enough to enter the United Church of Canada.

For Central, the outlook had begun to brighten when the interregnum following Hindley's departure was brought to an end with the calling of the Rev. Byron Stauffer, a Canadian then living in San Francisco. A journalist rather than a theologian by training, Stauffer arrived at Central in January 1919. Stauffer was a flamboyant orator who had a strong appeal for some. However, his career was marred by an egotism that seemed to care little for church discipline and by a weakness for drink. In the opinion of J.B. Silcox, "eventually drink 'got' him."[38] After only eighteen months at Central, he left for Toronto where he conducted services at Massey Hall in the hope that he might build up a following among those who had heard him five years earlier when he had been the minister at Bond Street Church. However, his hopes were not realized. He died two years later at the age of fifty-two.

His successor at Central was from Yorkshire, a man small of stature but big of voice, named George Laughton. Laughton's five-year pastorate saw the church return to a measure of stability under his strong preaching and steadying influence. But the financial pressures which had begun during the war had become a perennial problem. A second mortgage had to be secured, and the congregration was constantly contending with the problems of an aging facility.

It was during Laughton's time as pastor that Central and Crescent became United Churches. The issue of church union brought to a head those divergent attitudes exemplified in an earlier period by Silcox and Pedley. There were some Winnipeg Congregationalists who felt that union was a positive and faithful response to the spiritual needs of the nation. There were others who guarded their denominational loyalty and viewed union with suspicion.[39] And there were a good many in the middle who saw church union simply as an acceptance of the inevitable. For Central itself, it was becoming clear by the mid-twenties that, with or without union, it would not be possible for all of the large Protestant downtown churches to survive.[40] As the United Church came into being, Central's main concern seems to have been to avoid becoming the new denomination's first casualty in downtown Winnipeg.

Laughton departed for St. James Church in Montreal in 1926. As the Church went through the process of adapting to United Church polity – including the procedure for calling a minister – it made a decision which seemed to speak of its intention to maintain its individual, independent Congregational character. It called to its pulpit a colourful, dynamic and independent-minded preacher, the Rev. P. Campbell Morgan.

Morgan, son of a well-known English evangelist named G. Campbell Morgan, came to Central from Cincinnati, Ohio. What the people knew of Morgan was that he had a strong pulpit appeal and a reputation for packing churches. What they did not know was that, in coming to Canada, he left behind a bevy of American creditors to whom he owed some $6,000.[41]

To outward appearances, the first part of Morgan's pastorate was a resounding success. The church was full again, and Central had once more a pulpit whose incumbent was in demand as a preacher and lecturer all over the continent.

Behind closed doors, matters were different.[42] Pursued by some of his creditors, Morgan resorted to borrowing from members of the church. He also managed to win concessions from the church in the form of manse furnishings and salary increases. Eventually, much of his salary had to be paid directly to his creditors' trustees. In time, Morgan managed to reduce his American debts by over $4,000, but in the meantime, his penchant for spending incurred new and unnecessary debts which, in the view of a Presbytery investigation, tarnished both his personal reputation and that of the church. Further, a dispute over the reimbursement Morgan expected to receive from the church for the preaching missions he was in the habit of conducting caused considerable resentment in the congregation.

By 1929, Central was a house divided. Morgan's popular following was still large, but to many of the church officers he had become an embarrassment and an encumbrance. In a decision made behind closed doors he was forced out, but the result was a split congregation.

In a sense, the worst was yet to come. In an effort to salvage Morgan's career, Winnipeg Presbytery assigned him as "stated supply" at Zion Church. Zion, once a great Methodist congregation, had fallen into decline. Situated between downtown and the north end, it seemed to have a future only as a mission. But Morgan saw an opportunity to take his personal following from Central with him. It is certain that Zion's membership experienced a sudden, if shortlived, increase after Morgan's arrival. And in the opinion of some at Central, he positively enticed people away from his former church.[43] Others, disillusioned by both minister and church, disappeared from church rolls altogether.

At Zion, financial and other problems continued to dog Morgan's steps. The details of the so-called Zion Church case lie beyond the scope of the present study. Suffice it to say that a presbytery commission concluded, in 1932, by recommending that Zion Church be closed and that Morgan be expelled from the ministry of the United Church of Canada.[44] Before Presbytery had a chance to act, Morgan resigned, withdrew from the United Church, and eventually departed for a Presbyterian Church in the United States.

For Central, Morgan's pastorate and its aftermath had done irreparable harm. It could safely be argued that the church's days were numbered in any case, but the split which Morgan brought about so reduced the membership and sapped the congregation's strength that, in the coming Depression, it simply had not the resources to maintain itself.

The dubious honour of cleaning up after the Morgan debacle fell to the Rev. Andrew D. Reid of Nova Scotia. Reid was a solid, dedicated minister, but he faced an impossible task. When he accepted a call to Chalmers Church in 1932, the congregation felt that they were at the last ditch. Short of funds, they decided to gamble. Two theology students from Wesley College, Bill Hughes and Stanley Knowles, were invited to share the work between them. On his ordination the following year, Knowles took over the pulpit on his own and served for two more years. He was the last minister of Central United Church.

Crescent Church, meanwhile, had been doing rather better. Certainly it experienced no similar catastrophes. In 1927, in fact, it had undertaken a building project that included the addition of a full basement. With Augustine and Fort Rouge Churches, Crescent had even, as far back as 1916, sponsored what was called the Sunshine Mission – the precursor of Harrow United Church. Hailed in its early days as the prototype of "Winnipeg's First Union Church,"[45] the enterprise became the Stafford Street Mission before being established at its present location.

As church union approached, the people of Crescent made an effort to arrange joint events with the other Fort Rouge churches, particularly with Fort Rouge Methodist. By 1930, looking at the cost of maintaining two buildings and at the duplication of services, the two congregations began to discuss amalgamation. It was not until 1935, however, that the congregations agreed to spend two years conducting services jointly at Fort Rouge, and to continue Sunday school and young people's activities at Crescent. The union was finally completed in 1937, when Crescent–Fort Rouge United Church was voted into existence by large majorities in both congregations. Crescent's building remained in use for some purposes, but being the smaller and less substantial of the two, it soon came to be seen as unnecessary. It was sold to the St. John Ambulance organization, and is at present the site of an apartment block.

In the mid-1930s, the last act in the drama of Central Church was being played. Already dedicated to the social gospel, Stanley Knowles was attracting growing attendances at his evening services. Until the Board closed them down (pointing to the high cost of fuel), he conducted as well afterservice forums on topics like "Has Capitalism Failed?" and "The Essence of Socialism." J.S. Woodsworth, John Queen and Ralph Maybank were prominent speakers at the forums. With the demise of this platform, Knowles turned to radio and saw to it that most of his broadcast sermons dealt with social themes.[46] Although Knowles financed his broadcasts entirely apart from the church, the Board was less than supportive. When the opportunity came for him to contest the Cooperative Commonwealth Federation nomination in Winnipeg South Centre, he took it, won the nomination and resigned from Central, effective 30 June 1935.

That spring, it was discovered that the rafters of the church building were rotting and the roof was in danger of collapse. Already heavily mortgaged, the church simply had no resources to cope with the necessary renovations. The city engineering department condemned the building, and the congregation was forced to make an early start on its recent tradition of worshipping with First Baptist Church[47] during the summer months. There was no future. Knowles was later to remark that he had brought the roof down on Central Church.[48]

An impressive saga had come to a sad end. In 1936, facing the inevitable, the church leaders wound up the congregation's affairs. The furnishings had already been disposed of. In April, the wrecker's ball fell on the building. An R. Billinkoff had bought it for the value of the materials. Eventually the YMHA building was built on the site.

It may be dangerous to speculate on the ifs of history, but it is probably fair to guess that, if it had not been for church union, Congregationalism in Manitoba would have disappeared by means of a gradual decline. As it was, it disappeared quickly and by absorption, although the spirit of Congregationalism continued to influence the United Church of Canada.

The causes of fatal weakness in the Congregational Church in Manitoba and the West were many. At the outset, the Church in the East seemed undecided about whether to concentrate on the establishment of colonies or on direct evangelization. The debate was never really resolved. Where colonies were established – as at Wood Bay, Landis and Saltcoats – the churches were limited by small numbers and isolation and, in some cases, by denominational competition. Where a small core of declared Congregationalists set out to attract others to the church – as in Winnipeg and Brandon – the dedicated core remained relatively small.

Working from a small base and entering the field rather late, the Congregationalists were at a disadvantage from the beginning. Whether one thinks of the earlier period when the CCMS took responsibility for western expansion or of the later period when the CES took over, one finds the Church's efforts repeatedly hampered by limitations of money and personnel.

Hugh Pedley, as we have seen, felt that the West was an ideal field for the introduction of Congregational polity. But, as the membership records show, western Canadian pragmatism expressed itself in a casual crossing over of denominational lines rather than in a flocking to the Congregational cause. For people with the breadth of vision of a J.B. Silcox, this phenomenon was no reason for regret, but for the Congregational Church it proved fatal. In good times, Central Church, particularly, attracted crowds to hear the great preachers of the day. But while a core of dedicated workers carried on through thick and thin, the crowds came and went with the preachers. They seem to have lacked a sense of loyalty to the church. They appear, in a sense, to have asked not what they could do for the church, but rather what the church could do for them. And their preoccupation with personalities betrayed a shallow understanding of worship and of the church's character and purpose. Typical was the remark of a young woman in James L. Gordon's time who, on hearing it rumoured that Gordon would accept a call to a church in the United States, wondered aloud where on earth she would go to church if the great man were to leave the city.[49]

Congregationalism in the West was a denomination with shallow roots. It was distinguished by some dynamic and fearless preachers, but it was also at times at the mercy of scoundrels. It had some able and dedicated lay leaders, but it was unable to broaden and deepen an enduring base of support. The result was a measure of instability that makes the Church, in retrospect, look like something of a will-o'-the-wisp.

And yet the spirit of Congregationalism lives on. As one wag has it, at the time of church union, the Presbyterians were afraid of being swallowed by the Methodists, and the Methodists were afraid of being swallowed by the Presbyterians, and when they were not looking the Congregationalists swallowed them both.

Certainly the United Church in western Canada today is characterized by an at times fiercely independent congregational spirit. It is a spirit beloved of many lay people at the congregational level and one that tends to be loathed by presbyteries. For better or worse, the system that Pedley extolled and that some Congregationalists feared would entirely pass away in 1925 has left its mark on the United Church of Canada.

Head, heart and purse:
The Presbyterian Women's Missionary
Society in Canada, 1876–1925

Margaret E. McPherson

Since we have gained an intelligent interest in missions, we are imbibing its spirit. Through our heads our hearts are reached and through heart interest, purse interest is kindled and we are looking with longing desire to the spread of the Gospel news, to full missionary ranks and full missionary treasures.[1]

The Presbyterian, Methodist and Congregational forebears of the United Church of Canada brought theological, liturgical and organizational traditions to church union in 1925. They also brought their respective women's missionary societies, well-established associations with national structures "created by women, supported by women and administered by women."[2] The amalgamation of these societies in 1926 to form the Woman's Missionary Society of the United Church of Canada established a strong organization with a million-dollar budget and over four hundred workers in the field;[3] it united women who, whether cognizant of the fact or not, were ready to move out to every field of service in the church and in society.

Although hundreds of women worked in these societies to further the mission and ministry of Canadian Protestant churches both at home and abroad, only a small number of the societies' leaders can be named, and few details of their exploits are known. Recently, however, encouraged by the work of women's history scholars, church women have been stirred to search out long-neglected records in order to file a claim on the place of women in the pre-union history of the United Church of Canada.

In this article, I focus on one of the forerunners of the United Church Woman's Missionary Society, the Presbyterian Women's Missionary Society of Canada (Western Division) (PWMS), and more specifically on one the PWMS's parent organizations, the Presbyterian Woman's Foreign Missionary

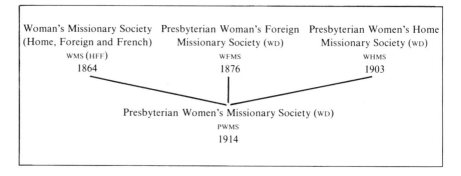

Figure 1
Formation of the Presbyterian Women's Missionary Society (Western Division)

Society of Canada (wfms), and on Amanda Norris MacKay, one of the pwms's early leaders in Manitoba. As well, I consider how the Canadian women's missionary movement of the late-nineteenth century related to the feminist movement of that period. Such reflections seem most appropriate now, in the 1980s, since United Church members are struggling with issues of inclusive language and the changing roles of men and women in the Church.[4]

THE IMPETUS

The formation of the Woman's Foreign Missionary Society of the Canadian Presbyterian Church was not a sudden inspiration. Influences were abroad in the world tending towards such an event. Women's societies had been for some time in operation in the Old World and in the United States. Hearts were stirring also in the Canadian Church.[5]

The genesis of the women's missionary movement in Canada benefited greatly from experiences of Protestant women in both Europe and the United States during the nineteenth century. Feminists struggled for equality and autonomy for women in educational, political and legal systems; at the same time, they sought equal rights for women in the established religious organizations.

One area in which the growth of women's influence in religious affairs was significant was in the Sunday school movement. Involvement in Sunday school not only offered women opportunities for administration and organization, but also "it raised their importance in other peoples' eyes and in their own."[6] In some congregations women were in the majority as Sunday school teachers and as the movement became an established middle-class Protestant

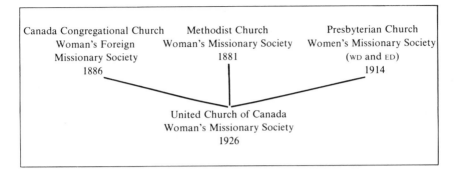

Figure 2
Formation of the United Church of Canada Woman's Missionary Society

convention, they exercised considerable influence over the young of the church – often to the chagrin of the male clergy.[7]

Early religious sects such as the Quakers, Shakers and the Christian Scientists endorsed a distinct feminist component which offered a real alternative for women who wanted more active roles in church affairs.[8] Dorothy Bass, an American professor of religious history, argues, however, that it was the sect called Evangelicals who were the catalysts in the emancipation of women in both religious and secular spheres.[9]

Technological changes in Great Britain and North America that took production of goods out of the home and into industrial shops had helped to alter the role of women in society. Confined to a tedious and unsatisfying role, many women became restless and responded eagerly to calls for aid in alleviating the social problems created by the industrial explosion. Rapidly growing cities spawned vice, poverty and misery. At the same time, the settlement of the vast frontier challenged Christian denominations to provide a Christian presence. By convincing women of their important role in redeeming a "wicked" world to righteousness, evangelical churchmen enlisted the energy and passion of spirited women for evangelical crusades.

Lydia Child, a nineteenth-century American author and abolitionist, used the old story of the sorcerer's apprentice to illustrate the expansion of women's involvement in society. The apprentice bewitched a broom into a living being but was unable to change it back into a broom. "Thus it is with those who urged women to become missionaries and form tract societies . . . they have no spell to turn it into a broom again."[10] From a western Canadian perspective a more appropriate metaphor is the old adage: no use

TABLE 1

Terms used by the Presbyterian Women's Missionary Society

Auxiliary	An auxiliary consisted of a group of women from a small district or from a single congregation who gathered to study and to raise monies for missionary work.
Presbyterial	A presbyterial was formed from a group of auxiliaries in a geographical region comparable to an established presbytery.
Provincial Society	The first provincial society was established in 1914 to facilitate the work of presbyterials within its bounds.
Dominion Board	The first board was established in 1876 to coordinate mission work from the national level.

closing the barn door after the horses have escaped. Once freed to exercise their many talents, women would not be corralled again.

Missionary societies organized and administered by women for women, were among many societies, clubs and unions that emerged from the feminist drive of the nineteenth century. Spurred by both the feminist spirit and Christ's command to carry the Gospel to the world, "more females became involved in woman's missionary society work after the Civil War than in all areas of the social reform and women's rights movement combined."[11] Most Protestant denominations approved the establishment of women's missionary societies but frequently placed restrictions on the scope of their work. Activating women in the task of evangelizing the world did not mean that women were to become full partners in established church structures. On the contrary, they were still denied membership on church boards and committees, and could not vote on church affairs. Still, in spite of the limitations imposed on church women, the societies flourished.

For Canadian church women, the struggle for broader participation in church life was similar to that of their sisters in both the Old and New Worlds. Even in obtaining the right to form their own missionary societies, Canadian women had to overcome considerable prejudice and finally succeeded only because of support from the foreign and home missions committees who were desperate for workers.

THE SOCIETY

The object of the Society was to aid the Foreign Missions Committee in the support of its work among heathen women and children, to interest women and children of the Church in this work, and to call forth in a systematic way their prayers and free will offerings in its behalf.[12]

Canadian women had been engaging themselves in mission work in fragmented ways for some years before attempts were made to coordinate women and mission work. Records indicate that as early as 1856 Presbyterian women in Scarboro Township (Ontario) had formed a foreign missionary association to support two orphan girls at a school in India.[13]

The PWMS[14] that existed in 1925 was itself a merger of three Presbyterian women's mission societies. The oldest and smallest group, the Woman's Missionary Society (Home, French and Foreign) was based in the Montreal area. It had its origin in 1864 with the founding of the Ladies' Auxiliary Association in Connection with the French Mission Work in Montreal.[15] The largest branch, the WFMS, was organized in 1876 to assist the church in meeting increased demands for foreign mission work. Although formed to support mission work abroad, the WFMS understood "foreign" to include native Indians, Chinese, French and, later, Eastern Europeans who were living in Canadian communities. It was not until 1903 that the third branch, the Presbyterian Women's Home Missionary Society, (WHMS) was established to address purely Canadian mission needs.[16]

The major thrust to organize the WFMS came from the Foreign Missions Committee of the Presbyterian Church. A notice was placed in the Toronto daily papers calling a meeting of women to consider the formation of a woman's society for foreign missions.[17] At that meeting, held 17 February 1876, two leading churchmen, Rev. Dr. William MacLaren and Rev. Dr. Alexander Topp, conveyed the Foreign Mission Committee's desire that such a society be organized in a manner similar to the way the societies in the American Presbyterian Church were organized. A committee composed of fourteen women and the two men was quickly struck to lay the foundations for the new society. By 21 March 1876, the WFMS was duly formed, with a constitution, by-laws, a board and appointed officers, and a definition of the objectives of the organization. Fifty women enrolled at the first monthly meeting on 4 April 1876 at Knox Church in Toronto. Two months later the General Assembly of the Presbyterian Church endorsed the constitution and recommended the WFMS to the Church at large.[18]

The nature of the mission work women were expected to assume was clear: the work was confined to "heathen women and children." To accomplish this, the WFMS was to enlist women and children in the task and to include, "in a systematic way," prayer and money. This prescription was carefully followed and proved to be highly beneficial to the health and growth of the WFMS. The basic organizational units were the auxiliary for the women, and the mission band for children. Over the first few years auxiliaries sprang up in nearly every settled area of the country. The WFMS motto, "The World For

Christ,"[19] adopted in 1883, reflected the growing aspirations of the society. Its escalating crusade relied on educating women about mission needs, moving their hearts and then causing them to open their purses, a process which presented an interesting dilemma. In order to provide and staff hospitals and schools for heathen women and children, the WFMS needed to enlarge its base of support; but in order to build this support, it needed specific projects towards which to direct an appeal for funds. One popular way to fan enthusiasm was to call on missionaries and their spouses who were home on furlough to speak to gatherings of women. Such was the situation when the first WFMS auxiliary in western Canada was formed in Winnipeg in 1884. On 24 October 1884, a group of Presbyterian women in Winnipeg had held a meeting at Knox Church to hear an address by Mrs. J.F. Campbell, wife of a Canadian Presbyterian missionary in central India. Stirred by her words, the women decided to follow the example set by their Presbyterian sisters in the East and to form an auxiliary to the WFMS. Membership in this new auxiliary was drawn from the three Presbyterian churches in Winnipeg: Knox, St. Andrew's and St. Giles. From the fifteen members who made up the auxiliary, officers were elected, with Janet King, wife of the principal of Manitoba College as the first president, Mrs. D.M. Gordon and Sophia Pitblado as vice-presidents, Margaret Taylor (afterwards Lady Taylor) as treasurer and Minnie Campbell as secretary.[20]

During its first year the Winnipeg Auxiliary made only limited progress. The trauma of the Riel Rebellion in the spring of 1885 and the attention given to providing food and relief supplies for both civilians and troops detracted from interest in mission work. By the end of 1885, however, the auxiliary had swung into action again. Raising funds for foreign mission work went hand-in-hand with meeting the needs of people in the immediate community. Mission work involved not only preaching the Christian faith, but also alleviating physical distress with material goods, commonly referred to as "supply." The first report of the Winnipeg Auxiliary noted that a sum of $100 had been forwarded to the head WFMS office.[21] The first supply list included the following message: "Five sacks of clothing were sent to the Indians at Edmonton, one sack of clothing, one sack of oatmeal and twenty-five gallons molasses to Rev. Geo. Flett, Okanase Reserve near Strathclair, Manitoba, three sacks clothing to File Hills Reserve and yarn and flannel costing $8.75 to the Assiniboine Indian women who can knit and sew, also ten sacks clothing and $9.00 in cash to white settlers who suffered severely from prairie fires."[22]

One example of the work the women of the Winnipeg Auxiliary did in meeting local needs was to open a school for the small group of Chinese men who had settled in Winnipeg in those early days. The YMCA provided a room for classes. Fourteen WFMS members volunteered to teach the five Chinese men who attended the first class. But soon, the number in the class grew and the men were said to "evince great delight at being taught to read and write our language."[23]

The Brandon missionary field was being cultivated at this time by Jessie Turnbull McEwen (wife of Donald McEwen). Having been active in Ontario with a variety of feminist causes before moving west, Jessie McEwen is credited with founding auxiliaries around the Chater, Humesville, Rugby and Brandon communities and with forming Brandon Presbyterial, the first presbyterial in the West in 1886. (A presbytery was a court of the church consisting of all the pastoral charges within its prescribed bounds. *Presbyterial* was the term given to a level of organization of the WFMS to coordinate the work of auxiliaries in a region which corresponded approximately to that of the presbytery.) McEwan was also instrumental opening a YWCA hostel in Brandon and organized the first chapter of the Council of Women there.[24] One WFMS member said that McEwen was the first woman she ever saw on a platform or heard address a meeting![25]

In 1888 the Winnipeg Auxiliary, now much enlarged, voted to disband in favour of forming WFMS auxiliaries in each congregation, the first congregational auxiliary in Winnipeg was thus organized by the Augustine women. These new auxiliaries gathered together on 12 February 1889 and formed the Winnipeg Presbyterial.[26]

The Dominion board of the WFMS had laid its foundations carefully. Organizing auxiliaries and distributing literature were among its first concerns. The board set about at once to secure "direct missionary intelligence." Correspondence from missionaries in the field was circulated to auxiliaries. In 1884 a publication called the *Monthly Letter Leaflets* was begun, for which an annual subscription was twelve cents. By 1900 this publication was called *Foreign Missionary Tidings*, cost fifteen cents annually, and had 16,500 subscribers.[27] Not only did this kind of literature provide "head interest" but it also stimulated "heart interest." Unable to become missionaries themselves, thousands of women lived vicariously through the experiences of women active in the field. Each auxiliary would have a designated missionary to correspond with, to pray for, and to support with small remembrances. Personal visits from missionaries home on leave inspired auxiliaries to even deeper commitment. Minnie Campbell, in her 1896 Annual Report, referred to mission education as the facts which "are fuel to flame the fire."[28]

During the earliest stages of the foreign missionary movement the wives of missionaries represented Christian women in the foreign fields. The wife was there not as an evangelist, however, but as a support for her spouse, to care for his health and material needs. Like a Judaic woman, the glory of the missionary's wife came through caring for her husband; as her husband was successful, so was she. Nevertheless, women perceived the role of the missionary's wife to be an important one, granting her – if the President's Address from the 1889–90 Annual Report of the WFMS can be so interpreted – an equally valuable place in mission work. The president stated "that a man is not half a missionary till he gets a wife. This is to aid and comfort him in the work and to set up the shining light of a Christian home in Heathen darkness, even if she is not allowed by home duties to take charge of a school or engage in more active outside work."[29]

Ironically it was the social customs of some foreign cultures that enabled Christian women to become missionaries in their own right. Foreign mission committees came to realize that in many countries where mission fields were established, the local women exerted considerable influence within the family circle, especially in educational and religious matters. At the same time, it was customary for these women to be limited in their contacts with the outside world, particularly with men. Successful evangelization required reaching these women and only women missionaries would be able to make the connections. Once the door was opened to them, unmarried, educated Christian women suffering from the constraints placed upon them by "women's proper role" eagerly prepared themselves for mission work, welcoming the accompanying opportunities for travel and independence. Increased interest in missionary societies resulted from the move to employ women and as the number of auxiliaries grew, so did the number of women in the mission fields.

During its early years the WFMS faced formidable obstacles to its growth. Overcoming amused condescension or scepticism of church members or even outright disapproval from some clergy took time and patience. Still, indifference or patronizing attitudes could be handled more readily than other difficulties, such as those faced by many rural auxiliaries in the West. Poor crops, a lack of leaders, long distances to travel to meetings and bad roads challenged even the most faithful. However, neither inclement weather nor impassable roads stopped women such as Jessie McEwen. One expedition involved two sisters who had a pony but no vehicle: "They rode to the McEwen farm where there was no horse but a harness and buckboard. Hitching up their pony, they took turns one driving Mrs. McEwen to the meeting and the other riding in a box behind on the board. Often there were only 3 or 4 could get to the meeting but they kept on believing that where 3 or 4 were gathered in the Master's name He was in the midst of them."[30]Setbacks occurred when members moved on to take up homesteads in other districts. In one instance only one member and no officers were left in a scattered community. "This energetic little woman believing that though the workers are gone the work must still go on, resolved to reorganize the auxiliary and succeeded in interesting those who had never belonged before."[31]

The growth of the Mission Band Program had its own particular problems. Referred to as a "nursery and feeder"[32] to auxiliaries, the Band Program aimed at indoctrinating children with the importance of missions and with disciplined givings. Some bands were solely for girls, others for boys, and some were for both boys and girls.[33] Twelve years was generally the upper age limit for membership. Appropriate names, all very descriptive of their objectives, were chosen: Cheerful Givers, Willing Workers, Earnest Workers, Helping Hands, Faithful Workers, Busy Bees. The success or demise of a band was directly proportional to the degree of commitment and creativity of its leaders. Thus the WFMS paid considerable attention to leadership training and to providing resource material for mission bands.

From the very beginning the women relied on "divine guidance" to direct their organizational efforts. Prayer continued to hold a prominent place in the WFMS activities throughout the years. As well as having a particular missionary to pray for, the women were asked to observe an hour of prayer on Sundays from 4:00 to 5:00 p.m.[34] Prayer cards for each month were prepared and distributed to assist members in this aspect of their spiritual life.[35] Members took turns leading in worship at meetings. Amanda MacKay, in an address to the Brandon Presbyterial in 1936, reflected on how women who had never before been called on to pray in public felt about leading in worship, and the effect it had on meetings. "Very few women at that time had ever taken part in meetings of any kind, as there were no societies for women except the Ladies' Aid and *they* did not have programmes. Most women would tell you that they could not pray or read the Bible in public and as for writing a paper on any subject, it was beyond them – so they thought, so that for a long time, it was hard to keep up interest in meetings with so few willing to take part."[36]

If a woman could not be a missionary for Christ in a foreign land, she could at least support one, and women did support missionaries in ever-increasing numbers. In an appeal to rouse mission workers, an early journal writer pleaded, "Let every lady who feels that she would be a missionary, go to work at home, and she may, by every dollar raised, teach her heathen sisters."[37] To advance the work to which they were committed, the society used head and heart interest to kindle purse interest. "The system adopted by the WFMS was one of absolute simplicity, and as it proved itself throughout the years, of great efficiency."[38] An annual WFMS membership cost one dollar. A life membership fee was introduced in 1883;[39] it cost $25 and could be bought by an individual or by an auxiliary in honour of one of its members. Each member was expected to contribute money according to her ability at the regular monthly meeting. Mission bands devised their own ways of raising funds. One was "talent money" – money realized by a member by using such particular talents as sewing or gardening. Another was the distribution of "mite boxes" – small boxes that members could use for regular donations. Annual thankofferings were begun in 1885.[40] The establishment of the Scattered Helpers in 1889 gave the WFMS a structure within which to enlist women in remote places in a type of associate membership.[41] Literature was sent to the Scattered Helpers regularly, which enable the WFMS to maintain lines of interest for future development.

The principle of giving for the whole of mission work and keeping decision-making at the Dominion board level was strictly observed. This strengthened the WFMS and enabled it to finance projects that individual groups would never have been able to support: "Minute attention to detail, watchfulness against waste of funds or extravagant expenditures, and voluntary service in every department kept the cost of management down to less than two percent (2%) all through the Society's existence."[42] The members were sensitive to the effect their money-raising might have on the general coffers of the Church. In the 1901 Annual Report celebrating the twenty-fifth anniversary of the WFMS, the president commented, "The Society has not detracted from other schemes of the Church but has been an incentive to more liberal giving."[43] In the same report she cautioned the membership to "guard against the temptation to allow entertainment or even study to take the place of prayer in our meetings."[44] The spiritual dimension of the WFMS continued to be paramount, as shown in the annual reports which included the entire texts of the presidents' addresses and committee reports. In the reports, God is eloquently thanked for the prosperity of the Society, for sparing the workers for another year of work, for answering prayers. Although women were denied the right to preach from the pulpit, the reason was certainly not any shortage of ability or shallowness of spirituality. WFMS women were strong of faith and their expression of faith was articulate.

Almost from its inception the WFMS was pressed to include home missions work under its umbrella. The WFMS understood its mandate to be directed at "heathen women and children" which included native Indians, Chinese, and French living in Canada. Financing missionaries already at work required tight control of funds. Yet requests to designate funds for other projects kept arriving from auxiliaries. Some even believed that with so many crying needs locally, foreign work should be abandoned and the WFMS should be turned into a home missions society.

In Manitoba, James Robertson was named superintendent of home missions in 1881, and he soon began to agitate for the women in Winnipeg to organize a home missionary society. He found sympathetic women in Margaret Taylor, Penelope Baird and Marion Bryce, and by 1891 the first Home and Foreign Missionary Society in Canada had been formed at Augustine Church.[45]

In her address to the 1889 Annual Meeting of the WFMS, the president, Mrs. Thomas Ewart, cautioned the members about disloyalty to the goals of foreign work and the distractions of "new emergencies, new causes, new woes" on the work already pledged.[46] However, the same Annual Meeting heard a report from the Brandon Presbyterial which indicated that home missionary societies were being formed: "In one or two districts, owing to urgent needs of funds for Home Mission work we hear of a Home Missionary society flourishing, side by side with our Woman's Foreign Missionary Society, and both flourishing, so that we need not fear that our cause at home shall in any way suffer from our continued efforts in Foreign Mission work."[47] While some home missionary societies were organized and while some local auxiliaries responded to home front needs, the response was fragmented and uncoordinated on the women's part. The major responsibility for home missions work in the Presbyterian Church fell to the Home Missions Committee.

One of the most pressing problems facing the Home Missions Committee was created by the large numbers of prospectors and entrepreneurs stampeding into the Canadian Northwest in search of gold. Distressing conditions in mining camps, the hardships of cold weather, and the geographical isolation all contributed to a call for help, particularly medical help. In 1898 a group of Presbyterian women in Toronto met with members of the Home Mission Committee to develop a plan for sending Christian nurses to the Klondike. The following year the Atlin Nurse Committee started its campaign to raise funds to equip and send two nurses to begin this medical relief work[48] at Atlin, B.C. Rev. Dr. John Pringle described the experience which moved him to establish the first Presbyterian hospital in Canada in 1900: "On a very cold night I visited the tent and cabin used as a hospital. There I found Miss Mitchell caring for three sick men. The tent was 12×14 and had a stove in the middle of the floor, around which, as near as safety would permit, were the three canvas cots. The nurse sat almost against the stove, her fur coat buttoned round her. I could not sleep that night. . . . In the morning I said 'I am going to build a hospital.' "[49]

Just as the Foreign Mission Committee had called on the talents and vigour of women for foreign work, so the Home Mission Committee decided to challenge the WFMS to include "evangelistic, medical and educational" concerns in Canada under their pervue.[50] Rev. James Robertson's first attempt in this direction in 1901 failed but his fervent pleas for help continued. The Home Missions Committee then turned its attention to the Atlin Nurse Committee and, aided by this concerned group, was successful in 1903 in creating what was the third parent organization of the PWMS, the WHMS.[51] With this organization established, the Atlin Nurse Committee disbanded and turned its work over to the WHMS, whose motto was "Canada for Christ," and whose watchword was "humility and service."[52]

The object of the WHMS included support of medical work, cooperating with the Home Missions Committee in raising funds, and "engaging in any other work of a kindred nature that the Committee may deem it advisable to have taken up."[53] Facing the same organizational and fund-raising problems as the WFMS, the WHMS had an advantage – the experience of the older sister organization. Using the building tools of head, heart and purse interest again, the WHMS developed first of all an efficient educational component. A travelling secretary, a monthly magazine named *The Home Mission Pioneer*, educational leaflets, a circulating library, lectures and lantern slides were provided to fire the enthusiasm and compassion of women for home mission needs.

Any discussion of the WFMS and the WHMS would be incomplete without reference to the ambitious project undertaken by them in forming a training school for women missionaries. Named the Ewart Training Home, it opened in 1897 in Toronto under the joint management of the WFMS and the Foreign Mission Committee of the Church.[54] When the Deaconess Order was established in 1908 by the General Assembly, the Church itself assumed responsibility for the school, re-naming it the Missionary and Deaconess Training Home.[55] The WFMS continued to provide financial support.

For over ten years the WFMS and the WHMS functioned separately but similarly. It became obvious that the similarity went beyond structure and organization since the two groups drew upon a common pool of church women for membership with many women working for both societies. Eventually, after much negotiation, the two societies decided to combine with the smaller Woman's Missionary Society (Home, French and Foreign) from Montreal, to form a new society. On 15 May 1914, 1,327 auxiliaries with 52,000 members and 656 mission bands from the three active mission societies of the Presbyterian Church (Western Division) joined to become the PWMS.[56]

Until 1896 only two presbyterials existed in Manitoba and they reported directly to the Toronto Board. By that year however, auxiliaries were springing up regularly and everywhere as the province became more densely settled. Brandon Presbyterial became known as the Mother of Presbyterials because it produced, in order, the presbyterials of Glenboro, Portage la Prairie and Minnedosa.[57] Considerable shifting of auxiliaries took place as new presbyterials were formed, the last one at Dauphin in 1913.[58] The West also had an abundance of home missionary society auxiliaries. When the WFMS and WHMS amalgamation took place a new administrative level, the Provincial Society, was created to cope with the enlarged amount of work new embraced by the PWMS.

Up to this time, leadership at the national level was located mainly in and around Toronto. After the merger, vice-presidents were named from across the country, but most of the committee work still fell to the women in Ontario. Attendance at the WFMS Annual Meeting was not limited at first but by 1889 resolutions to restrict representation were presented.[59] Such a decision reflected increasing numbers rather than exclusivity. At the annual meetings, reports were heard from all the various committees, presbyterials and, later, provincial societies.

Strong leaders were now emerging across Canada. In Manitoba such competent women as Amanda Norris MacKay were called on to continue the traditions of the early years and maintain the enthusiasm the WFMS had worked so hard to establish.

A MANITOBA LEADER IN THE PRESBYTERIAN WOMEN'S MISSIONARY SOCIETY

She was among the earliest of our Presbyterial officers and was continuously in the work longer than almost any other. The value of the work she did can never be estimated in this and in any other Presbyterial but also along other lines, the YWCA and the Free Kindergarten. Her hands were never idle where there was Red Cross and WMS supply work to be done. She was always ready to give of herself even when one felt she had done her share.[60]

The temperature registered thirty-five degrees below zero (Fahrenheit) when the train chugged to a stop and deposited a passenger at the siding of the tiny settlement called Neepawa, Manitoba. The year was 1883. Amanda Norris MacKay had arrived at her destination.

Born in Princeport, Nova Scotia, 15 August 1858, Amanda was the eldest daughter of Matthew and Mary Johnson Norris.[61] Matthew was a sea captain and a ship builder – a man of talent and considerable prestige in the community. Shipbuilding records indicate that he built at least six vessels in the yards along the Shubenacadie River in the 1870s.[62] Trade with the Caribbean countries and with the United States was thriving and provided the Norris family with a comfortable living.

Amanda Norris MacKay
(Photo courtesy of Westminster United Church, Winnipeg,
Manitoba.)

Amy, as she was affectionately known, was a resourceful and determined child. Few stories of her early years have survived but one she often told summed up her nature. Amy was anxious to learn to crochet but her mother, fearing the small child might hurt herself on the sharp crochet hook, vetoed the activity. Undaunted, the little girl bent a pin, took a spool of thread and started in to master the technique.[63] Such spirit was to become a trademark of her life.

Only limited records which would indicate the extent of Amanda's formal education are available in Nova Scotia but apparently her academic achievement was sufficient to allow her admission to the Nova Scotia Teachers' College in Truro in 1876.[64] After one year of teacher training she was ready for her first job.

Amanda had taught school for two years before she married Angus Daniel MacKay on 24 November 1879.[65] Angus was a young telegraph operator working for the Intercolonial Railway at Brookfield close to where Amanda was teaching. In 1883 he moved west to Manitoba with the new Canadian Pacific Railway (CPR) and was assigned to Neepawa. Amanda stayed for six months with his parents at Lovat, Pictou County, until Angus had prepared a home for her.

In an interview given to the *Winnipeg Tribune* for the column, "An Album of Winnipeg Women," Amanda said: "I left Truro on a beautiful fall day, wearing a light suit and overcoat; I arrived in Neepawa six days later, 35 below zero. I had changed cars 10 times, travelled all the way in day coaches, lost my trunk and box of wedding clothes and books. The belated things arrived in February; even then I was glad to see my winter coat, I hadn't been very comfortable in my fall outfit and ladies' clothing was not for sale in town."[66] The delay in the delivery of her belongings, compounded by the isolation she experienced because of geography and weather, called upon Amanda's resourcefulness, and she put her time to good use. A literary and debating society was founded when she lived in Neepawa, at which topics such as the desirability of a railway to Hudson Bay were addressed. The Presbyterian minister in Neepawa at that time, Rev. D. MacRae,[67] invited her to use his library. Amongst the books she selected were the works of Thomas Carlyle; reading his works, particularly *Sartor Resartus*, helped shape her philosophy on the importance of work and the "sin of not working."[68] In 1885 the MacKays moved to Portage la Prairie and it was there that Amanda embarked on her missionary work and social reform activities.

According to her own account, Amanda MacKay's introduction to the Presbyterian WFMS came about because of her participation in a local community project. In her article, "Notes on the Early History of the Indian

Industrial School, Portage la Prairie," she described the events that led to the formation of the WFMS in Portage in 1886.[69]

Following the Sioux uprising in the Dakotas during the 1860s, a band of Indians had settled near Portage la Prairie. During the summers they lived in tents near the town but moved to poor shacks in the bush for the winter. They roamed the plains hunting, fishing and existing as well as they could. When the federal government wanted to place them on the newly established reserve at Griswold, many preferred not to move. Half of the group remained around Portage la Prairie. Life was very difficult for them in spite of many kindnesses shown by the townspeople and new settlers. Some seasonal work was available, old clothes were given to them, and meals shared with them. Unfortunately, some residents were unscrupulous in dealing with the Indians and added to their problems by selling them liquor.

Amanda and her friends had observed the plight of these people, but it was the events surrounding the Riel Rebellion in 1885 that finally precipitated action. The Indians in Portage were approached by Indians from the reserves in the West to join the rebels' side in the confrontation, but they rejected the idea. Amanda and other Presbyterian women had for some time felt an uneasiness when praying in church for missionaries and missions in other parts of the world, and said, "Our minds turned to pagans in our streets and we were not very happy, and no doubt the rebellion that year intensified these feelings. We felt we should be doing something to teach them about the Prince of Peace and His interest in them."[70]

One day in early January 1886, Amanda visited the home of Mrs. John MacLeod whose husband, a merchant in town, was one of the elders of the Presbyterian Church. The conversation immediately turned to the plight of the Indians. The women decided to try to help. A meeting of interested women was called and a petition to establish a mission to the Indians in the Portage area was forwarded to Brandon Presbytery. The request was rejected on the grounds that the Home Mission Committee had more than it could handle already, but the presbytery recommended that the women open a mission themselves. So they did!

They opened a day school to which Indians old and young were invited; they rented, cleaned and repaired a small building, they provided daily lunch, made clothing available, and hired a teacher. The group of women decided to call themselves the Indian Missionary Society, and in Amanda's words, "[we] pledged ourselves to provide daily lunch week about and carry it to the school. We canvassed the town for clothing and though many laughed at us and said we were undertaking a hopeless proposition they nevertheless gave us all the clothes they could spare and we needed it in the months ahead, and we also needed both faith and patience."[71] They raised money for supplies by soliciting donations, and by putting on a concert, but "where was the clothing to come from?" The town was apparently so cleared out of surplus garments that "the inhabitants had barely more than their business suits and their Sunday clothes."[72] A suggestion was made that they appeal to the new WFMS in Ontario which had sent out bales of clothing to other Indian missions at Prince Albert and Round Lake. Amanda was asked to make the appeal: "So I as secretary was directed to write, asking if they could help us and telling them what we were trying to do. I had never written to any society or organization and that letter cost me some sleep, but the fate of our school in which we were so deeply interested by this time, was at stake, so the letter was dispatched."[73]

A positive response came quickly: the WFMS offered to take over responsibility for the school, make it a boarding school and pay the entire expense. All that was asked in return was that the Portage women form an auxiliary to the WFMS. They gladly accepted the offer.

The Portage Residential School was but one of a growing number of schools for Indians opening in the West. Some of these institutions were under the jurisdiction of missionary societies; some were sponsored by Christian churches themselves, such as the Presbyterian Church of Canada; others were founded and maintained by the federal government. The establishment of residential educational institutions was a popular solution to the problem of how best to assimilate Indian people into the mainstream of Canadian society. Divergent views on land settlement and the different cultures of Métis and Indian communities were believed to have contributed to the Riel Rebellion of 1885. To prevent a similar uprising it was considered essential to accelerate this assimilation process. The churches saw great merit in sponsoring these schools. At the same time that a "Canadianization" process was going on, the Gospel message could be shared and the physical distress that so many Indian children were experiencing could be alleviated.

The residential school system, and particularly the original motive for opening the schools, has come under severe criticism in recent years. However, to the credit of the Portage la Prairie women, even if the means of helping had been unwise and the motivation suspect, the concern of the women for the suffering of the Indian people in the community was genuine and their effort to lessen it was generous. As a by-product of establishing the school, the head, heart and purse interests of the Portage women were channelled into the swelling women's missionary movement of the day.

By 1893 Angus and Amanda had moved again, this time to the growing city of Winnipeg.[74] Angus had left the railroad to assume the treasurer's duties for the Northern Elevator Company. The MacKays immediately became involved in the fledgling Westminster Presbyterian Church and poured their energies into the work of that congregation for the rest of their lives.

Amanda experienced her first election to office when she became secretary of the newly-formed Brandon Presbyterial – quite a leap of faith for a woman who not long before had lost sleep over writing her first piece of official correspondence. This administrative experience and her passion for the WFMS were soon put to use in Winnipeg. Over the next thirty years she held various offices in the WFMS. From 1904 to 1914 she served as president of the Winnipeg Presbyterial and in 1914 became the first president of the Manitoba provincial board formed when the foreign, home and Montreal branches united. In 1917 she was elected for a three-year term as a vice-president of the Dominion board. She relinquished this office to Helen King Gordon (wife of Charles W. Gordon) in 1920 but became honourary president of the Winnipeg Presbyterial and continued to counsel, to encourage and to train new leaders.[75]

Amanda's interest in mission work was not confined to carrying the Gospel to foreign fields. Shortly after her arrival in Winnipeg, she was approached by a Mrs. H. Chown who asked her to assist with the establishment of a free kindergarten program in the area north of the CPR tracks and west of Main Street. The Free Kindergarten Association, an ecumenical group consisting of Anglican, Baptist, Methodist and Presbyterian women, sponsored the kindergarten project.[76] Amanda, keenly interested in education, accepted the offer and pursued this work for nineteen years.

During her early years in Winnipeg, Amanda also became involved in volunteer work to aid European immigrants settling in the city. The temporary housing provided for these new citizens was in railway sheds which also served as immigration halls. Church women visited the sheds, offering assistance. They understood that settling into a new land with different customs and a new language called for considerable adjustment on the part of the settlers. Amanda was touched by "the stolid frightened women";[77] her own experiences on arriving in the West were still fresh in her memory.

It became apparent to the church women that ongoing contacts with these new Canadians and some form of long-range aid were needed. Once again concerned Presbyterian women asked their church presbytery to take on mission work, this time in the northern section of Winnipeg, and once again the presbytery recommended the women do something about the problem themselves.[78] So the women called a meeting – this one at St. Stephen's Church on 5 April 1907 – at which the Winnipeg Presbyterian Women's Union was formed.[79] To provide the kind of support they felt was needed for the newcomers, this latest alliance of Presbyterian women opened a mission shelter called the House of the Open Door at 732 Alfred Avenue. "[The Mission] began with a Kindergarten and a Deaconess to visit the homes of the people and a committee was appointed to select a site for the school. I remember tramping up and down the streets of North Winnipeg west of Main for days with other women looking for a suitable place."[80]

The mission opened in October 1907.[81] A building costing approximately $3,150 was constructed; $700 was provided by the Church Extension Committee and the rest was contributed by members. The building contained a schoolroom, sitting-room, bedroom, bathroom and kitchen. Harriet Ormond was hired as deaconess, Miss Perry as kindergarten teacher with Miss Carey as assistant. Mothers' meetings, boys' and girls' circles and Sunday school classes were all under the direction of volunteers from the various Presbyterian congregations. Christmas parties, picnics and a fresh air camp were held. The church women believed that providing Christian nurture involved not only evangelizing but it also involved providing shelter, if needed, education in nutrition and child care, and language training. Such work was seen as the expression of Christian love as well as a means of improving Canadian society. It was practised by various Christian denominations. Indeed, "for Methodists and Presbyterians, even as concern for the immigrants and for the nation were inextricably related, so there was no attempt to separate the temporal from the spiritual good for the one reinforced the other."[82]

The mission needed money. Amanda was one of the leading fund-raisers; in fact, when she turned her charm to the task of convincing people to reach into their pocketbooks, she was successful: " 'What are you bothering about these people for?' a citizen asked her as he dutifully handed over his cheque for the venture. 'Well, for one thing' answered Mrs. MacKay, 'if we do not reckon with these people, in a few years they will reckon with us.' "[83] Amanda's frank comment suggests motives other than just Christian charity in providing aid for immigrants. Perhaps fears that the Anglo-Saxon establishment might lose economic or social control, or that another rebellion might erupt, were in her mind. Work was already underway to assimilate native Indians and she believed that similar efforts were needed to convert the immigrants to Canadian ways as quickly as possible.

By 1910, the mission had become too small for the demands made on it. About the same time, the Dufferin Avenue Presbyterian congregation decided to move north because the population was expanding in that direction. In conjunction with the Alfred Avenue Mission, the Dufferin Avenue congregation purchased a new site on Burrows Avenue. The two groups formally united to form Robertson Church and Robertson Memorial Institute.[84] The Women's Union continued to support the Institute financially and administratively. Amanda MacKay was named to the board of the new enterprise.[85]

During her years in Winnipeg, Amanda MacKay suffered bouts of illness that required long convalescences. As early as 1889 she travelled to California for health reasons. While she was away again in 1916, recuperating from a serious illness, Angus died suddenly at home.[86] Following his death, Amanda's sister Mary, a widow herself, came to live with Amanda in the MacKay home at 150 Sherbrook Street. From there the two women took the short walk to Westminster Church for worship services and missionary meetings. By the 1940s Amanda had retired from official responsibilities in mission work. Yet the call to work was still strong. In October 1941, in a letter to her niece in Nova Scotia, she wrote: "My sister is fairly well and I am fine. We are both working every minute for the Red Cross. I knit a pair of seamen's socks every week and she knits 2 pairs ordinary socks. I also sew at the church 2 afternoons every week and all day the last Thursday. The war is awful and no sign of letting up."[87] She gave an address in June 1942 to the Portage la Prairie Presbyterial. In a letter to her niece following this event she reported, "Had the last meeting yesterday. Brought home a big bag of yarn to knit during holidays but can sit on the verandah and do that."[88] On 19 November 1942, after a short illness, Amanda died.[89]

Amanda Norris MacKay exemplified the middle-class woman who found within a women's missionary society an acceptable place for expending her energies while at the same time developing her administrative and leadership skills. Always "Mrs. A.D. MacKay" to her associates, in her correspondence and in her social contacts, Amanda upheld the traditional image of woman as homemaker and helpmate. Because the MacKays had no children, Amanda had fewer family responsibilities than the average woman did. Yet, unlike many of her co-workers, she does not appear to have joined in the struggle for suffrage or in the crusades of the Woman's Christian Temperance Union. Her age – she was of the older generation of women in the missionary societies – and her recurring illness may account for the limiting of her interests to the Church and its auxiliary organizations.

Amanda's Christian convictions and her philosophy of work were inter- woven, however, with hidden aspirations that suggest a different woman – one who lived with unresolved conflict between inner desires and the con- straints of tradition and convention. It would be surprising indeed if she did not harbour convictions, even in private, that were sympathetic to new social reforms. Her whole life witnessed to her concern for the underprivileged and needy, whether abroad or at home. Although she was of middle-class paren- tage, was educated and socially and financially secure herself, she must frequently have crossed class barriers in her contacts with people in the Indian school, the Free Kindergarten and the Robertson Mission. Whether aware of it or not, Amanda underwent radicalization.

During the 1930s, she followed the growth of the Cooperative Commonwealth Federation (CCF) party with considerable interest. She was excited by the social reforms advocated by the new political group. She told her niece about billeting a delegate to a CCF convention and commented, "[The CCF] are going to do great things when they get into power, but I'm afraid I won't live to see it!"[90] Perhaps the most revealing of her memoirs was recorded in a memorial editorial after her death. Amanda is quoted as saying, when observing young women graduating from university, "What I would have given for that chance! I would have been a politician."[91]

IN RETROSPECT

Restricted by a patriarchal society, church women in the nineteenth century sought to enlarge their spheres of influence in church life and at the same time to respond to the call of evangelism by embracing the concept of women's missionary societies. These societies were founded by "highly cultured and well-trained women"[92] intent on keeping the organization in harmony with the larger church while at the same time providing outlets for women to expend their energy and expand their experiences. While the cries of feminists seeking autonomy for women in all facets of life were certainly heard by all church members, the responses among church women to them were tempered by the maternal feminist stance adopted by the majority of church women, a position which emphasized the importance of women's maternal qualities in shaping the next generation and in effecting social reform. It attracted large numbers of women and clearly diverted the direction of the feminist movement. Radical feminists who sought equality outside of domestically defined roles for women turned away from religious affiliations encumbered by patriarchal roots to pursue the quest through secular structures. However, for active middle-class Protestant women to gain any ground in church life, they were driven "to gain power through the exploitation of their feminine identity as their society defined it."[93] They had little choice but to operate out of the milieu of their day. Women chose the "higher feminine" doctrine to "open up more fields of competence for themselves in religion and society while still maintaining an idealistic and redemptive role model."[94]

Criticism may be directed at the missionary societies, particularly at the motives of the organizers, their band-aid approach to problems, and their restricted vision of women's role, but it is clear that the women's missionary societies succeeded in meeting short-term goals for women by providing sufficient autonomy and opportunities for success. The fact that church women channelled their energies into organizations exclusively for women may have diverted them from seeking equality in wider religious and secular fields, but the consequence of establishing their own societies and learning new skills was real, long-term liberation. The PWMS and its parent organizations provided a substantial legacy for women in the twentieth century.

In pursuing their mission goals, PWMS women formed strong bonds with each other, both within their local communities and across the nation, as well as with foreign women they would never meet. Spreading the Gospel of Jesus Christ to heathen lands would not only convert women to Christianity, but would also free them from what were perceived, by Christians, to be the oppressive customs of non-Christian cultures. Also, as women met regularly in their auxiliaries, studied the literature provided and discussed the nature of mission work, their attention was directed away from their own homes and families – their vision was broadened. Church women began to examine the needs of their own society, and at the same time examined the traditions and attitudes that bound them together just as strongly as non-Christian customs bound the heathen women the missionary societies were aiming to liberate. As well as providing an avenue for consciousness raising, participating in a women's missionary society provided women with a sense of usefulness and worth which was independent of home responsibilities. This alone was an accomplishment for many women.

Rewards of another kind appeared. Church women developed skill in conducting meetings, keeping minutes, writing and presenting reports, handling money, preparing programs, speaking and praying in public. The skills were developed at the grassroots level and sharpened as women accepted leadership positions at presbyterial, provincial and dominion board levels. Moreover, these skills were transferable and many women, once equipped and confident from experience in missionary societies, gravitated to organizations focusing on specific social concerns: the Woman's Christian Temperance Union, the suffrage movement, the Women's Institute. Presbyterian women are not seen to have been as active as Methodist women were in the social reform movements – notably temperance and prohibition – that reflected the Methodist social gospel theology. They were, nevertheless, moving out into the secular world.

The shifting of skills and energy from church to secular spheres has been recognized and acknowledged since the early years of the societies. Minnie Campbell, the first secretary of the Woman's Foreign Missionary Auxiliary in Winnipeg, in her Annual Report of 1896, reflected, "Another benefit derived is the training which a large number of our timid earnest women are thus receiving for enlarged spheres of usefulness."[95] William O'Neill in *The Woman Movement* observed, "Having taken up one cause women found themselves with an increased capacity for others."[96] Wendy Mitchinson, a professor of Canadian history, concluded that not only did the missionary societies provide women with the opportunity to develop leadership and administrative skills, but, "these women became examples for other women to follow and to be proud of. The missionary societies altered the public's view of churchwomen from one of caretakers to participant."[97]

American historian Barbara Welter viewed the new opportunities for woman's participation in church affairs "less a victory than a strategic retreat by the opposition."[98] Whether in victory or in retreat, whether by conscious effort or as an unexpected by-product, women's missionary societies provided a forum for meeting the needs of many nineteenth-century women. Welter describes the societies as a "rare combination of church and socially-sanctioned activity and freedom."[99] There was a legitimacy about belonging to a church woman's organization. Even the most patriarchal father or husband could not object to the women in the household participating in such Christian effort. While leadership in the societies was provided mainly by the better-educated of the middle- and upper-class women who had larger financial resources and time available, the call to join and to serve was responded to by church women from all classes. Strong sisterhoods were forged through these organizations to supply friendship, social exchange, and support in times of adversity. Added to this were the opportunities the societies furnished for women to express their intelligence, to develop their talents, and to channel their abundant energy. It is evident that the women's missionary societies, in answering the call to mission, also made a contribution of great worth to the struggle for independence by nineteenth-century women.

Wendy Mitchinson suggested, however, that women in mission work did not perceive any relationship between themselves and the woman's movement, although she believed that their very struggles to carve out a place for themselves in the church, "made them a part of the larger effort to expand women's role in Canadian society."[100] A reading of the Presbyterian Society's annual reports substantiates Mitchinson's point. If any perception of a relationship between the Presbyterian Society and the feminist movement existed, it is not articulated in the annual reports. Glowing comments are made about other benefits women received. For example, in her 1900–1901 presidential address, Marion Shortreed said: "The growth of women's public influence during the past century has been unprecedented, not in missions alone; but in all church and philanthropic work she has manifested an ever increasing interest and activity."[101] Her remarks about the Society also included phrases such as, it "deepened spiritual life," "aroused latent talent," and "raised intellectual culture." Church women may not have acknowledged any direct connection between their mission involvement and the women's movement, but they did identify results of their efforts that benefited women – results in harmony with feminist goals.

Despite their passionate desire to share in mission work and their success in raising head, heart and purse interest, nineteenth-century women's missionary societies were not politically radical organizations. Their members were realistic and pragmatic in carrying out what they saw as benevolent and humanitarian work. Indoctrinated with an imperialist view, they believed they were providing a better world by denying other cultures. They worked within the established system and for acceptable goals. However, the question remains: Were these church women satisfied with their role or did they have covert ambitions and unspoken dreams of richer, more meaningful lives. Did they harbour feminist ideals?

Amanda MacKay apparently did harbour unspoken dreams. It is from a few of her letters and addresses to women's gatherings that have been saved, and from histories compiled by Amanda, that a reader catches a glimpse of her private feelings and a sense of her fears and hidden aspirations. Insights such as those provided by Amanda MacKay are invaluable to church women of the twentieth century, for it is by being aware of the aspirations of their foremothers and the traditions which constrained them that contemporary church women can appreciate the legacy bequeathed them. Participation in church life is important to many contemporary Canadian women because it shapes new sisterhoods, directs attention to current social needs and provides outlets for those women still encumbered by patriarchy. The legacy bequeathed by the women's missionary movement is simple but powerful; it is one of example, of evidence, of proof that when women work together, dreams can be realized. Whatever were the direct accomplishments of the early women's missionary societies, they unquestionably exerted a strong positive influence on the lives of Canadian women in the nineteenth century which, in turn, changed the role of women in the twentieth century.

John Mark King:
First principal of Manitoba College

Gordon Harland

When the Synod of Manitoba and North West Territories of the Presbyterian Church met in November 1899, several months after the death of John Mark King, first principal of Manitoba College, the members adopted a report which expressed the esteem in which they held him and the influence he had exercised among them. In this statement, nearly three pages in length, King's gifts as scholar, teacher, educational leader, administrator, churchman, pastor and personal friend were held up and eloquently described. "He was," says the report, "a leader of thought and a master of discussion in the General Assembly, and in this Synod he was the member above all others whose opinions were regarded with respect."[1] Clearly, King was a man who was greatly beloved and who had made his mark on the community.

KING'S EARLY YEARS

John Mark King was born in the village of Yetholm in the county of Roxburgh on the Scottish Borders in May 1829.[2] He received his master of arts degree from the University of Edinburgh where he studied with such influential scholars as Sir William Hamilton and John Wilson, the Christopher North of *Blackwood's* magazine. He also studied theology in the Divinity Hall of the United Presbyterian Church while hearing on Sundays such preachers as Dr. Guthrie of Free St. John's Church, Dr. Candlish of Free St. George's and Dr. John Bruce of Free St. Andrew's, men who made the Edinburgh pulpit of the time, as King put it, "exceptionally strong and brilliant."[3] His studies also took him to Germany, to the University of Halle, where he came under the influence of such spiritually intense teachers as Friedrich August Tholuck and Julius Müller. He was already deeply rooted in the evangelical

John Mark King (Photo courtesy of Ruth Gordon.)

tradition, which in Scotland reached back to the Erskine brothers and found its culminating expression in Thomas Chalmers, and at Halle he found that a similar orientation was receiving an attractive and moving articulation in Tholuck and Müller. It was this theological heritage, with its centre of gravity in the doctrines of sin, grace and regeneration, that King later represented in his preaching, teaching and writing.

One of King's most attractive personal qualities – his genius for friendship – came to the fore in his student years. He formed friendships that not only survived the separation from Scotland but which also, through thoughtful, regular correspondence and occasional visits, deepened across the years and lasted a whole lifetime.[4] In 1856 the United Presbyterian Church sent him to Canada as a missionary. He spent the first year helping to establish new congregations in some of the frontier settlements of Ontario. He was ordained on 27 October 1857 and had two pastoral charges. The first, starting in 1857, was the rural congregation of Columbus and Brooklyn in the presbytery of Whitby, the second, starting in 1863, was Gould Street Church in Toronto, which later became St. James Square Church. When King assumed responsibility for this church, it was a small, struggling, debt-ridden congregation, but his ministry was unusually effective and, during the twenty years he spent there, he built it into one of the strongest Presbyterian churches in the nation. It was a congregation that had in its membership many public figures such as Sir Oliver Mowat, Principal William Caven of Knox College and George Brown of the *Globe*. This congregation became widely known for its vigorous leadership in church extension and home missions, concerns which were always central in King's philosophy. The congregation was also known as the College Church, because of the large number of students from various faculties within the College who attended King's Bible classes. Indeed, it is striking to note the large number of ministers and laymen in western Canada who were at one time associated with King's congregation at St. James Square.[5] The place he came to occupy in the life of the Church was indicated in 1882 when Knox College selected him to be the first person to receive the degree of doctor of divinity; the following year he was elected moderator of the General Assembly.

The General Assembly of 1883 received a memorial from the Presbytery of Manitoba seeking the appointment of a principal and professor of theology for its new and struggling Manitoba College. The Assembly appointed King and this posed a real dilemma for him. His congregation and many others were strong in the opinion that he should stay where his influence was already large and established. Indeed, there were many who thought that there was no need for a college in Manitoba and that the Church had made a mistake in undertaking such work. Family reasons made the decision especially difficult. On 4 December 1873 he had married Janet M. Skinner, the principal of Morvyn House Ladies' College in Toronto. They had one son, John Ralph, and a daughter, Helen, who married the well-known minister and novelist Charles W. Gordon (Ralph Connor). King's marriage to Janet Skinner was marked by deep mutual devotion and support, but by 1883 they lived with anxiety because in June 1882, Mrs. King had undergone an operation for breast cancer.[6] However, after making the trip west to assess the situation for himself, he made the decision to come to Manitoba, and it is clear that the decisive factors were conviction and duty. He believed in the central importance of the College in this vast new land and had a clear sense that it was his duty to come since the future of the College had become uncertain because of financial problms.

KING AS PRINCIPAL OF MANITOBA COLLEGE

Manitoba College had been built during Winnipeg's speculative boom in real estate, but by 1883, when King arrived, after the bubble had burst, it had incurred a debt of $40,000. A bleak situation faced the new principal. "Money," he wrote to his wife on 24 November, "is a very scarce article with Winnipeg people at present," and three days later he wrote, "Such is the financial condition of this city and province, & such the claims and needs of the congregations," that little help could be expected in the task of reducing the debt of the College.[7] The situation was further complicated by the confused state of the College accounts. He describes them to his wife as "a deep sea"[8] and, continuing the metaphor in a later letter, he reported, "I am getting near the bottom of the old accounts but it has been a great deep."[9] He wrote to his wife every other day and from these letters it is clear that he was taking firm control of everything, overseeing every detail. "I have paid today," he wrote on 7 December, "all or nearly all the bills for November, going round to the stores myself. I got a small discount at some and arranged to have reduced prices at others. Instead of American coal oil at 50 cents per gallon, I am to get a barrel of Canadian not much, if at all inferior, at 33 cents."[10] He ordered chairs and tables for the college,[11] was anxious about how many of tons of coal and cords of wood were burned and, as the weather got colder, he looked "with very deep interest every morning to that wood pile."[12] This attention to the smallest detail was necessitated by the difficult financial situation he encountered upon assuming the task; but throughout his principalship, there was nothing connected with the College that did not receive his personal attention.

With equal energy he turned to the task of raising money. He wrote to ministers in all parts of the country to lay before them the needs of the College. "I have during the last two days," he told Mrs. King, "written twenty-nine such letters and I have still a few more to write."[13] During the summer of 1884 he went to Britain and Ireland to canvass for the College and in the fall he continued his canvass in Ontario and Montreal.[14] It was not a task he enjoyed, but he was so diligent and commanded such great respect that he was eminently successful at it. In a few years the debt was removed, the College was remodelled and doubled in size and before his death an endowment fund had been established. The confidence he so quickly won in the business community was kept throughout his life. Discussing King's abilities as a financial administrator, Colin H. Campbell, Q.C., wrote, "As a rule we do not look for skilled financiers in profound theologians and gifted preachers [but] . . . any country would have been honored to have him as finance minister, or any large financial institution as manager."[15]

The early years of King's principalship were marked not only by immense labour and great achievement but also by deep personal sorrow. Mrs. King died in Winnipeg on 13 September 1886 and in February 1888, when King was on a trip to Montreal on Church business, his son, who was nine, suffered an attack of scarlet fever and died before King could return. His close friend and collaborator, James Robertson, wrote, "Since you went west it has been with you sorrow upon sorrow."[16] Out of the discipline of sorrowing love came rich blessings for those around him. In the words of Thomas Hart, King's close friend and colleague at Manitoba College, "His sympathies, always a strong feature of his character, grew stronger, broader, deepened. . . . Always liberal, he became generous."[17] His preaching also gained in power and sensitivity. To honour his son he gave a scholarship in theology and to perpetuate the memory of Mrs. King he gave to the College a rose window which was designed by Henry Holiday on the subject of theology. The window was placed in Convocation Hall of Manitoba College and is now in Bryce Hall of the University of Winnipeg.[18]

Manitoba College flourished under King's energetic leadership. Not only did he succeed in placing the College on a sound financial basis, he also set high academic standards and had that great gift of leadership which called forth the best in faculty and students alike. Part of his influence came from his own teaching. He was widely acclaimed as an effective and demanding teacher and he carried an incredibly heavy teaching load ranging in the theological department from biblical studies and systematic theology to homiletics, and philosophy and German in arts.

Despite the many burdens he was carrying, King was determined to keep up his scholarly work through constant reading, some writing and by maintaining a close relationship with Scottish scholars. In the summer of 1891, he visited the University of Berlin, "to ascertain," as he puts it, "the present tendency of philosophical and religious thought in Germany, at one of the great centres of intellectual life." In a brief article in *The Manitoba College Journal* he gave vivid descriptions of the personalities and lecture styles as well as a view of the positions of some of the most eminent theological figures of the day such as Otto Pfleiderer, Julius Kaftan and especialy Adolf von Harnack whom he described as "the most brilliant and interesting lecturer to whom I have ever listened." The thinking of such men was not to be accepted uncritically, if at all, and King was protective enough to think it unwise for students to "betake themselves to continental seats of learning" before "their views of truth are somewhat matured"; nevertheless he felt that it was imperative that he know the thought of such scholars and that his students be alive to the issues at stake in the current theological debates.[19]

King was also concerned that the College should be vitally related to its own community. One of the ways he sought to do this was to have the College sponsor a rich offering of public lectures given by distinguished visitors and also by members of the College faculty. In a moving tribute to King, after his death, Elizabeth Parker dwelt on this aspect of his contribution, emphasizing how eager King was to see Convocation Hall filled up with people from all walks of life as he brought speakers such as George Adam Smith, James Orr and T.B. Kilpatrick from Scotland. Most notable among the series were the public lectures which King himself gave in three different years directed to the women of Winnipeg. One series dealt with biblical theology and another with moral philosophy, but the series which drew the largest and most enthusiastic crowd was on Tennyson's "In Memoriam." These lectures were published in 1898 in the book entitled *A Critical Study of "In Memoriam."*[20]

As the settlements of western Canada opened up, the needs of home missions in the west became particularly acute. To enable students to supply churches during the winter, a summer theological session was begun in Manitoba in 1893. This meant that henceforth King taught eleven months of the year. Clearly, it would have been impossible for him to accomplish all he did had he not brought to his high dedication great resources of energy and above all a careful and purposeful use of time.

WHAT GAVE KING'S LIFE UNITY AND DIRECTION?

The characteristics which were most obvious and frequently noted by King's associates were his sense of order, thoroughness, duty and boundless energy.

The sense of order pervades and shapes his view of the world, his sense of right relationships and the responsible life. God is a god who "orders all things" and that was, for him, a source of comfort and assurance. The good life was shaped according to the responsibilities attending place and vocation. James Robertson, the energetic superintendent of Presbyterian Missions in Western Canada, remarked: "He loved method, system, accuracy; and he strove that the business of the Church might be conducted decently and in order."[21] Thoroughness marked everything he did. He could not abide the superficial dabbler. In a series of lectures on pastoral theology given January 1890, King impressed upon his students the importance of having set times for entering the study and for remaining in it. There must be, he emphasized, a reason "such as you could plead before God for not entering your study at that hour every day of the week except Monday." "Begin your ministry in this way," he continued, and "it will become so natural, so almost necessary, that you will find it difficult to be courteous to the friendly visitor who threatens to interrupt the well established order of your intellectual world."[22] King was no academic recluse but this admonition illustrates how he viewed the ordered life – including the intellectual life – as a condition for discharging the work of the minister.

This careful ordering of life did not stifle affection, but instead channeled, controlled, and perhaps limited it. King was a man of profound affections, he had a capacity to live intensely and a deep need to receive love. The deep hurts and joys of life were alike caught up in his compelling sense of purpose, dedication and duty. He was, in the best sense of the word, a pietist for whom the religious relationship was the basic orientation of his life. It was this rich religious life in which a warm, intense piety was united with clearly defined and firmly held theological convictions which gave his life its unity and direction.

King died in Winnipeg on 5 March 1899 after a six-week illness, and was buried in Kildonan cemetery. There was not only the expected general out-pouring of grief but also a quite extraordinary expression of the sense of loss to the Church and the wider community. Dr. R.H. Warden, the general agent of the Presbyterian Church in Canada, said, "No man perhaps was more loved throughout the whole church than he was." Memorial services were held in Toronto, Vancouver and in various churches in Winnipeg. King had made his mark on the community. Principal James Walter Sparling of Wesley College spoke for many when he said, "No death has occurred in Manitoba since I came to it ten years ago that has, in my judgment, made so great a vacancy."[23]

KING AS THEOLOGIAN

To appreciate the distinctive role played by Principal King and the great respect with which he was held, we must consider the theological climate of the time and the way he entered into the theological debates during the closing decades of the century. In Protestant circles the age was marked by the rather sudden collapse of orthodoxy in the control of major seminaries, the debates over the significance of the new sciences, biblical criticism, the rise of liberal theology, the social gospel and the embracing of progressivist views of human nature and history. It was an age of great complexity, but these various movements did cast doubt on the Christian drama of redemption and even made it appear irrelevant. The central queston was still the nature of human nature. If, after all, humans were essentially good, harmless and rational creatures, if sin was merely the downward pull of our biological and cultural heritage, if historical development was itself a redemptive process, then the whole Christian understanding of human nature, the work of Christ, redemption and the ground of hope would have to be totally revised and perhaps dismissed.

Increasingly, a destructive polarization took place between those whose religious ideas and energies were centred in "the building of the kingdom of God" and those for whom the central task was the defence and preservation of the faith in its traditional formulations. This debilitating schism has found numerous expressions through the years and in one form or another it has persisted to the present day. Presbyterian churches experienced more than their quota of conflicts and heresy trials in these years. The new Presbyterian Church in Canada, which had come into being in 1875, faced such a crisis immediately after its formation in the famous heresy trial of the Rev. D.J. Macdonnell. It is to be noted that those who defended Macdonnell's position to the General Assembly were Principal Caven and John M. King. In Scotland the celebrated case of W. Robertson Smith brought the issue of biblical criticism into the consciousness of the wider public. In the United States the struggle was particularly fierce as a conservative position received vigorous and able leadership from the Princeton faculty led by Charles Hodge which clashed with a developing liberal approach led by the equally able Charles A. Briggs of Union Seminary in New York as well as other distinguished scholars such as Henry Preserved Smith, George Foot Moore and A.C. McGiffert. It was in the context of such conflicts that King articulated his theology.

There are no guides to the content of King's theological thought. Those few scholars who have written sketches of his life have uniformly acclaimed him as a theologian whose thought was distinguished by its clarity and depth.

The sketches are filled with adjectives of praise but there have been no attempts to set forth the character of King's thought. King published two books: the public lectures on Tennyson's "In Memoriam" and *The Theology of Christ's Teaching,*[24] a large set of class lectures published posthumously with an introduction by the Scottish theologian James Orr. Both works give valuable insight into King's thought. The best and quickest way to enter his thought is, however, to consider three significant public lectures he gave at the opening of the theological school sessions – one in 1893, one in 1895 and another in 1897. In these lectures he addressed some of the issues central to the controversies of the age and to his own concerns.

In 1893, King opened the summer session with a lecture entitled "The Spirit in Which Theological Enquiry should be Prosecuted." Clearly, the stress of the times dictated his choice of subject. Indeed, right at that time, although King made no reference to the fact, the General Assembly of the Presbyterian Church U.S.A. was meeting to hear and adjudicate the appeal in the case of Charles Briggs, who was being tried for his too liberal approach to the Bible. King's lecture reveals much about himself. He began by stating that the aim of theological enquiry is "to learn what the actual nature of the revelation is" which is given in Scripture and thus "to ascertain and define religious truth." Since this is its aim, the first requirement "for its prosecution is love of truth." And he emphasizes that he means love of "truth," not of "the truth." The distincion is worth noting. King's whole being was wrapped up in and committed to what he regarded as the truth of the Christian faith, yet at the outset of his lecture he urged that there must be a creative tension between the open, critical mind and the committed self. This is a high and rare attainment, he said, but he impressed upon the assembled students of theology that "it is a large and an essential element in the spirit which should animate you in the studies to be prosecuted in this place."[25]

The second element in the spirit proper to the theological enquiry that King points to in this lecture is a "large degree of caution" in "arriving at and announcing conclusions." Christian theology, for King, is not a harmless subject, remote from the interests and the issues of daily life. On the contrary, he thought, its "questions touch human experience at the most vital points," and the manner in which they are understood will have large consequence for the quality of the life, faith and hope of countless people. Moreover, what he called "the eager, restless spirit of the age" evidenced in the vigorous pursuit of biblical criticism, and the disposition to obscure the Church's affirmation concerning God in Christ, carries the demand for an appropriate caution. What King found offensive was not so much the new views, but the presumptuous spirit in which radical new positions were being announced with what he calls "an almost ostentatious defiance of the Church's feelings."[26]

He did not, however, offer any protection to the conservatives who had closed their minds. The posture of defensiveness, King well knew, is productive of error in all areas of life, but especially in religion. Or as he put it: "The unreasoning resistance to all change . . . is not one which can be commended. It is not courageous. It has at its root lack of confidence in truth. . . . And it is not wise, any more than it is courageous." Nothing could be more calamitous for the Church, King thought, than to create a "divorce between itself and the intelligence of the age." Moreover, he taught, theological enquiry is not something to be tolerated as a necessary evil; it is to be encouraged. And it is to be encouraged not only in the interests of the theological enterprise but "in the interest of spiritual life, with which it might so often seem to be at war." He stated this bluntly: "The maintenance of healthful religious life in a community for a lengthened period is incompatible with intellectual slumber. . . . The connection between thought and life," between "the play of intelligence and that of moral feeling," he continues, is so close "that we cannot long have the latter without the former." Apologists or preachers who will bless the age will have a spirit at once "philosophic and devout"; they will have as their aim a capacity for "seeing deeper into truth, rather than seeing more completely round it, setting it in its due relation to the permanent and universal needs of man." The idea that truth exists in "relation to the permanent and universal needs of man" was central to King. The idea recurs frequently in his lectures, and it was always delivered passionately. The deepest conviction he had, and the one which integrated his thought, is that it is precisely the great doctrines concerning sin, the Incarnation, the Atonement, and the work of the Holy Spirit which meet our deep and universal need for meaning, forgiveness and for vision. Because of this, scholars and preachers who impugn or ignore these central doctrines of Christian faith, instead of being up to date are actually ceasing to have a message relevant to humankind's greatest questions and needs. In this lecture given in the summer of 1893, with the British Hegelian and Gifford lecturer Edward Caird in mind he asks, "What could a Christianity thus emasculated do for its recipient? How unequal it must prove to the demands of human need."[27]

The same concerns prompted King to choose the doctrine of the Atonement as his subject for the opening lecture in 1895. This central doctrine is of vast significance for the whole understanding of Christianity. The Atonement is "as gracious as it is vast" and it is being either badly misunderstood or "simply put to the side," so he was determined "to show where we stand in this Institution" on the matter.[28] King acknowledged that there are numerous influences accounting for the shift in concern taking place. He points specifically to three: (1) a proper reaction "against a crude, coarse, almost a commercial view of the atonement"; (2) the widespread interest in the histori-cal Christ with its predominantly ethical views of his life and person; and (3) the fact that many feel the lack of a clear connection between belief in the doctrine and the development of personal goodness that must be the living result of faith.[29] These protests represent a positive gain. Nevertheless, he stressed that an understanding of Christianity that does not have this doctrine at is centre goes against the "whole drift and tenor" of scriptural teaching, fails "to supply any adequate reason for the Incarnation," and proceeds on "a radically defective view" of the human condition.[30] The ethical, humanitarian emphasis coming to the fore in theological circles possesses real strength, but it has a fatal weakness: it is, as he puts it, not "adequate to the full strain of human need."[31] This old doctrine of the Atonement, of Christ's sacrificial and sin-bearing love is the truth that meets the human situation. "To preach," he says, "with this truth left out, in however cultured and gracious a style is – to use the apt illustration of Mr. Denney's fisherman – to fish with a hook without a barb. Men will take your bait; the age is in love with moralizing discourse; but you will not take the men."[32] This was an eloquent and strongly argued lecture and would appear to have received considerable attention. Indeed, Mr. William E. Dodge, a trustee of Union Theological Seminary in New York, ordered a hundred copies for distribution among the students of that seminary.[33]

King returned to a similar issue in 1897 in a lecture entitled "The Purely Ethical Gospel Examined." This lecture is, perhaps, the finest in this series. Ethical concerns were, of course, central to King and he acknowledged that there had been recent positive gains in securing a fuller recognition for the ethical dimensions of the gospel than there had been in former periods of the Church's history. Nevertheless, a purely ethical Christianity which seemed to be gaining popularity "is seriously and painfully defective, if it does not indeed change the centre altogether, and thus throw even the truths which it retains out of their proper relations."[34] Its deficiencies are closely interrelated, and they are visible in all crucial areas. Its view of humanity is sentimental, lacking in realism and "not set" as he puts it, "to the key-note supplied by the [Pauline] Epistles."[35] In the writings of St. Paul, "sin is . . . not a mere weakness, a simple defect" but an "enslaving power which has seated itself at the very centre of man's being."[36] The moralism of this ethical approach is such that it fails to understand sin properly in relational terms with the result that what is lost to view, he says, is "the alienation *from* God which is at its heart."[37] Perhaps it should be said that King, in stressing the reality and dynamics of sin, was not at all concerned with emphasizing the littleness of humankind. Instead, he urged his readers to see themselves in the full dimensions of their beings, in their capacities for both good and evil, in what Pascal called the grandeur and the misery of man. It is in the relationship to God that we see the full measure of human loss indicated by the word *sin* and also the true greatness of human beings pointed to in the word *regeneration*. The inevitable consequence of this misreading of the human condition is the obscuring both of the necessity for, and the greatness of, Christ's work in redemption and regeneration. And further, such a reduced gospel cannot, King thought, be expected to nurture a piety of great depth or earnestness. "Where it is in the ascendant, religious life will be apt to droop, or to degenerate into something little better than a moral cult."[38] "For myself," he went on, "if I could believe that it was to become the prevailing type of teaching with the Churches of the Reformation, I could anticipate nothing else than their signal and continous decline."[39]

In these three lectures King addressed a few of the hotly debated issues of his day and in the process clearly revealed where he stood. He was assuredly conservative, he stood "in the old paths," but he was not narrow. He understood modern thought, he was open to its strengths, and he saw with exceptional clarity its weaknesses. There are no doubt many reasons why the Canadian churches did not suffer anything like the deep cleavage over the fundamentalist–modernist controversy that the American churches did, but surely one reason was the presence in our theological colleges of open-minded conservatives like John Mark King. Indeed, this was the sort of evaluation made of King by the great biblical scholar, George Adam Smith. King had managed to secure Smith to lecture at the summer school in Manitoba College and, when he left Winnipeg, Smith wrote a moving letter to King which showed his esteem:

. . . I thank you very affectionately for your generous trust of me and my efforts. I am fully aware that a great deal in the somewhat bungling attempts of us younger men to obtain fresh conceptions of God's truth must seem crude & raw to the larger experience of our elders. But if there is anything that will keep us sober & cautious it is the sympathy & confidence of older men like yourself, whose knowledge of God's word & experience of the religious life is so much deeper than our own can be. . . .[40]

Theology was for King a very practical as well as an intellectually demanding discipline. He often urged his students to preach the great doctrines of the faith, not as pieces of an abstract system of thought, but in the most intimate relation to the universal need of people for meaning, consolation and regeneration. Only the great doctrines, he emphasized, were adequate "to the full strain of human need."[41] Sustained theological reflection was necessary if the tasks of the preacher and the pastor were to be fulfilled.

After King's death, Father Drummond of St. Boniface College spoke in a press interview of his association with King, of the philosophical discussions they had had, and how he, a Roman Catholic, felt more at home with King's thought than he did with that of most other non-Catholic thinkers. He remarked also on King's intellectual power and his capacity to inspire a zeal in his students for philosophical study, and continued on to say that "the University has lost in Dr. King a representative of old world culture, whose opinions had great weight with the more thoughtful members of our body."[42] This remark emphasizes a basic quality about King: his genius was to hold together qualities and concerns which frequently get separated. In him a deep piety was united with a rigorous intellectual life; pastoral sensitivity was combined with shrewd business acumen and administrative skill. He was, as Father Drummond put it, "a representative of old world culture" but he was no alien misfit in this new and bustling land. He embraced this new frontier, had a vision for it and gave himself unstintingly to its people. This capacity to hold together qualities and concerns frequently divorced marked the whole of his life. He had told his students that the apologist or preacher who would bless the age "must have a spirit at once philosophic and devout." This was John Mark King's own achievement and through it he blessed both the Church and wider community.

"Keeping Canada God's Country": Presbyterian school-homes for Ruthenian children

Michael Owen

In the preface to *Enduring Witness*, John S. Moir makes a rather remarkable statement. Religion, he writes, "has been such a vital life-force in creating present-day Canada that no apologies are needed for our attempts to examine and explain its influences on ourselves."[1] If indeed no justification is required for the investigation of the religious influences on Canadian life, then historians must reproach themselves as professionals for largely neglecting the effect of the church as a social, intellectual and cultural agent in Canadian history.

The difficulties hindering the integration of church history with newer fields of study such as the history of women, children, labour and ethnic groups are not unfamiliar to the social historian. Many records of churches, church societies, and individual actors have been and remain scattered, inaccessible or lost to the researcher. The historian confronts a paucity of published biographies, memoirs and, especially, scholarly studies of church-related social movements in Canada. While doctoral candidates may be slowly reducing the "endless themes begging for investigation," there are a considerable number of topics still unexplored. In this essay, I examine one of these themes: early twentieth century Prostestant efforts to integrate non–Anglo-Saxon immigrants into Canadian society and, in particular, the "school-homes" for Ruthenian (Ukrainian) children sponsored by the Presbyterian Women's Home Missionary Society (WHMS) to evangelize and Canadianize the non–Anglo-Saxon "new Canadians" of the Northwest. These school-homes were part of a wide range of institutions founded by the Protestant churches in the first two decades of the twentieth century in order to integrate European immigrants into Canadian society.

The Presbyterian Women's Home Missionary Society (Western Division) grew from the Atlin Nurse Committee, which was formed in response to the

Rev. John Pringle's appeal for nurses to relieve hardships and sufferings in the Klondyke. The WHMS was formed in 1903 and aimed to aid the Home Mission Committee "by undertaking nursing and hospital work" in the newer districts of the nation and by raising funds. By 1914 the WHMS had assumed the financial obligation for seven hospitals, eleven mission fields, seven school-homes, eight deaconesses, as well as for workers in the "stranger" and Jewish departments, the loggers' missions in Northern Ontario, and, in part, for the Ukrainian students at Manitoba College, the Ukrainian Church and the Robertson Memorial Institute in Winnipeg. By 1924, one year before the mission stations joined with the newly formed United Church of Canada, the WHMS school-home system had expanded to ten schools, accommodating approximately 190 boarders. In addition, the WHMS inaugurated a vigorous program of missionary education through its journal, *The Home Mission Pioneer* (after 1914 *The Missionary Messenger*) which had an initial distribution of ten thousand. By 1914 it had grown to a circulation of twenty-three thousand.[2]

When early-twentieth-century Canadian Presbyterians analyzed foreign immigration, they perceived Canada as a leading Christian and British nation possessed of a special mission to evangelize the world. However, the missionaries, church members and concerned Canadians believed that the church must first transform Canada's own territory into "His Dominion." This Presbyterian vision of Canada as "God's country" apparently assumed a homogeneous national value system committed to evangelical truth and British-Canadian customs and world views.[3]

However, in the early twentieth century, Canada was facing the immigration of "groups who did not share" this British and evangelical Protestant heritage and national sense of mission.[4] Between 1900 and 1915 Canada received, in proportion to its population, more immigrants than did the United States at any time in its history. The charts prepared for the 1913 Pre-Assembly Congress and the Report of the Board of Home Missions and Social Service to the 1914 General Assembly showed the huge numbers of foreigners entering Canada and shocked Presbyterian stalwarts. In the thirteen years prior to 1912–1913, 2,537,582 people immigrated to Canada. Of these newcomers, 689,539 (or more than twenty-five percent) were immigrants from countries which had no cultural links to Great Britain. The task before the nation and the church of absorbing hundreds of thousands of foreign settlers and making them into complete Canadians was, in the opinion of Presbyterian leaders, "herculean."

The presence of massive numbers of non–Anglo-Saxon and non-Protestant settlers raised major questions for Presbyterians who were also

Canadian nationalists. To these guardians of Canadian values, even the idea that being Protestant and Anglocentric was different from being a real Canadian was a real challenge. How then could these foreigners ever become true Canadians? Would their presence hinder the moral and social progress of the nation? Would they become "stepping stones" toward the establishment of the Kingdom or stand in its way? The battle to make these immigrants "Christian Canadians," or as close as it was possible, was the challenge assumed by the Canadian Presbyterian Church and its auxiliary, the WHMS.

The Presbyterian belief in a special destiny for the Anglo-Protestant culture in Canada left the Church no option but to set up evangelical and social service missions for non-British and non-Protestant immigrants. It was not so much love for the foreigner as it was fear of their destructive powers if left to fend for themselves which caused the Church to help the immigrants. Presbyterians saw it in terms of self-defence; they wanted to preserve in western Canada a culture which fused British-Canadian nationalism (Imperialism) with Protestant and North American Utopianism. Left to themselves, the foreigners might place the Presbyterian vision of Canada as "the city on the hill," or as the perfect Christian nation, beyond reach.

Historians John Webster Grant, N. Keith Clifford and Marilyn Barber argue that Protestant Canadians viewed the immigrants' "presence as a threat to the realization of their vision and reacted by demanding that the newcomers conform to their way of life or their entry be restricted." Scholars stress those sides of the churches' Canadianizing programs which responded to the immigrants' social and political threat rather than those which expressed Christian brotherhood and socialization.[5] Their interpretations emphasize Canadian Protestants' expectations of conformity to the heritage of political democracy, British culture and evangelical Protestantism. This is the accepted historical exegesis of the Canadian response to the non–Anglo-Saxon immigrant and captures the essence of the Presbyterian home mission enterprise.

In the early 1890s Presbyterian home missionaries had sounded a warning that the foreign influx might swamp the British population. Since the larger numbers of central and southern European immigrants who arrived after 1900 were considered to be ignorant and possessed of "little religion worth the name," home missionaries urged that every effort "be made to discourage too large an influx of [this] alien population."[6] Whereas "a nation is builded of its people," Home Mission Superintendent Rev. James Robertson argued that the Northwest should be secured by Canadian and British settlers. Large colonies of non-British settlers in this centre of nation-building, "where they will remain undigested, unassimilated, a foreign, unsympathetic, unhealthy element in our body politic," were, in Robertson's view, a threat to the Canadian nation.[7]

Christian nationalistic sentiments, often expressed in negative tones, permeated Presbyterian journals and the reports of Presbyterian boards. For example, one correspondent for *The Presbyterian* warned that the Northwest might not remain a Canadian and Protestant territory. Surveying the rapid settlement of Orientals, Mormons, Eastern Europeans and Americans in the Northwest, he asked: "Shall we . . . assimilate these people and mould them into Canadian citizenship, or will they remain as a distinct people, in the country but not of it, perpetuating their social and religious ideals under the aegis of the British flag?" Canadians must "either lift them up to our level or be dragged down to theirs. Unless they are assimilated and educated and evangelized," the correspondent cautioned, they will become a "source of danger and weakness rather than strength."[8] The way to greatness for Canada lay in continued attachment to, involvement in, and leadership of the Empire; greatness for Canada lay in the traditions of Ango-Saxonism.

Early in the twentieth century the worst fears of Presbyterian home missionaries seemed to have been confirmed. The commissioner of the North West Mounted Police claimed "that the foreign born population of the North West Territories equals that of British birth."[9] The Presbyterian Home Mission Committee demanded that these foreign immigrants, "accustomed only to the lowest planes of social and intellectual life" and "far removed from us in their ideals and aspirations as well as in their speech and modes of living,"[10] be assimilated and moulded into Christian Canadians. An editorial in *The Presbyterian Record* asserted that "only solvent that will fuse these varied nationalities into one, and make them brothers all, is the Gospel of Jesus Christ . . . . [It placed] the responsibility for giving them that Gospel . . . with those who now have that Gospel . . . . Or, to put it in another way . . . as Christians, as patriots, the privilege of shaping the future of Canada, lies with the present Christians of Canada; and that responsibility is discharged by each doing the little, or larger part that opportunity presents and ability permits."[11]

The conversion of foreign immigrants to both evangelical Protestantism and British parliamentary democracy, the inseparable element of Anglo-Canadian self-perception, was more than a challenge to the Presbyterian Church – it was a duty to the nation and an obligation before God.

Not all Presbyterians saw eye to eye on the details of Canadianization. "To some it was the melting pot, to others it was assimilation to an essentially Anglo-Saxon standard." R. Craig Brown and Ramsay Cook argue that individuals like novelist Ralph Connor, (the *nom de plume* of Rev. Charles W.

Gordon of St. Stephen's Church, Winnipeg) "made no distinction" between the two approaches.[12] Yet to the Women's Home Missionary Society, there was a distinction. Presbyterian women perceived Canadianization as a one-way process of assimilation, the final stage of which "amalgamation" "occurred through interbreeding and intermarriage."[13] The steadfastness with which early-twentieth-century social and religious reformers, including many prominent Canadian Presbyterians, view the premature intermingling of races as the source of moral, physical, intellectual and social decay, places them against the American melting pot idea. To many, including Rev. Charles W. Gordon and WHMS President Mrs. John Somerville, the intermarriage of Canadian and "foreign" young people before the "foreign" population was uplifted socially, culturally and religiously, engendered great anxiety about the deterioration of the rising generation.[14] Presbyterian home missionaries believed that assimilation, or the near "obliteration of ethnic differences" through education, should precede amalgamation. Few Presbyterians, indeed few Canadians, believed that the process of assimilation could be accomplished within one generation.

The WHMS, behind its banner, "Canada for Christ," rose to confront the massive influx of hundreds of thousands of "foreign" immigrants who, in their view, threatened to engulf the nation. As self-appointed guardians of Canadian values,[15] WHMS members and missionaries seized for their church new national responsibilities, including an obligation to educate and acculturate these new arrivals, especially those who settled in isolated prairie colonies. It was the preceived need to preserve a "Christian" and British Canada from the ravages of the "barbarous" hordes that led the WHMS to initiate an aggressive program of Christianizing and Canadianizing children of "foreign" immigrants. In seven prairie settlements (near large Ruthenian settlements at Teulon, Ethelbert and Sifton, Manitoba; Wakaw and Canora, Saskatchewan; and Vegreville, Alberta)[16] school-homes were adjoined to existing medical (hospital or dispensary) missions. The Teulon and Vegreville missions, prototypes for all other Presbyterian school-homes in the West, resembled the contemporary Presbyterian residential and day schools for French-Canadian girls at Pointe-aux-Trembles, Quebec, and the Methodist school-home for Ruthenian children at Wahstao.[17] The goal of both the Ruthenian school-homes and the French schools was Canadianization and "Christianization."

Two characteristics distinguished these prairie home missions from Presbyterian city missions or purely evangelical missions. First, the clients were primarily children, isolated from their parents and culture.[18] Second, these children, residing in an unfamiliar boarding home or a mission hospital, were pressured to reject their cultural heritage and, in many instances, their religious beliefs in favour of a synthesized and idealized British culture and an evangelical Protestant religion. These WHMS educational missions illustrate how Canadian-Protestant fear of change threatened by massive foreign immigration merged with the social gospel mission to uplift the social, moral and religious life of the immigrant. The WHMS education missions were patriotic, evangelical and practical. They responded to the immediate social and educational needs of the foreign immigrants while guarding and promoting a parochial Presbyterian vision of Canada as a Christian nation.

While the WHMS expressed its concern about the perceived threat of non–Anglo-Saxon immigrants, by 1910 its strident anti-Catholic and anti-foreign rhetoric had given way to a more positive, evangelical and social welfare, if nevertheless nativist, program. It emphasized the assimilation of new Canadians into Canadian society through the "uplifting" of their moral, social and religious life. The fear that assimilating the foreigner would alter the Canadian character immeasurably was tempered by a humanitarian appeal to raise the low standard of living among foreigners on the frontier. As defenders of Anglo-Protestant Canadian culture, Presbyterian women did seek to counter the alleged threat of alien or foreign radicalism and the danger of malcontents through the extension of evangelical mission and national schooling.

The form and content of the educational missions, and indeed all missions to the non–Anglo-Saxon immigrants, were shaped by the society's nation-building and evangelical agenda. Although they were socializing and prose-lytizing missions, the medical and educational missions represented a "gentler kind of assimilation [which] arose from sympathy not dread."[19] It was hoped that they helped to counter what non–Anglo-Saxon immigrants saw as anti-immigrant and anti-Catholic hysteria. The WHMS response to the need of the nation and the non–Anglo-Saxon may be viewed in a three-fold manner: first, "the humanitarian task of introducing the immigrants to the country . . . [and] providing them with the essential services," often in the form of "bales" of clothing, shelter or medical services; second, the Canadianization or nationalization of the foreigner; and third, evangelism, the inculcation of Protestantism or "pure Christianity."[20] In the WHMS missions to the Ruthenians of the Northwest, these reactions were so interwoven as to be virtually indistinguishable.

As with other Protestant agencies, the WHMS continued to be wary of immigrants who were not Protestant and "lacked desirable Anglo-Saxon qualities." The WHMS acknowledged that eastern Europeans were Christians who adhered to the Orthodox or Catholic churches, but regarded these churches "as backward and authoritarian."[21] The WHMS's commitment to evangelize the eastern European immigrants, in true social gospel fashion, was buttressed by the belief that assimilation would not be complete until "Christianization" (conversion to evangelical Protestant values) occurred. Thus the WHMS educational and medical missions fit within historian Howard Palmer's typology of nativism, which links social reform, religious reform and anti-foreign nativism closely together. While Palmer rightly argues that the Canadian church perceived the eastern European immigrants as "stumbling blocks" hindering the achievement of the social gospel goal of a truly Christian society, he emphasizes the Church's shift from an evangelistic to a secular reform motivation. Yet his essentially secularist analysis of a Protestant-directed reform impulse confirms both the religious and nationalist foundations of the Protestant vision of "His Dominion." In addition, "this nationalistic religious vision of 'His Dominion,' " as historian N. Keith Clifford states, was "at odds with the concept of a pluralistic society."[22]

Although occasional letters to the WHMS *Missionary Messenger* did expound on a modified "pluralist" concept of the nation, they were clearly in a minority. When the Rev. William D. Reid, the Rev. H.A. Berlis and the Rev. Max Kinsale gave an address to the Pre-Assembly Congress of 1913 entitled "Non–Anglo Saxons in Canada" they confirmed the mainline Presbyterian rejection of a pluralistic concept of Canada. A decade and one half of close association with the foreigner had strengthened, not lessened, the Church's attachment to Anglo-Protestant conformity. Notwithstanding their dread of the foreigners' effect on Canadian society, and perhaps because of it, Reid, Berlis, Kinsale and the WHMS responded to the Ruthenians' threat with an appeal for medical, educational and social services, each infused with an evangelistic fervour and an understanding of the plight of the foreigner. It must be conceded, however, that the Presbyterian press, including the WHMS *Home Mission Pioneer* and *Missionary Messenger*, was often more strident, emphatic and less conciliatory than were the missionaries in the field.

All WHMS missionaries had ambivalent attitudes toward the Ruthenians; their reports to the WHMS mingled feelings of foreboding, bewilderment and optimism. They worried about whether the Church could fulfill its mission to the tides of immigrants sweeping ashore. Would the Church be able to extend the Gospel to these multitudes of foreigners? They wrote with horror of the great masses of foreigners, of their poverty and of the ignorance, immorality and irreligion which seemed to prevail in foreign settlements. The missionaries in the field, however, held out hope that, with mission assistance, they would improve the spiritual and moral character of the foreigners, and proclaimed the promise of public education and evangel for the aliens. But confusion also permeated missionary views: confusion about how best to deal with the multifaceted problems posed by alien immigrants, how best to approach and uplift these strangers, and how to interpret their responses to the Presbyterian mission enterprise.

The threat posed by foreign immigrants was confirmed by missionaries who were anxious that assimilation did not occur without the Church's participation. Such a process, in their view, would imperil Canada's destiny as a Christian nation.[23] While the Ruthenians of Northern Alberta had but "an imperfect knowledge of language, ideals, and institutions,"[24] Southern Alberta Ruthenians carried from Russia "not only customs, and ideals, but also its problems." Dissatisfied with the assimilative process, the home mission superintendent for Southern Alberta, the Rev. William D. Reid informed subscribers of *The Home Mission Pioneer* that Ruthenians had "little sympathy for our laws and language and would like to be left alone to build up a Little Russia in Canada." It was evident to Reid and other missionaries that the Canadian church must intrude into the social, religious and educational life of the Ruthenians to ensure that they obeyed Canadian laws and understood their duties and privileges as Canadian citizens. In the January 1913 *Home Mission Pioneer*, Methodist J.S. Woodsworth impressed upon WHMS members the importance of immediate action: "Aside from altruistic motives we cannot afford not to care for the foreigner. Our welfare and theirs are inextricably interwoven. If we neglect them and their children, the neglect will inevitably reflect upon us and our children."[25]

The goal of Canadianization meant that foreigners, and especially their offspring, must embrace specific Canadian values: loyalty to the British-Canadian ideas of country, King and God and an acceptance of Protestant morality with its ideals of sobriety, diligence and hard work, cleanliness and purity.[26] Convinced that they could give the immigrants "that social and moral uplift to fit them for their new responsibilities" as Canadians,[27] the WHMS sent out missionaries to educate, evangelize and care for the foreign settlers in the Northwest. The WHMS determined that its most important work was "the Christian education of the foreign children coming into our country."[28] As the children might prove most receptive, missionaries moved on to specific Presbyterian doctrines propagated through the public prayers and sermons of the ministers and the Sunday school, bible classes and mission bands attached to the missions. Proper assimilation, as a one-way process, demanded that only the best of Canadian values, ideals and habits be imparted to the new Canadians. Presbyterian women believed that this packaged way of life must be imparted to the Ruthenian children before they could truly become one with the Canadian people.[29] The new Canadians would, therefore, be remade in the best image of the "Canadian" in the shortest possible time.

As astute observers of "the immigrant problem" in the years between 1900 and 1914, WHMS members believed that "to make the most of the foreigner coming to our shore, we must give him the very best possible environment."[30] The wisdom of contemporary American scholarship on the immigrant problem had convinced many of the need for medical missions and school boarding homes. "Our hospitals and mission houses are great factors in this [evangelical and national] work, and in the training of the foreign children committed to the care of the doctors and nurses a noteworthy step in advance has been taken. The opening on a larger scale of a home for children . . . at Vegreville, is a still further effort to touch and sweeten and uplift the homes of our foreigners."[31] These nation-building, educational and evangelical services, argued the WHMS missionaries, ensured that the Presbyterian Church would play a central role in assimilating and Christianizing the foreigners.

The focal points for the assimilationist sentiment of the WHMS missionaries in the Northwest were the school and church. Historians of immigration invariably identify the host society's faith in education as the essential mechanism of assimilating the newcomer.[32] Canadian Presbyterians viewed the public school and the church as naturalization agencies. "The Church and the school are the bond, the cement that [will] bind these people together into a solid, loyal, whole," claimed *The Presbyterian Record*. "Without the Church and the school a community or nation rapidly disintegrates and hastens to its fall."[33] The church and the public school, WHMS missionaries concurred, were the two agencies that must cooperate to mold these Ruthenian children "into sturdy and loyal citizens."[34] Public education and evangelical Christianity were the "only gastric juices capable of digesting these foreign elements, whose traditions are in some cases hostile to ours. Let the church supply the Christianity. . . . The education, on a sound moral Bible basis, the government should give."[35] The mind's eye of *The Record*'s editor envisioned a mass of eastern Europeans, adherents of ecclesiastical institutions which were portrayed as backward, oppressive, ritualistic, idolatrous and anti-intellectual. "If alien peoples filling our country are to be a strength to our country," asserted *The Record*, "there must be a church and school, and the school under decidedly religious [Protestant] influence." The school, Presbyterian Church members believed, would supplant the European immigrants' "backward" culture, non-democratic politics and religious "superstitions" with ideal Canadian cultural attributes, especially the Protestant work ethic, habits of social and personal hygiene, and concepts of temperance, political purity and religious idealism.

Presbyterian missionaries, therefore, forged close ties with this "splendid instrument in the Canadianizing of our immigrants." In 1903 the Home

Mission Committee employed student-missionary John A. Cormie as their agent among Manitoba's rural Ruthenians. Cormie, with the financial support of the committee, encouraged the Ruthenians to construct three schools, which were later absorbed into the public school system. In addition to financing the construction of these schools, the Church maintained their teachers for three years.

Experience, however, had convinced the WHMS that "national" schools in the western provinces were inadequate for the task before them. Qualified "Canadian" teachers were scarce. The "foreign" teachers, educated at one of the special provincial normal schools,[36] often lacked proper training in pedagogy, were unfamiliar with the English language, or were uncommitted to the "Christian" and Canadian curriculum of the schools. Hence, it was believed that these teachers undermined the nation-building mandate of the public school. Dr. Alexander Jardine Hunter, medical missionary at Teulon, warned that "there is a danger of the country being filled with half-educated young men looking for easy places in teaching . . . – an army of incompetents looking for public employment" who did not improve the quality of life in the Ruthenian community or instruction in the public school.[37] The solution to these difficulties was to train up a cadre of Ruthenian youth who would be educated in the public school and receive "Christian" religious teaching and moral training.

Since 1904, WHMS mission staff had boarded immigrant children so they could attend the public school. In 1909, Dr. George Arthur, medical missionary at Vegreville, made representations to the WHMS executive to construct a school-home. WHMS executive and missionaries saw these proposed boarding homes for immigrant children as an opening to extend the evangel, to train these children in Canadian habits, bolster the nation-building role of the public school, and serve the educational needs of the Ruthenian children. The WHMS school-home became the key auxiliary of the Church to the public school near Ruthenian colonies.[38] In spite of the problems associated with pioneer prairie education, WHMS members in the East were assured that Ruthenian children could be educated and were eager to learn. In a 1909 *Home Mission Pioneer* article, E.E. Sprague, WHMS nurse at Wakaw, Saskatchewan, exuded confidence in the virtually untapped ability of foreign children after she "visited the public schools of the three sections in the vicinity of the Hospital – Hungarian, Galician and Bukowinian respectively – schools just opened a few months." While the schools' foreign students wore peculiar "garb and head-dress" they were "anxious to learn" and "made wonderful progress, some of them having already exhausted three readers" in six months – remarkable progress indeed for students who did not know "a word of

English to begin with, and never saw even the outside of a school house before." At the Galician school, Sprague observed that "everything, reading, writing, spelling was done with an enthusiasm" seldom witnessed in the "Canadian" schools of Ontario.[39]

Other missionaries also reported Ruthenian school children getting ahead of their Canadian-born classmates, taking all of the school honours.[40] By themselves, these reports might be enough to convince the WHMS women that educational mission work would succeed among the Ruthenian population and, thereby, justify the society's continued financial support of the school-home established at Vegreville in 1910. Also, since 1904, medical missionaries had boarded young Ruthenian patients at the mission hospital or dispensary, so that they might attend the public school. The school-homes were similarly expected to enable more Ruthenian youth, deprived of public education because they were too far away from the school, because of lack of schools or because of parental indifference, to mingle with Canadian-born students and thus imbibe the public school's "Christian" philosophy. Only in the public school, WHMS missionaries asserted, "could these foreigners best be taught proper English, morality, cleanliness, and the need for pure air in their homes, and hygiene in general," knowledge assumed lacking in the Ruthenian household.[41]

To WHMS missionaries, the pressing need of Ruthenian children, who would one day become leaders of their people, was ethical and moral training. WHMS missionaries maintained that Christian morals and ethics were the spiritual framework for reading and writing. Dr. George Arthur of the Vegreville mission claimed that "secular education alone" was not enough – it required the teaching and practice of moral precepts to form effective young Christian Canadians. Dr. Alexander Jardine Hunter, medical missionary at Teulon, agreed that "the real problem is to give them a rightly balanced view of life and moral principles of action."[42] He thought that these traits were best inculcated in the positive environment of a good Christian home, and the average Ruthenian home did not qualify. According to Presbyterian missionaries, the school-home would supplant the Ruthenian children's deficient upbringing with a sound evangelical Christian and ethical view of life.

The moral climate of the "typical" Ruthenian home mirrored its physical disposition. The average Ruthenian home was portrayed as dirty, poorly aired and unhygienic. Claimed an unidentified author in the June 1915 *Missionary Messenger*:

We realize more fully the meaning of the words poverty and ignorance . . . as we picture to ourselves one Ruthenian home. . . . The house consisted of one large room with a wee window (plastered in tight with mud and manure) which let in no air and little light. For furniture there was a home-made table, a bench and a kind of cupboard. Nothing that bore the slightest resemblance of a bed could be seen. In one corner of the room was a huge mud stove and extending from this the whole length of the room was a pile of potatoes. There was a fire in the stove (although it was summer), and beside it on the potatoes lay the fevered mother and her three-days-old child. Under them was a mere handful of straw while for a covering was a sheepskin coat. In such conditions of poverty and dirt is it to be wondered that ignorance and superstition prevail, that disease is everywhere rampant, and that death gathers in a large harvest![43]

Presbyterian women reasoned that the inborn tendencies, "some base and degenerating," of Ruthenian children could only be "held in check" in the "Christian" home. The only practical alternative to the Ruthenian household was the system of school-homes operated by Presbyterians or other Protestant groups within close proximity of efficient public schools at which selected Ruthenian children could board. The routine, organization and curricula of the school-homes were designed to provide Ruthenian children with the "discipline" and "loving care and watchfulness" of the idealized Christian Canadian home.[44] No matter how laudable the school-home scheme was, however, it was too expensive and too impractical, logistically, to extend to *all* Ruthenian children in the Canadian Northwest. Therefore, most young Ruthenians, of necessity, remained with their parents in the Ruthenian colonies for their upbringing and education.

The WHMS missionaries found themselves caught in a dilemma. They firmly believed in the traditional importance of the home as a character-forming institution and as a centre of moral instruction. The image of the "Christian" mother as "the real guardian of the world's morals and ideals"[45] permeated Presbyterian views of the family. But WHMS missionaries feared that the "uneducated and superstitious" Ruthenian mother (with whom the major child-rearing responsibility lay) lacked essential knowledge to transmit to her children Canadian ideals, morals and domestic habits. While Presbyterian missionaries decried any undermining of the home's religious and educational duties, they championed the school-home scheme which, by emphasizing its Protestant and Canadian characteristics, subverted the customs and authority of the Ruthenian family. Acknowledging the "benefit of a refined educated mother in the home," WHMS missionaries were convinced of the absolute necessity that young Ruthenian women "who are to have children in the formative years of their life, be educated."[46] Only if educated in a "Christian" and Canadian home environment would the homes of these young Ruthenian women be "refined." Consequently, both George Arthur and Frank O. Gilbart, medical missionaries at Teulon and Sifton, respectively, urged upon the WHMS the responsibility to train the girls as Canadian homemakers.[47]

The WHMS executive continued to ensure that the residences were ruled by the knowing heart and hand of a Christian matron; discipline, hard work, hygiene and Christian love would be the world of residents who attended the nearby public school. The ideal boarding homes, Dr. Arthur suggested to the WHMS executive, would be in the charge of "good Christian women, where ten [Ruthenian] children at a time might be taught Christian principles and trained in household duties, – these children of course should attend the public school."[48] The WHMS executive and medical missionaries claimed that the school-homes provided unequalled opportunities for Galician children to attend public school, but "at the same time gave them the advantage of all the good influences possible, kindly Christian training in the home, and attendance at church and Sabbath School."[49] The Ruthenian children were taught "the value of truthfulness, industry and integrity, to honor the highest and best in life, and [were] point[ed] through it all to the Saviour Jesus Christ."[50] The children, isolated from the negative influence of the Ruthenian settlements, were awash in Christian principles, beliefs, knowledge and habits. The social and moral environment of the school-home would, its organizers hoped, offer a model for the Ruthenian scholars to carry back with them when they returned, educated and "Christianized," to the Ruthenian settlement.

What are we striving to do in the "homes"? asked "Grandma" Arthur, matron of the Vegreville school-home and one of the "cultured Christian women" who devoted "careful attention" to the religious and moral welfare of the children. Her answer: impress persistently upon the minds of the boarders "the right moral and spiritual influences."[51] The necessity of surrounding the boarders with "right moral and spiritual influences" was such that the Rev. Mr. Lang, minister and teacher at Vegreville, enforced a "rule that none of the children go home for weddings." The Ruthenian wedding was "a most degenerating thing. With the extended length of the festivities, the great gathering of people, men, women and children, and excessive drinking, crimes of greater and lesser degree are inevitable. . . . The boys, even the youngest, are urged to drink."[52] Apparently, the work of the school-home could be undone if the children were not carefully governed and prevented from participating in the traditional patterns of Ruthenian life.

Religious training was overt and systematic in the school-homes. At the Teulon residence, the boarders attended morning worship and were taught the "Lord's Prayer, the sermon on the mount, the twenty-third psalm, the ten commandments, and other scripture passages. . . . On Sunday they attended the Ruthenian church in the morning, . . . Sunday School in the afternoon, and the Presbyterian Church at night."[53] A description of the life of the Vegreville school-homes, with "prayers, consisting of a few verses from the psalms and gospels . . . and the Lord's Prayer" after breakfast, illustrates the commonality of experience and the pervasiveness of religious instruction. In addition, hymn singing was a "very popular" form of religious inculcation, in which the children "sing the tune before they know a word of English." Hymns and Psalms were thought to instill in the children a sense of religious enthusiasm and were thought to be a part of an effective evangelistic strategy. Christina Reid, head nurse at Sifton, explained this emphasis: "The teaching, memorizing of the Scripture, etc., is what is going to fit [the Ruthenian children] to be intelligent, useful Christians. We hope soon to see some of them accept Christ as a personal Saviour."[54]

The duties of Protestant Ruthenian ministers, who were associated with the Presbyterian Church through the Independent Greek Church, were also important features of the religious education of the youthful Ruthenian boarders. The Rev. Maxim M. Zalizniak, a Ruthenian minister, served as a catechist to the Vegreville students and taught them "to read and sing in their own language." At Teulon, the boarders attended Sunday morning service in the Ruthenian Church under Mr. D.D. Perich, a Ruthenian missionary. "In the afternoon," Perich also instructed "a Bible Class of twenty Ruthenian children."[55] This training, conducted in the vernacular, was considered invaluable to the future Ruthenian missionaries because it would allow them to communicate the truths of evangelical Christianity in traditional ways *and* in their own language with their less acculturated clients. In addition, the presence of Zalizniak, Perich, the Rev. Maxim P. Berezynski, the Rev. Sigismund Bychinsky and other Ruthenian Protestant ministers[56] and services in the Ruthenian vernacular they conducted may have comforted the Ruthenian children: these people were familiar anchors in a sea of strangers. By their presence, the Ruthenian ministers served as models of success and acceptance within the Anglo-Protestant world. They were "foreigners" who had achieved a modicum of religious and social acceptance in the Protestant society.[57]

The secular training offered in the WHMS mission stations varied, depending upon the expertise of the missionaries, the needs of the mission and the facilities at hand. Generally, the Ruthenian young people were instructed in the mode of Canadian homemakers. This training, demanded by Presbyterian missionaries acquainted with the Ruthenian household, would redress the influence of the Ruthenian "home" environment[58] and impose the hygienic and economic standards of Canadian home life. Matrons and missionaries offered residents models of good house-keeping habits. However, practice was thought to be more effective. Therefore, as boarders in the school-homes, Ruthenian young people received practical training in "proper" methods of

work and house-keeping. At the Vegreville residences, Dr. Arthur explained
that the boys were "being trained in all the work necessary about the house;
[to] do all the bedmaking, sweeping, dishwashing, washing of floors, etc., etc.
. . . They also take care of the two cows and the poultry."[59] In addition to
teaching the children appropriate work habits, these duties contributed to the
goal of making each mission as self-supporting as possible. The notion of
self-support was an important one for all Protestant missions and one which
was impressed upon the boarders.

The boys, argued one missionary, "must have educated Christian wives,
for Ruthenians are great advocates of early marriages – if they are to measure
up to the full requirement of missionary life and that is what we are training
them for – to be missionaries to their own people."[60] In a letter to *The Home
Mission Pioneer*, Dr. George Arthur claimed that the Vegreville mission
hospital demonstrated what might be done with the Ruthenian girls. Arthur
and his mother had employed in the hospital and in their home a number of
"green" Galician girls. These girls were "taken into the kitchen and laundry
of the hospital and trained cleanly and orderly habits of living, and in right
and proper methods of housekeeping." Since these foreign girls "marry
young," the Arthurs trusted that the habits learned by the girls in the mission
and the English settlers' homes in which they served as domestics would
"remain with them."[61] Presbyterian missionaries anticipated that training the
girls as Canadian-styled mothers and in Canadian domestic sciences, and
training the boys as self-supporting men and in practical household duties
served to transmit Canadian values and habits of domesticity to the Ruthenian colonies.

The WHMS continually assessed the progress of its home missions. The
three criteria of success employed by the society and their missionaries were:
the cultural assimilation of the Ruthenian children under their care; the
children's acceptance of the tenets of evangelical Protestantism; and, the
demand for the services of the school-homes. In a letter to Mrs. Edward
Cockburn, "A Progressive School Boy" residing in the Teulon residence
expressed his "hope to see every one of the Ruthenians, or as they call
themselves sometimes, Ukrainians, to become Protestants and to put away
the old Catholic doctrine." Nicholas D. Halaberry, a resident at the Teulon
Boys' Home, wished to study theology and medicine following the model of
the Rev. Dr. Alexander J. Hunter, head of the Teulon mission, so that he
might "help the Presbyterians to bring about [the] reformation of our people"
or, in other words, to assist the Ruthenians to become Protestants and "true
Christians."[62]

Another "typical" case was "Mike – a Ukrainian boy of 15," who "eagerly
availed himself" of the school-home's opportunities. His progress in the

public school was noticeable and he was expected to prepare "for Normal School and for a life of independence and of unusually capable service." At the school-home he learned "the meaning of personal and home cleanliness; and the chief events of Bible history; all the passages selected by our Church for memory awards and many others; and, best of all, he has been led to give his heart to Christ and to realize that life's true purpose is to help others towards God. What investment can we make that will bring richer returns?"[63] Female boarders were also trained to be important agents of social change in their communities and their achievements were measures of the missions' success. In a 1916 review of educational work among Ruthenian females, "organized but a few years," the WHMS was encouraged by the example of two Ruthenian girls who were maintained, clothed and trained in Teulon, then sent to Winnipeg to complete their education. These young women, as teachers of "their own people," had "justified the faith that was placed in them." The WHMS expected that, in time, more Ruthenian women, "educated under Christian influence," would become "Christian teachers and workers and leaders among their people."[64] Finally, reporting on her tour of the WHMS missions, Jean Kipp, its travelling secretary, observed that "the chief ambition" of Ruthenian youth was "to be entitled and worthy of the name Canadian."[65] Although dissatisfied because greater educational opportunities could not be provided, Presbyterian women and missionaries justified continued support for the school-home scheme on the basis of such reports of assimilation to Canadian and Christian norms.

The ever-increasing number of requests for accommodation in WHMS school-homes led the missionaries to conclude that their missions answered a need among the Ruthenians for education and "true Christianity." *The Missionary Messenger* editorialized that "the foreigners themselves are growing more and more appreciative of what is being done for their children. . . . Parents are . . . anxious to have their children educated and, at the same time be under the care of cultured Christian women."[66] There seemed to be no shortage of boarders for the school-homes. As late as October 1918, Rev. J.H. Edmison claimed that "no difficulty has been experienced in securing pupils. Parents are anxious to secure educational advantages for their children."[67] The evangelical Protestant climate of the school-homes did not deter Ruthenian parents or their children. Many of the youth who boarded at these school-homes, and those built in the last years of the World War I and immediately thereafter, may have been adherents of the Reformed Greek Church (the former Independent Greek Church) and so had already accepted the tenets of evangelical Protestantism. The letters of missionaries to *The Missionary Messenger* and to the Board of Home Missions and Social Service indicate that after 1917 many of the children were Ukrainian Orthodox.

Unfortunately, there is no record indicating whether the "successes" were students of "Protestant" background or of Ukrainian Orthodox Church background. To the WHMS women and to their supporters this did not matter; the missions' success was confirmed by the overwhelming demand for accommodation in their school-homes by Ukrainian public school students.

The explanations for the success of the school-home missions (demand for accommodation, educational and social mobility of the students, and a nascent evangelistic spirit among the students) offered by the mission staff emphasized the missions' utility to the Ruthenians. Available historical data do not suggest that Ruthenian parents sent their offspring to these church-directed boarding homes for the religious education provided or for the benefits of cultural assimilation. It is probable that the requests for accommodation reflected the Ruthenians' acceptance of the public school as the means of upward social and economic mobility and felt the exposure to Protestantism not nearly as effective in changing the home religion as did the missionaries.

Thus, in spite of the WHMS's portentous claims of success, that children who went to the school-homes did indeed go on to become teachers, ministers, doctors and businessmen,[68] it is unlikely that these school-homes and their religious agenda had much effect in changing the culture of the Ukrainian community of the Northwest. The rapid growth of the Ukrainian Orthodox Church and a Ukrainian nationalist movement in the Northwest before and during World War I,[69] the decline of nativism[70] and the integration of the Ukrainian community into the social, political and economic structures of the western provinces undermined efforts to impose a Protestant religion on these people. Histories of the growth of the Roman Catholic and Ukrainian Orthodox churches in western Canada, in spite of the initial concern of these sects with the development of the Independent Greek Church,[71] virtually ignore the existence of Presbyterian school-homes and other Protestant mission activities among prairie Ruthenians.

Since the public school system was not fully extended across the Northwest until the 1930s, the school-homes undoubtedly offered educational opportunities for some Ruthenian children before then. (There were 100 boarders in 1915 and 187 in 1924.) With the establishment of schools near all Ukrainian communities, and with the onset of the Depression during the thirties, the school-homes, now operated by the United Church of Canada, gradually closed. Finances dwindled and requests for accommodation declined. Yet for the Presbyterian Women's Home Missionary Society and for the United Church Woman's Missionary Society, the efficacy of the school-homes – which had been maintained through the economic slump before World War I, through the difficult war years and through the optimistic post-war years when the demand for school accommodation had increased – had already been proven. These school-homes, WHMS executive and missionaries believed, had helped to provide a brighter future for the Canadian West. The Ruthenians were becoming Christian Canadians. "His Dominion" seemed secure.

Nellie L. McClung (Photo courtesy of Provincial Archives of British Columbia, 3985–7.)

Nellie L. McClung:
A part of a pattern

Carol L. Hancock

A brilliant woman, wise and witty,
Forceful, fearless, good and gritty,
With tongue and pen, in terms strong,
Upholds the right, condemns the wrong.[1]

So begins a poem written to pay tribute to Nellie L. McClung and now to be
found tucked in her own papers. The poetry is not particularly subtle, but it is
a nice example of the sentiment that often greeted Nellie L. as she preferred to
sign herself. There was, however, another side to the response people had to
her. She was once caricatured as a mosquito and was nicknamed "Calamity
Nell." Although some magazine and newspaper articles hailed her as "Joan
of the West," others called her "Lady Terror" and "Windy Nellie." In 1935, a
column in Toronto's *Mail and Empire* published the opinion:

Nobody living in Manitoba 20 years ago will ever accept the current fallacy about Nellie McClung
that she is wishy-washy; for in bringing the Roblin government to destruction, she showed more
pluck than any man in the province and equal intelligence. Of the filthy abuse poured on her, all
fortunately is forgotten, leaving only the derisive tag, Salvation Nell, to carry abroad the
suggestion of a virago, which is as false a notion of the author of "Sowing Seeds In Danny" as
that she is too sweet. The truth is that she has a lively mind, strong character, and a keen sense of
humour.[2]

It can be seen, even from this tiny sampling, that opinions about Nellie L.
McClung were varied. And for good reason: she herself was a complex and
multi-talented worker who approached a wide spectrum of issues. Critics
have often found fault with individual dimensions of her work and missed the

richness of her particular contribution. In this article, I present a glimpse of what she did offer, with particular focus on her years in Manitoba and her contribution to its history, both secular and ecclesiastical.

If we are to gain some insight into the way McClung perceived her own contribution, we need not try to find great and distinctive works which were hers alone. In the preface to her second autobiographical volume, she did express some wish to be remembered, but she expressed little desire for individual attention or fame. Rather, she saw herself as part of larger enterprises, and she knew that she had offered her share to large tasks. Her own words were simple and powerful: "In Canada we are developing a pattern of life and I know something about one block of that pattern. I know it for I helped to make it, and I can say that now without any pretense of modesty, or danger of arrogance, for I know that we who make the patterns are not important, but the pattern is."[3] In this article I discuss the ways in which McClung was part of Manitoba's history, how she helped shape it, and, coincidentally, I will suggest some of the ways in which her Manitoba years shaped the rest of her life. McClung, it must be realized, was forty-one years old before she left Manitoba for Alberta.

Although it is certainly appropriate to include McClung in a history of Manitoba, it should be noted that she would also have a significant place in a similar work in either Alberta or British Columbia. A tourist travelling through western Canada might be surprised to find her honoured so often, by cairn, plaque or museum.

McClung's two autobiographical works, *Clearing in the West* and *The Stream Runs Fast*, furnish us with her own version of her early history. *Clearing in the West*, published in 1935, recounts her history up to the time of her marriage to Wes McClung. *The Stream Runs Fast*, not published until 1945, picks up the story of the newlywed couple in 1896 and continues the narrative.

Her contemporaries were always aware of how important her religious faith was to her, and she always asserted that it began with her own family. Born in 1873 in Grey County, Ontario, Nellie Letitia Mooney was the youngest of six children. Raised by a strict Scottish Presbyterian mother and an Irish-Methodist father, she claimed that her own consciousness was a mixture of both traditions.

Spurred on by Nellie's oldest brother, the family moved to Manitoba in 1880 and homesteaded near present-day Wawanesa. Carefully taught that career and homemaking could not mix, Nellie L. chose a career and headed off to Winnipeg in 1889 for a five-month teacher-training program. The next year she taught all eight grades in a school at Hazel, three miles from

Manitou. It was there that she met her future mother-in-law, Annie E. McClung, wife of the local minister, the Rev. J.A. McClung. She also heard discussions about women receiving the vote, about homestead rights, the Women's Christian Temperance Union (WCTU) and prohibition. Her diary reveals a passionately romantic young woman who claimed no thoughts of becoming a reformer herself. Nevertheless, her journals reflect rapid changes and an enthusiastic idealism, apparently inspired by Dickens:

As I read and thought and marvelled, a light shone around me. I knew in that radiance what a writer can be at his best, an interpreter, a revealer of secrets, a heavenly surgeon, a sculptor who can bring an angel out of a stone. And I wanted to write; to do for the people around me what Dickens had done for his people. I wanted to be a voice for the voiceless as he had been a defender of the weak, a flaming fire that would consume the dross that encrusts human souls, a spring of sweet water beating up through all this bitter world to refresh and nourish souls that were ready to faint.[4]

In spite of these sentiments, her focus was still centred on her own education and the next few years were occupied with study at the Winnipeg Collegiate Institute and more teaching, this time at Treherne. The McClungs had also moved there, and under Annie McClung's tutoring, Nellie continued to support the WCTU.

Nellie married Wes McClung in 1896 and quickly became pregnant. The indignation which pervades her account of her pregnancies is evocative of her fully developed crusading spirit: ". . . why had not something been found to save women from this infernal nausea? What good was it? If it had been a man's disease, it would have been made the subject of scientific research and relieved long ago. But women could suffer; it kept them humble!"[5] By 1901, there were three McClung children, and even though they were a pivotal part of her life, Nellie's journal for 1 February reads: "With three small children and a house to run, you can imagine what sort of frame of mind I'm in. In fact, the frame is all that is left of my mind."

In the midst of the chaos of children and home, she tried to find time for writing. Some of McClung's earliest attempts produced short stories and articles for the Methodist Sunday School Publications. Very short stories were also to be found in "Jewels," a production of Sabbath School Publications for the Presbyterian Church in Canada.

Nellie L. always said that the "blame" for the start of her writing and speaking career had to be laid upon her mother-in-law. Annie McClung urged Nellie to enter a short story contest sponsored by *Colliers* in 1902. Overwhelmed by a myriad of household chores, Nellie needed direct urging to rearrange her priorities. "If you wait until you are ready to write, you will never write," she was told. "Don't you know that conditions are never perfect? Life conspires to keep woman tangled in trifles."[6]

Nellie McClung's first speaking engagements were also prompted by her mother-in-law. Annie McClung had helped keep Nellie's involvement with the WCTU very active, and Nellie wrote that she felt the first "stirrings of ambition to be a writer at a WCTU convention in Manitou in 1907." She had not been a delegate to the provincial conference before, but she was a member and declared that she was "simply thrilled" when asked to give the address of welcome on behalf of the local unit. With her usual sense of humour, she reflected that the success of her speech probably owed a lot to the quality of the banquet which preceded it but whether or not anyone else would recall her words, the experience made a lasting impression on her: "For the first time I knew I had the power of speech. I saw faces brighten, eyes glisten, and felt the atmosphere crackle with a new power. I saw what could be done with words, for I had the vision of a new world as I talked. . . . It was not ideas I was giving them exactly, but rather ferments – something which I hoped would work like yeast in their minds."[7] That was only a beginning. Annie McClung supported a project in Winnipeg which needed money (the WCTU Home for Friendless Girls, called the Williard Home) and when in 1908 it occurred to Nellie that funds could be raised by public readings from her recently published book, *Sowing Seeds in Danny*, she was on her way to a public-speaking career. McClung would often respond to pleas from organizations with special projects. In her files are many references to speeches and pamphlets presented on behalf of the Woman's Missionary Society (WMS). An order for the Easter Thankoffering Service was distributed by the WMS and gave her the credit for being its author. In an undated pamphlet entitled "An Insistent Call,"[8] she reflects the attitude toward missionary work which was common in her day. Sarcastically responding to those she called "superior people," who said others should be left alone, she asked her question and then answered it: "Is our Christian civilization such a boon that we should go out of our way to pass it on to other people? I believe it is – and we should."

McClung wrote the preface to "Organized Helpfulness," the report for 1911–12 of All Peoples' Mission in Winnipeg. A review in a local newspaper hailed her contribution and said that she "sounded the key-note of the mission" when she wrote:

The missionary spirit in our churches is changing, evolving, advancing. . . . To clothe the poor has ceased to be our highest conception of our duty to our neighbour, for somehow the idea has been borne in upon us that our neighbor, poor though he may be and ignorant and 'foreign', is a man of like passions as ourselves, and that old clothes alone will never satisfy the hunger of his heart, nor clear us of our responsibility. What he needs is just what we need – it is understanding, fellowship, companionship – the human touch. Absent treatment and long-distance methods cannot be effectively used in missionary work.[9]

McClung's efforts touched both ecclesiastical and secular spheres. Her work in Winnipeg was not limited to church and women's groups, but also involved a political activism which had begun quite simply. At a Local Council of Women meeting, after concerned discussion about the plight of women workers in small factories, she and another woman were assigned to lobby the government for the appointment of a female factory inspector. Their strategy was direct and uncomplicated. They arranged to meet with the premier, Sir Rodmond Roblin, and were able to convince him to tour some of the factories with them. Before the tour, Roblin said he felt that "there was too much idleness now, with electricity and short cuts in labor. As a boy he had worked from sunrise, and before, until the shadows of evening fell, and enjoyed it. . . . These young girls in the factories whom we thought were underpaid, no doubt . . . lived at home, and really worked because they wanted pin-money. . . . Most of the women in the factories, he understood, were from foreign countries, where life was strenuous."[10] Nellie and her co-worker endured these platitudes in silence.

The tour took them to unventilated, foul-smelling, overcrowded basements. McClung wrote later that she knew the premier would soon bolt away from them, so they spared him nothing. They showed him the hopelessly inadequate toilet facilities; there was no need to point out that the plumbing had gone wrong. Declaring that he never knew such hellholes existed, Roblin resisted further education. "Now, Sir Rodmond," they said, "do you still think that these women are pleasurably employed in this rich land of wide spaces and great opportunities?" Roblin responded, "I still can't see why two women like you should ferret out such utterly disgusting things." The exercise had some usefulness, because it did draw the situation to the premier's attention. However, he said that all he could do was check up on the work of the present inspector (a male); he had "too much respect" for women to let one of them take on the job.

That was McClung's first association with Premier Roblin, but it was by no means her last. Her involvement with the struggle for women's suffrage brought her into direct confrontation with the government, culminating in 1914 in what would be known as the "women's parliament."

Because the Local Council of Women had many members who were not willing to involve themselves in highly controversial issues, some of its members, including McClung, formed a new, more activist, group called the

Political Equality League. One member of the new organization, Lillian Beynon Thomas recounted a story of a skit which had been put on in Vancouver by the University Women's Club there; the new group seized the idea for similar development in Manitoba. McClung had nothing to do with organizing the event, since she was out of the city, but when she returned the scheme was explained: the group would send a delegation of women to the Legislative Assembly then in session to ask for the vote. They counted on Roblin's refusal. In all their previous attempts, he had irrevocably and condescendingly rejected the requests. He respected women, he said. He lifted his hat when he met women, he said, but nice women would not want the vote. Nellie's feelings about such gestures were clear. "We went there asking for plain, common justice, an old-fashioned square deal, and in reply to that we got hat-lifting. I feel that when a man offers hat-lifting when we ask for justice we should tell him to keep his hat right on. I will go further and say that we should tell him not only to keep his hat on but to pull it right down over his face."[11]

The delegation was received at the Legislative Assembly at 3:00 p.m. on Tuesday, 27 January. Anticipating that the premier would refuse their request for the vote, the women planned to parody the confrontation the following evening, 28 January. They would stage their play at the Walker Theatre. Roblin did not disappoint them. As Nellie wrote later, he could have pricked their "beautiful balloon" and "taken the flavour out of every bit of their humour," by making some concessions, but, she declared, she needn't have worried. "The orator of the old school ran true. He was at his foamy best."[12] Roblin waxed eloquent on the afternoon of 27 January and gave Nellie all the material she needed. Next day, the papers carried a detailed report of the encounter and that night, at the Walker Theatre, Nellie led a cast who portrayed a women's parliament considering the petition of men to vote. As the premier of her own parliament, she presented a burlesque of all the unctuous arguments so favoured by Sir Rodmond. Hilarity ran high, and the papers of the following day were full of the latest McClung-Roblin altercation.

Using a person's own words to defeat him or her was a favourite strategy for Nellie L.; it was only natural that she would have employed the method in yet another struggle. She told the story of a speech she delivered in Ninga, Manitoba, to illustrate the inequalities for women. The story featured a wealthy farmer who had willed his three farms to his three sons. His daughter had received a feather bed and a cow, and his wife was guaranteed her "keep" with one of her sons – no money, just her keep. One of her male listeners challenged Nellie's disparagement of the situation. The widow would be thankful to go on living in familiar surroundings, he declared; what need had a sixty-five-year-old woman for money? McClung said she allowed several seconds of silence to "jell" that remark and then retorted: "I thank you sir, more than I can tell you. You have completed the story better than I could ever have done it. What does a woman of sixty-five need of money? Say it over, all of you."[13]

If someone were to argue now that McClung's political escapades and endeavours do not fit well with accounts of her contribution to the Church in Manitoba, then one could only be reminded that the two were always inter-woven in her life. Any deliberate separation would have been perceived by McClung as inappropriate. A newspaper account of an address to a WMS group in Portage la Prairie in 1914 makes the point clearly:

Mrs. McClung said that according to her outlook as a Christian, the franchise and the missionary movements were synonymous. She took as one illustration Mary and Martha and compared us to them. Mary recognized the Lord's visit as a red letter day and an opportunity to learn of greater things. Martha was too busy with the smaller things, just as today women are sometimes too busy housecleaning to give wider things even a thought.[14]

Although not usually named as a major figure in the social gospel move-ment, McClung certainly occupied a place within it. An overarching dimen-sion of the social gospel was its concept of humanity and its emphasis on the social applications of the Gospel. Its proponents were optimistic about the possibility of rconstructing and correcting society by applying democratic Christian principles.

A speech delivered by McClung around 1914 provides an interesting overview of her position within social gospel circles. Entitled "Social Respon-sibilities of Woman," the speech began with a call to women to leave behind the emphasis on acts of individual charity and join the cause of justice for all. The themes and illustrations of the speech were often repeated. Inter-woven with acknowledgement that women's energies were often misdirected was an awareness that they were encouraged in their misguided pursuits by dominant ideologies. She believed that

. . . so long as women are content to distribute blankets and coats, to make strong garments for the poor, to deal with the symptoms of poverty, paying no attention to the causes, all is well, all is smooth sailing. There is [much in] our charity that is transitory, vain, fleeting, ineffectual. Xmas dinners to hungry people is a deed of Christian charity incumbent upon all, and yet its effects are soon gone – the people are as hungry the next day as ever.[15]

She argued that charity too often had little real effect in changing the situa-tion. She told the story of a "kind old gentleman," who found a sick dog lying in the glare of the sun at the side of a road. Touched by compassion, the man climbed down from his carriage. Carrying the dog into the carriage's shadow, he told it to lie there and take refuge from the sun's rays. Then the man got back into his carriage and drove away.

The story echoed for her the Gospel parable of the good Samaritan. Never one to be limited by strict adherence to fact, McClung presented her own version of that story:

Once there was a man who was attacked by thieves and left, beaten and robbed, on the road from Jerusalem to Jericho. The priest and the Levite, when they encountered his broken body, fussed about the state of the times: "Dear, dear, how very distressing, I don't know what the road is coming to." The Samaritan took the man to shelter and made provision for him, ". . . actually spending money on him." Then she added her major variation. In her re-telling, the Samaritan had occasion to travel the same road the next day, and encountered another victim. On the third day, he found two more ". . . and while he was caring for them, he began to do some revolutionary thinking, – he hunted up some other good Samaritans, he even tried to interest the priest and the levite, he hunted up his old shotgun, and they all went down the line, gunning for thieves. They determined to clean up the road!"[16]

Women, she said, were beginning to learn the same lesson: "For centuries they have been acting the good Samaritan by their philanthropies, their private and public charities, their homes for the Friendless, for orphan children, Free Kindergartens, Day Nurseries; they have been picking up the robbed, wounded and beaten. Now they are wondering if they cannot do something to clean up the road. Investigation is taking the place of resignation."[17] McClung would not accept a pietism which separated faith and works. Listing such social evils as prostitution, sweated industries and alcoholism, she insisted: "If we sit down under these things, gently acquiescent, we become in the sight of God a partner in them. Submission to injustice, submission to oppression is rebellion against God."[18]

Political involvement was for McClung a natural outgrowth of religious commitment. In older days, McClung declared, God spoke through the mouths of His servants the prophets, who administered the legal as well as the spiritual affairs of the state. This was evidence that the Church's tradition supported political involvement. If politics had become corrupt, there was all the more reason to supply a "purifying influence." People might readily accept that what went on in the four walls of their homes was their affair; now it was to be understood that the home had expanded until it became the whole state.

McClung believed that to encourage people to actively witness to their Christian faith would help increase the range of the Gospel's effect. In a pamphlet written for the Board of Home Missions of the United Church,

McClung appealed to the ninety percent of the people of Canada who, according to her sources, did not attend any church: "We do not presume to judge the spiritual condition of anyone, nor are we taking church attendance as the sole criterion of conduct. But this we do know. That if the other ninety per cent would give as much time, money and energy to the spread of the Gospel as the ten per cent who do go to church we could reach every part of this country with the Gospel message."[19]

Consistent with the philosophy of social Darwinism, McClung was optimistic about the continued development of the human race. It had been Christ's plan, she said, to establish a church that would break the chains of the captive and preach deliverance to the poor, a church that would pull the mighty from their seats and exalt the humble and meek. Even the disciples misunderstood him, "and squabbled among themselves to see who was going to get the portfolios in the new Cabinet," but in spite of everything, Christ's message took root and spread. Humanity was moved relentlessly, albeit reluctantly, forward and took the message with it.[20]

McClung's belief that the principles of Christianity could transform the world did not blind her to the fact that the transformation had not yet taken place. Christianity had not failed, she asserted, but civilization had failed. Christianity as a religion for the individual was not given its proper scope:

The principles of Christ have not yet been applied to nations. We have only Christian people. You will see that in a second, if you look at the disparity that there is between our conceptions of individual duty and national duty. Take the case of the heathen – the people whom we in our large-handed, superior way call the heathen. Individually we believe it is our duty to send missionaries to them to convert them into Christians. Nationally we send armies upon them (if necessary) and convert them into customers! Individually we say: "We will send you our religion." Nationally: "We will send you goods, and we'll make you take them – we need the money!" Think of the bitter irony of a boat leaving a Christian port loaded with missionaries upstairs and rum below, both bound for the same place and for the same people – both for the heathen "with our compliments."[21]

Another of McClung's concerns was church union, a concern she shared with other social gospellers. She believed that if the church could overcome its divisions it would be more likely to serve society effectively.

Although the debate over the ordination of women was not a major issue for Nellie L. during her Manitoba years, it can certainly be argued that the roots for her sentiments on that subject stemmed from her early experiences. Nellie found the experience of public-speaking an intoxicating one and, having learned that the "power of speech" could influence or instruct an audience, she never forgot the significance of speech-making.

Indeed, her campaign for ordination often included mention of her frustration with the ways in which women were silenced. Her sharp and witty chapter, "Women and the Church," in her 1915 book, *In Times Like These*, gave early witness to her perception. "Women have until the last fifty years been the inarticulate sex," she wrote, "but although they have had little to say about themselves they have heard much. It is a very poor preacher or lecturer who has not a lengthy discourse on 'Woman's True Place.' " If women had found it difficult to follow a straight and narrow path, she declared, it was not for lack of advice to pursue it. Men had great confidence that they knew where women belonged. "Man long ago decided that woman's sphere was anything he did not wish to do himself, and as he did not particularly care for the straight and narrow way, he felt free to recommend it to women in general."[22]

Tied in with this enforced silence of women, McClung contested, was a masculine domination over the teachings of the church. The result was a loss, to the Protestant religion anyway, of the idea of the motherhood of God. The image of father/God could not always be helpful. "There come times when human beings do not crave the calm, even-handed justice of a father nearly so much as the soft-hearted, loving touch of a mother, and to many a man or woman whose home life has not been happy, 'like as a *father* pitieth his children' sounds like a very cheap and cruel sarcasm.' "[23] It is interesting to note that McClung's thoughts are often a mixture of radical and conservative perceptions. Even as she challenged the treatment of women, she still wished quite traditional roles upon them whenever the topics referred to home and family.

A consistent theme in McClung's writing and speaking, whether before, during or after her concentrated work to have women ordained, was her discontent with the way the church let women down. She felt that it gladly took women's labour, patronized them for it, and then refused any proper credit for their contribution. In 1915 she wrote:

Women have certainly been allowed to labor in the church. There is no doubt of that. There are many things they may do with impunity, nay even hilarity. They may make strong and useful garments for the poor; they may teach in Sunday-School and attend prayer-meeting; they may finance the new parsonage, and augment the missionary funds by bazaars, birthday socials, autograph quilts and fowl suppers. . . . The women may lift mortgages, or build churches, or any other light work, but the real heavy work of the church, such as moving resolutions in the general conference or assemblies, must be done by strong, hardy men![24]

It is important to understand something of the controversy inherent in the whole question if we are to understand McClung's part in it. Records of Proceedings for the meetings of the Presbyterian and Methodist Churches prior to union show that both congregations were working on the issue. The 1922 General Assembly of the Presbyterian Church made reference to the work of a committee assigned by the 1921 meeting to the task of reflecting on the admission of women to theological colleges, as regular students, with a view to ordination. The Assembly was not prepared "to foreclose this question either positively or negatively. . . ." The report acknowledged the contribution of women but cited no particular demand for the ordination of women and the difficulty of that ministry as reasons for its decisions. "In view of the variety, the intimacy, the gravity and the burdensome nature of the work of the Ministry on the one side, and in view of the limitations, necessarily involved in the fact of sex on the other, the Assembly is not prepared to direct that women be ordained to the office of the Ministry."[25]

The issue was raised again the next year, this time by a resolution from the Presbytery of Saskatoon. It asked the Assembly "to take such steps as will permit the ordination of women who have completed a full theological course and who are under appointment by a Board of the Church, under the same conditions as obtain for men."[26] A remit sent out by the Assembly and brought back in 1924 showed mixed reactions from the presbyteries who responded. Fifty percent of the polled presbyteries failed to respond and almost half of the group who did respond still favoured no action.

The Methodist Church was also addressing the question. The forerunner to the issue had been an earlier resolution asking for equal rights and privileges for women and men in Church membership. That resolution passed unanimously in 1918 at the Canadian Methodist Assembly but a second resolution, that the ministry be opened to women, caused heated debate. The issue was referred for consideration at the local level in the Quarterly Official Boards.

Nellie L. was given a chance to make her views known at the Methodist Ecumenical Conference in England in 1921. She was the only woman delegate from Canada, and on the eighth day of the conference she was invited to respond to an address entitled, "The Awakening of Women." Accounts of the reaction reveal delighted surprise at her directness. She began by claiming that the title was at best misleading:

The woman of fifty years ago who carded the wool, spun it, wove the cloth to clothe her family, made the clothes without any help from Mr. Butterick or the *Ladies' Pictorial*, brewed her own cordials, baked her own bread, washed, ironed, scrubbed, without any labour-saving devices, and besides this always had the meals on time, and incidentally raised a family, and a few chickens and vegetables in her spare time, may be excused if she did not take much interest in politics, or even know who was likely to be the next Prime Minister. But her lack of interest was not any proof that she was asleep – she was only busy![27]

After expressing her disagreement with the stance the Church usually took on issues affecting women, McClung spoke very specifically on ordination. She suggested that if the ministers who opposed the ordination of women had a real vision of the work of the ministry, they would welcome women to the pulpit. "They confess their inability to deal with the new spirit of unrest among women. They rail at the present fashions and habits of women, and yet in their denunciations they must be conscious of the futility of their censure. Does it never occur to them that though they have failed to reach the women, some one else might be more successful?"[28]

The topic of church union rather overshadowed that of ordination but, after 1925, the issue was brought to the forefront again. The request from Saskatchewan Conference to ordain Lydia Gruchy effectively denied the excuse that there were no eligible female candidates, but it was eleven years before she was finally ordained. Nellie L. was a delegate from Calgary to the General Council held in Winnipeg in September 1928 and became a member of the sessional committee charged to consider the replies from presbyteries on the question of ordination of women and bring a recommendation to the floor. Because of sharp disagreement among the committee's members, the recommendations when they came were not as progressive as many had wished, but they were worded in such a way that the committee members could all support the report. The central declaration asserted that there was "no bar in religion or reasons to the ordination of women to the ministry." No opposition was raised to the report, apparently either because supporters felt that it at least opened the door to future decisions or those in opposition felt that the liberal declaration need never be translated into action. A disappointed Nellie L. declared: "People can be too careful. I heard of a man who could not buy a calendar because he was afraid he would not live the year. I thought this was only a story, until I sat in this committee."[29]

McClung did not abandon the issue. She debated the question in public, wrote articles and gave speeches. She systematically challenged all the justifications for barring women. In a major article in *Chatelaine* in September 1934, she reflected on the 1928 Council and said that she had to sadly admit that the ordination of Lydia Gruchy was "killed" by the indifference of some of the women. When a woman representing the WMS interrupted her prepared statement with an aside that declared it was just as well that the WMS had not been asked its opinion because it would have been very conservative, Nellie said she knew the day was lost. "If the Woman's Missionary Society did not favor ordination of women, the matter was settled. I knew it was the end. An idle word, carelessly spoken, had put back the clock. And how the men who had opposed ordination loved her for her few words!"[30] What made the incident particularly galling was the fact that the woman was only making her personal comment, and was not representing the WMS position!

Lydia Gruchy was finally ordained in 1936, but there is evidence that the whole debate left a lasting mark on McClung. In an essay entitled "The Long Road to Freedom" which appeared in a collection entitled *More Leaves From Lantern Lane* in 1937, she reflected:

It is a long time since Erasmus, in a burst of enthusiasm, said he would wish "that even women might read the Gospels!" but it has taken the full five hundred years to convince the "brethren" and fathers of the Church that women have the same ability to understand the Scriptures as men, and the end is not yet. . . . The United Church of Canada has at last endorsed what Saint Paul said more than eighteen hundred years ago, that there is no 'male or female bound or free', but all are one in the service of God.[31]

Nellie L. McClung's career was just as diverse in the second half of her life as it was during those first forty years spent mainly in Manitoba. She became a member of parliament in Alberta, continued her active participation in the United Church, and expanded her writing into regular newspaper columns. Her involvement in the Person's Case[32] was just one more facet of her struggle for justice. Wherever she went, she left her mark on the communities in which she had lived.

Nellie L. McClung's own words leave us with a vivid impression of her contribution: "Certainly I do not want to pull through life like a thread that has no knot. I want to leave something behind when I go; some small legacy of truth, some word that will shine in a dark place. I never could believe that minding one's own business was much of a virtue; but it's a fine excuse for doing nothing."[33]

Salem Bland, 1912 (Photo courtesy of Western Canada Pictorial Index.)

Salem Bland and the spirituality of the social gospel: Winnipeg and the West, 1903–1913

Richard Allen

The social gospel has been seen by its critics as a superficial movement, concerned only with meliorating social relationships, confusing the redistribution of wealth with the coming of the Kingdom of God and generally divesting the gospel of its spirituality. In the same vein it is easy to view Salem Bland, the Methodist mentor of the social gospel on the prairies, simply in terms of his role in the more obvious moral and social reform causes of the period between 1903 and 1919, his expanding relationship with urban and rural progressivism, and his increasingly radical politics after 1913.[1]

Salem Bland's struggle to fashion a social gospel for the Canadian prairies, however, was nothing less than a quest for a spirituality appropriate to an age of great collective undertakings. The quest was an urgent one and led from the nature of the soul to the meaning of culture, from the devotional life to the arts, from academic study to social action. Life was lived in relationships; grace was everywhere. What Bland fashioned, in effect, was an alternative Protestant ethic, best described by Luther's admonition, "you are each other's priests." The critical years in that quest lay in the ten years that followed his arrival in Winnipeg in 1903.

A PRAIRIE VISION

On 17 September 1903, as newsboys in Winnipeg's dusty streets hawked the Monday afternoon papers with their announcement of his imminent arrival, Salem Bland was near the end of a long serpentine journey across the Laurentian Shield.[2] Three months before, sitting in the study of Eastern Methodist Church in Ottawa, rereading the Pastoral Address of the recent Montreal Conference, he had underlined the words, "The North-West has special demands upon us . . . Methodism has there the opportunity of its history. A springtime has come."[3] He did not know that at summer's end, Dr. J.W. Sparling, principal of Wesley College, Winnipeg, would be standing in that same room demanding that Bland come to his college to teach church history and New Testament. He had asked before. This time he had come in person, and would not be denied. In a matter of days, Bland was on his way.

Remarkably well read and an exceptionally fine preacher, Bland at forty-four was widely regarded as one of the brightest ministers in the Church. He was also radical, a single taxer, a defender of labour's right to organize and a proponent of extensive state provision of cultural amenities and social schemes to equalize conditions in society. He believed that business combination would nurture a more social spirit, but urged cooperation and public ownership as congenial vehicles for that spirit. Bland had been active in prohibition campaigns. He was the president of the Ottawa Lord's Day Alliance, and advocated a union of Protestant churches. He was also – and this may have been the nub of Sparling's determined arguments – immensely popular with young people. The decision to teach at Wesley College had been made, and now he was heading for the open prairie.

Already the prairies had found a place in his vision of an ultimate Protestantism which he was convinced would emerge from the spiritual strife, the intellectual debate and the material struggles of the new century. The immensity of the land ahead conjured for him the image of a pure faith that could exist without reliance on external authority; it would be a faith dependent only on the grace of God. Surely such a country would grow not only great crops but also men and women of large stature and spirit, and a society fresh in its purposes and uncommonly responsive to human need.[4]

THE PROTESTANT ETHIC AND THE COMMERCIAL ELITE

The earliest preoccupations of Europeans on the prairies had, of course, been furs – and then wheat. Churchmen in the West had expressed an uneasiness about the all-consuming passion each of these staple commodities evoked. A Presbyterian colleague of Bland's, Charles W. Gordon, alias Ralph Connor, declared that "the West had not to fight against agnosticism so much as love of wheat. Let a man get filled up with wheat, and you could get nothing else into him, tho' you offered him heaven."[5]

Wheat brought settlers. Following Bland's train into the Winnipeg Canadian Pacific Railway (CPR) station was the 147th immigration train of 1903, bearing 140 Hungarians and Galicians.[6] Wheat brought the expansion of the rail system, land speculation and the transformation of the prairie commons[7] to private property. Wheat brought banking, insurance, investment and marketing services. It brought machinery dealers and hardware chains. Wheat, in short, brought the revolution that incorporated the West into the modern world of commercial and industrial capitalism and subordinated it to the driving centres of investment in central Canada and across the Atlantic.

Bland was not long in meeting the primary agents of this revolution. J.A.M. Aikins, his host during his first weeks in Winnipeg, was founder of the most prestigious law firm in the city, counsel for the Western Division of the CPR, the Department of Justice, solicitor for several banks, and a director of the Imperial Bank and the Great West Life Assurance Company. At the College Board, if not around Aikens' table, he would have met J.H. Ashdown, Board chair and hardware prince of western Canada, who held bank and mining directorships, a founder of the city and of the Board of Trade. R.T. Riley's successful business career had won him the presidency of the Board of Trade and numerous directorships. Rodmond Roblin, the Conservative premier, was on the College Board too, and, because he promoted elevator companies and organized the Ranching and Grain Growing Company, he was legitimately considered a grain merchant.[8]

These men were the patriarchs who had brought Ontario to the banks of the Red, the Assiniboine and the Souris Rivers, overturning the bi-cultural institutions of a society delicately balanced between English and French, Protestant and Catholic, the "bloods" and the "breeds." The victories of municipalities and school districts over parishes, of the old Liberal formula of "rep by pop" over communally based constituencies, and the establishment of public nondenominational school systems had all been their victories.[9]

And these were the men to reckon with in prairie Methodism. Wellschooled in Protestant concepts of the use of time, talent and treasure, they devoted themselves to church, Sunday school and college, to advancing the YMCA and YWCA, to assisting charities, hospitals and the Childrens' Aid. They listened attentively when James Henderson of the Missions Department declared that "the money-power of the world is greatest in Christendom, just because Christianity has given man the best possible control of himself and of the forces of nature around him." But Christian men and women had to Christianize that money-power by imitating the self-giving sacrifice of God: "Your wealth is yourself," Henderson said, and he thought that the secret of the larger life and of greater prosperity was to give more and more and more.[10]

As a group these men were by no means motivated by simple greed or hindered by narrow vision. Aikins, if he can be allowed to speak for them, was concerned about how children could acquire a sense of identity and destiny and become the breed of strong-minded citizens would would mould the nation in righteousness.[11]

The Methodist commercial élite in Winnipeg, however, in the early 1900s, were heirs of highly individualized doctrines of justification by faith and the priesthood of all believers, the Protestant slogans that denied the right of any power to stand between an individual and God. Transformed by the commercial classes of the seventeenth century, the Protestant ethic came to justify the individual manipulation of property, and fuelled the expansion of the spirit of capitalism. The priesthood of all believers became, in effect, a priesthood of property. It now justified a structure of economic relations which Bland increasingly considered unChristian, and it had generated a type of spirituality which, if it satisfied ambitious burghers, was quite inappropriate, he thought, to a new social age.

He was not long in saying so. In the course of three notable and highly acclaimed addresses a month after his arrival, he predicted that prairie society would become one of catholicity and reconciliation, congenial to the new social ideas pushing their way forward in the churches. The older parts of Canada had grown up in an age of individualism, an expansive era that had seen the "crackling and peeling of old restrictions." Liberal freedoms had been a great advance, but many old tyrannies had vanished only to make way for new. The palms had gone to the strong and the powerful, and it had been a hard time for the less able. Was it too much to think, he asked his new public, that, on the prairies, common people should come into their own?

God's word, spoken in the fellowship of prairie churches, he suggested, would lead them to church union. But the spirit of reconciliation could not end there and leave an economy that separated people from each other and divided society into the propertied and the unpropertied. The prairies should be a land of public ownership. He was quite explicit: private enterprise had undertaken what the public had been either too timid or stupid to do, "but we deserved to be fleeced and were great fools if we placed human nature any longer under such circumstances."[12]

The point did not arouse open protest. Perhaps it was lost in the general acclaim for the three addresses whose ideas ranged broadly over the West and the nation, continent and empire. Perhaps the remarks were heard in terms of current sentiment that had created in Winnipeg the first publicly owned asphalt plant in North America. The Winnipeg business community was already eyeing the possibilities of making electric power publicly owned as a way of reducing costs. But Bland's intent clearly went far beyond local business concerns.

He was little concerned with the materialism or petty immorality of the time, which he put down to passing boom conditions. Such behaviour was too easy a mark for successful religious and humanitarian people who otherwise ignored the unChristian network of relationships they were committed to in the world of commerce and industry. Material pursuit was vital and urgent, Bland oberved, and a true spirituality did not reject it, but was concerned with the way in which the pursuit of wealth was ordered. Whether or not Bland's point was taken up at the time, his debate with the commercial élite of prairie Methodism had begun.

THE NEW SPIRITUALITY AT WESLEY COLLEGE

Bland's heroic attempt to fashion an alternative religious vision for the prairies was played out in a number of forums – in the classrooms and extra-curricular activities at Wesley College, in the programs of the Ministerial Association, at the Manitoba and Saskatchewan Conferences of the Church, at summer camps, and through hundreds of speaking engagements throughout the West.

Bland early established a reputation among students for his Sunday morning YMCA conferences at the College, and he was in considerable demand as a speaker at the popular Literary Society meetings, not to mention the Church young people's organizations.

Wesley College students had already been introduced to the social gospel, probably through their YMCA and YWCA organizations which brought them in touch with North American and British student movements. One Wesley College student, in 1898, explaining the significance of missions, touched most of the bases of the new spirituality: "We are knit together by a common brotherhood [in a world] ruled by the creator and a system of reciprocity. [Missions means lifting] our voice in [sic] behalf of our stricken brother [which in turn] lifts our own hearts to a higher plane. . . . Let us get out on the broader field of human interest and affection where we feel the world's anguish and hope and strivings. . . . 'Social solidarity' is a maxim now of sociologists. There is no such thing as purely individual righteousness."[13]

That student's view was entirely consonant with the conviction that Bland himself had struggled to secure for himself, that "culture is an enlargement of experience. It is the power gained . . . to enter into other lives and modes of thought foreign to our own."[14] He cautioned students that if there was anything to be learned from human experience, it was the readiness to foreclose the future, to lower the shades of life, to settle for some little idolatry.[15] They should not let the great gift of self-consciousness arouse an anxiety which could build walls around the self and dam up the tides of life. Nor should they indulge in the "evil dreams of our separateness" from which arose all sorts of oddities and incongruities.

Whether he spoke on the arts, on prayer or on the nature of the soul, Bland sought to convey a sense, both realistic and mystical, that life was lived in relationships. The arts were designed to enlarge human sympathies. The painter drew us into his feelings, the novelist engaged us with the afflictions of others, and the dramatist involved us in personal and social dilemmas of life.[16]

The devotional life, in Bland's view, did not consist simply of two or three seasons of prayer or a half hour of daily Bible readings. Instead, prayer opened the individual soul to the soul of life itself. And reading the great spiritual testaments of the ages opened the mind to the choicest of spirits from Augustine to Wesley. The devotional life entailed fellowship, because God's truth comes to us in fragments and people need to share these fragments with each other. The condition Jesus laid down for his presence was that two or three be gathered together. Bland emphasized that this should not be limited to a cozy circle of like-minded friends, because in principle we can never be complete until we have embraced the Russian, the Oriental and the African philosophies.[17]

Every dimension of life, Bland claimed, offered help in the nourishment of the Christian life. Every mood of nature and the body, even social life and athletics, could be means of grace. And academic study prompted the humble obeisance of the mind before the ordered structure of other minds and of God's world.[18]

God's own strategies were social, Bland claimed. In His plan for the restoration of humanity, God chose a people and a church to nurture the way of reconciliation in the world at large.

Bland was prepared to concede that personality was a separate source of will and action, and he preserved a sense of mystery about the nature of the soul. But he insisted that the soul was not a separate entity like a boiler one could take out, repair and polish, then replace. The soul was not separate from the body or its environment. Salvation, he had long claimed, entailed full health and wholeness of life.[19] It was a false and unChristian spirituality that simply counselled a personal quest of individual blessedness.

Bland was not alone in developing these spiritual dimensions of social Christianity among Wesley College students. Others among the faculty, like William Osborne and W.J. Rose, and local preachers, like A.E. Smith and J.S. Woodsworth, amplified the vision. James Elliott and George Blewett, in Wesley's Chair of Philosophy, systematically drew out the full implications of the vision. Both men were philosophical idealists: Elliott, like Bland, was schooled in his idealism by John Watson at Queens, and Blewett studied at the great centres of idealist thought in Britain and Germany. "God," Blewett said, "is the home of persons." Individuals become persons as they laboriously struggle for a larger consciousness of the good of others or, in other words, as they take up the tasks which affirm membership in the family of God. To do otherwise was to be alienated from the source of one's own life and growth.

Blewett's ultimate vision, like Bland's, was therefore a society in which the attainment of the good by one "consists in its attainment by others, and in the last analysis by all."[20] It followed that social institutions which obstructed that objective were inimical to the spiritual quest of Christians, and merited not submission, but transformation or repudiation. To undertake the task of social change was to find one's proper relation to the larger mind of God. Christianity, in a broad sense, was as inescapably political as it was spiritual.

If this disturbing conclusion led to attacks which charged the social gospel with abandoning a proper spirituality, the evidence remains that Bland and his colleagues were fashioning a spiritual quest on high Christian grounds.

BIBLICAL FOUNDATIONS FOR A WESTERN CITY

Outside the College, Bland's first areas of action were the Methodist Ministerial Association and the Manitoba and Saskatchewan Conferences. His involvement in the Ministerial Association after mid-1904 was possibly the critical – though not the only – element that transformed what had been desultory gatherings into a breaking ground for new thought and a clearing house for concerted action. All the denominations had been scouring the country for a cadre of preachers whose prophetic ministries would indelibly imprint the new West. The Methodist Ministerial Association in Winnipeg in 1904 reflected the results. With the ranking statesmen of the Church in Winnipeg and College men like Bland and Blewett joined with forceful middle-aged and younger figures like J.H. Morgan, Robert Milliken, J.S. Woodsworth and A.E. Smith, the intellectual level of the Association's proceedings leapt dramatically upward. At the end of 1904, theological students were permitted to join student ministers at Ministerial meetings, and the meetings were never the same again.

The range of interest among the group was wide: Bland demonstrated critical methods in the study of Galatians, Blewett spoke on Christian mysticism, and Woodsworth reviewed varieties of religious experience. There were papers called "Labour Organizations and Labour Ideals" and "Socialism and Individualism in Christian Work." Sometimes serving on the program committee, occasionally drawing on his students for reviews, often making presentations, always forcing the pace of discussion, Bland became the dominating presence in the Association for the next half dozen years.[21]

In mid-1904 Bland joined the central figures of this group in launching a western Methodist weekly paper. For some reason the church's official paper, *The Christian Guardian*, had never taken hold in Winnipeg.[22] Other Methodist publishing ventures were sprouting in Victoria and Assiniboia, but the self-consciously progressive Methodist clergy of Winnipeg felt the need of a paper that would chronicle their remarkable growth, monitor western development and articulate the challenges of advanced Protestant thought and reform in the West. With Milliken and Morgan as editor and associate, and Bland contributing and supporting, a twenty-page publication was soon reaching most Methodist homes in the district. Although it eventually lost out to the Victoria-based *Western Methodist Recorder*, the paper vigorously pressed Winnipeg Methodists to "go into the city" and engage themselves with its deepest problems.[23] The city, of course, was Winnipeg.

Few if any of the clergy in Winnipeg had ever experienced the tumult of rapid urban growth which the western boom precipitated in their community. The problem of the city was on all their minds: it was the great collective of the modern age to which they had to address their gospel. On the one hand, urban social problems caused most of them to shift away from preoccupation with a personal gospel, and on the other, the reality of urban divisions challenged central tenets of Bland's social gospel.

The railway had long since split Winnipeg in two, but Bland's arrival coincided with the great CPR expansion which irrevocably divided the city, separating the foreign immigrants and English working-class districts from the middle classes around the business centre of the city and the wealthy along the riverbanks. Industrial conflict escalated as Winnipeg's commercial and industrial base expanded. The immigrant working class was badly abused by housing speculators, employers and by the *Free Press*, which lightheartedly approved of CPR police disciplining them whenever they caused trouble.[24] Civic elections were fought over police efforts to contain "social vice" in the red light district; utilities and transportation barons fought with advocates of public ownership for control of power, gas and street railways; and debate on private property rights impeded the sanitary reforms necessary to keep small-pox, diphtheria, tuberculosis, and especially typhoid, at bay.

Despite the reality that confronted him, and despite the agrarian bias of many of his co-religionists, Bland held a large and hopeful view of the city. It was easy, he thought, to see the city only in terms of its darker aspects. But the existence of homes, hospitals, schools and missions had to be acknowledged as well as the squalor, illness, ignorance and immorality, and the most delicate refinements of culture alone with slums and taverns. The city was the centre of the greatest intensity and variety of relationships and of the greatest intellectual activity of the land. It was "the birthplace of reforms and revolutions, the fountainhead of change." Ultimately, the city was not so much a product of economic acquisitiveness as it was of human sociability, in which people ministered, however imperfectly, to each other's needs. The Bible could be cited to legitimate such views. It declared that the highest wisdom "uttereth her voice in the streets; she crieth in the chief place of concourse, in the opening of the gates. . . ." The Jews left the villages for the cities of Capernaum and Jerusalem, Bland observed. Indeed, although the Biblical drama began in a garden, it ended in the city.[25]

In 1905, as Bland stepped up the pace of his public activity, he enlarged on the challenge of urban reform thrown out by the new Methodist paper. In Moose Jaw, Winnipeg, Carman, Emerson and Portage la Prairie he sketched the characteristics required of the new "saints for the age," and outlined the evolutionary roots of and prospects for a cooperative social order.[26] Before a Christian endeavour youth rally in Winnipeg he presented his mandate of Christian socialism and laid out a comprehensive program for an urban reform administration which included: reservation of parks and riverbands for the people; sanitary reform and municipal ownership; more and better schools, hospitals and asylums, municipal art galleries, libraries and free concerts; and, adequate wages for workers and recognition of trade unions.[27] Not surprisingly, the Winnipeg Labour Council soon asked him to address them. By mid-1905, when the Union of Canadian Municipalities met in Winnipeg, Bland launched a series of sermons about the city.

The urgency of civic social action inspired the Manitoba Conference of the Church in June; the Winnipeg District called for support for the new newspaper, for institutional urban church work, and for putting All Peoples' Mission on a proper legal basis so it could get on with the formidable task of serving North Winnipeg. William Osborne and Robert Milliken organized a committee to develop a movement for municipal political action based on the activities of the Epworth Clubs and the Young Men's Clubs of the Church.[28]

While Bland associated himself with Osborne's Municipal League, which at the end of 1905 went into action on the issue of prostitution, he was quick to castigate the middle class for its "out of sight, out of mind" position on prostitution, and berated segregationists who wanted to restrain the police on the issue of prostitution but who would at the same time unleash the police on the slightest perpetrator of a crime against property.[29] And at St. Stephen's Young Men's Club, amid the December campaign, he said that it was the great disparity of wealth which was the central economic issue facing the city, called once more for the widest possible extension of public ownership, and declared that an inspired people, in company with God would remake the city in terms of its own underlying cooperative spirit.[30]

The inspiration that prompted these quests lay, for Bland, in that foundation of radical monotheism in western culture, the Bible. At both the Manitoba and Saskatchewan Conferences, therefore, he established a year-round program of modern Bible study for members. The topics for discussion, the readings and the approach bore directly upon the cause of reform: Amos holding the plumb-line to crooked structures of power; the Sermon on the Mount with its reversal of priorities of the present age; James on the perils of private wealth for the soul; Paul on the unity of spirit amid a diversity of traits and talents. All were critical to mounting a reform campaign of broad, basic and durable proportions in Winnipeg and the West in the decade prior to World War I.[31]

THE RELEVANCE OF THE KINGDOM OF GOD

For Bland, himself, as his teaching progressed and as he tried to encompass a larger reality, the search for biblical foundations for the social gospel was an ongoing quest of huge proportions. He read voraciously on New and Old Testament themes, in church history and apologetics, in philosophy and social criticism, not to mention general history, biography and fiction.[32]

Once a devotee of Paul, Bland had come to appreciate how far Paul's rigorous training as a Pharisee in Hebraic law, the peculiar nature of his conversion, his long, fierce conflict with the Judaizers of the early church and the Colossian heretics had deeply influenced, and limited, his articulation of the gospel. Up to a point, Paul's Christology could be harmonized with an evolutionary world view, with which Bland's generation was absorbed. Paul's lack of interest in the life and teachings of Jesus, however, his fascination with the death of Jesus, his struggle with the Judaic law, his clear separation of divine and human natures, and his elaborate theology all ran in another direction.

For a time, the fourth Gospel, the Book of John, provided a more congenial theological ground on which to gather social Christian arguments. It was indeed quite natural that the evolutionary idealism which so much impressed Bland in the mid-1890s should lead him into long and serious study of the Book of John, with its theme of life-giving incarnation. John portrayed Christ as springing from the original source of life, which he so fully represented that he himself was the source of abundant life. More than Paul, John read the character of Christ back onto God, so that God was clearly seen as self-giving love. Moreover, John's naturalistic images of vine and branches nicely fitted social themes and an evolutionary scheme. Not only was all this more congenial to Bland's purposes, but John himself, like Bland, had undertaken to render the gospel in new clothing for a new generation. The appeal is not surprising. John's words were addressed to the neo-Platonic idealists of Asia Minor. In short, John appeared to be the relevant gospel for the new century. But Winnipeg, the labour movement and the writings of Adolph Harnack, the great German scholar, changed that in 1905.

The hard reality of social problems in Winnipeg sat in such utter contrast to John's elegant metaphor of the word becoming flesh that by 1906 Bland was speaking of him as walking the world on tiptoe.[33] Bland's encounter with the Winnipeg Labour Council in 1905 was his first engagement with serious Marxists. He was asked to present his reform Darwinist address, "Four Steps and a Vision," and the effect of the resulting debate was such that he did not deliver the piece again.[34] Although he never fully adopted historical materialism, he maintained an ongoing respectful relationship with the Labour Council which encouraged the growing realism and radicalism of his religious and social thought. From that point on he appears to have joined the growing debate over the adequacy of idealism as a master philosophy for the age.[35]

It was Adolph Harnack, however, who shifted the centre of Bland's New Testament interest from John to the "historical Jesus" of the synoptic gospels with their recurrent metaphor, the Kingdom of God. Bland read Harnack's immensely influential book *What is Christianity?* in 1905, and in early 1906, in an exciting address, he harnessed Harnack's concept of the Kingdom of God to the cause of urban reform.[36]

By 1900, New Testament scholarship had isolated the Parables in Matthew, Mark and Luke as the core of the teaching of Jesus – and the idea of the Kingdom of God as the key to the Parables. The Parables were immediate and earthy. They dealt directly with the daily inter-personal encounters, and expressed God's sovereignty.

Bland's excitement over the connection of a political analogy like the Kingdom of God with the heartland of Jesus's teachings is evident in the ideas that tumbled over each other in his addresses to the Ministerial Association and the Saskatchewan Conference in 1906. This clearly biblically based idea thereafter displaced reform Darwinist arguments in his promotion of the Christian social reform. This shift to a more biblical apologetics for the social gospel was widespread in North America at the time, but Bland articulated it directly from its European roots and not from its American branches; the Canadian social gospel was not just a reflection of its American counterpart.

Bland was not above creating his own parables addressed to the clashing movements of the time: "Watch the big press in the *Free Press* basement – so complicated, things moving in all directions at once, yet with no clash, no check, no destruction." God's kingdom was an organized world, Bland declared, and the teaching which proclaimed it was a "doctrine of social Christianity summing up all schemes of social reform, all municipal and national action, gathering them up into one organic whole, rooting them in Christ."[37]

Bland's reading of Harnack's works did not, however, cause him to adopt Harnack's rather courtly moderation in social reform. For one thing, Harnack "arrived" in Winnipeg on the eve of the street railway and Vulcan Iron Works strikes which initiated twelve years of intense industrial conflict in the city. But quite apart from that radicalizing development, unlike Harnack, who largely disposed of the Old Testament, Bland maintained his footing in the prophets even while he kept his eye on the New Jerusalem of the Book of Revelation. The result was a growing radicalism of which Harnack would hardly have approved.

Nonetheless, there remained in Bland's character and in his thought – and hence in his teaching of the social gospel – an unresolved but engaging tension between the spacious concepts of the "larger consciousness" born ultimately of Greek idealism and the temporally urgent ones born of Hebraic prophecy and apocalyptic. Those varied moods of cultural reflection and social compulsion endured to enrich the Christian social movement in Canada.

THE RENEWING SPIRIT AND PRAIRIE POLITICS

The Winnipeg campaign for civic righteousness – which saw Protestant clerics and laymen involved in moral and sanitary reform issues, conciliating industrial conflict, campaigning for public power, women's suffrage, and reform of civic government – merged in 1905 with provincial politics. The Roblin government, whose liquor policies were increasingly unacceptable to moral reformers, would have eventually to face the electorate, and clerical activists and their principal lay supporters were soon in the thick of political battle. Critics wondered whether political preachers were not betraying historic Protestantism, sowing discord in the church, and compromising themselves with political entanglements.

The issues for Bland – as for many – went well beyond temperance concerns. Roblin's one attraction was his interest in public ownership of utilities, but his penchant for selling land to individual and corporate speculators, rather than selling directly and cheaply to settlers themselves, opened up yawning possibilities of corruption (which indeed marked the rest of Roblin's years in office). Bland attacked Roblin in an open letter, and his name was blazoned in the headlines; Aikens made an abortive effort to have Bland removed from his post at the College.[38] Whatever the influence of Bland's intervention in the campaign, Roblin won handily.

By 1906 Bland was in heavy demand as a speaker throughout Manitoba and Saskatchewan. His own graduates were now fanning out across the prairies. They claimed him as the single most influential person of their college years, and were always forceful in duplicating his message. They and others called for his presence, and he responded until time and energy gave out.

"Come if you can, Doctor," wrote John Lane of Swan River in May 1907, "we do not often have college men come to the frontier points."[39] E.S. Whittaker of the Moose Jaw YMCA importuned Bland to lead Bible study at a young people's summer school being inaugurated that summer. Local preachers lacked the power to inspire young people, he said and, "if we can have a part of the good things the East is enjoying all the time, we will be happy." Would Bland come and "help us launch this new order of Christian culture for the West?"[40]

So the requests came in: people were hungry for inspiration, full of hope as to what the West might become if it were shaped properly. Many requests had to be refused. Since 1904 Bland had been accepting almost fifty invitations a year to speak and preach. In 1907 requests came from Moose Jaw to Toronto, and in 1908 they came even from the west coast.

Some of the western brothers in the Methodist ministry – Wellington Bridgeman at Neepawa, for example – were affronted by the elements of modernism creeping into the western pulpit, and expressed their "frustration and anger when faced with things arising out of metropolitan sophistication."[41] The heavy demand for Bland's services, however, suggests that it was not the predominant mood of the pre-war prairies to beat a retreat before the modern world. Bland's promotion of church union, a major part of his message to the gathered congregations at prairie points, was a case in point. He spent no time on the economics of multiple congregations in small towns, but linked the prairie experience to the mixing of creeds and cultures throughout the world. Comprehensiveness was necessary in the church as never before, and with it a new receptiveness to other traditions. Where oriental or immigrant cultures were consistent with Christianity, it was necessary to endorse them, he suggested, and he cited historic and biblical authority.

The task, Bland said, was to discover what was "vital – common – universal – always – and around this to gather the educated and the simple of every class and race." In linking this task with "the spirit of these broad-flung prairies," Bland presented the church union movement as part of the destiny that called his listeners to be both prairie people and modern men and women. It was a compelling challenge. That he thought them capable of it was a flattery they could hardly ignore.[42]

Whether it was at Crystal City, Cypress River, Stonewall, Neepawa, Holland or Carberry, local presses sang the praises of his captivating style and the substance of his message: "The popularity of Dr. Bland is sure to draw large congregations," the *Selkirk Weekly Record* announced;[43] *The Killarney Guide* observed that "as a speaker he is bright, attractive, forceful, and profound"; "The Doctor is known throughout the West," it added, "as a great student of social and political problems."[44]

Bland's widespread preaching engagements brought him into extensive contact with local leaders of the Manitoba and Saskatchewan Grain Grower's Associations which expanded rapidly between 1903 and 1913. Their mounting power, their rootedness in prairie Protestantism and their indefatigable promotion of the cooperative ideal tempted Bland, as it did others, to think in terms of a new party that would regenerate politics in Canada. Invited to address the provincial conventions in 1912 and 1913, he came close in Saskatchewan of provoking a decision to initiate a third party.[45]

While both church union and the "new politics" would have to await the conclusion of the World War I, both projects were symbols by 1913 of the desire for an institutional break with the past which Bland's social and religious visions helped to generate. The new spirituality of the social gospel was in search of new wineskins.

A TIME FOR DECISION

In Winnipeg and at the College, other developments were pressing Bland to a break of a similar order. The social problems of Winnipeg multiplied with the forced pace of rapid growth. If the "instant duty of Christianizing the social, economic and political order," as he put it in 1908,[46] was not to be dissipated, solid information and clear social thinking were urgent. In 1907, addressing the first convocation of the University of Saskatchewan, Bland had called for courses of sociological study in the new institution. The next year the issue became a live one at the Manitoba Conference of the Church, and Bland was soon involved in setting up such a program at Wesley College.

A great laboratory for the study of social problems lay at hand in the North End. Young J.S. Woodsworth, who was assigned to All People's Mission just north of the tracks in 1907, was already involving students in social studies, urging them to go on and form a social settlement, live among the immigrants, learn their language, and help them fight their battles. Such

an immersion would lead to critical examination of the structure of society –
and to its reconstruction.[47] Bland was close to Woodsworth from 1907 to
1913, when Woodsworth left All People's. He was frequently at the Mission,
and shared with Woodsworth an increasingly warm attachment to the Winnipeg labour movement.

In 1910, when another provincial election was anticipated, Bland called
for a new workers' party in the province.[48] In May, when the Manitoba
Labour Party was formed, it very nearly won a seat with Fred Dixon as
candidate, but went into decline thereafter.

The extent of Bland's association with labour in Winnipeg was not
entirely clear, but his growing interest in farm and labour politics coincided
with a declining participation in the Methodist Ministerial Association. In a
significant sermon, delivered early in 1911, entitled "The Christ without the
Camp," he suggested that one of the essential ideas of Christianity is that
Christ is ever outside the settled places and practices of society, and in every
age calls his followers into the lonely unknown places of which it is only
known that He is there."[49] A new note of anxiety appeared in his sermons,
that is, that the Church had become too settled, too encrusted – even too
heavenly (heaven, too, could become one of those settled places, a habitual
category) – to respond to the call of the spirit. The Church had to come down
from the clouds and break out of its institutional confines to regain its
vitality.[50]

It was now evident to Bland that, to become a movement again, Christianity also had to disentangle itself from the existing economic order, many, if
not most, of whose protagonists sat in the pews of the churches. Among those
property owners who refused to share civic political power with non-property
owners were some prosperous church members. They were prominent among
those who contested the attempts of working people to organize and bargain
collectively, without which workers were forever divided against each other in
a "free market" of labour. And there were some wealthy members of the big
churches, as Woodsworth's experience in North Winnipeg made plain, whose
prosperity was bought at the expense of Winnipeg's newcomers, who were
charged exhorbitant rents for confined, insubstantial and unsanitary quarters.

In 1903, on coming to Winnipeg, Bland had asked "whether the evangelical churches are going to show a spirituality strong enough for the strain that
is coming on them. [They] have to accommodate the greater number of the
wealthy and official classes, which they never had to do before. Will they
remain true to their traditions of spirituality?"[51]

By 1913 the answer was reasonably clear: it was time for plain speaking
and confrontation. The question was not just whether there would be further

social progress, but whether the Church would be part of it. Clear divisions were the order of the day.

Asked to preach at Grace Church, Winnipeg's wealthiest Methodist congregation, in August 1913, Bland unleashed an uncompromising assault on the state of the Church. Using Winston Churchill's recent novel, *The Inside of the Cup*, he held up the mirror image of a congregation generously supporting good causes – missions, charity, hospitals – while their daily economic actions dispirited, deprived and diseased the poor. Shocked by the recognition that his church largely represents forces opposed to real Christianity, the minister in the novel turns from inoffensive orthodoxy to militant revolt. The church, Bland declared, was still the hope of the world – but novelists, not preachers, are stating the new ethical standards of our age, and socialists and single taxers are exhibiting the enthusiasm Christians once had. All Christians had to share the blame for allowing economic conditions to become so corrupt that "you cannot expect a businessman to live a Christian life today . . . . We must begin the great work of attacking all the cruelties of our commercial life, all the rascalities of high finance, all the abominations of our political system."[52] Bland's sub-title made the issue entirely clear: "Religion no substitute for Justice." The point was not that religion was superfluous, but that the radical monotheism to which Bland subscribed elevated justice above the trappings of religion.

There is no record that Bland was ever invited to preach at Grace Church again. But it was not because the radical social gospel which Salem Bland had fashioned in his first ten years in Winnipeg had abandoned Christian spirituality for entirely secular schemes and superficial nostrums. It was rather because a rich and profound spirituality, at once traditional and modern, would not permit him to speak other than he did. Whether or not the commercial élite of Winnipeg would be overthrown, they had at least met their match, and an alternative Protestant ethic in Canada was well on its way to becoming the spirit of Canadian socialism.

The Labor Church in Winnipeg

Vera Fast

When J.S. Woodsworth wrote "The Old Order changes and so also one's ideas of God. . . . As with the ideas of God, so with the idea of worship . . . ,"[1] he was reflecting upon a spiritual evolution which had occupied him and others like him for many years, an evolution which in Manitoba eventually gave birth to the Winnipeg Labor Church.

The conception of the Labor Church lay in the heritage of the social gospel movement. It is beyond the scope of this paper to detail all that is involved in the term *social gospel*.[2] Certainly its theological roots lay deep in reactions to seventeenth-century Protestant scholasticism: pietism, rationalism, and especially, British idealism.[3] In simplistic terms, pietism provided resistance to an entrenched orthodoxy; rationalism encouraged an emphasis on Christianity's social and ethical commitments; and British idealism contributed a mixture of empiricism and idealism, found in the writings of T.H. Green and Edward Caird, among others, who taught that the developing moral self-consciousness of humans combined with equality and kinship were the highest ideals desired by God.[4] In essence then, "the social gospel rested on the premise that Christianity was a social religion, concerned . . . with the quality of human relations on this earth. . . . It was a call for men to find the meaning of their lives in seeking to realize the Kingdom of God in the very fabric of society."[5] From this common background emerged three divergent emphases: the conservative, progressive and radical.[6] Conservatives stressed personal ethical issues, saw sin as individual wrongdoing and advocated legislation as a means of reform. Radicals, on the other hand, viewed society as so saturated with evil that personal salvation without social reconstruction was impossible, but for such a gargantuan task, the activities of the immanent God were immediately available. From this latter group sprang those who later advocated

Marxist solutions, both economic and political, to bring about societal reconstruction. The vast majority of social gospellers, the progressives, fell between
these two extremes; they assimilated aspects of both platforms but transmit-
ted them, as Richard Allen puts it, "in a broad ameliorative programme of
reform."[7]

Although elements of all three positions were undoubtedly found within
the ranks of the Labor Church, it was comprised largely of progressives and
radicals. Men such as J.S. Woodsworth, Salem Bland and William Ivens were
certainly progressives, while A.E. Smith stood staunchly with the radicals, as
did R.B. Russell and William (Bill) A. Pritchard. The tensions and polariza-
tions created by this dichotomy proved to be a factor in the demise of the
"Humane, lovable and progressive religion" which the Labor Church sought
to disseminate.

BACKGROUND OF THE LABOR CHURCH

J.S. Woodsworth, a Methodist minister, very early in his career had problems
with the traditional doctrines of the historical church.[8] After attempting to
resign from the ministry in 1907, he was appointed superintendent of All
Peoples' Mission in Winnipeg, and from this base sought to implement his
philosophy that true Christianity must identify itself with those who are
oppressed. He saw workers and immigrants, and above all, *alien* immigrants
as the "oppressed," and he analyzed one cause of their misery as their
alienation from religion. "Alas," he wrote, "this is the most serious danger
which besets our immigrants – the loss of the old faith in the new land."[9]

In 1910, seeking to alter this situation, Woodsworth organized Sunday
afternoon meetings known as the People's Forum, which provided, in his
words, a "pleasant and profitable" afternoon for those who had no place to
go, and at the same time attempted to "break down racial, national, religious,
political and social prejudice" among the various nationalities.[10] There were
lectures on scientific, economic and social subjects, as well as entertainment,
while "a religious atmosphere was not lacking, the effect in part, perhaps, of
the oft-repeated motto, 'Thou shalt love the Lord thy God and thy neighbour
as thyself.' "[11]

A popular speaker at the Peoples' Forum was Salem Bland of Wesley
College, a convinced and eloquent advocate of the social gospel.[12] Another
was A.E. Smith of Brandon, a fellow Methodist clergyman, equally concerned with social justice, who felt that "the Gospel of Jesus was the proclamation of a new social order of human society,"[13] and that Jesus "was to be
cherished because he died as a leader of the people, for his principles and in
protest against the unjust rulers of his day."[14]

The influence of these men – Woodsworth, Bland and Smith – upon William Ivens, the founder of the Labor Church, is difficult to exaggerate for, as a theology student at Wesley College, Ivens was magnetized by the brilliance of Salem Bland, he was a friend and admirer of Woodsworth, and he was the successor to Rev. A.E. Smith at McDougall Methodist Church in Winnipeg.

Ivens assumed his pastorate at McDougall Methodist Church in 1916 with great promise and the self-imposed task of reaching workers who were not attending church but were still interested in religion. The message was clear, said Ivens, that "only through the common people, the world of labour, would the re-Christianization of the church and Christianization of society take place."[15] With A.E. Smith as predecessor and with Woodsworth and Bland both active in city pulpits, this obviously was not a new message, either for Methodism in general or for McDougall Methodist in particular, and had Canada not been at war, Ivens could conceivably have enjoyed a long and successful ministry at McDougall. However, Canada *was* at war, and as the issue of conscription intensified, Ivens's unabashed pacifism became an exceedingly irritating thorn in the flesh of McDougall's Official Board.

Woodsworth shared Ivens's views on militarism and though neither used the pulpit on more than a few occasions to voice their convictions, both used the public press and personal speaking engagements to speak out energetically against the hostilities. In their pacifism, Ivens and Woodsworth stood alone among leading Methodist ministers,[16] for even Ivens' mentor, Salem Bland, staunchly supported Canada's war effort.

In the face of such clashing ideals and the emotionalism inherent in times of conflict, the tension at McDougall Methodist Church in 1918 became, understandably, intolerable. The board and a great majority of the congregation felt strongly, along with other Methodists, that Canada's involvement in World War I was just, a cause blessed by God. The pastor felt equally strongly that all war was wrong and that the highest form of patriotism was obedience to the spirit of the gospel of Christ, whatever the price.

Added to this was the uneasy matter of Ivens's involvement with labour, both in his efforts to church the workers and his active participation in the Dominion Labor Party as well as in local labour and union activities.

Antagonisms congealed. On 21 March 1918 the McDougall Methodist Quarterly Board met and by a vote of eleven to two asked Ivens to resign. When he refused, the matter was referred to the Stationing Committee of the Manitoba Methodist Conference. Although petitions and letters were received on Ivens's behalf, the Stationing Committee decided to remove him from McDougall Methodist and offered him another charge in Winnipeg. Obviously they were not hostile and did not censure his religious views, his

William Ivens c. 1890 (Photo courtesy of Western Canada Pictorial Index.)

ability or recent speeches and activities.[17] But from Ivens's statement to the Board that dismissal from McDougall would mean leaving the ministry, it was also quite apparent that he would refuse another station (since *any* church would share McDougall's view of the war) and that he felt bitter over what he considered a lack of freedom to express his convictions.

Ivens, at his own request, was left "without station" for a year and in August 1918 accepted the editorship of the *Western Labor News (WLN)*. At the same time he gathered a group of friends around him and commenced the organization of a labour church. When the case was reviewed a year later, his request to be left again without station was denied, and on refusal to accept a charge, he was located, that is, deprived of his position as a Methodist minister. By now, however, the Winnipeg Labor Church was well established and was the focus of his interest and energy.

FORMATION AND FORMAT OF THE
WINNIPEG LABOR CHURCH

The concept of a labour church was not new. In Manchester, England, John Trevor, convinced that God was now working through the labour movement as He had once worked through the Church, formed an organization in 1891 which he envisaged as the means by which its members "consciously co-operated with God in the process of human evolution," and which he named the Labor Church.[18] For a time it proved immensely popular, and it is likely that Canadian labour churches were patterned after this British experience. Surprisingly, however, there is at present no documentary evidence to support this contention. However, the literature does contain casual references to British labour speakers, hymn books were purchased in England and Sunday School teachers with "Old Country experience" were sought. These facts indicate a very real influence, even if not an overt connection with the British labour experience.[19]

In any case, no one single cause for the formation of Winnipeg's Labor Church can be isolated. Rather, it was the end result of "experience with people's forums, social gospel preaching and religious socialism,"[20] as well as disenchantment with the organized churches' stance on participation in war and, in Woodsworth's view, a "revolt against denominationalism and formality and commercialism in the churches – a hunger after righteousness and spiritual truth."[21] Out of this background and with these high ideals, William Ivens met with a group of the like-minded on 8 July 1918, in room 10 of the Winnipeg Labor Temple. S.J. Farmer, future leader of the Manitoba Cooperative Commonwealth Federation (CCF Party) and then head of the Dominion Labor Party, chaired the gathering while Ivens gave the message. Two hundred enthusiastic people that day signed cards reading: "I am willing to support an independent and creedless Church based on the Fatherhood of God and the Brotherhood of Man. Its aim shall be the establishment of justice and righteousness among men of all nations."[22] The motto of the new organization was to be, "If any man will not work, neither shall he eat."

Immediately upon formal organization, the Labor Church plunged into a delirium of activity. Church notices in the *One Big Union* (*OBU*) *Bulletin* of 1919 and the *WLN* of 1918–19 promoted women's guilds, young people's societies, study classes on Thursday and Friday evenings (with subjects such as public speaking, economics and industrial history), choirs and orchestras. On Sundays, besides the regular services, there were "religious classes" and "economics education" classes. When J.S. Woodsworth joined the organization as secretary in 1921, he conducted many of the educational programs personally, considering instruction of the working class to be of prime importance. He also formulated a unique Sunday School curriculum, combining the teachings of socialism with those of Scripture. One section, for example, is labelled "The Fight with the Machine: (a) Tools of production in the hands of a few: (b) The new slavery – men, women, children; (c) The work of Jesus, Luke 4:18."[23]

Labor Church services were characterized by informality and freedom of expression. Woodsworth described them as opening "with devotional exercises, more or less after the Methodist form, but the platform was open to anyone with a message and there was considerable freedom of discussion."[24]

The WLN of 22 August 1919 provides more detail: "The meeting was opened with a selection by the orchestra . . . the audience sang a labor hymn. The reading of a prayer printed in the program by J.S. Woodsworth in which the audience joined, followed by a reading of a Psalm by Dr. Bland. The choir . . . rendered Gounod's 'Nazareth.' "

The press reports such responses in the Labor Church as clapping, even after prayers, audibly voiced expressions of approval or disapproval, and occasional booing and laughing. Sermon topics were as unfettered as behaviour was, and ranged from "The Immorality of the Profit System" (7 February 1919, Wm. Ivens), to "The Old Time Religion – Is It Good Enough for Me?" (20 November 1920, W.D. Bayley), to "Shelley as a Revolutionary Thinker" (29 March 1923, J.A. Cherniak). At one branch there was a series of lectures on health ("The Human Body, Its Health and Its Diseases"), while another had a series called "Evolution in the Light of Modern Knowledge." Topics and speakers were endlessly varied and each branch was free to choose both.

Labor Church services have been described as political meetings held in a religious setting, their tone illustrated by the frequently sung labour hymn:

When wilt thou save the people, Lord,
O God of mercy, when?
The people, Lord, the people,
Not crowns and thorns, but men.[25]

William Ivens also composed hymns which appear in the *People's Church Hymns*, without identification. One of these, untitled, particularly reflects the strident socialism of the Church:

We knelt before kings, we bent before lords;
For theirs were the crowns, and theirs were the swords;
But the times of the bending and bowing are past,
And the day of the people is dawning at last!

We cringed before gold, we deified wealth;
We laid on its altar the life and the health
Of manhood and womanhood, childhood and youth;
But its lordship is doomed in this day of the truth.

The strength of the state will lavish no more
Than making of wealth and making of war;
We are learning at last, though the lesson comes late,
That the making of man is the task of the state.

Great day of Jehovah, prophets and seers
Have sung of thy coming thousands of years.
Thank God for each sign that the dark night is past;
And the day of the people is dawning at last.[26]

In addition to writing hymns, Ivens was a very popular speaker, a distinction he shared with Woodsworth, W.D. Bayley and Fred Dixon.[27] Women figured largely among those for whom the day was dawning at last, as might be expected in Manitoba during this heady period. They also became popular speakers. A Miss Flett, sister to Mrs. Fred Dixon, carried the suffrage banner, and from the Labor Church pulpit "pleaded with women, the newly enfranchised electors, to spend their time informing themselves on the national issues so that injustice might be wiped from the face of the earth. . . ."[28] The Church was also addressed by Agnes McPhail, first woman member of parliament from Ontario, Elsa Brandstrom from Sweden and, of course, the energetic and devoted Beatrice Brigden, who assumed major responsibility for the Brandon Church after A.E. Smith's departure. Such leaders' wives as Lucy Woodsworth, Mrs. Fred Dixon and a Mrs. Hancock were frequent speakers at branch churches, and while positions of power were firmly occupied by men, women were given more prominence in the Labor Church than they were in any other major denomination during that period.

For men or women who wished to associate formally with the group, William Ivens asserted that basis for membership did not "rest upon a belief in a theological syllogism. Anyone . . . shall be eligible for membership who believes in the need and possibility of a better day for human society, and who is willing to make some systematic, consistent and constructive contributions of thought, time, influence and means toward that end. . . ."[29] This declaration of intent is so broad as to be virtually meaningless, but it does give credence to Richard Allen's statement that "Ivens may not have believed that one man's religious testament was as valuable as any other's, but this was the tendency in his thought. In his rebellion against the authoritarianism of 'dogmatic religion' . . . Ivens' grip on any principle of authority was dangerously weakened."[30]

The Labor Church did not adhere to a creed but it did endorse a statement of faith:

We the members and supporters of the Labor Church believe:

1 That the Labor Church came into being, not by the will of any one individual, but in response to a far-reaching desire on the part of the common, toiling people, for a broad-minded, social religious organization, to champion their cause, and to provide expression, in a congenial social atmosphere, for their ideals and longings for freedom, justice and truth.

2 That justice, equity, righteousness, a square deal to every man, a practical, co-operative brotherhood, in the economic as well as in every other realm of life, are the foundations and essentials of religion.

3 That the person who possesses a passion to make these a reality in all departments of human society and life is in the truest sense a religious person, worthy of fellowship with any and all religious people, and that all such should be welcomed to the fellowship of the church.

4 That a person's theological views are a personal affair with which no one has a right to interfere, and that each person must be free to his own interpretation of Truth.

5 That genuine practical love for humanity, based on truth and experience, is the proper and sufficient guiding principle of life.

6 That the present system of society by which a person can obtain an income or amass a fortune out of the industry of the worker, without directly or indirectly doing any productive work, is essentially unjust and immoral.

7 That it is the first duty of the church to point out and denounce this injustice and wrong and to blaze the way to a system that shall be essentially just and moral.[31]

While these statements contain social and political implications as well as moral obligations, they have no theological strength and reflect the social gospel movement in its vaguest and most fluid form. This was perceived by some of its leaders, and J.S. Woodsworth verbalized the concern when he addressed a group at the Strand Theatre in 1920. He realized that there were those within the Labor Church, he said, who had not questioned the doctrines of the established denominations, and there were those who "had imbibed the ultra materialistic doctrines of the self-styled 'Scientific Marxian School' of Socialism. They rejected all religion as superstition. The majority were betwixt and between." He continued, "While the Labor Church refuses to be bound by dogmas, we believe it is essentially in line with the teachings and spirit of Jesus of Nazareth." Then he presented a statement which seems to have been the closest the Labor Church ever came to formulating a theological statement of faith. He referred to the aspirations of the Labor Church as the "religion of the future," and that it was to be:

(1) *Progressive* – dynamic not static; (2) *Scientific* in its spirit and methods . . . not afraid of the truth; (3) *Practical.* . . . Right relationships with our fellow men are more important than speculative Orthodoxy . . . ; (4) *Social* in character. . . . The emphasis is on social salvation; (5) It will be *Universal.* When we evolve a religion that is big enough and broad enough and loving, it will make a universal appeal.

He elaborated:

The Labor Church believed in "A spiritual interpretation of life; a continually developing humanity and religion; the establishment on the earth of an era of justice, truth and love. The Labor Church Stands For: (1) *Fellowship.* We welcome all men and women irrespective of creed, class or race; (2) *Education.* We seek to know and spread the truth . . . ; (3) *Inspiration.* By association we stimulate one another to truer thoughts, higher aspirations and nobler living.[32]

In discussing this "religion of labour," Douglas Pratt writes:

God seldom was described in personal terms but rather as an immanent power propelling the world onward and upward toward a more just social order – the power that was at work in the Labor movement. . . . Jesus' humanity was stressed and he was described as differing from all great teachers in degree but not in kind. . . . Pauline theology was viewed as a corruption of the simple gospel. . . . The Kingdom of God was defined as "social salvation" . . . [while] ethics were dependent on knowledge; . . . immortality "a subject on which one must suspend judgment, awaiting further scientific evidence"; and prayer was autosuggestion because "each person must answer his own prayers."[33]

One of the side effects, as it were, of these efforts by the Labor Church leaders to develop their own religious philosophy was the questioning of the practice of traditional forms of worship and discipline. One of these practices was the saying of "Grace before Meat." W.A. Pritchard "ridiculed the idea of praying for daily bread when the workers produced all. What would they think of a band of hungry wolves who caught one by one a heap of jack rabbits and then, fixing their eyes upon the north star, said, 'Give us this day our daily bread.' "[34] After experiencing similar reactions against the practice, Woodsworth formulated the following table prayer: "We are thankful for these and all the good things of life. We recognize that they are a part of our common heritage and come to us through the efforts of our brothers and sisters the world over. What we desire for ourselves we wish for all. To this end may we take our share in the world's work and the world's struggles."[35]

In addition to the new form of table prayer, Woodsworth wrote that the "Church is considering the advisability of some sort of dedicatory service to take the place of the conventional 'Christening' . . . [and] we have not yet evolved a 'prohibition' method of expressing good fellowship (as in the drinking of toasts)."[36] Certainly, a strenuous effort was being exerted to "make all things new" and meaningful.

THE WINNIPEG GENERAL STRIKE AND THE LABOR CHURCH

J.S. Woodsworth wrote that "the Labor Church of today is essentially one of the products of the strike." The remark must be taken in context, but certainly there was a direct relationship between the growth of the Church and the Winnipeg General Strike of 1919. Although a study of the strike is outside the scope of this paper, it is necessary to consider a few details to show how the lives of the Labor Church leaders and people were interwoven with those of the strikers. In many cases these people were one and the same.

The strike began on 1 May 1919 and became general on 15 May. There are various interpretations of the causes but generally it is now agreed that the strike grew spontaneously and that the demands of the workers were reasonable.[37] However, emotions were running high on both sides and William Ivens was frequently the instigator of controversy. Richard Allen says "that while reports of Ivens proclaiming a Soviet rule in Winnipeg 'emanated from hostile sources,' " and "although it is impossible to find anything overtly seditious in Ivens' writings there is little doubt at all that he was often injudicious."[38]

J.S. Woodsworth, not resident in Winnipeg in 1919, had previously arranged to come for meetings, and on 8 June he arrived according to schedule. The next day, Rev. Dr. McLean of First Presbyterian Church noted, "Rev. [sic] J.S. Woodsworth . . . came all the way from Vancouver and addressed the Bolsheviks last night at the Labor Temple. . . . It is a sad thing that the Bolsheviks are being supported by three Methodist ministers."[39]

And support the strikers (not the Bolsheviks) they did, these three Methodist ministers, Smith, Woodsworth and Ivens. Woodsworth and Ivens, especially, were constantly moving among the men, addressing crowds that overflowed the various buildings rented by the Labor Church and reassembled out of doors, or in the Industrial Bureau. The *WLN Strike Edition* (#8, 20 May 1919) records: "Winnipeg has never had a church service like this in all her history. It was throbbing with interest and enthusiasm. The people felt that here was one church that really did voice their sentiments at this hour and they thronged the place. . . ." The *WLN Strike Edition* (#14, 2 June 1919) published the statement: 7500 People Pack Labor Church. . . . Thrilling, pulsating, wonderful was the meeting of the Labor Church in Victoria Park on Sunday night. The Industrial Bureau had been refused, so the enormous congregation of from 7,000 to 9,000 that surged into the park stood for three hours and listened with rapt attention. . . ." But the enthusiasm and sincerity of the Labor Church, as well as that of the strike leaders, were about to be tested.

In the early hours of 17 June 1919, William Ivens was arrested and his home searched for seditious literature. Also taken into custody were John Queen, R.B. Russell, A.A. Heaps, A.E. Bray, R.J. Johns and G. Armstrong, most of whom had participated to some degree in the Labor Church and were active leaders of the strike.[40] Woodsworth was arrested a few days later. Fred Dixon went into hiding. The Labor Church leadership was experiencing its baptism of fire.

However, on 25 June 1919, when public meetings had been banned, when revenue was petering out and many working-class families were on the verge of starvation, and when there was abundant evidence that the federal government was determined to use force if necessary, the strike was called off.[41] At the strike's termination, and in spite of labour's defeat, the Labor Church was at its zenith: not only did it experience great public popularity, but it also had martyred leaders to celebrate.

THE PROGRAM AND GROWTH OF THE LABOR CHURCH

In July 1919 J.S. Woodsworth preached his first sermon after release from prison, a dramatic sermon entitled "The One Big Church," in which he summarized the effect of the strike on the Labor Church and looked into the future: "As many as 10,000 men and women gathered to gain strength and encouragement for the coming week's fight. The 'Church' became a 'movement' – a spontaneous movement of the people – an insistence upon a social code of ethics, a revolt against denominationalism and formality and commercialism in the churches – a hunger after righteousness and spiritual truth, a sense of fellowship in suffering and inspiration."[42]

For a while it seemed as though this "one big church" might become a reality, for the Labor Church was "throbbing with enthusiasm" and life. On 23 July 1919, the WLN exulted:

The anniversary service of the Labor Church on Sunday last proved the vitality of the movement . . . thousands were turned away. The Meeting was electric and throughout throbbed with enthusiasm. . . . The applause was wonderful and unusually prolonged even for a labor meeting. . . . Everywhere the emphasis was upon a religion for life as opposed to a religion for death. It was life, full, robust, pulsating, pregnant. . . . Mr. Woodsworth made a strong plea for justice to the foreign born. . . . He was followed by F.J. Dixon . . . R.B. Russell . . . W.A. Pritchard . . . Mr. Ivens. . . . Where there was one church a year ago there were now eight. The membership was increasing faster than plans to cope with them were worked out. . . . The church must [now] investigate four principal realms of thought: religion . . . humanity (relationships, national and international) . . . form of government (Parliamentary or Soviet) . . . [and] industry. . . .

Salem Bland, on a visit to Winnipeg, also encouraged the Labor Church to "think big," but not in revolutionary terms: "This church . . . would then have a grander future than either Roman Catholicism or Protestantism." On 15 August 1919, WLN comments: "Dr. Bland's further remark that a revolution in a democracy like Canada would be a crime was received in silence. . . . 'No,' he declared, 'revolution in Canada is an evil dream, an evil dream inherited from the old world.' " Clearly this was not a message to which all Labor Church adherents were receptive.

PROBLEMS AND DECLINE OF THE LABOR CHURCH

While the years between 1919 and 1921 were years of expansion and growth[43] (the WLN of 11 July, 1919 lists nine locations and one more was added in November) they were not years without problems, and most of them were structural. Then followed "the slow and dragging years" during which the problems became more acute and the decline of the Labor Church in Winnipeg was more apparent.

Although the Winnipeg General Strike had, in many ways, been a positive time for the Labor Church, William Ivens personally experienced considerable emotional trauma, both before and after his trial, becoming almost paranoiac in his relationship with the public press and the established denominations. The *OBU Bulletin* (13 December 1919) did little to mitigate the tension: "Ivens is in hot water these days," it reported. "If he sings, Mr. A.J. Andrews says the hymns are songs 'Calling on the People to Rise.' Now it is claimed that his prayers also are part of a seditious conspiracy. The newspapers seem to be somewhat mixed over these prayers. It is evident that it is out of their line. One of them says that Ivens called upon God to aid the revolt, while another declares that Ivens prayed for guidance during the revolution."

Ivens felt himself to be spied upon and under constant pressure. In his address to the jury he said, "I expressed my convictions freely in the Methodist Church and they had to wait until the Labor Church came before they laid hands on me.[44] Because I left the Methodist Church and started the Labor Church I am dogged by spies."[45] This kind of pressure took its toll.

When the case came before the Court, Ivens, together with Queen, Pritchard, Armstrong, Johns and Heaps, was charged on seven counts: seditious conspiracy to excite contempt against the law and to set class against class; conspiracy in connection with the Walker Theatre meeting of 22 December 1918;[46] conspiring to bring about an unlawful general strike in 1919; conspiring to destroy the confidence of the people in the government; conspiring to endanger the lives of citizens and forming unlawful associations of employees to break contracts; conspiring to establish a soviet form of government in Canada; common nuisance during April, May and June 1919 because by their acts they endangered life and the property of citizens.[47]

When he addressed the jury in his own defence, Ivens spoke for a total of twenty hours,[48] concluding, "I am still going to stand for what I believe to be justice, truth and right. I shall help every cause I believe to be just by the exercise of whatever brain I have. I won't use force. I don't believe it is right. My fate is in your hands, my destiny is not. My destiny is in the hands of the Almighty and myself. I ask for a verdict of 'not guilty.' "[49]

Although Ivens expressed himself with courage, eloquence and sincerity, he was, nevertheless, found guilty and sentenced to one year each on the first six counts and six months on the seventh, to run concurrently, and entered Stony Mountain Penitentiary on 6 April 1920.

While Ivens was imprisoned, the Labor Church was administered by the central governing body of the Church, consisting of a president, general secretary, vice-president, and an executive of four members. These officers, elected annually at a general meeting of all branches, were a functioning body with or without Ivens. However, Ivens's personality was a strong unifying factor, and when he was elected to the legislature in 1920, while still in prison, and took his seat on his release, it spelled the beginning of the end, for his attention was increasingly absorbed by his legislative duties while the Church relied more and more on "outside" speakers. In 1926 Ivens graduated from the Manitoba School of Chiropractors and thereafter practised chiropractic as enthusiastically as he did politics and the ministry. He was also active in the National Anti-Vaccination League, which further depleted the time he gave to the Church.

With Ivens now rarely free to pursue his duties in the Church, J.S. Woodsworth accepted the position of secretary in June 1921, but in the fall of that same year he also was elected to public office as member of parliament for Winnipeg North Centre. This left the Labor Church without the undivided attention of either one of its strongest leaders, and to further complicate the situation, F.J. Dixon, W.D. Bayley and John Queen, among others, all active and frequent speakers on the Labor Church circuit, also assumed public office, leaving less time for Labor Church activities. Yet, surprisingly, the dangers of a divaricated leadership were not apparent to the politically impassioned directors. Woodsworth is quoted as saying to his wife upon leaving for Ottawa: "I can leave the Labor Church now with things in good shape and everyone enthusiastic.[50]

But all was not well in spite of continuing enthusiasm. The General Strike and the subsequent trial of Labor Church leaders had drawn the attention of the Royal Canadian Mounted Police (RCMP); while in Parliament, Senator Gideon Robertson made a damning attack upon the organization, grouping it with the Jewish Bolsheviki Party, the Anarchist Communists and the Bulgarian Bolshevists, to name but a few.[51] This official suspicion and condemnation was certainly a factor in the decline of the Labor Church, for it alienated those within the Church who had no desire to be identified with subversion, now that the Strike was over. It also created another problem.

There has been speculation that up to this point the Labor Church might be welcomed into the Methodist fold as an experiment in church and labor relations.[52] Certainly the Methodist connection was strong. Many of the Labor Church's most active leaders were or had been Methodist ministers, both the Edmonton and the Winnipeg Churches began initially under the Methodist umbrella, the denomination was openly sympathetic to the needs of labour,[53] and men like Salem Bland could continue to work freely within its ranks. Then too, William Ivens quite noticeably moderated his reckless criticism of the organized church in the 1920s and indicated that the Labor Church would like to cooperate with all who had the interests of the working man at heart.[54] However, when Lieutenant Colonel C.F. Hamilton of the RCMP contacted T.A. Moore of the Methodist Evangelism and Social Service Department to discuss the Labor Church, any hope of rapprochement disappeared, for from this point, the Methodist leadership relied on RCMP reports for its facts on Labor Church activity and these reports were not always accurate or objective. For example, Hamilton concluded that the Labor Church was not a religious but an irreligious, or an anti-religious device, designed for the teaching of revolutionary socialism under the cloak of religion; that it contained no spark of religion, Christian or otherwise; and that it was a conscious piece of hypocrisy, designed to attract a certain type of person of Christian principles who was interested in social problems and troubled over the attacks made upon the church for not solving them.[55]

The Methodist Church, especially in the person of T.A. Moore, accepted these reports, where "all the purple passages with revolutionary implications were presented out of context,"[56] as the whole truth. Allen notes that later in the Hamilton–Moore correspondence, Hamilton revised his opinions about Ivens, Woodsworth and others from being "revolutionaries" to simply being engaged in "humanitarian talk, . . . but by then the damage had been done."[57]

Dr. Chown of the Methodist Church, more generous in his attitude than were Rev. Mr. Moore or Colonel Hamilton, still insisted that a class church was contrary to Christian teaching, although Salem Bland argued that the "Labor Church may be a class church, but so, unfortunately are large numbers of other churches,"[58] and therefore, he contended, the Labor Church was justified in providing a congregation in which workers could feel accepted. Be that as it may, the fact remains that the Methodist Church finally and firmly rejected the Labor Church as an experiment in labour-church relations. This rejection proved to be one further cause in the decline of the Labor Church, for it left no alternative for those members who wished to retain the religious aspect of the Church but to return to the various denominations when the anti-religious elements within their ranks became militantly dominant, as happened in some areas of the city.

The division between those who wished to adhere to the Christian faith and those who saw the Labor Church only as a political platform from which to propagate socialist or Marxist propaganda – the tension between progressives and radicals –steadily intensified after the incarceration of the leaders, while the difficulties in steering a middle course were multiplied. By the mid-1920s the Labor Church policy of an open pulpit was being blatantly misused by some: "According to R.B. Russell, the views of men like Joseph McCabe ('Rationalist') and Marshall Gauvin ('Atheist and Free Thinker'), frequent visitors at Labor Church gatherings, became increasingly prominent and helped to undermine the eroding foundations of the new religious movement."[59] Ivens's view was that "for the socialist movement to become divorced from its religious roots was for it to begin to die. In spite of this conviction, however, less and less religion was to be found in Labor Church programmes."[60] For many, in this lack of creed and doctrine lay the strength of the Labor Church appeal, yet when worship of God could no longer be readily discerned in the Church, indeed, when overt antagonism to Him was not uncommon, then the "Church" ceased to exist and unmitigated secularism prevailed.[61]

With continual decline obvious, especially after 1926, the OBU gradually reorganized the Labor Church Sunday Schools into union children's classes, in some cases merely picking up where the Labor Church had left off,[62] while the Independent Labor Party advertised lecture forums almost identical in format and content to those of the Labor Church, often with the same speakers in the same locations.[63]

As for the Labor Church itself, in the words of F.L. Paulley, it seemed merely to "dwindle out of existence."[64] Since the Church owned no buildings and possessed few assets at this point in time, it appears that the religious aspect of the organization was simply absorbed into the political – a triumph of secularism.

CONCLUSION

Although the Labor Church disappeared as far as the Winnipeg public was concerned, it was not altogether a failure. It raised pertinent questions on social, economic and moral issues; it gave women a much more prominent place in its organization than was common for that day; it provided fellowship and strength to immigrants, labourers, strikers, the unchurched, the "Oppressed." It acted as a gadfly in Winnipeg's "Christian" community. There was also that intangible "something" left in the lives of thousands of Labor Church adherents, so that, in Beatrice Brigden's words, "they could never think in the same narrow way again."[65]

Yet possibly the most important legacy that the Labor Church left Winnipeg, and indeed Canada, was its influence on the leadership of the still-future CCF Party, for included among that party's founders were J.S. Woodsworth, William Ivens, S.J. Farmer and William Irvine, all active Labor Church leaders.

Why then did the Labor Church "dwindle out of existence"? Richard Allen suggests that because there was no "large, self-conscious" working class in Canada the Church was not a viable institution in this country. Yet even in Britain, where such a socio-economic group did exist, the Labor Church did nor survive. Certainly a return to the traditional denominations after the first flush of enthusiasm and the aggravation of the Strike had disappeared, erosion by organized labour and the intense political involvement of its leaders took their toll, but in the final analysis it was internal weakness rather than external pressure which caused the collapse. Basically, the leadership generally and William Ivens particularly were overly simplistic in assessing both the problems of society and the competence of their church to redress these problems. But more than lack of erudition was the absence of a sound theological basis which militated against its success as a "church." It was this doctrinal poverty which ultimately became not only a cause for its decline but constituted the determining factor in its demise, for it deprived the leadership of weapons in a spiritual warfare. As Douglas Pratt points out, "in disparaging all theology, [Ivens] failed to appreciate its vital necessity as the foundation of that faith which works through love; and it was this failure that prevented the Labor Church from having more than a temporary effectiveness in the promotion of social justice. Its concern for the Christianizing of society, while neglecting the Christian nurture of its people, led it to become merely the religious expression of a social philosophy, and later, with increasing secularization, to lose its identity as a religious movement."[66]

R. Morley, writing in the *Labour Prophet* at the inception of the British Labor Church, thundered: "Christianity must go, and a humane, lovable and progressive religion must take its place."[67] In Winnipeg, between 1918 and 1927, while Christianity looked on critically, the "humane, lovable and progressive religion" had come, and without taking Christianity's place, was now gone. What sphinx would arise from its ashes to again challenge the complacency of mainline churches?

J.H. Riddell (Photo courtesy of Western Canada Pictorial Index.)

Principal J.H. Riddell:
The sane and safe leader of Wesley College

Gerald Friesen

Wesley College, the centre of Methodist higher education in the Canadian prairies, was a hotbed of reform doctrine during the decade of the western boom before 1914. It was a quieter place in the inter-war years. The exciting atmosphere of debate stimulated by Rev. J.S. Woodsworth's work on immigration, W.F. Osborne's critique of the Methodist Church and Salem Bland's advocacy of political change was less in evidence after World War I. Instead, new teachers such as Watson Kirkconnell and Arthur R.M. Lower imparted a different tone to college life. Students were exhorted to develop "character" and to display an interest in scholarship but were not pressed to become crusaders for social reform. Though subtle, the change was decisive. The radicals, whose social gospel roots encouraged a critique of the capitalist economic system, gave way to moderates whose evangelicalism demanded personal repentance and whose political caution required that reform be gradual and respectful of tradition. John H. Riddell, principal of Wesley College from 1917 to 1938, represented the forces of "sane and safe" reform. His influence was crucial in changing the political and social tone of College life in the inter-war years.

Riddell was born on a farm in the Humber Valley near Bolton, Ontario, on 1 November 1863. He had three older half brothers, but was the first of seven children born to James R. Riddell and his second wife, Ann Jane Jefferson. Ann Riddell, a devout church member, had converted from the Anglican to the Methodist Church at a revival service. James R., a Presbyterian from County Monaghan in Ireland, joined Ann in the Wesleyan Methodist connection at the time of their marriage. Their children were raised in the disciplined manner of the age. They were accustomed to daily morning worship, in which father led in prayer and read a passage of Scripture, and they accepted firm prohibitions against theatre, card games, drink, tobacco and unnecessary activity on Sundays. Three of the boys became ministers, one became a doctor and one stayed on the farm, while one girl married and the other remained at home.[1]

The intervention of a local teacher gave John an extra summer of studies and consequent admission into high school in 1879. Two years later, he was ready for the practical training course in education known as "model school," in Brampton, and in January 1882, at the age of nineteen, he started his teaching career. Convinced by his classroom experience that he should secure further education, Riddell returned to Collingwood High School to prepare for the matriculation examinations and, in the autumn of 1886, he travelled to Cobourg to enroll in Victoria University. For the next four years, he combined work and study in remarkable quantities as he proceeded toward his bachelor of arts degree. In his last year, he edited the college newspaper, helped to introduce the Young Men's Christian Association (YMCA) to the student body, and won a silver medal in general proficiency and a gold medal in mental and moral philosophy.

After his graduation, Riddell was posted to Manitoba, where he had served in 1887 as a summer teacher and supply minister. As the Methodist missionary in the Cartwright district, he travelled the countryside meeting his new parishioners and holding Bible classes and church services wherever the opportunity arose. In 1892, after two years on the circuit, he was granted the bachelor of divinity degree by his college and invited to assume the dual position of assistant minister at Grace Church, with responsibility for a new charge, Young Church, in west-end Winnipeg, and lecturer in Latin and Greek at Wesley College. He accepted the heavy responsibilities and was soon immersed in church and student life in the prairie metropolis. He married Florence May Armstrong of Holmfield, Manitoba, on 12 June 1894, and two years later became the father of a boy, Harold Gordon. In these busy years, Riddell aided in the establishment of the YMCA among the students and organized a Sunday-morning class for "fellowship and meditation." He cheered at football games, helped to set up the college newspaper, designed the Wesley College crest, lectured to study groups and founded a Methodist Church summer school for young people. He also studied in Chicago for two summers to improve his own knowledge of the classics and spent two summers in Europe, where again he travelled and studied. Riddell was, clearly, a young man of energy, ability and dedication. He worked well with his five colleagues on the Wesley College staff and was promoted from part-time to full-time faculty member in 1898. He undertook a number of modest administrative responsibilities and helped to draft, with Professor Thomas Hart of Manitoba College and Professor Coombs of St. John's College, the basis of the classics course which served the university for the next half century. His zeal and toil ensured that he would be asked to assume further obligations.

The Manitoba and North-West Conference of the Methodist Church offered another challenge to Riddell as he entered middle age. The rapid growth of population in the North-West Territories warranted the establishment of a college, and he was asked to become the founder and principal. Alberta College, located in Edmonton, opened its doors in the autumn of 1903 and soon became an important institution of secondary and university education. Riddell served as teacher and administrator in Edmonton, became a father for the second time (Robert Gerald was born in 1908) and played an active part in city affairs as well. In the days of the Alberta boom, he had a hand in many land transactions, including the choice of sites for the General Hospital, the Library and the new Alberta College South. Riddell went to the University of Chicago in 1911 to take lectures in sociology, a discipline which he established at Alberta College upon his return. The University of Alberta granted him an honorary doctor of laws degree in 1913 in recognition of his contributions to the province. The darkest part of his Edmonton years came in 1915 when his elder son, who had left university to enlist in the Mounted Rifles, fell ill at the Front. Riddell travelled to France to be with him, and there the boy died in February 1916.

A year later, in the spring of 1917, Riddell faced a crisis of a different kind. The principal of Wesley College, the popular Dr. Eber Crummy, had resigned under unfortunate circumstances. Having failed to secure its first choice, the board agreed that Chairman James H. Ashdown should approach Riddell. He was well known to Ashdown – indeed, had been offered the principalship in 1912 by the powerful merchant – and agreed with his views upon college life and the church. Riddell was probably feeling unsettled and, certainly, he interpreted the appointment as a Divine intervention. He accepted the position immediately. With the news of his selection, he wrote later, "such acute criticism occurred in some quarters, that the Board practically ran for cover. The Chairman alone stood his ground and remained till the time of his death, my constant friend."[2]

The problems at Wesley were many and complex. There was something "uncanny, disturbing, perplexing around the halls of this Institution," Riddell wrote, which was indefinable but worrisome.[3] He knew that he was replacing a well-liked principal in Rev. Crummy and that the simultaneous departure of two social gospel "radicals," Professors Irwin and Bland, still rankled with many students and citizens. Even the continued existence of the College was in question. Enrollment had declined sharply in the war years and College finances were approaching a crisis. A number of senior faculty members had been transferred to the University of Manitoba when the Presbyterian and Methodist colleges discontinued arts instruction in 1914–15, and had been replaced by new teachers when the Methodist Conference reversed its decision and recommenced arts instruction a year later. Moreover, in these days of turbulent political debate, a portion of the faculty wished to save money and preserve jobs by replacing the principal with a faculty committee. Riddell, on the other hand, with the powerful support of J.H. Ashdown and the board, believed that one individual must be responsible for the operation of the institution. His selection by Winnipeg's Methodist leaders was no accident.

Then, in 1920, Riddell made a decision that caused further serious disruptions in College life. The principal was considered by some members of the Methodist community to be neither a great scholar nor an impressive public figure and, partly in order to allay this concern, Riddell hired W.G. Smith of Toronto as professor and vice-principal. Smith's arrival in the summer of 1921 marked the beginning of a year-long struggle for control of the College which eventually resulted in board intervention on Riddell's behalf. The crisis is considered later in this article, but it may be noted here that Smith was fired, several other faculty members resigned, and Wesley slowly returned to more stable circumstances.

Riddell remained the senior administrative officer of Wesley until its complete merger with the Presbyterian Manitoba College in 1938. Upon his retirement, he turned his exceptional energy to writing and other church-related community activities. He died in 1952. Few Methodists had been so influential in shaping the institutions of higher education in Manitoba.

The character of college life is a vague and elusive thing. The role of an administrative leader in affecting the tone of its dormitories and classrooms is even more obscure. But no one would deny that differences of character do distinguish colleges or that administrators can alter the atmosphere of an institution. Riddell's stewardship at Wesley endured for twenty-one years. His personality and opinions inevitably affected the academic, physical and financial arrangements of the College and were communicated to the students.

The principal's job was a demanding one. Riddell was expected to supervise the faculty and students and to teach as many hours as his colleagues did but he was also responsible for the boilers and the roof and the repair of the steps. He arranged for the rinks and the playing field. He managed the budget, the investment of the trust funds and the campaigns for donations. The decision of the college board to buy him a membership in the Winnipeg Board of Trade because "his attendance brought the work of the College prominently before that body of men" was simply one acknowledgement of his role in the operation of a business and in public relations.[4] After his first year as principal of Wesley, Riddell reported to the Manitoba Conference of the Methodist Church that he had taught twelve hours each week in Church history and New Testament, had travelled fifteen thousand miles on College business, had spoken on forty public occasions, preached ninety times to seventy-five different congregations and acted as chief administrator of the College.[5] What kind of mark could be leave upon College life when he was preoccupied by so many responsibilities? Despite his travels, Riddell left a very clear stamp indeed.

Wesley College during Riddell's tenure as principal was a small and closely knit family of about four to six hundred students and twenty-odd faculty members. Its academic year opened in late September, ended in April, and was punctuated by the examination periods and student celebrations that have been a part of university life for generations. The social calendar started with a formal reception for students and the initiation of first-year students. It was marked, next, by the flags and pennants and cheers of the Hallowe'en parade; Hallowe'en activities were followed, in turn, by skating and hockey and basketball. All too soon, the students were dispatching Wesley Christmas cards and studying feverishly for their examinations. There were meetings of the drama and literary and history and choral clubs, a few curling matches and skating parties, and then it was time for class photos and preparation for the biggest events of the year, the seniors dinner and grads' farewell. The rhythm seemed unchanging throughout the two decades of Riddell's principalship and, indeed, differed little from the pattern of the late nineteenth or even the late twentieth century. After all, what was there about college life that could conceivably be changed?

An air of predictability was also evident in the daily round. When the first bell sounded at 7:30 in the morning, noise erupted in the men's and women's residences as a hundred students rushed to claim toilet facilities and sinks with plugs. Doors banged and warnings were left with sleepy roommates – "two minutes left" – and then the second bell announced breakfast. By 8:30, when the early mail was distributed, the students who boarded in city homes were streaming up the walk and the serious business of the day commenced. From 9:45 to 10:00, there was a pause between lectures for daily chapel service and then classes resumed until the lunch bell rang at 12:30. The residence students headed off for such favourites as corn soup and shepherd's pie while the rest unpacked sandwiches and perhaps bought a cup of coffee in the canteen. Afternoon lectures and study would give way to recreation and talk, perhaps a skate on the rink or a gathering to hear a saxophone recording. After dinner, residence students met at the Sparling Hall reading rack, where they read the comics pages of the newspapers more readily than they did the editorial sections, and then they might debate current issues and religion. Secluded corners of the lounge were sometimes in short supply, it is said, but the 7:30 study bell recalled the diligent to the task at hand. The last bell at 11:00 prompted an outburst of noise and argument but, within half an hour, all was silent again.[6] There was nothing here, it might seem, to distinguish this small college from several dozen others in Canada or, indeed, hundreds of others in North America.

The distinctive traits of Wesley College, the Methodist Church and Riddell himself were evident, nonetheless, in several aspects of College life. Chief among these distinctive characteristics were faculty caution in the face of the students' misbehaviour, faculty concern for the academic progress of individual students, and faculty resolve that the College should develop the character as much as the intellect of its charges. The ideal was expressed in a resolution of the Wesley College Board, a resolution that Riddell himself had pressed: "The final end of education is character making, not the imparting of information. We believe that toward this end an invaluable contribution is being made by our Church through the maintenance of such institutions as Wesley College, where not only high standards of scholastic achievement are preserved, but distinct assistance and impulse to Christian living."[7]

Faculty worries about student behaviour were expressed annually during autumn initiation rites, when the professors tried to regulate the rougher activities or to abolish them altogether, but were also evident when such issues as smoking, drinking and dancing arose.[8] The Wesley College Board, in line with the rules of the Methodist Church, expressed "its strongest disapproval of the use of tobacco by students and wishes as far as possible to guard its students against the formation or continuance of a habit which it regards as injurious. . . ."[9] Alcoholic beverages were forbidden; if unwary undergraduates were caught breaking this rule, they were dealt with severely. In April 1922, when province-wide prohibition was still in force, a committee chaired by Riddell held twenty hours of hearings into a case in which several residence students took liquor to their rooms. The committee recommended to the College faculty that two of the young men be dismissed and never again permitted to enroll in Wesley. At a formal evening session of the entire faculty, Riddell delivered reprimands to six others involved in the disturbance, warning them "firmly and kindly and with a depth of feeling, of the dangers which lay ahead of them should they continue to pursue the course which had brought them to the place where they now found themselves."[10] A similar case in 1932 inspired an investigation in which the board of directors sought to establish "if there was genuine sorrow for their [the students'] actions, and a desire to live so that such a thing would not occur again so far as they were concerned." In the end, three Wesley students were forbidden to enroll in 1933. After a more serious disturbance in 1934, three students were told they would never again be permitted to enter the College.[11] The rules in these cases were clear and the punishment for infractions was severe.

Dancing was a more difficult problem, as Riddell was to discover. He had been raised in a home where dancing was forbidden and had never altered that view, despite the changing social atmosphere in the early twentieth century, because he feared that dancing encouraged "unwholesome conduct."[12] As late as 1926, Wesley College officially forbade dances. Indeed, when a group of graduating students in the class of 1926 arranged that the annual senior dinner at the Fort Garry Hotel be followed by a dance, the Wesley faculty issued a public statement dissociating the College from this "informal event." The professors recognized that such questions of behaviour were "largely matters for individual conscience," the statement declared, but they did not wish to offend "the convictions and traditions of many good friends of Wesley College." The conclusion of the faculty statement, probably written by Riddell and Professor Watson Kirkconnell, was a stern admonition: "The President and Faculty trust, however, that the recognized and cherished loyalty of the students to their college will induce them on this and on every occasion to so conduct themselves that they will help the College that they love to do her best work in the world."[13] Riddell could not prevent students from dancing. Dismayed by the number of student social activities, he and his faculty colleagues resolved in 1928 to require that students "spend at least four evenings per week in pursuit of their studies." Despite these strictures, they received yet another unwelcome missive from the students in October 1928 again requesting that "mixed dancing" be permitted in the music room between 7:00 and 8:00 p.m. on Wednesdays. In 1931, the faculty acceded to the request for one dance hour per week but were still concerned about students' socializing and had established yet another committee: "The end to be achieved is the regulation or the restraint of social activities." One casualty of this student campaign was Riddell's conviction that the College must never be associated with dancing. In 1930 he issued a formal statement to the faculty acknowledging his defeat. In this unusual document he agreed that dancing might not be wrong – "I quite readily recognize that many people just as good as I and perhaps better, dance with a clear conscience" – but he maintained that the College was "a sacred place for the reasons that it has been intimately associated with the religious ideals of a great denomination. . . ." Changing students' views and perhaps the Methodist union with the Presbyterians had altered the situation: "For the purpose of securing better control and thus preserving in the highest degree possible the honour of the College and the students," Riddell said, he would accept the *faculty's* decision to recognize and to supervise dances.[14]

Drinking and dancing among the students were just two of the difficult social questions faced by the Wesley College staff. Faculty attention to student deportment was also evident during regular reviews of student performance. The extraordinary concern for the students' academic and social development was, indeed, one of the most striking features of staff meetings during Riddell's administration. It appears that attendance forms were regularly filled out by the instructors and that absenteeism elicited a written warning to the students and, on occasion, to the students' parents. Christmas examination results were reviewed and, where appropriate, students were placed on probation for one month. Students who "failed to respond" to several warnings were "asked to discontinue." The parents of delinquent students were also contacted and, on occasion, were invited to be present when their children were reprimanded.[15] The Wesley College record in the annual university-wide competition for grades and scholarships was a matter of great interest to the faculty and was monitored with careful attention. Because awards, punishments and progress were discussed in full-scale meetings of the faculty, the career of every student was reviewed once or twice a year during Riddell's administration. Such attention was priceless.

The spiritual life of the students was a matter of even greater College concern. In his letter of appointment to a new staff member, Riddell noted that Wesley students must do well in the University of Manitoba examination competition but he added that the arts faculty at Wesley existed "primarily for the spiritual contribution it may be able to make to the life and well-being of the community."[16] After several years of debates among students and faculty over compulsory attendance at chapel services, a new calendar entry was drafted: "As an educational institution under Christian auspices, Wesley College is primarily concerned with the moral and spiritual welfare of its students. With this end in view students are expected to attend morning worship as part of their regular daily program; and they are expected to attend Divine Worship on the Lord's Day at such churches as their parents or guardians may direct."[17] Though Riddell failed in his attempt to secure board participation in the disciplinary activities of the College, he did win a board statement which might serve as a statement of the College aim: to cultivate "a sane, wholesome, intelligent attitude to the principles and organizations of the Christian religion, with a view to securing the finest type of leadership for the people."[18] And he also instituted the custom of welcoming each College graduate into his office after Recognition Day, the annual awards ceremony in the spring, to convey "his sincere blessing and the Book which may be carried through life as a guide."[19] Bible study was compulsory in the high school branch of the College and four Bible classes were convened weekly in the university branch. The principal had a personal interview with every student and, together with the faculty, tried to ensure that students would be required during their College years to face the "great moral and spiritual issues" of life.[20] Wesley College under Riddell provided a carefully supervised and thoroughly religious experience for its students.

If Riddell emphasized personal discipline and the character-building qualities of student life in Wesley College during his years as principal, he was only accentuating what had always been strong points in the Methodist institution. He differed from his predecessors, however, in other aspects of his educational and political philosophy. As is the case with any educational leader, his views were implicit in his teaching and scholarly work, on the one hand, and in his administrative practices on the other. In each sphere, Riddell possessed such positive attributes as energy, determination, self-confidence and a cautious reforming spirit. But to this catalogue should be added less attractive characteristics, including stubbornness, highhandedness, complacency and a strain of anti-intellectualism. The result of this combination of qualities was a less radical, less adventurous Wesley College than had existed before 1914.

Riddell himself believed that the two outstanding achievements of his administration were his defence of a downtown location for undergraduate arts instruction within the University of Manitoba and his financial management of Wesley College.[21] He acted with tact and statesmanship in these matters, it is true, and could take pride in the results. He also emphasized his role in the construction and renovation of College buildings and the development of the College library. Again, his contributions were important. But these were the normal duties of an administrator and would detain us only if they were done badly.

Riddell's attitude to scholarly inquiry is less easy to discern. He was not a scholar himself, as he sometimes acknowledged, and he seemed uneasy with that aspect of College life. His own speeches on ceremonial occasions tended to stress such virtues as self-discipline, perseverance and independent judgement. He regularly taught Latin, Greek and the New Testament but he had little advanced training in those fields. When he founded the discipline of sociology at Alberta College, it was after a single summer of sociological studies in Chicago in 1911.[22] He pursued this interest in Winnipeg,[23] taking a special study leave in the summer of 1927 to visit the eastern Canadian provinces and examine their governments' social legislations, but the demands on his time were undoubtedly too great to permit further research while he remained principal.[24] When he turned to writing after his retirement, he chose such topics as the penal system, the community responsibilities of church leaders, the social history of Canada, and the history of the Methodist Church in western Canada.[25] These studies bore witness to his remarkable energy and industry but they were the work of an intelligent lay observer, not a scholar or specialist. Two of them, the social history and an undistinguished autobiography entitled, significantly, "*Gateways to a Life of Service*," never found a publisher. Riddell was simply too busy to develop the scholarly interest and skills usually associated with university leaders.

His record as an administrator of scholars was similarly uneven. The faculty of Wesley College had undergone a period of crisis when Riddell was appointed in 1917, as could be expected. The abrupt departure of a well-loved principal, Rev. Eber Crummy in June 1917, and the simultaneous dismissal of a famous radical, Salem Bland, left prairie Methodists in turmoil. Bland and his followers believed forever after that "moneyed interests," including J.H. Ashdown and men who shared his social philosophy, had threatened to withdraw their financial support and close Wesley College rather than endure its association with the radical social gospellers. Subsequent Church investigations did not sustain Bland's charge: a financial shortfall was said to be justification enough for his departure. But Riddell's appointment had indeed been facilitated by his old friend, J.H. Ashdown.[26] The connection was logical. Riddell shared Ashdown's conviction that one person, not a committee of social gospellers, should be responsible for the day-to-day administration of the institution. And Riddell was not a political radical. His cautious – even evangelical – views on social reform and personal conversion were undoubtedly more congenial to Winnipeg's Methodist businessmen than Bland's denunciations of individual profiteers and the capitalist system in general.

Riddell's political caution and religious evangelicalism were revealed during the most serious academic crisis ever faced by Wesley College. When two of Wesley's most able scholars, W.T. Allison and D.C. Harvey, resigned in the summer of 1920, Riddell was sufficiently conscious of his own shortcomings to launch a search for academic staff who might restore Wesley's credentials as a respectable university-level institution. By chance, the leading

Methodist candidate in what must have been a small field was Dr. W.G. Smith of the University of Toronto. Smith had laboured for ten years to separate the discipline of psychology from the department of philosophy at Toronto and had just started work in experimental psychology that, he hoped, would establish the subject as a proper "science." At this stage in the development of Canadian arts faculties, when psychology and sociology were not widely recognized as distinct disciplines, his enthusiasm for laboratory work and reliance upon scientific measurement were advanced, or at least unconventional, so his decision to leave Toronto, where he had finally won a niche for the new approach, was an unusual step. He agreed to join the Wesley faculty because he thought he was being asked to shape not just a discipline or a faculty but to have a leading part in the rebuilding of the post-war West. This was the era of the Winnipeg General Strike and the progressive movement, of course, and the community must have seemed open to new approaches; moreover, having just completed a survey of Methodist colleges in Canada, Smith would have perceived the importance of Winnipeg as the metropolis of the prairies and of Wesley as the leading Methodist institution west of Toronto. He assumed that he was being invited to direct Wesley's contribution to the new order in Canada.

Riddell did not have a clear plan for Smith's work at Wesley and did not understand the range of his new colleague's ambitions. The misunderstandings were apparent in the letters of appointment in the spring of 1921. Riddell secured board approval of Smith's hiring in February but did not finally ascertain his responsibilities until May. In the interval, various combinations of teaching and administrative responsibilities were canvassed. It was eventually concluded that Smith would be professor of philosophy and sociology, a position fraught with difficulties because the University of Manitoba did not utilize the narrower approach to the social sciences; and he would be a senior administrative officer with the resounding but potentially empty title of vice-president in "charge of the academic side of the work of the College."[27] In neither position would Smith find a secure, comfortable or defined role. What is worse, perhaps, Riddell was having second thoughts even while he was arranging Smith's responsibilities. In the small group at Wesley, he was hiring a professor who would take over his own specialty of sociology; he was offering the "academic leadership" to this new man; and he still did not know Smith's political views or even his religious perspective. The unanimous opinion of Methodist leaders in Toronto seemed to be that Smith was a "brilliant psychologist and inspiring teacher" but also that he had been an unreliable radical a few years earlier and was still inclined to that side of the theological spectrum. As Rev. J.H. Arnup of the Methodist Foreign Missions

Office told Riddell, "There seems nothing in common in your views on evangelical religion. . . . One [Smith] would be like a fish out of water (as it seems to me) in a red hot revival meeting, and the other [Riddell] perfectly at home."[28]

During the appointment negotiations, Riddell explained his political perspective to Smith in a most revealing letter. Concerning the teaching of sociology, for example, Riddell said that "the general situation [in Winnipeg] . . . requires very careful study and very sane handling" because of the 1917 crisis at Wesley involving Salem Bland and "because of the general situation in the City." He suggested that "the recent strike with its peculiar emphasis and its unfortunate developments coupled with the vigorous propaganda carried on in the parliamentary session in favour of what is generally regarded as an extreme social and industrial programme, make for us a very sensitive people." Riddell, by contrast, was committed to what he called "sane and safe leadership" and, therefore, wished to hear Smith's views on the "industrial, social and economic propaganda" being aired in Winnipeg. His concern was to welcome "sane constructive social and economic policy," Riddell wrote, but he wished to emphasize that "any unwise advocacy of radical measures would at this juncture here be fatal to us and to the larger cause we seek to advance in this new land."[29] Riddell was a cautious reformer, in short, and would do nothing to reinforce the labour radicals at City Hall or to alienate close friends like J.H. Ashdown.

His caution and his alliance with Ashdown saved Riddell from a severe personal reverse in the following year. Smith arrived at Wesley with great plans for change and proceeded to implement them with little or no reference to his principal. Riddell's friends feared that he was being bypassed by the newcomer and were doubly concerned when Smith's reforms roused opposition within the philosophy-sociology examining committee at the University of Manitoba. Soon, factions formed around Riddell and Smith within the Wesley College faculty and the board was forced to intervene. In the end, Smith refused to accept Riddell's leadership and commenced an attack upon him and the College. In one dramatic episode, Smith convened a luncheon meeting at Eaton's cafeteria in which he told a number of Methodist ministers of his concerns about the moral conditions and the scholarly atmosphere at Wesley and produced a "French safe," presumably from the residence, as proof of his allegations.[30] The Wesley College Board did not accept Smith's arguments. It terminated Smith's contract in July 1922 and then endured a year of legal actions, first in the Methodist Court of Appeal, then in the Court of King's Bench and finally in the Winnipeg District of the Methodist Church, where Smith charged Riddell with having uttered falsehoods.[31] The board supported Riddell throughout the battle, despite the dissatisfaction of a minority within its ranks and despite the resignation of several highly respected faculty members. Riddell remained principal, Smith left in disgrace, and the annual round of lectures and meetings and student events resumed as if they had never been interrupted. The confidence which Ashdown placed in Riddell in 1917 had been reciprocated by the support of those Board members who shared Ashdown's perspective in 1922–23.[32]

Riddell displayed greater decisiveness but no better judgement a decade later. In 1932, three years after hiring two promising historians, Arthur R.M. Lower and Jack Pickersgill, the principal informed the latter that his services were no longer required. Riddell explained that "the welfare of an institution was greater than that of its members" and that Pickersgill's position would be better filled by Riddell's own son, Gerald, who was then studying at Oxford. Pickersgill stood his ground and, in a remarkable letter, informed his principal that he doubted "whether the principle of reasonable security of tenure for its [Wesley College's] staff could be compensated for by an incidental advantage." Pickersgill won and the principal lost face.[33] The episode was an unfortunate reminder of his informal approach to higher education.

Riddell continued to be principal of Wesley College until its complete merger with Manitoba College in 1938. After his retirement, he spent his time addressing the social issues which had always interested him. In one of these works, he wrote something approaching his own epitaph:

My highest interest in life found expression in a longing to make men and women, boys and girls, capable of fulfilling their divine mission in the world. . . . I was never a brilliant student, never a great scholar. I knew something about a lot of things, but was never an authority on any one thing, but I did love my fellowman and was always ready to toil and sacrifice that his well being might be promoted.[34]

The statement was characteristic of his self-deprecation but it did not do justice to the man. Riddell was a vigorous, hearty, hard-working, efficient and courageous man. In his younger days, his great popularity was due, as one observer recalled, to "his spiritual passion and deep sympathy, so that he was a great-hearted comrade to many a student. . . ." His personality did not change dramatically in later years but the demands on his time became nothing short of extraordinary.[35] He continued to labour for a better world. He had no patience with "idle, careless, thoughtless time-serving" students;[36] his sympathy rested with those who displayed "courage, kindness, constancy and candour coupled with an undying determination to make life better."[37] And how would this be achieved? Riddell was an evangelical, not a social gospel advocate. He believed the crucial institutions of society were the state, the church, the school and the home rather than the social class or the trade union or the political party.[38] And he believed that, in the end, individuals were responsible for their own fate: "Joy in life consists in serving, in being hopeful. Of my difficulties I can say they've all been helpful in the end."[39] These were the opinions of a sane and safe administrator. Wesley College was a reputable competent institution under Riddell's leadership but it had lost the spirit of its earlier days.

A heritage of healing:
Church hospital and medical work
in Manitoba, 1900–1977

Raymond R. Smith

Kathleen Mullen was the first superintendent of the Elizabeth M. Crowe Memorial Hospital in Eriksdale, about ninety-five miles north of Winnipeg in the Interlake region of Manitoba. In 1927, she reported that "although this little hospital, accommodating only 7 patients, has been in operation for only two years, it is already proving too small. Its territory is extending and patients are coming from long distances. The dispensary work is one of its active phases, 811 out-patients and 55 children having been examined, and 532 prescriptions made up. Besides this, 137 bed patients were given care, 49 of which were surgical cases, and 21 maternity. Many children are treated. One little lad was brought in with his arm taken off above the elbow. The bone had to be removed but no surgeon's saw was available, so one (a saw) was borrowed from the local butcher. The lad made a wonderful recovery and was thankful to have his life spared."[1]

The report shows the kinds of experiences the doctors and nurses had in their medical and hospital work for The United Church of Canada during the first decades of this century as they responded to the challenges of service and mission on the frontiers of western Canada. What they lacked in facilities, they endeavoured to make up with ingenious improvisations.

As the tides of immigration from Europe began to sweep over the prairies of western Canada in the late nineteenth and early twentieth centuries, many Christian denominations became aware of opportunities to expand their horizons and influence. All three traditional methods of Christian ministry were employed – preaching, teaching and healing – with particular emphasis on teaching and healing. The Presbyterian Church was aggressive in this expansion, in 1900 establishing medical missionaries in the Ukrainian Dauphin Colony at Sifton, and later at Ethelbert. In 1902, mission work was begun at Teulon, followed in 1920 by the establishment of medical services at Amaranth and Pine River. Soon after church union in 1925, hospital units were established by The United Church in Eriksdale and Gypsumville.

The Methodist Church, active in establishing medical missions in other parts of western Canada, did not begin work in Manitoba until 1923 when a small hospital was opened at Vita. There are no records of medical work initiated by the Congregationalists in Manitoba, but their ministry in western Saskatchewan had some medical aspects.

It is significant to note that, whereas the hospital and medical work were generated by concern in the national structures of the Methodist and Presbyterian Churches (at that time only men), the supportive programs were established by the women of the Church. The Presbyterian Woman's Home Missionary Society was particularly influential in providing funds and personnel for medical ventures. In later years, the Woman's Missionary Society of the United Church, before its integration with the Board of Home Missions in 1962, was a prime source of support for medical missions in Canada. In Manitoba, only the hospital at Vita came directly under the responsibility of the Board of Home Missions prior to 1962, with all other Church medical and hospital work under the aegis of the Woman's Missionary Society. The vision and initiative of the women of the church was a vital factor in the development of this practical expression of Christianity.

SOUL AND BODY: EVANGELISM AND HEALING

In the latter part of the nineteenth century, the federal government, largely through the initiative of the Honourable Clifford Sifton, embarked on several ambitious programs to colonize the West. The churches saw in this influx of settlers an opportunity for growth and evangelism, and established mission centres in areas along the new western frontiers. A significant group who came to Manitoba were the Ruthenians, also called Galicians, and finally referred to as Ukrainians. They came from Galicia, a province of Austria touching the south and west boundaries of Russia. On their arrival in Canada, some settled in Dauphin Colony, an area around Sifton. Others established homes near Teulon, where they were close to settlers of French, German, Polish, Norwegian, Swedish, Icelandic and British origin.[2] By 1912 there were eight thousand non Anglo-Saxon settlers in southern Manitoba, spreading as far as Ethelbert. The land on which they settled was generally poor. Much of it was bush and stones and very hard to clear, and some was swampy and entirely unfit for agricultural development. There was poverty, sickness and distress; the settlers worked hard but had little to show for their efforts except a determination to survive.

In 1900, Dr. James Robertson, Superintendent of Missions for the Presbyterian Church in western Canada, appointed Dr. J.T. Reid as medical missionary to the Ukrainians at Sifton. Reid was a physician who had graduated from the Montreal Theological College. He did not bother much with the "missionary" side of the work, but concentrated on the medical needs of the community. It was not long before he opened another medical centre at Ethelbert.[3]

The program of "soul-winning," however, was not to be entirely neglected. It gained momentum with the appointment in 1902 of the Rev. R.G. Scott and the Rev. Campbell Munro to minister in the Dauphin Colony. However, they were quickly foiled in their hopes by the language, cultural and religious inclinations of the settlers. Their initial failure led both Scott and Munro to go to Winnipeg to earn medical degrees. This was to be the means by which they could approach the settlers in their variety of needs. Both men maintained home bases in the Dauphin Colony, and Mrs. Scott, along with a nurse, Christina Reid, carried on the work in Sifton during the winters. Scott spent the summers visiting and holding services, as well as doing some medical work.[4] A similar arrangement prevailed at Ethelbert, where Mrs. Munro, a trained nurse, turned one room of her home into a hospital ward and for two years cared for the sick of the community by herself.[5]

Meanwhile, Dr. Alexander J. Hunter, who had practised medicine for four years in Ontario then took theological training, volunteered for service among the new Canadians in the Teulon area; he arrived in 1902. In March 1914 writing from his experiences in the Ruthenian (Ukrainian) district of Teulon, Hunter states: "When the writer was sent out as a missionary to the Teulon district nearly 12 years ago, it was thought it might be possible to induce the Ruthenians to come out to religious services, but this was soon found to be impracticable, and that for two reasons. In the first place, the people and the missionary spoke different languages and could not understand one another. In the second place, the people were mostly prejudiced against Protestantism. Some of them were devout Greek or Roman Catholics, and had been taught to look on Protestantism with horror. Others were skeptical socialists, who regarded all churches as devices of the rich for humbugging the poor."[6]

The Presbyterian Church, nevertheless, persisted in its concern to bring its form of Christianity to the new settlers, in spite of the differences and difficulties of language, culture and religious persuasions. Mrs. H.M. Kipp, Secretary of the Woman's Home Missionary Society, wrote in 1908 "that the ministry of healing would have to go hand in hand with the preaching of the gospel if desirable results were to be obtained."[7] In 1906, the Rev. Campbell Munro describes his house at Ethelbert as "a preaching place, registry office for servants, a hospital and dispensary, a dwelling place for the missionary and family. The principal work is Sabbath School work and healing the sick"; he also noted that medical work was the means of entrance to the homes.[8]

Between 1919 and 1938, when Dr. Samuel Eshoo was in charge of the Ethelbert Hospital, Sunday Services and prayer meetings were held each week. There is no record of the attendance or of the effect of these religious services on the commuity. Lenore Kirk (formerly Schaldemose), who was a nurse at Ethelbert between 1927 and 1929, states that these services were the "social event" of the week: "Everyone went and had tea and lunch and took time to visit with their neighbors."[9]

The experience garnered at Sifton, Ethelbert and Teulon was used as a guide when medical work was initiated in other areas of the province. When work was begun in Pine River in 1920, a registered nurse, Kathleen Mullen, and an evangelistic worker, Queenie Walker, established a hospital and dispensary and also engaged in mission work. Later, when they were succeeded by Rose Bolton, a registered nurse, and Myrtle McArthur, a deaconess, Sunday schools were organized, religious correspondence courses were developed, Testaments distributed, and "lantern slide" lectures were given on the Christian faith, Protestant style, of course. A similar program was developed in Amaranth where Isabel Meikle, a registered nurse, served under the Woman's Missionary Society as both community nurse and Church worker. She was also a member of the local church board, a significant posting at that time, since such boards were considered male domains.

When work was begun in Gypsumville in 1928, the same team approach was used, with two nurses, Margaret Mustard and Annetta Sinclair. Mustard, in a publication entitled "Built By A Woman," recounts the experience of her involvement in the building of a church at Gypsumville, since such a facility was considered necessary for effective evangelistic endeavours.[10]

The Vita Hospital, established in 1923 by the Methodist Church, was no less concerned about winning souls, even though the hospital was located in an area devoid of Methodists. Woodmore Church, fifteen miles to the west, was the nearest Methodist congregation. Dr. Harold V. Waldon maintained a Christian witness in the hospital through regular worship services and personal and family evidences of a Christian lifestyle. At Eriksdale, while there was no particular emphasis on evangelistic endeavours, the nursing staff at the hospital provided Christian leadership in the local United Church as Sunday School teachers, as mid-week group leaders and as musical leaders for services.

The basic assumption of this medical work was that the doctors and nurses who staffed the medical centres provided by the Church possessed a sure and certain faith and had the means to communicate it. Ella E. Wray, a nurse at Ethelbert in 1914 writes, "A doctor who is not a thorough Christian, and is afraid to work, ought not to come."[11] Occasionally, there was a slip in this strict endeavour at "Christian" behaviour. At the Vita hospital, during a difficult operation, Dr. Walter W. Read was heard to utter a "swear word." The attending nurse reported him to the hospital board but also stated that "as the patient was under the anaesthetic the only ones affected were the nurses,"[12] so there were no serious consequences for this indiscretion. The incident underlines the attempt at strict discipline under which Church medical personnel lived and worked as they sought to make, through every possible way open to them, a Christian witness to the people they served.

Edward Shillito, in an article in the United Church Record and Missionary Review, summarizes the role of medical missionaries this way: "Medical Missions! The doctors and nurses are missionaries of the Gospel. It is no reduced faith which finds expression in their healing of the sick. It is the full faith of a Christian by which they live and serve; and in the presence of Christ they kneel side by side with evangelists and leaders, and all the company of His servants."[13] Thus in all the medical and hospital services initiated by the United Church in Manitoba, healing and evangelism occurred side by side.

THE NEED FOR BUILDINGS

The natural outcome of the establishment of medical work on the frontier was the erection of buildings. Very early, however, it became clear to Church workers that the settlers in the Dauphin Colony and Teulon had a fear of hospitals. In their experience, people went to a hospital to die. Church workers concluded that the best place to give medical treatment would be in the settlers' homes or, as second best, through an out-patient treatment program; therefore, most of the early medical work carried out by the Church in Manitoba, when Drs. Scott, Munro and Hunter practised medicine, was carried out in settlers' homes. This often presented difficulties. The people were very poor and were able to provide only for the basic necessities of shelter and warmth in their homes. Families tended to be large, so the houses were crowded. The farm animals were often kept in buildings attached to the houses. This, along with inadequate nutritional and poor sanitation habits, bred all sorts of diseases and ailments. A story is told of a nurse called to a home where a birth was imminent. She arrived just in time, and her first task was to wipe the straw off the newborn baby.

Soon after his arrival in Teulon, Dr. Hunter felt the need for a hospital building in spite of the attitudes of people favouring home care. He envisioned a building thirty by forty feet, two and a half storeys high; a builder in Teulon thought it could be erected for $1,600. He got $800 from the Home Mission Board, obtained a site from the CPR for a nominal sum, and provided most of the balance himself; he then engaged Epenaetus Jones to build the structure at the agreed estimate. Hunter was not the first or the last to be caught in the uncertainties of cost estimates, and the actual cost on completion was $2,600. Financial problems were the least of Hunter's concerns, so he quickly signed a promissory note to Dr.George Bryce of Manitoba College for the difference in cost. The note was used by Dr. Bryce to procure the needed funds from a bank, and the hospital opened as planned in 1904.[14] Hunter repaid the loan over a period of time.

In 1906, writing to Mrs. H.M. Kipp, secretary of the Woman's Home Missionary Society, Dr. Hunter stated, "Between medical supplies, horses, stable, and other things used in the practise, Mother and I have now about $5,000 invested here. It is not a profitable investment financially, as I think I spend more on the practise, some hundreds of dollars every year more than the fees amount to."[15] The important concern was not the building or the money, but the service they could render to the people of the Teulon area. As time went on, the facilities were improved, so much so that in 1913 Dr. Hunter could report, "Our hospital is made over and modernized. We have a splendid cement basement where before there was only a hole in the ground under the building, and we have steam heating and our own waterworks. One room has been fitted up as an operating room"[16] As the years went on, many additions and repairs were made, and in 1954 the hospital building, along with approximately ten acres of property, was sold to the hospital district for $7,500. A new hospital was erected by the municipality. The Church, through the Woman's Missionary Society, cooperated for a further five years in meeting operating costs.

Church medical work had similar beginnings at Sifton and Ethelbert. There is no record of a building in Sifton but the work is referred to as a hospital unit. It appears that a residence was used as a dispensary and hospital until the work in Sifton was phased out in 1924. Ethelbert, however, did get a hospital in December 1915 when a twenty-three-bed unit was opened at a cost of $10,000. "It was bright, airy, warm and substantial, with its own water and sewage systems."[17] Dr. F.A. Gilbart was in charge at the time and Nurse Elizabeth Bell, who had rendered such sterling service at Teulon, took over as matron, where she remained until her retirement in 1938.

The Ethelbert Hospital received a charter in 1917 under the Charitable Association Act from the Lieutenant-Governor of Manitoba, Sir James A.M. Aikins. The charter authorized "the carrying on of a general hospital for the care of the sick and disabled." The hospital was a three-storey building located on the main street of the village. The main floor comprised a sitting room, kitchen, dining room, a doctor's office and a ward for patients; the second floor was used as wards and accommodation for the head nurse; and the remainder of the nursing staff shared the third floor. In 1916, the Church purchased the nearby lumber yard property "to keep out undesirables and prevent a fire-trap being close to the barn," and used one shed for vehicles and the other for a henhouse. The hospital at Ethelbert was closed in 1957, and later was sold to the Ukrainian Greek Orthodox Parish.

The Pine River Hospital Unit, opened in 1920 and closed in 1946, used a vacant school building and developed a small cottage hospital. Facilities were meagre. The water supply was poor so the hospital, like other residents in the area, melted snow in winter for laundry purposes, and used barrels to catch rainwater in summer.

When the work at Sifton was discontinued in 1924, the furnishings and equipment were transferred to Amaranth where Nurse Isabel Meikle operated a dispensary and community nursing service. In 1929 the Woman's Missionary Society decided to transfer the Amaranth work "to a more needy area." After consultation with the Manitoba Government Medical Services, the home missions superintendent and the Woman's Missionary Society leaders chose a new site at Gypsumville, the location of limestone mining. The Gypsum Company provided a building at a nominal rent, and nurses Margaret Mustard and Annetta Sinclair were appointed as medical workers. Mustard (later Crookes), reports that, while the house was owned by the Gypsum Company, "the furniture came from Amaranth, the kitchen range and heater required wood, there was no electricity or running water (which was 'hard' and had to be brought from the village pump), and they had to melt snow in winter for laundry purposes."[18] The formal opening of the Gypsumville Hospital Unit was a dinner given by the two nurses to members of the Woman's Missionary Society Conference Committee.

Mustard was not content to confine her activities to nursing and soon mobilized the community to build a church. The new church was opened in March, 1933, by the Rev. Dr. Charles W. Gordon, and the structure was debt-free. The hospital, with several improvements and repairs, remained in operation until 1957–58, when it was closed.

The hospital at Vita, in southeastern Manitoba, grew out of a small mission or social centre established by the Methodist Church. It was generally felt that the establishment of medical services at Vita, with an area population of about eight thousand people, would strengthen the mission there.[19] The people living there were largely of central European origin, they had very

Dr. Hunter on a house call. (Photo courtesy of Dolly Maksymyk.)

Elizabeth M. Crowe Hospital, Eriksdale, Manitoba. (Photo courtesy of Kay Forsyth.)

poor farming land, and the area was some distance from the nearest doctor. The funds for the hospital building, opened in 1923, came from the Home Mission Board. This building was a three-storey structure, was thirty-eight by sixty-six feet, and cost $58,000. The hospital could accommodate twenty-two patients plus staff, and had its own water system and electricity. In 1940, a thirty-foot extension was added to the north end at a further cost of $13,000. In June, 1955, a devastating cyclone (thankfully in which no one was killed or injured) caused damage requiring major repairs and renovations, costing a further $83,000. Some of this cost was covered by insurance. The property was sold to the Vita Hospital District in 1966 for $60,000, to be paid over a ten-year period in interest-free monthly payments. The formal transfer took place on 5 September 1975.

The hospital at Eriksdale grew out of a medical program of the Woman's Missionary Society, and "in 1926 a building was erected and equipped at a cost of $7,000, contributed by Westminster Church" [Winnipeg].[20] The hospital was small and even after an annex was added for a kitchen and staff dining room, it accommodated only fourteen beds and six bassinets. Toilet facilities were inadequate, the basement was damp, and the heating was unsatisfactory, but improvements were made. Only minor surgery was performed. A building for isolation cases was erected but it had to be used for storage and as a morgue. In 1958, a new wing was added, but it was soon clear that a new structure was needed. The Church and the community responded and in September 1963 a new hospital was opened with seventeen beds, five bassinets, modern X-ray and laboratory facilities, a well-equipped operating room, and spacious halls.[21] Before long, however, negotiations between the Church and the provincial government were begun, and arrangements were made for a transfer of responsibility for the hospital to the community (hospital district). The community was reluctant about this process: people tended to feel more comfortable with a church-sponsored medical service than they did with a government-run service. Nevertheless, the transfer was arranged, and was completed in June 1977 when the Church relinquished all formal involvement with the hospital. It is worth noting, however, that many local Church people continue to be active and involved in the welfare and administration of the hospital, so there is a continuing, informal input from the Church.

"So we built!"[22] The response was to the need for medical services and structures were built or acquired as each situation demanded. Changes and alterations were made, doctors and nurses were recruited, medical services were adjusted, and closing or phasing out was accomplished when new systems developed. The legacy lies not so much in the buildings as it does in the quality of service and devotion to duty rendered by medical personnel and in the grateful response of the people.

DEEDS OF LOVE AND MERCY

The 1956 Commission on Church hospitals, reporting to the 17th General Council of The United Church, stated: "In Church hospitals, it is particularly important that Doctors and Nurses, and in fact, all other staff, should, in addition to being well-trained, skillful and efficient in their work, be also persons of high Christian character, devoted to duty and bearing a Christian witness among those with whom they associate in the hospital and the community which the hospital serves."[23] In many ways this is an accurate description of the people who had been serving in the Church hospitals.

Foremost in this service was the country doctor. Whether the doctor was appointed by the church or placed in an area by some other agency, the work demanded from the doctor a selfless devotion to duty that commanded the respect and appreciation of the community. Joined with the country doctor in the healing enterprise were the nursing co-workers who also rendered stellar service, often with less recognition and prominence. "When the history of this country comes to be written, historians will find woven into the lives of Canada's early pioneers the impress of other lives, and foremost among them will be that of the Christian nurses, whose courage and faithfulness, tender efficient skill and great sacrifice were blended into one magnificent heroic, and patriotic service for God, country and humanity. All honour to such women, co-workers with the Great Physician."[24] These words are weighted with sentiment and jingoism, but they do show that the existence of the pioneer nurse in these new communities was surely a blessing. It is a significant oversight that their role has not been noted in Canadian history books.

From various records we find the following examples which indicate some of the extreme hardships and circumstances experienced by the people in the areas where the Church medical work was carried out:

In 1929, Dr. Hunter, in his work at Teulon, was called to a home several miles in the country to attend a women in labour. The husband was away working, trying to make some money to support his family of thirteen, one of whom had tuberculosis. The family had one cow to milk; otherwise their only food was flour and salt. Dr. Hunter bundled the mother into his vehicle and drove her the thirty-four miles to the Teulon Hospital. Soon after arrival, the family number was fourteen, but it is not likely the change in number removed their hardships.

Rose Anna Bolton at Pine River tells of being called to a home one day at 3:30 a.m., but there was nothing she could do to save the mother. With five children in the room, the grieving husband said to her, after thanking her for all she had done, "I will pay you someday when I have money. I have only $4 now, and I need it for the burial."[25]

In the 1927 Year Book, in a report on hospital work, among the diseases listed with which the doctors and nurses had to contend is "broken hearts,"[26] a diagnosis of the need to revive hope and courage in the face of so many difficulties and calamities.

Margaret Mustard arranged a dental clinic in Gypsumville in 1931, but the work was more than the visiting dentist could handle. So she was instructed quickly in the art of extracting teeth and, in a ten-day period pulled "93 teeth using the painless extraction method!"[27] Deeds of love and mercy often required more than love and mercy!

"In 1927 Dr. Samuel Eshoo at Ethelbert covered 4, 175 miles in his errands of mercy and visited 555 patients. Dr. Eshoo says, 'No medical missionary can make money and answer the real purpose of his work at the same time!' Often he felt he should be giving money to the patients rather than charging them for his services."[28]

In order to communicate with and better understand the people in the Teulon area, Dr. Hunter studied the Ruthenian language and became proficient in using it. "I am discovering," he wrote, "many interesting things in Ruthenian literature and, just now, am preparing a pamphlet on the history of the people."[29]

On one occasion Dr. Hunter was called to a maternity case and asked the husband if he could be reimbursed for the $7 livery charge. The husband indicated he was unable to pay and Dr. Hunter, sizing up the situation, ended up providing clothing and other help for the family.

On 20 February 1951, Nick Ruzycki committed suicide. Nick had been with the Ethelbert Hospital for thirty years. As a boy he came to the hospital with an injured leg and remained there, going to school and doing odd jobs as the hospital became his home and life. Nick became a Sunday school teacher in the local church, and was a model caretaker at the hospital. For over twenty years Nick was the doctor's chauffeur and interpreter. Nick took his own life because he did not want to be a burden on anyone in his old age, but he left a legacy of trustworthy, honourable, and faithful service to everyone at Ethelbert Hospital.

When a tribute was being paid to Dr. Harold V. Waldon in 1934 for his faithful service at Vita, a patient had a conversation with Rev. Scott Leith, then the minister at Ninette. Asked if he knew Dr. Waldon, the patient, in broken English replied, "Yes, yes, him send me here. Him most like Jesus any man I know."[30]

Margaret Mustard recounts her first Christmas at Gypsumville when a man was brought in at 5 a.m. with symptoms of a ruptured appendix. He was taken to Winnipeg on a stretcher in a baggage car on the train, accompanied by Miss Mustard. When she returned on December 27, thankful that the man survived, she brought a primrose plant. People came from far and wide to see this beautiful plant blooming in winter. From then on the hospital tried to have seasonal flowers in the unit at all times.[31]

Dr. Hunter recounts an early experience: "In the first year no diphtheria antitoxin could be obtained readily, and we saw some tragedies. One of my first experiences was being called to a Ukrainian home when the disease was raging. It was a little log cabin about ten by fifteen. All one side was taken up by a bed and a large clay stove. One child had died and was laid out, with candles burning. Four more were sick and crawling over the bed and over the top of the stove, gasping for breath. The place seemed filled with the stench of the disease and was crowded with neighbors watching the children's dying agonies. I had no antitoxin and could only use old fashioned remedies. I was very thankful that two of the children recovered. One had died of the disease two weeks before, so out of six children in that home, only two were left."[32]

Though there was much tragedy and sadness, sometimes there was a touch of humour. On one occasion, Dr. Waldon at Vita encountered a unique medical request. A woman came to him three times asking for an operation since her friends appeared to feel this was a status symbol in the community. When Dr. Waldon refused the request on medical grounds, he was approached by the woman's husband with an interesting argument to support the request. "It's near Christmas," the husband said. "You give her operation for present." There is no record of such an operation.

A few weeks after her arrival in Gypsumville, Alice Gordon, R.N., tells of a woman who travelled seven miles on horseback to have teeth extracted at the hospital. Six teeth were removed "without pain." The woman rested for a while, had some supper, agreed to return later for more extractions, and then rode home dressed in sweater and breeches. If the nurses and doctors were made of sterling stuff, many of their patients were similarly blessed.

As the writer of Hebrews asks, "And what more shall I say?"[33] The record of the work of the doctors and nurses in the eight areas where the Church established medical work could easily be the subject of a substantial treatise.

CHOOSING NAMES

The simplest way to name an institution is to use the name of the geographical area where it is located, and most of the Church medical units in Manitoba were named in this way. The work at Sifton, Ethelbert, Amaranth, Pine River, Gypsumville and orginally at Teulon assumed the name of these communities, and are recorded as such.

The Teulon Hospital, founded by Dr. A.J. Hunter, was known as the Teulon Hospital for several years. Because Dr. Hunter's medical and community work made such an impression on the area, it acquired the name The Hunter Hospital. Records do not indicate when or how this change was made, but it appears to have occurred about 1920. No hospital was more suitably named, for Dr. Hunter rendered singular service from the time of his arrival in Teulon in 1902 until his death in 1940. At that point the hospital was officially renamed Hunter Memorial, and the name has not been altered despite the change in ownership.

Dr. Hunter was not only involved in establishing medical work in Teulon, but he was also instrumental in building two school homes that provided an opportunity for a high school education for many children in the outlying areas. In addition, his acquired understanding of the Ukrainian language enabled him to translate many gems of Ukrainian literature into English, thus providing a bridge between the central European settlers and those of Anglo-Saxon origin. The concluding sentence in his book, *A Friendly Adventure* sums up his spirit: "Let us join together as Canadians and seek the best things from whatever country they may come."[34] The hospital at Teulon remains a witness to his concern and dream.

The hospital at Vita, like the one in Teulon, originally took the name of the community. In 1943, with the death of Janet A. Cruise, widow of a Winnipeg contractor, the residue of her estate was left to the United Church of Canada on condition that the hospital at Vita be named The William Edmund Cruise and William Foresst Cruise Memorial Hospital. Since the residue was about $33,000, this was a very tempting proposition to the Board of Home Missions. The local hospital board was asked to make a recommendation on the name change, but the final decision would remain with the Board of Home Missions. At a meeting of the Vita Hospital Board on 30 June 1943, "it was recommended to the Board of Home Missions that the name of the hospital be changed to meet the requirements of Provision No. 7 of the Janet A. Cruise will, dated 13 December 1938."[35] The funds from the estate were used for "property improvements." Stationery and other official items at the hospital were changed to reflect the new name but the hospital board continued to use the name Vita Hospital Board in subsequent minutes. The community did not accept the name change either, and "Vita Hospital" continued to be the usual way of referring to the building. In the late 1950s, when the hospital administration was transferred to the community, the acquired name was dropped, and it was once again officially called Vita Hospital. One wonders what name the hospital might bear today had Dr. Waldon's name been suggested, since Waldon rendered such faithful service from 1927 to his retirement in 1958.

From its beginning, the hospital at Eriksdale was called the Elizabeth M. Crowe Memorial Hospital. Elizabeth Crowe had been a devoted worker and generous contributor to women's work in Westminster Church, Winnipeg. She served on the Woman's Missionary Society Conference Committee, seeking out a site for a new hospital in the Interlake region. She did not live to see the fruits of her labour, but did see some of the plans for the hospital since a member of her family was the architect in charge. The women's organizations of Westminster Church provided $5,000 to erect a memorial to Elizabeth Crowe and it was decided as a "memorial to her services and benevolent donations"[36] to name the hospital at Eriksdale after her. Today, even with all the changes in administration and new construction, along with the transfer of the hospital administration to the community, the name of Elizabeth Mona Crowe remains in the community as a continuing tribute to her work.

FINANCING THE SERVICE

Since the medical services of the Church were administered through national structures, most of the funds for capital and maintenance expenditures were provided by national funds of the Church. In some instances, as in Teulon, an effort was made to raise local money but was usually not successful. Both the Woman's Missionary Society and the Board of Home Missions recognized the importance of the healing ministries of the Church and provided generously from their limited budgets. But there was always need for more funds. Doctors and nurses quickly learned how to stretch dollars and to improvise when money was not available. At all times, the national bodies of the Church remained sensitive and concerned about the capital and maintenance needs of the medical units, and responded as best they could.

However the most significant aspect of the story of medical financing is found not so much in the efforts of the national structures of the Church, as it is in the contributions of the doctors and nurses. At Vita it is reported that Dr. Waldon never sent out a bill. "If people want to know what they owe," he reported, "they call and ask."[37] A story from Vita relates that an appendix operation could be paid for with one quart of cream, a dozen eggs and a bag of cucumbers! On another occasion a man brought in two bags of potatoes in payment for medical services, with a further promise: "Anything I have more than I can use for myself, I will give the hospital free."[38]

Dr. Hunter tells of two payments he valued "more than any others."[39] He had visited a colony of European settlers about twenty-eight miles from Teulon three or four times a year. At the end of seven years he received his first payment: a pair of elk horns. On another occasion he attended a maternity case fifty-five miles from Teulon, accompanied by a nurse, Miss Grant. The baby arrived before the doctor and nurse did, and all was in good order, so Dr. Hunter did not charge a fee. However, the family insisted he should receive some remuneration. Noticing that jack pine grew in the area, Dr. Hunter suggested they might transplant some in his Teulon yard. The people readily agreed, and for years the pines graced the doctor's home as a reminder of this trip.

Dr. Hunter also writes about a happy experience in 1932 when he received an overdue payment. "About 28 years ago a little French baby arrived in our hospital. I remembered the case, but had quite forgotten that the baby had never been paid for. The French folk remembered, however, and just a few weeks ago, a younger sister of that baby came to pay the debt. What pleased us most in this little incident was the confirmation of that old Scripture text, for this was truly after many days."[40]

There was often a lack of information in the community about the financing of the Church's hospital work. Apparently people did not inquire, and little or no effort was made to inform them. Dr. Ruth Fryer, serving in the Ethelbert Hospital in 1951, received an invitation to speak to the local Chamber of Commerce, normally a male bastion. She told them about the actual cost of services rendered through the hospital. The Chamber was amazed to learn that the Church had given over half a million dollars to the Ethelbert Hospital since 1919. Out of this revelation, the members of the Chamber of Commerce agreed to form an advisory board comprising three people from each village and municipal council. As a result of this new interest and concern, a new washing machine was procured by the community and vegetables were provided, so that the hospital staff no longer needed to plant and maintain a garden for hospital needs. As well, many repairs were made to the building.

Efforts were made to recruit resident doctors for each of the hospitals, but several times when there were vacancies, arrangements were made with a nearby doctor to serve the hospital needs. This happened at Eriksdale where the services of Dr. Gudmundur Paulson of Lundar were used for many years. Dr. Paulson made his own financial arrangements with the patients, but it is likely he was often paid in kind or received little or nothing except the gratitude of the people. At Gypsumville the matron of the hospital made arrangements for occasional visits by doctors and dentists, and minimum fee guarantees were usually made.

The salaries of the doctors and nurses were paid by the appointing body: either the Woman's Missionary Society or the Board of Home Missions. There are few records of the amounts of remuneration, but a report in 1956[41] states that nurses received $100 to $125 per month plus maintenance (room and board). One can assume that it had taken many years for salaries to reach this level. Some of the doctors, such as Dr. Waldon at Vita, also served as area medical officer, visiting schools with immunization programs, and received additional renumeration for this service. However, there is no record of any doctor or nurse getting rich on their incomes. The meagre financial records of the hospitals that have survived do not contain complaints and demands other than comments about the need for more financial support to undergird the ministry. The reports do indicate that the hospital staffs shared in the privations and hard work of the people in their community as they endeavoured to maintain a meaningful level of medical service.

The advent of government-assisted medical services proved a great blessing to the hospitals, even though there were misgivings on the part of Church members about it. It did provide scales of finances for capital and operating costs that removed much of the financial pressure on the Church and, at the same time, it introduced another level of control. Manitoba was one of the provinces in the 1950s to share in the program that provided matching federal and provincial grants of $1,000 per bed for acute-care hospitals, $1,500 per bed for chronic-care hospitals, $500 per bed for nurses' residences, $1,000 for each three bassinets and $1,000 for each three hundred square feet of floor space occupied by X-ray, laboratory service, or out-patients departments. In the changeover, municipalities were given authority to assess residents for the capital costs of hospitals, and all three levels of government guaranteed to all hospitals the full cost of care of indigent persons.

At long last the major financial conerns of the medical and hospital work were met, but the new program disturbed the Church. The Board of Home Missions, sensing loss of control as well as a base for Christian witness and service, reacted to this government involvement. At its meeting held between 14 and 16 April 1953, the Board approved a motion: "While recognizing the fact that the State is to an increasing extent taking over the responsibility for the physical well-being of the individual, it is the opinion of the Board that the State, having shown an increasing awareness of the problem and having manifested its desire to cooperate with voluntary agencies and to assist in financing hospitals, the Church should continue to take a share in providing in certain areas for the care of the sick, with such modifications as may become necessary from time to time, and that therefore, our hospital ministry should be maintained."[42] Little did the Board realize what modifications would be necessary, and how quickly time would run out on the United Church hospital work in Manitoba.

END OF AN ERA

"The far-reaching influence of all our hospitals across Canada is something that cannot be demonstrated in statistics. Their significance lies in the healing ministries performed quietly and unheralded year in and year out and the influences asserted by doctors and nurses, not only on the sick, but also on the community life in general in each hospital area. Through these institutions our Church has opportunity, in part, to obey our Lord's command to 'heal the sick' and to do something real in bearing others' 'burdens' and so fulfill the law of Christ."[43] In these words Dr. Malcolm C. Macdonald of the Board of Home Missions summed up the essential purpose of the Church in establishing and maintaining medical work.

The centres of concern were largely frontier areas where newly arrived settlers faced the uncertainties of carving a new life of hope in new surroundings. That the Church was with them, even though the denomination may not have been their particular persuasion, was undoubtedly a source of blessing and comfort to many. However, times change and the role of the Church in its medical endeavours on the frontiers had to adjust accordingly.

With improved roads and transportation facilities and adequate services available in the larger centres of the province, many of the Church's hospitals were phased out. The opening of an adequate hospital in Dauphin had its effect on the Church's work in Sifton, Ethelbert and Pine River, and it was necessary to close them. By the mid 1950s, the medical work at Amaranth and Gypsumville had also ceased as other medical arrangements were established.

At Teulon, arrangements had been made with the municipality to assume responsiblity for hospital and medical services. By 1960 the only United Church hospitals operating in Manitoba were at Vita and Eriksdale. However, negotiations soon began in both these communities to transfer the hospitals to municipal control. As with the earlier attempts to negotiate transfers in other areas, these communities too were reluctant to change: it appeared that the hospital boards and people in the community had more confidence in the methods and systems of the Church than they did in the methods proposed by government agencies. With increasing medical costs, however, the transfer process was inevitable. Arrangements were made for a ten-year "rent to purchase" plan with the Vita community in which the property would be paid for at the rate of $6,000 per year in monthly instalments. The final transfer of the Vita Hospital took place on 5 September 1975. The Elizabeth M. Crowe Memorial Hospital in Eriksdale was the last unit to be transferred, and this transfer was completed in June 1977.

The work that began with evangelistic enthusiasm in 1900 by Drs. Munro and Scott, and later with Dr. Hunter, and carried on by so many dedicated doctors and nurses over the years, continues in another form. The legacy of these church and community workers remains in the foundations of Christian service and witness they established, and in the lives of people in need of soul and body healing. The Church recognized the modifications needed and adjusted accordingly. The memories, however, will linger on, fulfilling the expectation of Reeve Joseph Kolickowsky at the opening of the Vita Hospital in 1923 when he said, "This hospital will save lives, stop pain, and dry up tears."[44] Such were the results of the medical and hospital work of the United Church in Manitoba as it fulfilled its three-fold ministry to people in the province. The work continues in the Hunter Memorial Hospital in Teulon, the Vita Hospital and the Elizabeth M. Crowe Memorial Hospital in Eriksdale, each a profound legacy to the vision and labour of men and women who "fought the good fight, finished the race, and kept the faith."[45]

Church union and western Canada

N. Keith Clifford

Fifty years ago, Dr. E.H. Oliver claimed that "the needs of the frontier inspired the vision and raised the issue of church union" in Canada. Furthermore, he asserted, that church union "was forced forward from the frontier of the prairies."[1] At the centre of his argument there were three propositions which invite closer examination. In 1923, Oliver declared that church union in western Canada was already an accomplished fact. In addition, he asserted that, unlike the situation in the East, there was no division in the West between the rural and urban churches on the question of union. Therefore, he concluded that it was not possible for the churches to back away from union. They had to move forward, in spite of some minor losses this might cause in eastern Canada, for otherwise they would lose the entire West.[2] Oliver's entire argument rests on these three premises. In this article I examine each of them in turn to determine whether they adequately reflect the different ways in which the three prairie provinces reacted to the church union issue.

In support of his contention that church union was an accomplished fact in the Canadain West, Oliver provided three pieces of evidence taken primarily from the Province of Saskatchewan. First, he cited the case of the cooperative union churches which resulted from the comity arrangements initiated in 1899 between the Methodists and Presbyterians.[3] Through these arrangements, according to Oliver, the Methodists and Presbyterians would each assume responsibility for the territory adjacent to alternate railway stations across the prairies.[4] By 1924, Oliver said, there were 350 places in Saskatchewan where this arrangement or some modification of it had taken place.[5]

Similar comity arrangements had been worked out in Alberta and Manitoba between the Methodists and Presbyterians. The Alberta Plan had

Edmund H. Oliver (Photo courtesy of Western Canada Pictorial Index.)

been used in 1911 by W.G. Brown of Red Deer, to demonstrate how a concrete and workable plan of federation (rather than organic union) had been devised by the churches in Alberta.[6] But Oliver did not mention the Alberta example because he was not interested in federation. He argued that all of the comity arrangements in Saskatchewan were "made tolerable only by the hope of church union."[7]

Next, Oliver brought forward the instance of the local independent union charges. He traced the beginnings of these churches to the establishment of an independent union congregation at Melville, Saskatchewan, in 1908. Oliver stated that by 1924 there were thirty of these congregations in Saskatchewan and they constituted "virtually a new denomination."[8] Again, however, he gave no indication of how many of these churches existed in Manitoba or Alberta.

Perhaps Oliver should not be faulted for his vagueness about these churches, indeed, very little is known about them. At the first meeting of the General Council of the United Church of Canada in June 1925, the General Council of Local Union Churches of Western Canada was represented by five ministers and five laymen, the most prominent of whom was the Honorable J.G. Gardiner. Three of this group were from Manitoba: the Rev. T.A. Munroe of Morris, John A. Young of Cypress River and J.J. Storey of Wawanesa.[9] The Rev. C.S. Elsey of Aneroid, Saskatchewan, president of the General Council of the Local Union Churches of Canada, signed the Basis of Union on behalf of these churches but they made no report to the first General Council of the United Church. As well, no separate record of their ministers and congregations was included in the *Record of Proceedings* of the first General Council. It is known that the Rev. John Reid was the travelling secretary of the General Council of Local Union Churches and that they published a newspaper. But the minutes of the council meetings, its publications and all other records have disappeared.[10] Consequently, it is extremely difficult to assess their significance or to determine the extent to which this "virtually autonomous denomination," would have constituted a focal point for the emergence of a new denomination in the West had union not taken place.

Finally, Oliver referred to the "double affiliation" churches which had come into existence after 1917. In these congregations, groups of Methodists and Presbyterians functioned as a single unit while keeping track of their members on separate rolls and contributing to the mission funds of both parent churches. According to Oliver, there were sixty of these congregations in Saskatchewan in 1924; a further twelve had triple affiliation and one had quadruple affiliation. Once again, however, Oliver provided no statistics for

Alberta or Manitoba, even though the addition of these figures would presumably have strengthened his contention that union was already an accomplished fact in the Canadian West.

This exclusive concentration on Saskatchewan is particularly curious because in the Presbyterian Synod of Manitoba, for example, the presbytery clerks put the union congregations under separate headings and indicated whether there was a Methodist or Presbyterian minister in charge.[11] Therefore, Oliver could have added another sixty union congregations from the Synod of Manitoba and he could have used these statistics to support his case that church union was already an accomplished fact in the West. But in Alberta and Manitoba the evidence was not as clear as it was in Saskatchewan. It appears that, by not mentioning Alberta and Manitoba, Oliver sought to leave the impression that the situation in these western provinces was similar to that of Saskatchewan.

The next question, therefore, is: how accurate was the Saskatchewan evidence which Oliver used to support his case? When he appeared before the Private Bills Committee in Ottawa, Oliver used a map showing the union churches in Saskatchewan with red dots indicating some form of union and black dots showing where the exclusively Presbyterian churches were located. In circulating this map and others for several different regions of Canda, he indicated that he was prepared to vouch only for the Saskatchewan map and that even it contained some errors. But these errors, he suggested, showed a bias against rather than for union and the map "should be even redder than it is."[12]

His claim that there were 440 union charges in Saskatchewan, however, was sharply questioned by several members of the Private Bills Committee. William Duff, the Liberal member from Lunenberg, Nova Scotia, for example, read part of a letter from the Rev. J.R. Graham of St. Andrew's Presbyterian Church in Assiniboia, which stated that "the map of church union in Saskatchewan is fearfully and wonderfully made." The map, Graham said, "gives only 1 Presbyterian charge in Assiniboia [that is, the Presbytery of Assiniboia], while it gives 38 union charges: as a matter of fact we have not a single union charge in our Presbytery."[13] Oliver, however, refused to admit any errors. He simply pulled rank and bluffed his way through, insisting that his information was more accurate than Graham's.

When this was questioned, Oliver admitted that he had not prepared his own statistics, but had used those provided by the superintendents of the Presbyterian and Methodist churches in Saskatchewan. Unfortunately for Oliver, however, the superintendent of missions for northern Saskatchewan, W.A. Cameron, was an opponent of union. Therefore, J.W. MacNamara, the organizing secretary of the Presbyterian Church Association, had asked Cameron for a letter commenting on the accuracy of Oliver's map. Duff, as the major parliamentary opponent of union, had a copy of Cameron's letter in front of him which, in part, read: "I doubt if the number of such congregations that call themselves union would be over 12, [and] if I were called to name those that were union churches I could not name half a dozen."[14] When asked to comment on this statement, Oliver again did not go into particulars. He simply pointed out that Cameron was responsible only for the northern half of the province and, therefore, did not have a complete grasp of the union picture in Saskatchewan.

In spite of further questioning that raised serious doubts about the validity of his maps, Oliver seemed determined to bluster his way through to the end. Thus, in summing up his presentation, he declared that there were 1,245 union congregations in Canada and "the advantage of union and the harmonious working of union, has become so well-known in the west that you could not organize anew the Presbyterian or Methodist district or denominational church."[15]

In some ways it is unfortunate that Duff did not make better use of Cameron's letter, for the portion which he read gave an inaccurate impression of the point Cameron was attempting to make. It is quite clear from this letter that Cameron was speaking of the whole of Saskatchewan and that he was making a serious attempt to provide accurate information. For example, he stated that there were thirty-two straight union charges in Saskatchewan which were organized into two presbyteries. In addition, there were forty-eight "double-affiliated" united charges. This kind of charge, Cameron thought, was working well in towns and villages in which there was room for only one church. "To my mind," he said, "the Presbyterian section of the united charge is in practically as close relation to the mother church as is the strictly Presbyterian congregation." Moreover, he continued, "so much has this type of union appealed to the people that since the double affiliated plan came into force over two years ago only three straight union churches have been formed." Finally, Cameron indicated that there were 228 cooperating points ministered to by Presbyterian ministers and missionaries, and 124 cooperating points ministered to by Methodist ministers or missionaries. In the 228 Presbyterian points, Cameron emphasized, all mission fields and nearly all augmented charges were included.[16]

The main point of Cameron's letter, however, was not the statistics but rather the interpretation of the statistics. Concerning "double affiliation," he said in his letter, "I believe that what appeals to people in it, is the fact that they have in this type, all the local advantages of union and yet are not cut off from the parent church." He made a similar point about the 352 cooperating points. Of these, 228 were totally Presbyterian in all respects. "Their church government," he said, "is wholly Presbyterian and everything about the church is carried on exactly as it is in the strictest Presbyterian congregation in Ontario."[17] The same was true of the 124 Methodist points: they were wholly Methodist. Therefore, if union did not occur they would remain as they were; in other words, they would not suddenly become a new united church of western Canada, as Oliver claimed. The only congregations which might continue toward forming a new church were the thirty-two local union congregations in Saskatchewan and the six local union congregations in the Presbyterian Synod of Manitoba, at Wawanesa, MacGregor, Beresford, Glenboro, Cypress River and Dryden, Ontario, as well as the union congregations in the Presbyterian Synod of Alberta.

If we read the evidence from this viewpoint, we get a picture quite different from that presented by Oliver. It is true that Cameron was an opponent of union, but he was not a major participant in the controversy. Consequently, while his figures are similar to Oliver's, his interpretation of them seems to be less politically oriented and therefore less biased. Unfortunately, however, it is Oliver's interpretation rather than Cameron's that the historians of church union have used.[18]

Oliver gave very little evidence to support his contention that there was no serious division between rural and urban churches in the West. In 1923, he simply stated that "the urban centres of western Canada are much more vitally related to the rural parts than the corresponding places in eastern Canada, and the urban centres of western Canada are giving way to rural opinion."[19] If this had been the case, then important differences between the urban churches of eastern and western Canada and their relations with their rural counterparts would have been apparent. But the important differences are not apparent. It is necessary, therefore, to determine what evidence there is to support this contention.

The only evidence which exists is the final vote of 1925 which determined whether individual congregations would go in or remain out of the United Church of Canada. From these records, it would appear that Oliver was on firmer ground when he pointed out the contrast in the relationship of the urban to rural churches in eastern and western Canada, for it is clear that the strength of the opposition to union was not in the urban centres of western Canada. Yet, when the results from Alberta, Saskatchewan and Manitoba are compared, some interesting differences appear.

In Manitoba, for example, the opponents of union barely had a toehold in Winnipeg and Brandon. Out of twenty-one congregations in Winnipeg and three in Brandon, only one Presbyterian church in each city was retained and in both cases they were among the smallest.[20] In the major Presbyterian churches in Winnipeg with memberships over a thousand (Westminister, Augustine, St. Stephen's and Knox) there were minorities who subsequently banded together to form First Presbyterian Church. But it is clear that the vast majority of Presbyterians and all the Methodists in Winnipeg and Brandon were in favour of union.

Why this was so is, of course, an interesting question. Among the many possible answers, one surely is the fact that there were several prominent national leaders of the union movement in Winnipeg: Leslie Pidgeon at Augustine, C.W. Gordon at St. Stephen's, F.B. DuVal of Knox and Andrew Baird at Manitoba College. Besides these men there were other local leaders, such as J.R. Mutchmor at Robertson Memorial, E.G.D. Freeman at King Memorial and J.A. Cormie, the superintendent of missions for the Presbyterian Synod of Manitoba who were strong advocates of union.

The control which these men exercised in Winnipeg was so effective that, when W.F. McConnell, the dominion organizer for the Presbyterian Church Association, arrived in Winnipeg, not one church would allow him to rent space for meetings. Therefore, he had to rent the YMCA cafeteria for evening meetings during the week and the Capitol Theatre for meetings on Sundays. In February 1924, however, the session of Norwood Presbyterian Church finally relented and agreed to allow the Presbyterian Church Association to hold a meeting in the church basement on the condition that there would be "no discussion or questions from the other side, for the sake of peace in the local congregation."[21]

Banks Nelson and W.F. McConnell were to be the featured speakers, and the prospect of such a meeting occurring in his church must have been an embarrassment to the minister, the Rev. D. McIvor, for, instead of attending the meeting, he went curling. J.A. Cormie, superintendent of missions and also an elder at Norwood Church, and E.G.D. Freeman of King Memorial, were not the sort who would miss an anti-unionist meeting, nor were they above using such an occasion to create as much disturbance as possible. As soon as McConnell and Nelson had finished speaking, Cormie immediately arose to read what he claimed was a statement from the minister of Norwood Church. The reading of such a statement was clearly against the rules laid down by the session, and Cormie was asked to sit down. As soon as he did so, however, Freeman requested the privilege of asking questions. This was an extremely sore point among the opponents of union, since at all the unionist's meetings they had always been prevented from asking questions. McConnell responded by offering to answer Freeman's questions if he were prepared to allow the opponents of union to hold a meeting at King Memorial. Freeman replied that only the session could grant such permission in his church, and there the matter ended.[22] But with this kind of pressure on them, it is not surprising that the opponents of union had a very difficult time making headway in Winnipeg.

However, the control that these unionist leaders could exert was less complete in the rural areas of the province. In spite of the fact that the opponents of union were not organized in rural Manitoba, they were able to retain Presbyterian congregations in Melita, Elphinstone and the Okanase Indian Reserve, Wellwood, Winnipegosis, Selkirk, Neepawa, Kildonan, Carberry, Hartney, Breadalbane and Lenore, Forrest, Blyth and Ninga. (Both Forrest and Ninga, it should be noted, had been points on former union charges).[23] The pattern in Manitoba appears to have been the reverse of what it was in many parts of eastern Canada where the centre of opposition to union was in the urban areas. It also appears to have been the reverse of what Oliver had in mind when he said that the western cities were "giving way of rural opinion."

The opponents of union fared somewhat better in Saskatchewan than in Manitoba. They did not secure a church in Regina, but retained one in Moose Jaw, one in Saskatoon and one in Prince Albert. In Saskatoon it was Mayfair Church, the smallest of the four Presbyterian churches in the city, but in Prince Albert it was St. Paul's, which, with its 473 members, was the largest and only Presbyterian Church in town. Saskatoon had among its Presbyterian Church members President W.C. Murray of the University of Saskatchewan and Dr. E.H. Oliver of St. Andrew's College, who were prominent national leaders in the union movement and who undoubtedly were able to exercise a high degree of pro-union control. But there were no such leaders in Regina. It is difficult to explain, therefore, why the opponents of union were unable to get a foothold in Regina. What is even more difficult to explain is how the Presbyterian Church Association, again with very little organization generally in Saskatchewan, was able to make a much better showing in rural Saskatchewan than in rural Manitoba. Anti-unionists succeeded in retaining congregations in almost every presbytery in the Synod of Saskatchewan, whereas they made no headway at all in several rural presbyteries in the Synod of Manitoba.

It is not difficult to understand why a few specific rural churches remained Presbyterian. St. James in Melfort is a case in point, for its minister was W.W. Bryden, the man who, following his appointment at Knox College in Toronto in 1927, led the Presbyterian Church in Canada out of the theological wilderness. But even Bryden was unable to take his whole congregation with him. It split, with thirty-six voting for union and fifty-four against. In other cases, for instance in Weyburn, where there was a sizeable self-supporting Presbyterian church with 377 members who voted overwhelmingly against union, there are no clues available in the existing literature to suggest why they remained Presbyterian. Even Peter Strang, the best authority on the Presbyterian churches in southern Saskatchewan, completely ignores the question.[24] What is clear, however, is that union was not quite as well-established in Saskatchewan as Oliver claimed it was and, as in Manitoba, there was more anti-union sentiment in the rural areas of Saskatchewan than in its cities.

The situation in Alberta was quite different from that in Saskatchewan and Manitoba. There was considerable opposition to union in the urban areas of Alberta. In Calgary, for example, the opponents of union retained three of the ten urban Presbyterian churches. But, more significantly, the largest Presbyterian Church in Calgary, Grace Church, with a membership of 1,072, was overwhelmingly anti-union. It was a centre of the organized opposition to union in Alberta from the beginning. In Edmonton, four of the ten Presbyterian churches remained out of the union. The largest of these, First Presbyterian, whose minister was D.G. McQueen, was the second largest Presbyterian church in Edmonton but it was the oldest Presbyterian church in the city and one of the most prestigious. The opponents of union retained the largest of the three Presbyterian churches in Medicine Hat, that is, St. John's, which had a membership larger than that of the other two Presbyterian churches put together. But notwithstanding this impressive showing in the urban centres of Alberta, it was in the largely rural presbytery of Red Deer that the opponents of union picked up their largest gains; seventy-five percent of the Presbyterian churches in this presbytery voted against union.

The reasons for the Red Deer Presbytery remaining Presbyterian are fairly clear. The minister of the Presbyterian Church in Red Deer was W.G. Brown, who was the most prominent and effective national leader of the Presbyterian Church Association in the Canadian West. He was supported by the clerk of Red Deer Presbytery, J.S. Shortt of Olds, Alberta, who, like Brown, would later become a moderator of the Presbyterian Church in Canada.[25] Both of these men were by far the most effective ministerial leaders of the opposition to church union in the West. Had there been many more like them, the story of church union on the prairies might have been quite different.

It is relatively easy to support an explanation of the impressive gains of the Presbyterian Church Association in Red Deer Presbytery, but there is little information available about the situation in the rest of Alberta and no evidence to explain why there was more opposition to union in the urban centres of Alberta than in urban centres of the other prairie provinces. The situation in Alberta, however, provides many examples for questioning Oliver's argument that there was no serious division between rural and urban churches in the West and that the urban churches of western Canada were "giving way to rural opinion."

The third of Oliver's propositions, that is, that the churches could not back away from union because they would lose the West, rests, as we have already seen, on a rather shaky foundation. The assumption that all the churches in the West would have followed the lead of a small group of local independent churches is most unlikely. Oliver's assumption that the whole of the West was like Saskatchewan will not bear serious scrutiny, because the three prairie provinces do not exist as a single unit which could easily be subsumed in a single category (such as the "frontier"). It is true that each of these provinces went through a "frontier experience" and parts of them, especially in the north, could still be considered "frontier." However, the frontiers of each province, and the responses to the frontiers, were quite different from each other. It is obvious today that they have evolved into three quite distinct social, political and cultural units. The differences among the provinces are also apparent in the realm of religion. They are apparent not only in the number of union churches and the relations between urban and rural churches, but also in the ways the governments of the three provinces dealt with the question of church union and the disputes which arose over property following union.

Manitoba was the only province in Canada where church union was treated as a government measure rather than as a private members' bill. Premier John Bracken, a former Methodist married to a Presbyterian, was responsible for this decision but he was strongly supported by several members of his cabinet, such as Attorney General R.W. Craig, a member of C.W. Gordon's congregation, and F.M. Black, the provincial treasurer, who was a personal friend of George Pidgeon, first moderator of the United Church. Introducing the church union bill as a government measure meant that members of the government were required to support the bill and were not as free to vote according to their consciences as they would have been on a private members' bill. It also meant that the bill passed with little or no amendment. Consequently, Manitoba was also the only province in western Canada which did not set up a property commission to deal with property disputes and cases of hardship among minorities.

All of this made things extremely difficult for the opponents of union in Manitoba, who were led by Judge H.A. Robson. Although Robson later became a leader of the Manitoba Liberal Party, he did not have a seat in the legislature in 1924, therefore he had to turn over the opposition to the church union bill in Manitoba to a non-Presbyterian, John Queen, the leader of Manitoba's Labour Party. Queen, who had been carefully briefed by Robson, did a very effective job of presenting the opposition's case. But he informed the house that personally he had no use for churches and he thought all of them were a menace to society. Describing them as "docile servants of a dominant class in the system," he said that he was opposing the legislation out of a sense of public duty, for he saw the church union movement as "an attempt to get a further strangle-hold on the people."[26] Queen's honesty, while commendable, made his opposition to the legislation more of an embarrassment than an asset to the dissidents. For while he raised all of the points which they felt should be raised against the legislation, he did it from a viewpoint that none of the opponents of union could accept.

In Saskatchewan it appeared as if the church union bill would have as little difficulty in clearing the provincial legislature as it had had in Manitoba. But in Saskatchewan the Liberal government of Premier C.A. Dunning refused to sponsor the legislation as a government measure. Moreover, the opponents of union in Saskatchewan had a strong lay organization led by Judge A.G. Farrell of Moosomin Saskatchewan; Farrell was able to enlist the support of Justice W.M. Martin, a former premier of Saskatchewan and the son of a Presbyterian minister who was very unsympathetic to their cause. When Martin appeared before the select committee on private bills on behalf of the opponents of union, therefore, the struggle in Saskatchewan proved to be much less a one-sided contest than it had been in Manitoba because Martin was able to subject the legislation to a critical scrutiny that few other people in the West could have done.

But because the sides were so diametrically opposed, to each other, it was impossible to proceed. Therefore, the Honourable A.P. McNab, chair of the select committee, asked both sides to meet in order to resolve their differences. The meeting failed to achieve any resolution, and McNab dismissed both parties. He referred several clauses of the bill to the legislative counsel, R.W. Shannon, to condense and redraft. Because of the anticipatory nature of the legislation, the Saskatchewan legislature reserved the right to pass retroactive legislation to bring the Saskatchewan bill into line with the federal legislation. It also introduced specific regulations regarding the holding of congregational meetings in order to vote on whether the congregation would enter the union. This recognition of the coercive character of the legislation as it was first presented to the provincial legislatures and the reservation of the right to deal retroactively with the legislation was hardly a victory for the opponents of union but it was an improvement over the treatment they received in Manitoba and it left the door open for the establishment of a property commission for the resolution of disputes and cases of hardship following the consummation of union.

In Alberta, as in Manitoba, the opponents of union were faced with a government which was in the hands of the United Farmer's Party, a group that was favorably disposed toward the idea of church union. Unlike the situation in Manitoba, however, Premier H.H. Greenfield of Alberta refused to take sides on the issue and therefore the legislation was introduced as a private members' bill. All of those making presentations to the Private Bills Committee on behalf of the opposition to union were Presbyterian ministers from Alberta. D.G. McQueen of First Church, Edmonton, argued that the legislation was coercive and confiscatory and would lead to the disruption of the Presbyterian Church. F.D. Roxborough, also of Edmonton, pointed out that in the fall of 1923 the vote on union in the Synod of Alberta had been thirty-two to twenty-eight in favour, and ever since, the resistance to union had been steadily growing. W.G. Brown of Red Deer took particular exception to Leslie Pidgeon's claim that the General Assembly had a right to force the Presbyterian Church into a merger. "The General Assembly," he asserted, "was the servant of the church not its master." J.S. Shortt of Olds indicated that he did not object to the principle of the majority having its way; what he objected to was the way in which the majority was seeking to drag others with them. His plea was that the Presbyterians who wished to remain out of the union should be left undisturbed and that the coercive clauses of the bill be eliminated.[27]

Yet, even though the ministers offered a creditable performance, they failed to influence the government, who seemed to be more impressed by R.B. Bennett of Calgary, legal counsel for the unionists. Consequently, the church union bill emerged from the Private Bills Committee virtually unaltered and passed its final reading on 12 April 1924.[28]

Manitoba was the only western province which did not set up a property commission. In the case of disputes, therefore, the dissidents' only option was to use the courts. It appeared as if the minority at Roland, Manitoba, were going to exercise this option but their suit was withdrawn before coming to court.

Property commissions were set up in Alberta and Saskatchewan, but the provincial legislatures refused to give these commissions mandatory powers and they did not enforce their findings with either legal or legislative action. Consequently, it was only in those situations where the contending parties voluntarily accepted the recommendations of the commissions that a satisfactory resolution of local disputes was possible. In a number of cases United Church majorities flatly refused to accept the commissions' recommendations. Thus the dissident minorities were denied any relief of the hardship which they claimed existed.

From this cursory comparison of the ways in which the three prairie provinces responded to the question of church union, it is apparent that there were a number of significant differences which are obscured when the provinces are indiscriminately lumped together and labelled the "frontier." In all fairness to Oliver, however, it should be noted that when he first formulated this argument he was acting not as an historian but rather as an ecclesiastical politician and forecaster who was seeking support for church union in eastern Canada and for the union legislation in the Saskatchewan legislature and the parliament of Canada. As a political forecaster, he was more accurate than most: ninety percent of the Presbyterians and all the Methodists in the three prairie provinces did in fact go into the United Church. But later, when he was acting as an historian, he used the same argument to support his contention that church union was a product of the frontier. It is at this point that problems arise because prophecy often does not make good history. Indeed, in Oliver's case it has tended to shut down rather than to stimulate further interest and research on the question of church union in the Canadian West.

Oliver's argument tends toward the abstract and the general rather than toward the particular and the unique. Vast generalizations have their place in historical writing. However, it is essential for scholars to penetrate these generalizations and begin to ask what really happened in Manitoba, Saskatchewan and Alberta before the interesting differences will begin to appear. Examination of these differences will stimulate further research about church union in western Canada. Then, and only then, will it be possible to tell the full story of church union in the prairie provinces.

The Chinese United Church of Winnipeg

Raymond R. Smith

The date of arrival of the first Chinese people in Winnipeg is not known, but by 1915 there were about seven hundred in the city. Following completion of the transcontinental Canadian Pacific Railway (CPR), the Chinese tended to work their way east, establishing themselves in the larger communities. Here they found places as cooks, launderers and similar occupations, establishing a reputation for thriftiness and hard work. Immigration to Canada was restricted, however, by a head tax imposed on Orientals by the Canadian Government.

In 1917, the Rev. Mar Sheung (also spelled "Sueng") and Wong Soon Hong founded the Chinese Christian Association, with about fifty members, and established the group at 418–410 Logan Avenue. The association limited its membership to those belonging to evangelical churches, and was designed as a centre of Christian fellowship and social enjoyment.

The Methodist and Presbyterian Churches shared in the spiritual oversight of the Chinese people. "Indeed, it is possibly here [in Winnipeg] that these two Churches had their first experience in cooperation and sharing a mutual responsibility."[1] The Methodist Church arranged the purchase of the Logan Avenue facilities for $3,000, but the mortgage was paid by interested Chinese and Occidental citizens of Winnipeg. Knox Church took a special interest in the Chinese people and several, when their English improved, became members of that congregation. "About a dozen churches of various denominations maintained Chinese classes in their Sabbath schools for many years, while Zion Church, in addition to this, maintained a Sunday evening class of about forty pupils as well as a night school during the week, with an attendance of ten to thirty."[2] In addition, some members from Grace, Young, and Westminster Churches came to help as teachers. These included Mrs.

T.B. Ross and her daughters Daisy, Molly, Lily and Agnes, as well as Messrs. Stewart, Houston, Heap, George Crocker, and J.A. McHaffie.

Two factors affected the work among the Chinese in Winnipeg. First, for many years after 1917 there was no local church administration to oversee the work. That responsibility fell to the national Home Mission Board of the United Church of Canada through its superintendent of Oriental missions west of the Great Lakes, the Rev. Dr. Smith Stanley Osterhout, who made infrequent visits to the city. On 24 September 1935, Rev. Kenneth Beaton of the national office wrote to Rev. Dr. James Miller in Winnipeg about the "Chinese mission" and commented regarding a request for a half-salary and transportation grant for Rev. and Mrs. Mar Seung. "It is hard for me to believe that such a request could have come forward without anybody in Winnipeg Presbytery being informed of it."[3] Even as late as 1947 Dr. Cecil H. Best, home mission superintendent in Manitoba, could write Dr. John R. Leng of the Home Mission Board in Toronto: "So far as I can see neither the Presbytery or the Superintendent has had very much to do with the Mission."[4]

Second, the Chinese ministers served several communities and their stay in one place was necessarily short. On 26 October 1936, the Rev. Dr. Harry B. Duckworth, chairman of the Chinese Work Committee, wrote to the Rev. William H.C. Leech, the presbytery home mission convener, stating: "The services which Mr. Chow [Rev. Yee Ching Chow] has been conducting when here seems to be pretty well confined to a meeting at 4 o'clock Sunday afternoon. The members of his little group carry on this meeting when he is absent. This meeting or service is attended by five or six men. There is said to be not more than a dozen Christian Chinese in Winnipeg."[5] Chow would arrive in Winnipeg on a Saturday evening and remain until Sunday of the following week, thus providing services two Sundays each month, as well as pastoral care during that week. The balance of his time was spent in serving other points in the province.

By the mid-1930s the Chinese Mission in Winnipeg had ceased flourishing. The building on Logan Avenue was in need of major repairs, the Sunday school had been discontinued, and, because of the strong desire of the older people to have their children learn Chinese, English classes were discontinued. But a faithful few persisted through this difficult time, and the nucleus of a Christian fellowship was maintained.

The turning point came in 1943 when the Chinese Mission formed a committee, comprised of Daisy Ross, Chen Hain Ken, Violet Quon, Frank Chan, George Crocker, whose intention it was to improve church facilities and programs. The Committee raised $144 and received a grant of $100 from

Chinese United Church, Winnipeg, Manitoba (Photo courtesy of Greg McCullough.)

the Home Mission Board, but it was soon obvious that more drastic measures were needed. In 1945, the Rev. Dr. Walter E. Donnelly of Young Church, who had been added to the committee, was named to head an expanded committee to raise funds for the Chinese Church and Community Centre. The Chinese people, through the leadership of the Rev. Fung Yu Louie, raised $6,000 toward the estimated cost of $33,000. On 13 November 1945, the Home Mission Board received a delegation from the Chinese Christian Association regarding a new church site on the north side of Pacific Avenue, between King and Princess Streets, and arrangements for purchase were quickly made. The Chinese people were encouraged to proceed with plans to erect a building to be known as The Chinese United Church. However, when the basement was completed in 1947 at a cost of $26,500, there were insufficient funds to complete the church. In fact it took ten years to clear the debt for the basement. The old building and site on Logan Avenue were sold in 1946 for $1,500, and the physical condition of the building may be assessed by a comment of the Rev. Dr. George Dorey of the Home Mission Board to the Rev. Dr. John A. Cormie, home mission superintendent in Manitoba: "I'd hate to pay $1,500 for that place."[6]

The Rev. Thomas Choy, who came from China to do post-graduate study at United College in Winnipeg, served as student supply in 1949, and became a full-time minister in 1952. It was the beginning of a new era. In his 1958 report, Choy noted that the congregation had thirty to thirty-five adults at worship each Sunday, a Sunday school with fifty pupils registered and an average attendance of forty-three; as well, there were eighty supporting families. He comments further on the work: "Over 50% of the Chinese population (800 in Winnipeg) are new immigrants who came to Canada since 1950. Except for a few truly converted Christians, these people had never before any connection with the Christian Church or heard the name of Jesus Christ. By faith they are either Buddhist-minded or none at all. Those who have been under pastoral care range from highly intellectual students to illiterate villagers."[7] Each Sunday afternoon at two o'clock Sunday school classes for children, English Bible class for youths and students, and the Bible class in Chinese for adults were held simultaneously. Church service was held at four o'clock in the afternoon (this time was chosen for the convenience of members who worked in the restaurants which were open late Saturday to the early hours of Sunday). Still, some did not get to church. Key leaders and workers in the period from 1952 to 1962 were George Crocker, Daisy Ross, Violet Quon, Thomas Faan, Frank Woo, Edwin Foo, Fletcher Argue, David Farn and Roy Mark, all of whom devoted loyal service to the Chinese Church, especially in the Sunday school and youth fellowship programs.

Significantly, on 13 March 1962, the Home Mission Board concurred in the action of Winnipeg Presbytery that the "Chinese Pastoral Charge be discontinued and the congregation be included in the Central Winnipeg Parish, with the understanding that suitable plans for a group ministry in the area be worked out."[8] The Rev. Steven Liao was the minister at the time, but the Central Winnipeg Parish did not "work out suitable plans for a group ministry." With pressures for ministry to other inner city needs, the inclusion of an ethnic congregation in the Central Winnipeg Parish added a component which the parish was not competent to handle. As a result the Chinese United Church became an insignificant part of the program of the parish, leaving the congregation very much on its own. After five years the relationship with the parish was dissolved and the congregation was restored to a regular pastoral charge basis.

In August 1968, the Rev. Samuel Choo became the minister of the congregation. His vision and energy inspired the congregation to complete the church facilities. The cost was $47,444, and the congregation first worshipped in their new sanctuary on Easter Sunday, 11 April 1971, celebrating the Sacrament of Holy Communion. Although the floor tiles were not in place and the interior was unpainted, it was a joy for them to return to their church home, a dream fulfilled. The dedication took place on 6 June 1971 with Conference and Presbytery representatives and many guests attending.

The building fund continued growing until the end of 1972, and there were more than adequate funds to cover the total expenditure of $73,192. But the vision was not yet complete. In 1959 the congregation had purchased a lot on the west side of the church property to be used for parking, and they now entered into negotiations to construct a senior citizens' home on that site after acquiring the adjacent property (the Cabinet Hotel) as well. The $1.9 million, eleven-storey building, including seventy-seven single units and eleven double units, was completed in February 1978 and named "Sek On Toi," a tribute of the people to "the old folk."

With the retirement of Rev. Samuel Choo in 1977, the congregation called the Rev. Kim Chuan Goh, and his evangelistic zeal and energy resulted in a dynamic youth program, a growing Sunday school, vigorous pastoral and fellowship efforts, and increased church attendance. Goh was succeeded in 1982 by the Rev. Wing H. Mak, who has given the congregation a strengthened organizational structure with emphasis on Christian discipleship, prayer, visitation, training sessions for Sunday school teachers, youth counsellors and church workers. The Sunday attendance at services averages about 110 people.

When the congregation celebrated its sixty-sixth anniversary in 1983, it could look back over years of hardship and struggle, as well as times of great expectation and joy, and know that God had blessed their endeavours in Winnipeg. The Chinese United Church has always been marked with a strong evangelical flavour, believing firmly in the love, guidance and blessing of God at all times. The Church has found a special and unique place in ministry in Winnipeg, and God has used the members abundantly for His purposes. In the words of Dr. Alexander Pan, an active lay leader in the congregation, "May God continue to bless this church and its ministry, not only to its own congregation and the Senior Citizens of Sek On Toi, but to extend its ministry beyond the Chinese community at large."[9] Such is their task and challenge, and their future.

MINISTERS OF THE
CHINESE UNITED CHURCH OF WINNIPEG

1917–1934	Rev. Seung Mar
1934–1935	Rev. C.C. Shiu
1935–1938	Rev. Yee Ching Chow
1938–1939	Mr. Ernest Chan, summer worker
1939–1944	Rev. C.S. Der
1944–1949	Rev. Fung Yee Louie
1949–1951	Rev. Thomas Choy, student supply
1952–1963	Rev. Thomas Choy
1963–1967	Rev. Steven Liao
1968–1977	Rev. Samuel Choo
1977–1981	Rev. Kim Chuan Goh
1982–	Pastor Wing H. Mak

George Roddick (Photo courtesy of Western Canada Pictorial Index.)

George Roddick:
A man with a dream

Murray McPherson

In July 1984 during the centennial celebration of Cornwallis municipality, the rural jurisdiction which surrounds the city of Brandon, Manitoba, the centennial committee acknowledged the contribution made by churches that had been in the area during the preceding one hundred years. Many congregations were named, but special attention was drawn to Brandon Hills United Church, the first congregation to be established in the district and the only one still holding regular services in Cornwallis Municipality in 1984.[1]

The events leading to the founding of the Brandon Hills congregation were unique. While the majority of new settlements in the West were eager to have religious establishments in their midst, most Protestant communities depended on home mission committees to initiate the formation of mission churches and to aid in building them. However, the Brandon Hills story is different; it is one of leadership and struggle in spite of discouragement and church bureaucracy. It is a story of determination, but primarily it is one of cooperation, of community cooperation in keeping the faith.

On the morning of the last Sunday of May 1879, the Rev. George Roddick conducted a service of worship in an area south of the Assiniboine River in what is now western Manitoba. Having crossed this river at Grand Valley (then in the North West Territory) the Roddick family and party of settlers who had accompanied them from Nova Scotia moved south toward the Brandon Hills where they terminated their journey. There, on that Sunday morning, the group of nineteen people gathered at the Roddick tent for their first worship service in their new land.[2] Such was the beginning of George Roddick's ministry in the West and the establishment of a congregation at Brandon Hills, a community of faith that has continued since that time.

George Roddick was born at sea 31 January 1831, while his parents, Robert and Lena Roddick, were enroute from Scotland to Nova Scotia.[3] The family settled at West River, N.S., and George attended school there before studying at Durham Hall, a Presbyterian theological school.[4] After he was ordained to the ministry in 1858, George Roddick was placed at the Presbyterian Church at Durham where he served for twenty-one years.[5]

In 1859 George married his cousin, Elizabeth Roddick, and the couple settled at Thornbank Cottage in the West River district.[6] There, four sons and three daughters were born to George and Elizabeth.[7] The difficulties of providing an education for the family and of acquiring sufficient land for his sons to farm in the densely populated valley, coupled with George's own missionary zeal, resulted in a family decision to emigrate to western Canada in 1878 when the youngest Roddick child was eight years old.[8]

Leaving the church and community which he had served for so many years was not easy. Nevertheless, early in 1879 arrangements were made for departure for the West as soon as weather conditions were favourable.[9] Rev. Roddick's parting from Pictou Presbytery was recorded in the presbytery minutes:

A highly appreciated minute respecting the Rev. George Roddick was read and ordered to be put in the Record of Presbytery. It expressed the faithfulness with which Reverend Roddick performed the duties of ministry in the West River congregation for a period of twenty years, the affection of the people toward him, the high esteem in which he is held by his co-presbyters, their deep regret in losing his services, and their prayer that he and his family may be brought safely to the distant place in which he proposes to make his abode, and that he may be long spared for labour in the Master's Vineyard.[10]

The news of the proposed emigration had drawn wide attention in Nova Scotia, and a sizeable number of people, including several members of his congregation at Durham, had indicated interest in accompanying the Roddick family. Consequently, in order to inform those joining his party, Roddick placed an announcement in the *Eastern Chronicle* on 27 March 1879, which read: "*Manitoba* The Reverend George Roddick here-by informs those who intend to proceed to Manitoba that his party will start by train on the 10th of April instead of the 8th."[11] On leaving Nova Scotia the group travelled west through Montreal and Chicago. Enroute they were joined by families from Ontario and the New England states who were also seeking new homes in the West. On arriving at St. Paul, Minnesota, they found that a new railroad had just been completed from St. Cloud via Emerson to St. Boniface, Manitoba. They boarded the first train north and reached their destination in St. Boniface on 17 April.[12]

In St. Boniface, they were welcomed by an old friend, David Murray, Winnipeg's chief of police, who arranged for a scow to take the party across the river to Winnipeg. During a brief stay in the city, the travellers purchased several oxen, a team of horses, and a number of wagons in preparation for their journey across the prairies as well as for use in anticipated farming activities. Roddick, in a letter to the *Brandon Sun* in 1898, recalled: "Our trip to Winnipeg was greatly enjoyed, with music, instrumental and vocal, to enliven the way. At St. Cloud the remark was heard, 'This is a jolly crowd, but the tune will be changed when they get out on the prairies of Manitoba.' As no palatial station awaited our coming, we were dumped with grips and trunks in the mud of St. Boniface. Now our troubles commenced."[13]

It is assumed that the troubles mentioned by Roddick related to the difficult days and weeks that he and his party faced as they made their way toward the "promised land" in the area known as the North West Territory. However, records of events show that his plan to establish a new Presbyterian church in the area was to face difficulties equal to the trip or to those of clearing land for farming. First he found that the Church leaders in Winnipeg were not supportive of his efforts and in some cases were downright opposed. He was perceived to be an outsider because he came from a small village in Nova Scotia and not from Upper Canada from which most of the Presbyterian leaders had originated. He was not sponsored by the Church and, in addition, his professional qualifications were seriously questioned; in fact the Presbytery of Manitoba took nearly two days to come to a decision on the validity of the documents from their sister organization in Pictou county.[14] They also questioned his vocational intent in coming to the West. Did he intend to be an active clergyman or did he intend to become a farmer and refuse to move to any pastorate to which he would be assigned?

In any event, George Roddick did attend meetings of the Presbytery of Manitoba during 1879, and following his presentation to the court, was appointed to take charge of Grand Valley and the Big Plains district.[15] The extent of the territory so described is somewhat ambiguous but local references indicate that his charge included the present Brandon area plus all the territory to the north and east including the area around the present town of Gladstone. Although the exact bounds of his pastorate are not clear, nor is the frequency of his visits recorded, he is known to have performed a number of weddings over fifty miles away from his home at the Brandon Hills.[16]

During his early years in the West, George Roddick ministered to many new communities, but always the idea of building a church in the area of his new home was foremost in his mind. Consequently, he informed the presbytery that he would give up serving the area north of the Assiniboine River but would continue to minister at Grand Valley, Brandon Hills and Milford. This decision led to the appointment of several Presbyterian ministers to work in the Big Plains area.[17] Roddick was pleased that these ordained men were coming, but he was somewhat distressed to learn that each was to be paid $300 per year while he was to continue work without a stipend.[18] Eventually the salary issue reached the presbytery where, in typical fashion, it was dealt with by referring the matter to Toronto. Roddick was not happy with this process but he was not deterred from continuing his work south of the Assiniboine River.

Concerned over Roddick's request for payment, the Church authorities requested the Rev. James Robertson, newly appointed superintendent of home missions in western Canada, to visit the Milford and Brandon Hills congregations to ascertain the validity of the request. As a result, Robertson made a trip to the area in the summer of 1881. Although no formal report is available, a description of the trip is found in a letter Robertson wrote to his wife.[19] Apparently Robertson found the members of the congregations interested in the development of new churches, but he was noncommittal in his reference to Roddick himself. Robertson's biographer, Charles Gordon, was more specific. He described Roddick (referred to as Mr. R.) as "a disgruntled missionary, unequal to the task of shepherding the flock."[20] It is unclear whether Gordon got this information from Robertson or from Presbyterian sources elsewhere. Robertson did write, "I found his influence is little. . . . I found moreover, that the Nova Scotians on the south side of the Assiniboine are few in number."[21] Nevertheless, Robertson recommended paying $300 to Roddick for expenses, with the comment, "It is better paid."[22] George Roddick's assessment of the meeting with Robertson is not recorded, but it is known that, in spite of lack of presbytery support, his determination to build a church continued unabated.

The rebuff by the Presbyterian Church, coupled with the fact that two of his sons married young women who were Methodists, led George Roddick to become a member of the Methodist Church in 1883.[23] Disassociating himself from the Presbyterians affected his plans to build a church at Brandon Hills. During the 1880s, church services were held by both Presbyterians and Methodists in private homes or in the schoolhouse. When George Roddick retired from active ministery to the community in 1883, the Presbyterian Church appointed first the Rev. Thomas Davidson as pastor, followed by John Mowat in 1884, J.M. Kelly in 1887 and D. Reese in 1889 before T.R. Shearer arrived in 1889 to serve the congregation for twelve years.[24] By this time the Methodist Church was also providing services from its Glen Souris Church a few miles distant. Roddick and his neighbours decided to build a combined, or union, church. Eventually the project took shape. In the early 1890s, plans for a building were developed and a building fund was established. Some years earlier, George Roddick had donated land for a cemetery; he decided to contribute an additional piece, adjoining the cemetery, for the church building.[25] James Baker, a neighbour of Roddick's, provided a plot of land for a Methodist parsonage.[26] The two congregations under the leadership of the Rev. T.R. Shearer (Presbyterian), and the Rev. John Lewis (Methodist) worked cooperatively and soon sufficient funds had been collected to start building.

Walter H. Shillinglaw, a Brandon architect, was hired to draw up plans for a white frame structure to resemble the church at Durham, N.S., from which George Roddick had come.[27] The plan did not call for a large building but it did incorporate a feature typical of Nova Scotia churches – an inverted table-top tower designed to accommodate a bell. The young people of the district (the Christian Endeavour Society) raised funds to provide the furnishings.[28]

Construction of the new sanctuary was completed during the summer of 1896 and by early autumn the church was ready for use.[29] Dr. John Mark King, principal of Manitoba College, had accepted an invitation to preach at the first service in the new building on 16 October 1896.[30] Following the dedication of the church, services were held regularly with the Presbyterian service in the morning and the Methodist service in the evening. The same choir and organist provided the ministry of music for both services, a custom which continued until church union in 1925.

Soon after the opening of the building a "bell fund" was established, and by 1900 a bell of suitable size and quality was found in an unused church in Nova Scotia. The bell was purchased, installed in the tower and ready for dedication on 24 May 1901.[31] Although the bell is not used regularly now, whenever it is sounded, its clear tones can be heard far across the rolling farmlands.

George Roddick continued to reside at Brandon Hills for a short period after the church was completed. However, as his wife had passed away some years earlier, he retired to Nova Scotia. After his death there in 1910, his daughter Mary, who was with him at this time, returned his body for burial in the family plot at the Brandon Hills cemetery next to the church he had worked to have erected in his time.[32]

During the years since the church was built, the Brandon Hills congregation has been served by a host of fine ministers of various ages and experience. Changes in transportation altered the extent of the community served by the church. Church union brought the dual ministry to an end and introduced the multiple-charge concept which saw the minister live in a neighbouring village.

In 1939, to commemorate the sixtieth anniversary of the founding of the community, a cairn was erected in the churchyard. The plaque thereon was unveiled by the eldest daughter of George Roddick, Mary Roddick Dunbar. In attendance were many of the original families, who, although very young when they arrived from Nova Scotia and Ontario, were by now the "old timers" of the community. This memorable occasion took place less than three weeks prior to the outbreak of World War II, another event which changed the membership and ministry of Brandon Hills Church.

The period following the war saw the city of Brandon extend to the south and east, threatening the existence of the church at Brandon Hills. Several families questioned the need to keep the small church open. However, the desire to continue worshipping in a rural setting was shared by enough rural and semi-urban families to keep Brandon Hills Church as part of the Wawanesa Pastoral Charge.

On anniversaries, people reflect on their roots, and once again a special anniversary – the Cornwallis Centennial – reawakened interest in the history of the Brandon Hills community, and the role the Church played in shaping the quality of life in the district throughout the years. The cooperative spirit that built a church and that enabled two denominations to share a building, still pervaded community affairs in 1984. This spirit is symbolized in the white frame church and the faithful congregation who worship in it as did their forebears.

Cadurcis:
A very rural church

Hartley Harland

Four miles south of Basswood, Manitoba, stands Cadurcis United Church, still serving an active community after a hundred years of the ups and downs common to most rural communities of western Canada. In many ways there is nothing special about Cadurcis. It is an ordinary church serving an ordinary community in an ordinary way, facing problems that affect small church communities throughout the western scene. In other ways it is quite unique.

Through the hundred years, members of five families, along with others that came and went, have given the continuous leadership that makes a little church in a rural setting a vital force and one able to survive. These families – the McNabbs, the McDonalds, the Murrays, the Thompsons and the Beatties – still make up well over half of the congregation. Although it has been at various times affiliated with Basswood, Newdale or Minnedosa, the Cadurcis congregation now meets regularly as a part of the Rapid City Pastoral Charge. One member of the congregation, Blaine Thierry, entered the full-time ministry and is now with the Canadian Bible Society.

Cadurcis has been very much a community church. It has been the centre of activity for all the people of the area, regardless of their religious affiliation. Even Roman Catholics have joined in worship. It is said that not one child has grown up in the Cadurcis area without attending the local Sunday school.

The community originated with a number of staunch Gaelic Presbyterian families who reached the area some time prior to 1880. These early settlers brought with them a deep reverence for things spiritual, as shown in the community they produced. Soon after their arrival they started building a church and a school, laying the foundations for the years to come. They showed an extraordinary adherence to the traditions of Presbyterianism. In the early part of the nineteenth century, congregational singing in the Presbyterian Church had been led by a designated church officer, called a precentor, who would lead the singing aided only by a tuning fork with which he would establish the pitch. During the 1870s, following a bitter controversy, the Presbyterian General Assembly allowed the use of pipe organs and other musical instruments during worship. But at Cadurcis, the precentor continued to lead the singing well into the twentieth century – long after neighbouring churches had invested in pump organs and pianos.

Because of the demanding standards of personal behaviour that were a feature of Scottish Presbyterianism, the days leading up to a Communion service would be a time of deep soul searching for members of the congregation. Only those who had confessed their sins and were truly repentant would be given permission to take Communion by the elders; and the elders took this responsibility very seriously. A case in point was the plight of a newly-married couple whose first child arrived rather sooner than was considered proper. Until the doctor in charge certified that the child had been born prematurely, the couple was denied access to Holy Communion.

The present building, the third structure in the life of the church, was officially opened in 1952. When fire, caused by lightning, had destroyed the previous building the year before, the congregation undertook at once the task of raising funds to build anew. The old building was rather small, allowing little space for the activities associated with the idea of church and community. The congregation had long been toying with the idea of building a basement for the church, but to put a basement under a building already considered inadequate was not practical. While the congregation was considering this new basement, they raised $1,000. The fire in 1951 resolved the problem, and soon the new structure, well-equipped with facilities to serve a new day, was erected. Did the words of the old hymn, "God moves in a mysterious way, His wonders to perform" find an echo in any of the people's minds?

Unlike many small prairie towns, Cadurcis has survived and flourished even within the shadow of the large modern town of Minnedosa, only nine miles away, because of its unusual stability and continuity of community feeling. Minnedosa supplies the people of Cadurcis with many of their material needs, but the local church carries on, providing them with spiritual strength. Supported by members of the original families who founded the community, Cadurcis United Church has been able to adjust to the times and still make its influence felt in the building of God's Kingdom.

Dand United Church

J. Clark Saunders

The community of Dand, Manitoba, is today little more than a spot on the map. Located between Hartney and Deloraine, it consists of a couple of farm houses (close enough together to be considered part of the village), the former school (now a community centre) and the United Church. A stranger driving by would have little idea of the unusual origins of that church or of the effect it has had on the people of the surrounding district over the past century.

The church at Dand is unique among the United Churches of Manitoba, having its origins among a group of Quakers (or Society of Friends). The 1880s and 1890s saw the arrival of families belonging to the Society of Friends in and around the area known as Chain Lakes – named for a string of little lakes in a valley just north of what is now the village of Dand. These Quaker families were variously of English, Irish and American stock, a few generations of which had lived in Ontario. They included Alfred and Sarah Mullett from Belleville, Sarah's sister Eliza and her husband, John Hodgson, from Sunbury, near Kingston, Henry James from Uxbridge (a widower who later remarried in the Chain Lakes district), and George and Eliza Baker from Dublin, Ireland.

The Quaker families brought with them the distinctive features of the movement begun by George Fox in the seventeenth century. They subscribed to no formal creed, emphasized the equality of all believers including women, observed no sacraments,[1] adhered to the principles of pacifism, and sought guidance through the "inner light." Their places for worship and the conducting of business were known as meeting houses. For purposes of organization, local groups would meet for what was called the monthly meeting. At the regional level there were quarterly meetings; and a national yearly meeting was held in Toronto.

Alma Dale (Photograph from *Golden Memories: A History of the Dand Community.*)

For the Quakers who migrated to the districts around Chain Lakes, a development among the Friends in late nineteenth-century North America had a significant effect. Worship among traditional Quakers consisted of silence, during which worshippers were free to offer thoughts, prayers or songs, as they felt led. There was no clergy to preach or lead the worship. However, in the years before 1900, a split between traditional Quakers and those who felt a need for a pastorate occurred. This latter group came to appoint individuals – often from within their own meeting – to visit the congregation and perform other pastoral duties and to conduct worship. Preaching in the formal sense became acceptable, especially at evening services, although worshippers still felt free to speak out if they disagreed with what was being said.

The Friends who settled around Chain Lakes were familiar with the idea of the pastorate. Had they practised only the traditional type of Quaker meeting, they might have isolated themselves from their Presbyterian and Methodist neighbours. As it was, when they took the initiative in establishing the first church in the area, their worship and organization was not so foreign to the other Protestants that they could not attend and feel comfortable. With the laissez-faire attitude that so many took toward denominationalism in the early days on the prairie – and with intermarriage between Quaker and other families – the Friends' Meeting House could become, in effect, the community church.

The catalyst that brought the new church together was the arrival in Hartney of Alma Dale. In 1898, the Canada Yearly Meeting had authorized Mrs. Dale to set up monthly meetings wherever she thought best in the Canadian Northwest. Leaving her husband to sell pianos in Toronto, she headed out to Hartney where she set up house. For some time, the Quaker families had been meeting in the Chain Lakes School or in the members' homes. But, on 3 January 1899, a significant development took place at a meeting at Mrs. Dale's new home. Present were Mrs. Dale (described as a "minister and missionary,"[2] a role and title few churches would have accorded a woman during this period), Henry James (called a "minister resident in this province,"[3] an indication of the leading role he had played in the little congregation) and members of the Hodgson, James and Baker families. The minutes indicate: "We sat down for worship realizing in a marked degree, the presence of the Master in our midst. After a time of silent worship several led in vocal prayer, after which our dear friend Henry James read a part of the 15th Chapter of John and spoke to us of the duty and privuleges [sic] of abiding in Christ. The discourse was a powerful one and the Spirit sealed it on many hearts."[4] In the business meeting that followed the worship, a group called the Hartney Monthly Meeting of Friends was formally inaugurated, and Mrs. Dale was asked to write the chair of the Society of Friends' Home Mission Committee requesting the group's attachment to the Yonge Street Quarterly Meeting.

In the months and years that followed the inauguration of the new group, Alma Dale, in spite of her precarious health, worked tirelessly on behalf of the congregation. She encouraged the use of music, set up a library with books from Uxbridge, and travelled widely to raise money from Quakers in Ontario and elsewhere for the construction of a meeting house. Progress on this last project was made quickly. A committee was formed, land was donated (by John Hodgson), construction proceeded, and on a stormy 15 October 1899, the meeting house was opened. Soon a stable as well as a cemetery with a vault were added on the surrounding property.

The life of the congregation in those early years shows a spiritual intensity and an evangelical zeal. Unlike some Quakers, whose doctrinal liberality led them away from orthodox Christianity, the people of Chain Lakes encouraged personal Christian commitment through the ministry of visiting Quakers and the conducting of preaching missions. Their young people were, in many cases, sent to complete their education at Pickering College, the Friends' school in Ontario. It was felt important that the young receive a Christian education.

In 1904, Alma Dale asked to be released from the pastorate. She spent part of the following three years in England and returned for a further year at the church in 1907. In the interim, Henry James was pressed into service as pastor for a short while until a replacement – one Harry Parry – was called from Ontario. It was on Mr. and Mrs. Parry's departure in 1907 that Mrs. Dale returned from England to the area and was given a stipend of $500 per year.

In 1908, Alma Dale felt compelled to resign once again. "No matter where I am," whe wrote, "this, our meeting, will have the largest place in my heart's affection."[5] The parting brought sorrow on both sides. The Friends in the district – and others who attended the meeting house – were left with a strong impression of her devotion and an indelible mental image of their pastor riding in her buggy pulled by two immaculately fitted-out cream-coloured ponies.

A succession of pastors followed Alma Dale. During John Metcalfe's incumbency (1908 to 1911) the congregation considered building a house for the minister. Although the idea of building was abandoned, a rental house was found so that Metcalfe could at least live in the district. In 1911, the Rev. Henry Sutton became the last Quaker minister of the church, his service there extending until 1923 and the eve of the congregation's entry into the United Church of Canada.

It is interesting to note the relationships between the Friends' Meeting House and the churches and Sunday schools of the surrounding districts. It had been common, since before 1900, for local school districts in the area to hold more-or-less regular church services in the country schools. Such services were attended by people of a variety of denominations. The Presbyterian minister at Lauder, for example, is known to have conducted worship in the West Hall district. Henry Sutton, in addition to his duties at Chain Lakes, led services at Regent, to the east of Dand, and at Luther School, to the south. Similarly, local Sunday schools were organized in some of the school districts and were often run as non-denominational community enterprises.

In 1919, the Chain Lakes School, to the north of Dand, and the Luther School, to the south, merged, and a consolidated school was built in the village of Dand itself. The Chain Lakes congregation began to use the new school for services and Sunday school in the winter months, and in 1922 a union Sunday school was formed to serve children and adults from the Luther area and surrounding districts. Sunday school attendance rose from an average of about thirty-five to eighty or ninety a week. Lay people from the Quaker Church continued to play a conspicuous part in the leadership of the larger Sunday school and did much to ensure that, for decades to come, Sunday school would be a family affair, with a large class of adults as well as classes for children.

It was against this background of a local union movement, and in anticipation of the national union that brought the United Church into being, that a deputation consisting of James Dunning and Clint Whetter Sr. was sent to Lauder to request affiliation with the Lauder-Melgund Pastoral Charge. The board at Lauder agreed to the request and settled on $400 as the Chain Lakes congregation's share of the minister's salary. The Rev. E.W. Johnson of Lauder then included Dand Union Church, as the congregation was then called, in his charge. In 1925, the church became Dand United Church.

One subsequent development of note took place in 1949 when the building was moved from its old site (now marked by a cairn on the east side of Highway 21) to the Village of Dand, where it now stands. A gallery had been built in the late 1920s to accommodate two classrooms, and now an addition to the south end provided a choir loft and two further classrooms.

More significant than the changes in the building itself have been the changes in the community. The post-war years brought a decline in rural population at Dand as it did in most parts of the province. The people of the church sometimes lament the changes that have brought a decline in the congregation. But, while numbers may no longer be what they once were, the people of Dand United Church – like their Quaker forebears – maintain a well-deserved reputation for Christian faith and community service, and for a high degree of commitment and competence. Their brothers and sisters in the church hope and pray that it may long remain so.

Blest be the tie

Sue Obee

Attendance in most churches decreases during the summer months. However, the reverse happens in Sioux Narrows and Nestor Falls, the two communities which make up the Lake of the Woods Pastoral Charge. With the influx of tourists and seasonal residents in the summer months, the population (which in winter is between six and eight hundred) rises to over ten thousand.

The two communities are twenty-five miles apart and are located between Fort Frances and Kenora in northwestern Ontario. The communities are young, and are very similar, yet each has its own distinct history and qualities. Road access was established to Nestor Falls in 1930 and to Sioux Narrows by the mid-1930s. Tourists from the northern and central United States were attracted to this sparsely populated area with its clean air, clear water and bountiful fishing and hunting. Without electricity or telephones and only limited road service, the early settlers were strong, daring and resilient. During the summers they worked from dawn to dusk in the infant tourist industry. When temperatures dropped to forty degrees below zero during the winters, survival became the prime concern for the inhabitants. There was little energy for anything else.

By the mid-1940s, the population in the two communities was large enough to support schools. Space in the school buildings, which were built during the 1940s, was used not only for regular classes but also for Sunday school classes and adult fellowship sessions which were conducted from time to time by visiting ministers and missionaries. Eventually, church services were held in the school. One of the residents of Sioux Narrows recalls: "The first service, held by United Church ministers, according to my diary, took place on February 15, 1950." This service was conducted in the school by ministers from Keewatin and Kenora.

By the mid-1950s, hydro and telephone services were established in Sioux Narrows and the population was growing; the citizens' dream of having a permanent place to worship could now be realized. On 24 September 1956, a meeting was called to consider establishing a congregation of the United Church of Canada at Sioux Narrows. The motion passed at that meeting was: "That this gathering request pastoral oversight of the new congregation of Sioux Narrows United Church by the minister of Knox United Church, Kenora, for the time being." At the end of the meeting, a sheet of foolscap with the heading "I desire to come into full communion in the United Church of Canada" was circulated. Ten people signed.

The inaugural service of the new congregation was held on Sunday, 14 October 1956. On the following Wednesday, officers were elected, a building committee was appointed, record books and a building lot were secured. Then they got down to work.

The church had no official name and when a bank clerk asked the treasurer for a name for the new account, she responded, "Lake of the Woods Chapel." And so, the Sioux Narrows United Church became and remains officially named the Lake of the Woods Chapel.

During the winter months of 1957 a building fund program was organized. A small grant was received from the Home Missions Office to start the project, but most building proceeded on a "pay as you go" scheme. There were a few large gifts, but it was the accumulation of the many small ones, given in the spirit of the widow's mite, that allowed work to continue. The church fundraisers made up in zeal what they lacked in knowledge of the United Church's basic fundraising policies. A boat raffle which they organized prompted a letter from the Kenora–Rainy River Presbytery which stated: "While Presbytery commends the interest, enthusiasm and concern that has been shown in an effort to raise funds for your new church building, it none-the-less wishes to advise that it will not tolerate a repetition of this type of scheme on behalf of the United Church." The fundraisers responded by rewording their advertisement to read "for the Sioux Narrows Community" (instead of "Church") which resulted in a donation of nearly $3,000 from people who wanted a new church in their community. Today, a sanctuary, a winter chapel, a Christian education room and kitchen facilities stand in tribute to those Canadians and Americans who worked (and continue working) side by side in Sioux Narrows to provide a place of worship.

The early church services in Nestor Falls as well were few and far between. In 1958, the results of a survey showed that the majority of Nestor Falls people wished to be affiliated with the United Church of Canada. A student minister served the community in the summer of 1958 and other student ministers served until 1966. Services were held in the school until a building program was started in 1963.

Palm Sunday has special meaning to the Nestor Falls Church: on Palm Sunday in 1959, the United Church minister from Keewatin baptized fifty-nine people (children and adults); the first service in the church was held on Palm Sunday in 1964; and the mortgage was burned on Palm Sunday in 1975.

In 1958, the church boards of Nestor Falls and Sioux Narrows met to make plans and dream dreams. They began their cooperative effort that year by sharing a student minister. They decided to issue a call for an ordained minister, a decision which resulted in the formation of a pastoral charge. In July 1966, the first ordained minister and his family were welcomed to the charge.

The United Church Women in both locations have been not only a source of fellowship but also a major contributing force in the life and the work of the Church. The women have cleaned and painted; they have raised funds through bake sales, rummage sales, craft sales and by publishing cookbooks; and they have shared in and contributed to the Christian education of the congregations. One major joint project of the United Church Women has been the furnishing and maintenance of the manse.

Like the Apostle Paul did, the United Church Women write letters. Unlike Paul, who wrote to churches, the United Church Women write to the people in their newsletters. Each newsletter contains Church and local community news. The newsletters are not theological epistles, but they do serve to maintain the circle of fellowship among those near and far during the long winter months.

Even though there was no cemetery in either community until well after the churches had been established, it seemed natural that deceased people would be remembered by family and friends with memorials to the churches as they were being built. Because of this each church could properly be called a memorial church; in fact, the winter chapel at Sioux Narrows is named the Memorial Chapel since all furnishings have been donated as memorials.

During the three decades after church union in 1925, the nucleus of faithful residents of Sioux Narrows and Nestor Falls was joined by interested American cottage owners to form a United Church which was also a "uniting" church. The challenge continues – that is, to maintain a ministry to and by two churches, each of whose congregations may drop to twenty in winter but may swell to over 150 in summer. Some members of the summer congregation are involved in the continuing life and work of the Church, some visit for only a few weeks, and others are one-time visitors. The charge is able to carry on because of the sustained support of United Church clergy from Fort

Frances, Emo, Rainy River, Keewatin and Kenora, and of other United Church personnel from Winnipeg and Thunder Bay. It is sustained as well by vacationing clergy from various American denominations, and by many others who are willing to share their musical talents. All these people have combined their labours, offerings and prayers to build and maintain the ministry in the Lake of the Woods Pastoral Charge.

The hymn traditionally sung at the end of summer in the Sioux Narrows and Nestor Falls United Churches (#376 in the old blue hymnary) well expresses the feelings of those who join in worship, whether they attend year-round or only in summer:

Blest be the tie that binds
Our hearts in Christian love.

A long goodbye to Mother Church

Ian Macdonald

CAST OF CHARACTERS

HOWARD ALBRIGHT, last recording steward of Grace United Church, Winnipeg.

LOUISE ALBRIGHT, his wife.

The REV. GEORGE YOUNG, first minister of Grace Methodist Church, 1868–1876.

The REV. W.L. RUTLEDGE, minister of Grace Church, 1887–1890.

ROBERT WYATT, a trustee of Grace Church, 1912–1921.

The REV. C.L. McIRVINE, minister of Grace Church 1920–1927.

The REV. RICHMOND CRAIG, minister of Grace Church, 1929–1936.

Time: July 1955

Place: Winnipeg

Howard Albright stares out the windows of his home at 54 Wilton Ave. He is in his sixties, finely featured, neat in appearance and assertive in bearing, even in his present distraction. His glasses give him a slightly professorial air but his manner is troubled. There are boxes and boxes piled in the living room. These are normal cartons; when the light dims, oversize cardboard cartons replace them.

The Rev. George Young (Photo courtesy of Western Canada Pictorial Index.)

HOWARD ALBRIGHT: I shouldn't have been away.

LOUISE ALBRIGHT: [Offstage] It wouldn't have helped.

HOWARD ALBRIGHT: If I had talked with Presbytery . . .

LOUISE ALBRIGHT: It would have made no difference. [*She enters and arranges flowers.*] You know that.

HOWARD ALBRIGHT: The vote was close enough – 32 to 25.[1]

LOUISE ALBRIGHT: Close enough doesn't count. They wouldn't have tried it if they didn't have the vote wrapped up ahead of time.

HOWARD ALBRIGHT: I suppose you're right. They've had their eyes on Grace as a money pot for some time. That's all they were interested in.[2]

LOUISE ALBRIGHT: It's all over and done with.

HOWARD ALBRIGHT: It's ironic. I spend my life in business and the one place I feel stabbed in the back is the church.

LOUISE ALBRIGHT: Why don't you write Dr. Dorey in Toronto . . . and appeal to General Council?

HOWARD ALBRIGHT: An appeal wouldn't work at this late date. Besides, when Dr. Dorey was in town for the meeting of Conference, he never even let us know he was here.[3]

LOUISE ALBRIGHT: That doesn't seem like the moderator; surely he knows you've been anxious to meet with him.

HOWARD ALBRIGHT: Just tiptoed in and tiptoed out. Oh, I'll write to him. Never fear.

LOUISE ALBRIGHT: Don't go writing him now. You promised to get rid of these boxes; no writing anyone until they're out of the house.

HOWARD ALBRIGHT: All right . . . what a job. . . .

[*He begins to rummage through the contents of one of the boxes, pulls out a pledge form.*]

HOWARD ALBRIGHT: Look, The Temperance Pledge.[4] Wonder if I still have mine?

LOUISE ALBRIGHT: Third drawer, middle dresser, Dear – but I don't think you should tear up your pledge just because they closed the church. [*She adjusts her hat before a mirror.*]

HOWARD ALBRIGHT: I won't. I'm tempted though. Are you off?

LOUISE ALBRIGHT: The Arthritic Association tea.

HOWARD ALBRIGHT: [Angrily] That's another organization that's lost its home![5]

LOUISE ALBRIGHT: Life will go on, Dear. We'll adjust. Now, promise me you won't read everything.

HOWARD ALBRIGHT: It's hard to put it all down, . . .

LOUISE ALBRIGHT: I know . . . but we have no alternative.

HOWARD ALBRIGHT: Grace is a church that served . . .

LOUISE ALBRIGHT: No Dear, Grace is just these cardboard boxes. Now get rid of them. [*They embrace tenderly, then, without a word, she exits. Albright looks around and blows the dust off a smaller box. He opens it.*]

LOUISE ALBRIGHT: She's right . . . I've got a church in cardboard boxes . . . what have we here . . . ? Oh, I remember him: George Young . . . [*He sits and reads, pausing to wipe his glasses, continuing to unfold old newspaper clippings. The spotlight narrows in on him keeping him half lit. The rest of the stage darkens except for one spotlight that picks up a man climbing out of a large box. He is the Rev. George Young, dressed in the style of the 1880s.*]

YOUNG: [*Rises and speaks to the audience. Albright does not notice him.*] I am George Young. I arrived in Red River in 1868 in time to be seized by Riel and imprisoned with all the others. It was I who heard the earnest prayers of young Scott and stood by him outside the walls of Old Fort Garry when Riel's firing squad martyred him.[6] It was I who rang the bell to show our fervent loyalty when we heard Sir Garnet Wolseley and his troops were in the vicinity of Kildonan and on their way to release the white prisoners in Fort Garry and put down the Rebellion![7] Three years later when we built the first Grace Church, they presented me with that very bell! I think it's in one of these boxes . . . [goes to explore the box then shouts] Albright!

HOWARD ALBRIGHT: What – how did you . . .?

YOUNG: Where's the bell? Have you lost the bell? Look for it, man!

HOWARD ALBRIGHT: I know you. . . . Aren't you George Young . . . !

YOUNG: Of course I am. Try that box over there. . . . Oh, say! Here's the plans for the first Grace Church. Some night that was. We built it on Main and Water three years after I preached my first sermon in a living room. I thought it would last for fifty years . . . but we needed a new Grace Church almost as soon as this one was finished.

HOWARD ALBRIGHT: I never saw that Grace.

YOUNG: You never saw a lot of things. Maybe the bell's in this box.

HOWARD ALBRIGHT: Look, these boxes are too light for a church bell and anyway, you're messing up my living room. [*The spotlight goes on and a deep sonorous voice speaks.*]

RUTLEDGE: It wouldn't be in that box anyway, Young; that box is mine! [*He is standing up behind the box. Slightly foppish, he is approximately forty-five.*]

HOWARD ALBRIGHT: Who are you?

YOUNG: Oh, not Rutledge. [*He glances up despairingly.*] This is Rutledge the Great, Albright. . . . I'd hoped I'd seen the last of you in 1890.

RUTLEDGE: Now George, your attitude is unbecoming.

HOWARD ALBRIGHT: Were you a part of Grace?

RUTLEDGE: A part of Grace! I baptized you, Albright. I served the new Grace church for three years. Check your baptismal certificate. W.L. Rutledge, that's me.

YOUNG: And check everything else when he's left.

RUTLEDGE: Mind your tongue, George. I served Grace well.

YOUNG: And yourself better.

RUTLEDGE: I left Grace in better shape than I found it. A new building, an enlarged congregation, and an active program of witness and service.

YOUNG: You could hardly have done any worse. Winnipeg was a boom town while you were at Grace.

RUTLEDGE: True enough – but I saw the prevailing wickedness of the city; degraded men and women lying in the very front of the chariot of Christian civilization.[8]

YOUNG: Rutledge, you're starting to sound like your sermons. If you'd been around in the early days we'd have used them for toilet paper.

RUTLEDGE: Different times need different leadership, George. You never understood that. The Winnipeg I knew was a young Chicago flexing its muscles, not a backwoods fort. The railway, grain, settlers, the distribution of merchandise – fortunes were being made. The city needed models of civilization and progress and a church like Grace to set the tone.

YOUNG: If that's your box, you can have it. Albright, get rid of him!

HOWARD ALBRIGHT: I'm not sure I can. I don't know how either of you got here; . . . my wife wanted me to clear out the living room. . . .

RUTLEDGE: Well, George I have no wish to disturb you. Grace wasn't a big part of my life.[9] [*He climbs back into his box.*]

YOUNG: Your type will always disturb me, Rutledge.

HOWARD ALBRIGHT: I wish you would both be a little more civil, and quieter; . . . this is River Heights.

[*A new voice cries out in pain.*]

WYATT: Hey . . . you're in the wrong box. . . . Get off my foot. . . .

RUTLEDGE: Sorry . . . I can't seem to do . . . are you sure?

WYATT: Look at the date, man. 1912 . . . one, nine, one, two.

YOUNG: Just ram him in anyway, Albright. Close the lid.

HOWARD ALBRIGHT: I can't do that, George, . . . he baptized me. . . . Who are you?

WYATT: I'm one of the Grace Church trustees, Robert Wyatt. Who are you?

HOWARD ALBRIGHT: I'm Howard Albright, the last recording steward of Grace, I suppose. And this is George Young, the founder and this is . . . where did he go?

RUTLEDGE: [*Sonorous voice*] I'm back in my own box and pleased with it! When I began in Manitoba there were only fifty Methodist ministers and only fifteen hundred members: when I left there were 175 ministers and nine thousand members.[10]

YOUNG: All I can say, Rutledge, is you slowed us down. We could have had twenty thousand without you . . . stay in your box! [*Rutledge disappears.*]

HOWARD ALBRIGHT: Mr. Young, George. . . . Don't you think . . .

YOUNG: [*Turning his attention to the new voice that has emerged*] Robert Wyatt . . . I don't recall you. . . . You were a trustee. . . .

WYATT: Right up to the time we had to resign in 1921.

YOUNG: [*Accusingly*] So you were the group that put Grace in debt . . . ?!

WYATT: It was not our intention, but . . .

HOWARD ALBRIGHT: It *was* the result.

WYATT: We were planning for the next Grace Church, the one that would serve the twentieth century. . . .

YOUNG: Was the building inadequate then? It was just newly built in '83.

WYATT: It was beginning to look a bit down at heel – and the city was changing. The land was valuable for business so we thought it a good opportunity to buy a new site, and sell the old one.

YOUNG: [*With contempt*] The old building wasn't good enough for you!

WYATT: Think before you speak, sir. It was being used almost to capacity. In addition to all our own programs we kept the club rooms open in the evening for young men and women to read or write letters home. . . . And we were kept busy helping people to find employment and rooms. The Business Girl's Bureau was formed in 1910 and we had a sewing machine that could be used each evening by arrangement with the office.[11]

YOUNG: I'm sorry, I see. Your time was taken up by the young and lonely . . . not so different from my day, really.

WYATT: Well, the big problem in the city, to put the matter fairly and squarely was . . . well, morals in Winnipeg were not in a condition very much to be desired.[12]

YOUNG: Never were, never will be.

WYATT: The biggest single factor was the bar with its attendant evils . . . paycheques not getting home, beatings of women and children, hunger and malnutrition. . . .

HOWARD ALBRIGHT: What did you do about it?

WYATT: We gave Nellie McClung her first public platform . . . and don't think that didn't raise eyebrows.[13]

HOWARD ALBRIGHT: With that kind of use, you should have just kept plugging along with the old building.

WYATT: Hindsight is easy, and cheap.

HOWARD ALBRIGHT: I don't hold anything against you personally. Planning had to be done, I suppose. It was just . . .

WYATT: How could we have known there would be a lull in the real estate and we'd be stuck with both properties?[14]

HOWARD ALBRIGHT: Some lull. It lasted until 1950, at least. Maybe longer.

YOUNG: Calm down, Albright – you'll die a bitter man.

HOWARD ALBRIGHT: It's just that . . . I feel I inherited the whole mess.

YOUNG: Well, the boxes are in *your* living room, man.

WYATT: We tried to sell. The new site, the old site. . . . We thought we'd solved the problem a dozen times but it never worked out.[15]

HOWARD ALBRIGHT: And the war was on, the old Hard and Dry Regiment[16] with all the sons of Grace was overseas . . . no one saw the interest mounting up. . . . I've heard it all before. . . . I was even there then myself, newly married with a young family.

WYATT: Look, between 1912 and 1920 we raised and payed $145,000[17] and still our debt was $412,000!

HOWARD ALBRIGHT: I'm sorry, I can't listen anymore. Just get back in your box, leave me alone. [*Sits down dejectedly*]

[*Wyatt crawls behind a box, legs out.*]

YOUNG: Go easy on him. It was the economy. And interest rates . . . I never knew they could be so hard. . . . In my day we just didn't borrow. Didn't believe in it.

HOWARD ALBRIGHT: You were well off. . . . He, watch it! [*He gets thrown off as McIrvine pops out.*]

McIRVINE: Ah, Howard Albright . . . you've aged so well . . . so very well!!

HOWARD ALBRIGHT: Mr. McIrvine?

McIRVINE: And you must be George Young.

YOUNG: Indeed, I am, but . . .

McIRVINE: Had a picture of you in my study . . . showed it to all the rich ones . . . you made me a lot of money, Mr. Young, and Grace

YOUNG: I did?

McIRVINE: When I'd tell them about you ringing the bells for release of Riel's captives and getting these same bells ringing in the towers of old Grace, why tears would glisten in their eyes and I'd hand them a blank cheque, or a pledge form and a pen.

YOUNG: I'm glad I was able to be of so much assistance but I don't think you need very much, the way you speak.

MCIRVINE: Oh, I've never been shy but I needed all the help I could get. In the end I really needed much more than I got. I died on the road, still trying to raise money for dear old Grace.

HOWARD ALBRIGHT: I remember. That was 1927. You were down east and your death shocked us all.

MCIRVINE: It took me by surprise too, Mr. Albright. I was so worried about Grace dying, I never thought I'd go first.

YOUNG: Quite a story, sir.

MCIRVINE: But not a successful one, Mr. Young. After seven years of hard campaigning in every part of Canada, we had raised $340,000 but with the interest still mounting, there remained $220,000 to pay.

YOUNG: That's incredible. In my day that sum would have bought Edmonton or Saskatoon or both. Why didn't Grace quit when you died?

MCIRVINE: To be truthful, they got an offer they couldn't refuse.

HOWARD ALBRIGHT: It seemed too good to be true at the time. Three businessmen,[18] all good churchmen, and men of considerable wealth, offered to buy the church for a dollar and take care of the debt themselves.

YOUNG: Where were they when you were dying on your feet across Canada?

MCIRVINE: Oh they were around. I'd hit them all up for good sums too. They just decided to clear this up and let Grace get on with being the church. . . . Let's see . . . It's probably this box we want. Craig . . . you in there?

CRAIG: No, over here, McIrvine. . . . How are you? [*Craig gets out.*]

MCIRVINE: This was the man the new owners picked, Richmond Craig.

HOWARD ALBRIGHT: Hello, Mr. Craig, you're looking well.

CRAIG: Albright! Good to see you again. . . . And Dr. Young, the pioneer.

MCIRVINE: I'll leave you now. I'm lecturing on fund-raising techniques at the Social Planning Council in half an hour.

YOUNG: But you're dead, McIrvine.

MCIRVINE: So are most of their speakers. Don't worry. I'll blend in fine. [*exits*]

CRAIG: An amazing man.

HOWARD ALBRIGHT: As you are yourself.

YOUNG: What kind of minister were you that three businessmen would pick you to run *their* church?

CRAIG: Oh, they didn't want it to be *their* church . . . not at all.

HOWARD ALBRIGHT: On the other hand, Richmond, they didn't exactly consult us about hiring you.[19]

CRAIG: True enough. James A. Richardson asked me to come to Winnipeg to do a survey of downtown churches, what the needs were, and what could happen from Grace.[20]

YOUNG: So . . . you're a surveyor.

CRAIG: No, an institutional social engineer.

YOUNG: A what . . . ?

CRAIG: I try to adapt old institutions to serve new needs and new opportunities.

YOUNG: There's more than a little of the snake-oil salesman in you. No wonder the businessmen liked you. Richardson must have hired you on the spot?

CRAIG: No, but he did come out to Vancouver two weeks after I'd finished and presented my report and told me the job was mine if I wanted it. And I wanted it.

YOUNG: It's good to get what you want, I suppose. Sometimes.

CRAIG: Well, along with the job, I got something I didn't want, the Great Depression. . . .

HOWARD ALBRIGHT: That's right. None of your plans could really be put into action. I'd forgotten . . .

CRAIG: I'd had rich dreams for an adequate staff to tackle the job.

HOWARD ALBRIGHT: We never ran out of work while you were here.

CRAIG: No, the bread lines grew, and the heat, and the boredom of the men was incredible. We started Goodwill Industries, recycling unusable items into jobs and affordable commodities – trying to get some positives going.

HOWARD ALBRIGHT: That was an idea that worked and still works well!

CRAIG: I wish I still worked well myself. After seven years, my health was so strained that I had to retire. Still, all in all, being at Grace was the best thing I ever did.

YOUNG: So, when you left, did they get another institutional . . . um . . . whatever?

CRAIG: No. Mr. Richardson died shortly after I left . . . the depression was still very much with us . . . the expansion of Grace's ministry that I had planned eight years previously didn't seem appropriate or possible.

HOWARD ALBRIGHT: It was all downhill from there, really, as I see it now.

CRAIG: Come now, Albright, W.G. Martin was a very able and very popular minister.[21]

HOWARD ALBRIGHT: True enough. And you could say much more about his gifts and it would all be true. But looking back . . . I wonder . . .

YOUNG: You mean Martin just held the fort . . . when people were expecting more?

CRAIG: If you knew Martin you'd never say that. No . . . W.G. Martin was a skillful orator, and an able and clever pastor. He kept Grace and himself full of use and in the public eye . . . I've got to go . . . look at the time. [*Climbs into box*]

YOUNG: But the Trustees wanted a different kind of church. . . .

HOWARD ALBRIGHT: [*Persisting*] They never said so . . . but I think so. . . . At least, they thought Grace and Richmond Craig was the right direction to go, or the most valuable to attempt.

CRAIG: [*In box*] Look, don't forget: after the Depression there was the war. Everything changed. Who knows what the trustees hoped for anymore. I think you're wrong, Albright. . . . Good-bye to you both . . .

YOUNG: [*Musing*] Maybe they just got old. Like me, and wanted everything done and in order before they shuffled off this mortal coil. . . .

HOWARD ALBRIGHT: You may be right. Well, if that was their intention, they shuffled off our mortal coil too.

YOUNG: What happened?

HOWARD ALBRIGHT: They transferred the title of the property to the United Church General Council. As it turned out, it was like being thrown to the wolves.

YOUNG: I remember some wolves nipping at the heels of John McDougall and myself near Lloydminster in '74, . . . but they were so mean-looking we figured they were Baptists.

HOWARD ALBRIGHT: [*Laughing*] Well, it took seven years, no, eight years of nipping but they finally got us. From May of 1947 to June of 1955 . . . just last month. It doesn't seem possible.

YOUNG: So you got et. If you fought a good fight, be satisfied in that.[22]

HOWARD ALBRIGHT: All we wanted, first and last, was to stay and be a congregation; we thought that was the best use of the property.

YOUNG: But . . . others thought differently. . . . Well, that's the church, Albright. Love it or hate it. It allows for different opinions.

HOWARD ALBRIGHT: Still, even with selling the property, I was sure that Presbytery would give us fifty percent of the proceeds to start a new Grace . . . somewhere in a new area. Why we saved them that much a time or two.

YOUNG: A new Grace in the suburbs, eh? It wouldn't seem the same.

HOWARD ALBRIGHT: Don't worry. It won't happen. Presbytery wouldn't guarantee us an amount or percentage from the sale.

YOUNG: That's odd.

HOWARD ALBRIGHT: It felt as if we'd no hope left. Nothing to go on with. Nothing to go to people in a new area with. So, we dissolved our fellowship.

YOUNG: And all that's left is these boxes.

HOWARD ALBRIGHT: That and a parking lot. Oh, they say it will be a merchandise mart by next June but I have my doubts[23] . . . ah, there's the car. [*Startled*] My wife's back. . . .

YOUNG: I'm looking forward to meeting her.

HOWARD ALBRIGHT: [*Ignoring him*] She wanted these boxes out of here.

YOUNG: So this may not be a convenient time.

HOWARD ALBRIGHT: Convenient time? If she finds out that you and Craig and Rutledge and McIrvine are here . . . why she'll . . . I don't know what she'll do . . . she doesn't like surprises.

YOUNG: Ah, few women do. . . . An extra seven for dinner used to raise the temperature around our dinner table too.

HOWARD ALBRIGHT: So you don't mind getting back in the box?

YOUNG: Not without my bell. I rang it for Wolseley. . . .

HOWARD ALBRIGHT: Look, I don't know where your bell is. I don't know if it exists or if its been melted down for ammunition or brass monkeys or whatever. . . .

YOUNG: Sorry, Albright, I'm not leaving without a thorough search. [*He crosses to a box previously untouched.*] Ah . . . promising. Old copies of the Guardian . . . look at these old heating pipes. . . . [*Leaning into the box*]

LOUISE ALBRIGHT: [*Offstage*] Howard, can you get the groceries from the car? I just picked up a few things after the tea.

HOWARD ALBRIGHT: Coming, Dear. . . . [*Quickly, Howard Albright grabs Young's legs and forces him into the box.*]

YOUNG: Hey! [*Muffled as Howard Albright closes the lid and sits on it*]

LOUISE ALBRIGHT: [*Entering*] What was that, Dear?

HOWARD ALBRIGHT: I said the time just flew by. . . .

LOUISE ALBRIGHT: It does that. . . . Look at this room! [*She looks at the huge boxes.*] Howard . . . what?

HOWARD ALBRIGHT: [*He gazes around a little sheepishly.*] I guess the boxes sort of took over, Dear. . . . It's hard to put so much life away.

[*Sound effects: a bell begins ringing in the distance.*]

LOUISE ALBRIGHT: You may have to choose between Grace Church and me. . . . Wait a minute, do you hear bells?

HOWARD ALBRIGHT: Yes, I do! [*Quietly*] He found it. . . .

LOUISE ALBRIGHT: What is it . . . a wedding . . . ? No it's Thursday afternoon. . . . [*Happy*] such ringing! [*Alarmed*] Howard, I think it's coming from that box! Howard?

HOWARD ALBRIGHT: [*Nods and looks at her solemnly.*] Wait till you meet Wolseley and his troops. And Riel!

YOUNG: Howard, calm down; tell me who's ringing the bell?

HOWARD ALBRIGHT: You want the truth . . . ? It's old George Young, Dear. He founded Grace and I guess he's ringing her out in style.

YOUNG: That doesn't make much sense.

HOWARD ALBRIGHT: Maybe not, but let it ring, George. . . . [*Throws open the lids of all the boxes*] Let it ring!

Curtain

APPENDIX I

Guide to the United Church Archives, Conference of Manitoba and Northwestern Ontario

Catherine Macdonald

The archival system of the United Church of Canada tends to mimic that of the federal and provincial governments of Canada. There is the national United Church Archives at Victoria University in Toronto and there are regional collections in each of the twelve conferences. The United Church Archives, Toronto, collects the records of the General Council and of the boards and divisions of the national Church as well as the equivalent records of the Methodist, Presbyterian and Congregational Churches. These kinds of records reveal the activities of the Church in the other regions of Canada from the perspective of the highest decision-making bodies. (See page 343 for a listing of materials relevant to Manitoba and northwestern Ontario in the national United Church Archives.)

Prior to the formation of the United Church of Canada in 1925, church records from all over Manitoba tended to drift into the colleges of the two largest uniting denominations in Winnipeg, the Presbyterian Manitoba College (founded in 1871) and the Methodist Wesley College (founded in 1886). This was not so much the result of administrative policy as it was of the efforts of a few influential church history enthusiasts. Of the two collections, the Presbyterian one was the most complete. It had been a labour of love on the part of the long-time professor of church history at Manitoba College, the Rev. Professor Andrew Baird. Baird's counterpart at Wesley had been the Rev. John Maclean, formerly an Indian missionary and latterly Archivist for the whole Methodist Church. It would appear, from gaps which exist in the Manitoba Methodist records, that Maclean never got the support he needed to run either the Wesley College archives or the national church archives.

The people attending the first meeting of the new Manitoba Conference of the United Church of Canada in June 1925, conscious of the need to preserve the history of the founding denominations in the region, formalized the tradition by passing a motion stipulating that the two colleges be the legitimate repositories for historic records of the Church. Manitoba College and Wesley College functioned cooperatively after 1925 and united formally in 1938 as The United Colleges, later simply United College. The formal union of the colleges in 1938 (and the sale of the Manitoba College building in 1931) effected the final merging of the two archival collections.

The Conference Historical Committee (later the Archives Committee) was given the job of gathering in material for the archives. Convenors of this committee often found the indifference of the rest of the Church to historical matters puzzling and disappointing. However their own enthusiasm pushed them to use precious leisure time to seek out church records. During the 1940s and 1950s, the dogged efforts of convenors like the Rev. A.W. Kenner, Dr. George B. King and the Rev. H. Gordon Harland, in particular, brought valuable material into the collection.

The organization of the material, once collected, was left to the staff of the United College library. Since very few people conducted research in the collection and there were many other calls on the time of the small staff, the archives were never fully organized. William Brooks, then a graduate student, made the first complete inventory in 1967. Still, the focus of the Church's strategy for collecting archives remained on collecting, and not on arranging and describing.

In 1967, United College ceased to be a church college and became the University of Winnipeg, an independent university funded by the province. Nonetheless, the new institution retained many aspects of its church heritage. Chief among these were the theology faculty and the church archives. In 1972, the library moved into new quarters in Centennial Hall. The new building housed a rare book room, which became the home for the University's rare book collection, the University archives and the United Church archives.

The collection had, by this time, received some attention from academic researchers but the lack of organization seriously limited the usefulness of the material. The United Church hired a part-time archivist in 1975 and a part-time assistant in 1978. Research access, on an appointment basis and with the help of University library staff, has been available since 1975. Because finding aids are still the weak point of the system, an additional part-time assistant was hired in 1984, whose whole time is devoted to compiling finding aids. Future plans include the development of a computerized inventory system that can easily be updated and that will allow the Conference Archives staff to send printouts of the inventory to other conference archives across the country as well as to the Central United Church Archives in Toronto.

The boundaries of the Conference of Manitoba and Northwestern Ontario are the boundaries of the Province of Manitoba plus northwestern Ontario up to and including Marathon, Ontario. Both Methodist and Presbyterian records prior to 1925 include some northwestern Ontario records. Prior to 1905, Manitoba was the centre of church activity for the North West Territories, as they were called then. As a result, some Methodist and Presbyterian records from Alberta and Saskatchewan for this period can be found in the collection. The absence of records from the other founding denomination, that is, the Congregational Union, is a cause for regret. Congregationalists were never numerous in the West, and what few records they kept seem to have been lost or dispersed to other archives. In spite of this, the United Church Archives, Conference of Manitoba and Northwestern Ontario, remains one of the strongest resources for the study of Canadian church and social history in the West.

DENOMINATIONAL RECORDS

Methodist Church

Although Methodist activity in Manitoba was inaugurated with the arrival of the Rev. James Evans at Norway House in 1840, no records of that early mission, which was sponsored by the Wesleyan Missionary Society in Britain, found their way to the Conference Archives. After almost twenty years of inactivity, the Wesleyan Methodist Church in Canada (after 1874, the Methodist Church of Canada) took up the work, sending the Rev. George Young to Red River in 1868. In 1883 the territory was given conference status and the Conference of Manitoba and the North West divided into six districts: Brandon, Pembina and Turtle Mountain, Portage la Prairie, Winnipeg, Saskatchewan, and Regina. In 1884, the Methodist Church of Canada united with three other Methodist denominations to form the Methodist Church. As settlement expanded in Manitoba and the North West Territories, further organizational changes took place:

1887 Morden, Deloraine, and Birtle Districts formed.
1889 Crystal City and Calgary Districts formed.
1893 Neepawa and Moosomin Districts formed.
1894 Lake Winnipeg District formed.
1895 Edmonton District formed.
1896 Carman District formed.
1897 Port Arthur District formed; Lake Winnipeg and Saskatchewan districts combined to form one district called Lake Winnipeg and the Saskatchewan District.
1899 Dauphin District formed; name of Lake Winnipeg and the Saskatchewan District changed to Indian District.
1903 Souris, Moose Jaw, and Red Deer Districts formed; Indian district renamed Lake Winnipeg District.
1904 Roland District formed; Alberta Conference and Assiniboia Conference created; Saskatchewan, Regina, Moose Jaw, Moosomin, Brandon, Souris, and Deloraine districts combined to form Assiniboia Conference (later renamed Saskatchewan Conference); Edmonton, Calgary, Red Deer Districts combined to form Alberta Conference.
1906 Swan River District formed.
1907 Rainy River District formed.
1910 Winnipeg District divided into Winnipeg North and Winnipeg South Districts.
1912 Brandon, Souris, and Deloraine Districts detached from Saskatchewan Conference and reattached to Manitoba Conference.
1923 Winnipeg North and Winnipeg South Districts reunited as Winnipeg District.

Minutes and Records of the Manitoba and North West Conference Held by United Church Archives, Conference of Manitoba and Northwestern Ontario
    Minutes 1883–1925
    Missionary Committee Minutes 1885–1903, 1910–25
    Stationing Committee Minutes 1886–1925
    Property Record Book 1901, 1916–17
    Board of Examiners, Annual Reports 1886–1904

Records Related to the Conference of Manitoba and the North West
    Methodist Ministerial Association Minutes 1899–1924
    Manitoba Conference Layman's Association Minutes 1917–25
    Deaconess Board of Management Minutes 1906–25
    Winnipeg Church Extension and City Mission Association Minutes 1911–24

Minutes of the Annual District Meeting and Ministerial Session
  Birtle District 1889–91, 1897, 1899, 1904, 1906, 1918, 1920–25
  Brandon District 1884, 1886, 1890–91, 1897–06, 1911–13, 1919–25
  Calgary District 1890, 1892, 1897, 1898–99
  Carman District 1897–98, 1905–21, 1923–25
  Crystal City District 1890–96, 1899, 1911–25
  Dauphin District 1904, 1919–24
  Deloraine District 1889–90, 1892, 1897, 1899–1902
  Edmonton District 1897, 1899
  Lake Winnipeg and Saskatchewan District 1899
  Lake Winnipeg District 1920, 1922–24
  Moosomin District 1897, 1899
  Morden District 1890–92
  Neepawa District 1897, 1899, 1901–09, 1911–16, 1919–23
  Pembina and Turtle Mountain District 1884–87
  Portage la Prairie District 1897, 1899, 1901–25
  Port Arthur District 1898–01, 1919–25
  Rainy River District 1918
  Regina District 1884, 1886–87, 1898, 1891–92, 1897–98
  Roland District 1918
  Saskatchewan District 1884, 1886–88, 1890, 1897
  Souris District 1903–06, 1915–20, 1922–23
  Swan River District 1919–23
  Winnipeg District 1884–04, 1906, 1924–25
  Winnipeg North District 1919–23
  Winnipeg South District 1910–14, 1916–23
  Winnipeg North/Winnipeg South District 1920–23 (joint district session)

Minutes of the Financial District Meeting
  Birtle District 1889–14, 1918–24
  Brandon District 1882–98
  Deloraine District 1889–07
  Morden District 1887–24
  Regina District 1885–99
  Winnipeg/Winnipeg North District 1895–22

Presbyterian Church
With the arrival of the Rev. John Black at Red River in 1851, the Canada Presbyterian Church inaugurated the first Presbyterian Church in the Hudson's Bay Company territories. The mission continued under the auspices of the Foreign Missions Committee until 1870, when the Presbytery of Manitoba and the North West was created. In 1884, the presbytery was raised to synod status and the new Synod of Manitoba and the North West divided into three presbyteries: Winnipeg, Brandon and Rock Lake. Successive changes in the organizational structure of the synod are listed below:

1885 Brandon Presbytery divided to form Brandon and Regina Presbyteries.
1887 Calgary and Columbia Presbyteries formed.
1889 Minnedosa Presbytery formed.

1892 Synod of British Columbia formed; Presbyteries of Columbia and Calgary transferred to new synod. ,

1893 Five existing presbyteries realigned into nine: Winnipeg, Brandon, Regina, Rock Lake, Minnedosa, Glenboro, Melita, Portage la Prairie and Superior.

1901 Regina Presbytery split into three presbyteries: Regina, Qu'Appelle and Prince Albert; Dauphin Presbytery formed.

1904 Minnedosa Presbytery split into Yorkton and Minnedosa Presbyteries; Melita Presbytery split into Arcola and Melita Presbyteries.

1906 Synod of Saskatchewan created; Regina, Qu'Appelle, Prince Albert, Yorkton, Arcola and Melita Presbyteries reorganized into new synod.

1906 Boundaries of the synods of British Columbia, Alberta, Saskatchewan and Manitoba readjusted to agree with provincial boundaries.

Minutes of the Presbytery of Manitoba/Synod of Manitoba and the North West Held by United Church Archives, Conference of Manitoba and Northwestern Ontario
    Presbytery of Manitoba 1870–84
    Synod of Manitoba and the North West 1884–1925

Minutes of the Synod Standing Committees
    Home Missions Committee 1884–1902
    Foreign Missions Committee 1890–1900

Minutes of Presbyteries
    Brandon Presbytery 1884–1925
    Glenboro Presbytery 1907–25
    Melita Presbytery 1894–1906
    Minnedosa Presbytery 1889–1925
    Portage la Prairie Presbytery 1884–1925
    Rock Lake Presbytery 1884–1925
    Superior Presbytery 1894–1925
    Winnipeg Presbytery 1884–1925

Minutes and Records of Presbytery Standing Committees
    Minnedosa Presbytery, Home Missions appointment book, undated.
    Winnipeg Presbytery, Home Missions Committee Minutes 1884–1908, 1922–23;
    Clerk of Presbytery, correspondence 1884–1900, 1902–05, 1907, 1914–24

The United Church of Canada
The United Church of Canada was formed in 1925 as a union of the Methodist Church, the Presbyterian Church in Canada and the Congregational Union of Canada. The new church borrowed administrative names and concepts from each of the uniting denominations. The "provincial" unit of administration was to be known as a conference, conferences were to be divided into presbyteries, presbyteries were to be made up of pastoral charges. Manitoba Conference was organized into nine presbyteries in 1925: Superior, Winnipeg, Rock Lake, Carman, Portage la Prairie, Brandon, Birtle, Dauphin and Lake Winnipeg. Successive changes in presbytery structure are listed below:

1926 Rainy River Presbytery formed.
1930 Name of Lake Winnipeg Presbytery changed to Hudson Bay Presbytery.
1937 Hudson Bay Presbytery split into Hudson Bay and Norway House Presbyteries.
1943 Rainy River Presbytery changed to Kenora-Rainy River Presbytery.
1961 Norway House Presbytery deleted, its charges added to Kenora-Rainy River, Hudson Bay and Winnipeg Presbyteries.
1961 Brandon, Carman, Rock Lake, Portage la Prairie and Birtle Presbyteries realigned to create four new Presbyteries: Brandon-Rock Lake, Carman, Birtle and Portage la Prairie.
1963 Winnipeg Presbytery divided into Selkirk and Winnipeg Presbyteries; name of Brandon-Rock Lake Presbytery changed to Brandon Presbytery.
1966 Dauphin and Hudson Bay Presbyteries merged to form Northland Presbytery.
1972 Kenora-Rainy River and Superior Presbyteries merged to form Cambrian Presbytery.
1981 Keewatin Presbytery formed.
1982 Name of Manitoba Conference changed to Conference of Manitoba and Northwestern Ontario.

Presbytery Minutes Held by United Church Archives, Conference of Manitoba and Northwestern Ontario
    Birtle 1925–60, 1967–75, 1984–
    Brandon 1925–78, 1984–
    Cambrian 1972–78, 1984–
    Carman 1925–57, 1960–79
    Kenora-Rainy River 1925–65, Executive Minutes 1965–72
    Dauphin 1925–59
    Northland 1967–84
    Hudson Bay 1929–54, 1961–66
    Norway House 1941–61
    Portage la Prairie 1925–79, 1983–
    Rock Lake 1928–61
    Superior 1925–72
    Selkirk 1963–76, 1978–81, 1984–

WOMEN'S RECORDS

Methodist Church
The first auxiliaries of the Woman's Missionary Society of the Methodist Church were formed in 1880 in Hamilton, Ontario. It soon became evident that a national organization was needed and the Dominion Woman's Missionary Society was duly formed in 1881. Although conference branches were authorized in 1882, the Manitoba Conference Branch was not formed until 1895. The Manitoba Conference Branch split in 1904 into the Manitoba Conference Branch and the North-West Conference Branch.

Minutes and Records of the Conference Branch Held by United Church Archives, Conference of Manitoba and Northwestern Ontario
    Executive Minutes 1917–26
    Annual Reports 1906–23

Presbyterian Church
The Woman's Foreign Missionary Society (WFMS) was formed in 1876. The first Manitoba auxiliary of the WFMS began in 1884. After this, auxiliaries began to spring up throughout the province as settlement continued. The first presbytery-level organization was formed in 1886 as the Brandon Presbyterial WFMS, and eventually most presbyteries formed presbyterial societies. The home missions groups were not as well organized as the WFMS was. Small auxiliaries and societies functioned more or less independently during the 1890s. In 1903, the national Women's Home Mission Society was created (WHMS) with the same organizational structure as the WFMS. In 1914, the WFMS and the WHMS combined to form the Women's Missionary Society (WMS) of the Presbyterian Church of Canada (Western Division). When the new society was formed, a new level of administration, that is, the Provincial Society, was created.

Minutes and Records of the Presbyterial Societies Held by United Church Archives, Conference of Manitoba and Northwestern Ontario
Brandon Presbyterial WFMS/WMS, Minutes 1893–1925.
Minnedosa Presbyterial WFMS/WMS, Minutes 1907–25.
Superior Presbyterial WFMS/WMS, Minutes 1912–25.
Winnipeg Presbyterial WFMS, Executive Minutes 1889–97; Minutes 1889–93, 1897–14.
Winnipeg Presbyterial WMS, Executive Minutes 1914–25.

The United Church of Canada
The new church retained some of the structural elements of its largest uniting denominations. In 1926, The Woman's Missionary Society (WMSWMS) of the United Church of Canada was founded. The WMS was structured with a Dominion board, conference branches, presbyterial societies and affiliated Canadian Girls in Training (CGIT) groups. Parallel in structure to the WMS was the Woman's Association (WA) which was the successor of the ladies aid groups at the congregational level. The WA was formally constituted in 1941, although World War II delayed its progress somewhat. In 1962 the WA and the WMS were replaced by a new organization, the United Church Women (UCW). The structure of the new organization was almost identical to that of the WMS.

Records and Minutes of Conference Level Bodies Held by United Church Archives, Conference of Manitoba and Northwestern Ontario
WMS Conference branch, Executive Minutes 1926–59; Advisory Committee 1934–46.
United Church Women, Minutes 1962–70; Annual Reports 1962–68.

Records and Minutes of Presbyterial Societies
Birtle WMS/UCW, Minutes 1926–62; North West Division Minutes 1953–58; Correspondence Book 1927–58.
Brandon WA, WMS/UCW, Minutes (WA) 1949–62; Minutes (WMS) 1926–61.
Carman WMS/UCW, Minutes 1954–67.
Dauphin WA/UCW, Minutes 1952–62.
North District (Selkirk), Minutes 1955–61.
Superior WA, WMS Minutes (WMS) 1926–62; Minutes (WA) 1952–61.
Winnipeg WA, WMS, UCW Minutes (WA) 1949–54, 1958–61; Minutes (WMS) 1925–28; Executive Minutes (WMS) 1928–62.

Miscellaneous Women's Records
  Winnipeg Women's Union (formerly Methodist and Presbyterian Deaconess Aid Societies), Minutes 1926–49.
  Fellowship of Professional Women, Minutes and Papers 1947–65.
  The Church Home for Girls/MacMillan House Project, Records 1945–76.
  Manitoba Canadian Girls in Training, Minutes and Papers 1952–73.

PERSONAL PAPERS

The Conference Archives collects the papers of prominent Manitoba clergy and laypeople. Important collections are listed alphabetically with the birth and death dates, where known, included in square brackets. The number following the square brackets represents the amount of shelf space the collection occupies.

ANDREW BROWNING BAIRD [1855–1940], twenty-four feet; Presbyterian missionary to Fort Edmonton, 1881–87; professor of church history, Hebrew and Old Testament at Manitoba College, 1887–1939; co-convenor of the Synod of Manitoba and the North West Foreign Missions Committee which oversaw Indian Missions on the plains, 1888–99; long-time clerk of Winnipeg Presbytery. Indian missions administration documents dominate the collection along with Baird's extensive private correspondence, including numerous letters from his family in Perth County, Ontario.

GEORGE BRYCE [1844–1931], three feet; founder and professor of science and literature at Manitoba College (1871–1909); chair of the Faculty of Science at the University of Manitoba (1879–1904); and historian of western Canada. The collection includes sermon manuscripts, the manuscript of an unpublished adventure novel and some correspondence.

JAMES DONAGHY, one foot; Presbyterian Indian missionary, amateur historian and photographer. Typescript histories of the Swan Lake, Long Plains and Okanese Indian Reserves, including excellent photographs.

JOHN A. DOYLE, sixteen inches; superintendent of home missions for Manitoba and Saskatchewan Conferences of the Methodist Church (1915–26); principal of the Brandon Indian School (1925–41). Sermon manuscripts.

FRANCIS M. FINN, one inch; Methodist minister at Roland, Chater and Brandon; formerly Roman Catholic. Small collection of sermon manuscripts mostly dealing with Protestant supremacy and the Catholic Church.

ANNIE R. GORDON, one inch; a typescript biography of the Rev. Andrew Gordon and his wife Annie Copp Gordon by their daughter, Annie R. Gordon. The Gordons were originally Bible Christians and Annie Copp Gordon had been a lay preacher of that denomination prior to their arrival in Manitoba.

HENRY KENNER [1832–1917], four inches; Methodist minister at Nelsonville, Russell, Thornhill and Winnipeg. Diary and sermon notebook, memoir of his ministry.

JOHN H. RUTTAN [1841–1943], three inches; Methodist missionary to Norway House (1874–79); minister at Meadow Lea, High Bluff and Portage la Prairie. Diaries of his time at Norway House.

CHURCH-RELATED AND INTER-CHURCH RECORDS

The Conference Archives welcomes the deposit of records by organizations with no formal ties to the United Church but whose work is closely related to the Church; or of groups which are supported jointly by the United Church and one or more other denominations. Among collections in this category are:

Records of the Inter-Church Task Force on Northern Flooding (1973–76), four and a half feet. Briefs, correspondence, press releases, supporting reference material documenting the task force's efforts to publicize the effects on the environment and on humans of the Churchill River diversion.

Manitoba Student Christian Movement (1923–73), six feet. Minutes and correspondence of the University of Manitoba and University of Winnipeg branches.

Records of the Winnipeg Ministerial Association (1955–70), eight inches. Minutes.

LOCAL CHURCH RECORDS

Since 1975 the Conference Archives has made an effort to gather in local church records, especially from churches that have closed, but also from active congregations who wish to safeguard their older records. Records of the local auxiliaries of the Methodist, Presbyterian and United Church women's groups are kept in this section. Along with these records, a typical local church collection would include minute books of the board and session, Sunday school records, youth group minute books, annual reports and photographs. Among the most extensive collections are:

Central Church, Brandon (1883–1957), seven feet. Records of Brandon Methodist and First Church Methodist; St. Paul's Presbyterian and First Church Presbyterian; Central United plus records of some smaller churches in the Brandon area.

Knox Shuniah Church, Thunder Bay (1911–70), seven feet. Records of Knox Church, Port Arthur/Thunder Bay.

Plumas-Lakeshore (1898–1975), eight feet. Records of Presbyterian, Methodist and United churches in Plumas and surrounding area including Glenella, Mekiwin, Langruth and Amaranth.

Russell-Inglis (1884–1975), eight feet. Records of the Presbyterian, Methodist and United Churches of Russell, Silver Creek, Angusville and Binscarth.

Transcona Memorial Church, Winnipeg (1911–78), seven feet. Records of the Presbyterian, Methodist and United Churches in Transcona and the surrounding area including Suthwyn and Springfield.

Trinity Church, Portage la Prairie (1880–1971), ten feet. Records of Knox Presbyterian, Grace Methodist, West Prospect Methodist, Burnside United and Trinity United Churches.

Westminster Church, Winnipeg (1892–1979), nine feet. Records of Westminster Presbyterian/ United Church.

MONOGRAPHS, PAMPHLETS AND PERIODICALS

The Conference Archives includes a small library. The monographs, whose content runs heavily to home and foreign missions, are almost exclusively books published by one or another of the founding denominations or of the United Church. Pamphlets have also accumulated, of which the most significant are those comprising the Church Union Pamphlet Collection (1905–52), eight inches. This is a relatively complete collection of pamphlets, broadsides, newspaper articles and drafts of legislation issued by both sides during the church union debate.

The serials section is not large but contains some scarce periodicals of regional interest. *Kanidayski Ranok* (Canadian Dawn), volumes 27 to 46 (1932–50) was a Ukrainian newspaper published first by the Presbyterian Church in Winnipeg and later continued by the United Church. *Progress* (1903–04) was a short-lived monthly journal published by the students of the Regina Indian Industrial School. A local church newsletter of unparalleled longevity, *The Robertson Broadcaster*, volumes 1 to 46 (1925–71) was issued by the Robertson Memorial Church and Institute in Winnipeg's north end.

The Central Archives of the United Church of Canada: A bibliographic note on Manitoba and northwestern Ontario

Neil Semple

In order to give the clearest picture of not only the extent, but also the nature, of the holdings of the Central Archives of the United Church of Canada in Toronto, this bibliographic note gives the primary sources rather than giving a simple list of holdings. In this note, the collections are divided into the following categories: (1) records of the United Church and its antecedent denominations; (2) personal papers; (3) periodicals; (4) theses; (5) special collections.

DENOMINATIONAL RECORDS

The Central Archives of the United Church collects and maintains the records of the national operations of the United Church and its antecedent denominations. In general, discrete collections are not maintained for Manitoba and northwestern Ontario. However, this region is well represented in the broader collections.

Methodist
The British Wesleyan Methodist Church oversaw mission operations in Manitoba, Northwestern Ontario and the remainder of the Northwest from 1840 to 1854. The Central Archives retains copies of the correspondence for British North America from the missionaries and the parent society in England between 1800 and 1867 as well as the minutes of the Wesleyan Missionary Society for 1814 to 1865. After 1854, the Wesleyan Methodist Church in Canada took over mission operations. Relevant correspondence is found in the following: the Enoch Wood and Lewis Peake Letterbooks (1868–80); Alexander Sutherland Letterbooks (1875–1906); James Allen Letterbooks (1906–18); Charles Manning Letterbooks (1907–26); and the James Shannon Letterbooks (1907–30).

Other Methodist records include: the Wesleyan (British) Missionary Society Notices (1816–92); the Wesleyan Methodist Church, Missionary Society Reports (1825–73); the Methodist Church of Canada, Missionary Society Reports (1874–83); the Methodist Episcopal Church, Missionary Society Reports (1858–83); the Methodist Church (Canada, Newfoundland, Bermuda), Missionary Society Reports (1884–1925); the minutes and general correspondence of the Methodist missionary societies.

The Central Archives also retains the Methodist Conference and District Minutes, some of which are in manuscript form (1824–1925). It also retains the correspondence of the General Conference of the Methodist Church (cnb) (1884–1925), the Committee on Education, including material on universities (1875–1925), and the Board of Evangelism and Social Service (1910–25).

Presbyterian

The Presbyterian records related to Manitoba and northwestern Ontario at the Central Archives are much more limited. Basically, they include the minutes, reports and correspondence of the Board of Foreign Missions, Western Section (1876–1925), and the Woman's Foreign Missionary Society (1880–1925). Some information is also found in the Board of Home Missions of the Presbyterian Church in Canada (1876–1925).

The United Church of Canada

Information about the United Church in Manitoba and northwestern Ontario is contained in nearly all the major collections of the Central Archives. These include: General Council, Executive and Subexecutive, Correspondence and Minutes and Reports (1925 to present); General Council, Special Committees and Commissions (1925 to present); Minutes of the Annual Conferences and Presbyteries (1925 to present); Committee on Law and Legislation, especially concerning property and estates; Board of Home Missions (1925–1971); Woman's Missionary Society, Board of Home Missions (1925–1961); the Board of Evangelism and Social Service (1925–1971); and the successor to all the boards dealing with work in Canada, the Division of Mission in Canada (1971 to present); and the Division of Ministry, Personnel and Education (1971 to present), the successor to the Board of Colleges and Secondary Schools (1925 to 1971).

Inter-Church Collections

The Central Archives contains large collections representing inter-denominational activity including: the Church Union Collection (1906–1925); the papers of the Dominion Alliance and the Canadian Temperance Federation (about sixty boxes); the Canadian Girls in Training (cgit) (thirty boxes); and the Student Christian Movement (100 boxes). Much of this material relates to these organizations' work in Manitoba and northwestern Ontario.

PERSONAL PAPERS

The personal papers listed here are those of individuals who spent a large portion of their careers in Manitoba or northwestern Ontario or who, through their national work for the church, represented significant aspects of this region's social and historical development. The papers are listed alphabetically with the birth and death dates included in square brackets.

ANDREW BROWNING BAIRD [1855–1940], twenty-two reels, copies of papers from the United Church Archives, Conference of Manitoba and Northwestern Ontario; professor at Manitoba College.

GEORGE BARNLEY [1816–1904], one reel, copies of journals between 1840 and 1845; missionary in western Canada.

JOHN WESLEY BELL [1847–1929], one box; temperance leader.

JOHN AND JAMES BLACK [1818–1882], one box, correspondence copied from the Archives of the Conference of Manitoba and Northwestern Ontario and the Alexander Ross papers.

SALEM G. BLAND [1859–1950], fifteen boxes, sermons and addresses; taught at Wesley College and was a national leader of the social gospel movement.

ROBERT BROOKING [1813–1893], one box, journals, sermons and miscellaneous papers; missionary at Norway House between 1839 and 1859.

FREDERICK L. BROWN, one box, daily diaries, especially related to northern Ontario between 1890 and 1933.

JOHN DUNCAN BYRNES [1869–1935], one box, reports, addresses and diaries between 1917 and 1930; superintendent of home missions, concerned with New Ontario.

ALBERT CARMAN [1833–1917], twenty-seven boxes, papers; last bishop of the Methodist Episcopal Church and general superintendent of the united Methodist Church, was involved in sending missionaries to Manitoba.

SAMUEL DWIGHT CHOWN [1853–1931], seventeen boxes, papers; Albert Carman's successor.

EBER CRUMMY [1861–1939], one box; principal of Wesley College.

GEORGE AND ALICE DOREY [1884–1963], five boxes, papers; secretary of the Board of Home Missions.

JOHN EDMISON [1871–1928], one box; involved with home mission work in the West.

JAMES EVANS [1801–1846], papers; British Wesleyan missionary in Manitoba, papers held at Victoria University.

WILLIAM J. GALLAGHER [1894–1964], eight boxes, mostly sermons, from the Board of Evangelism and Social Service.

JOHN F. GERMAN [1842–1918], one box, papers, typescript of correspondence between 1878 and 1881.

ARTHUR HAMES [1849–1931], one box, memoirs; missionary in Manitoba.

ARVI HEINONEN [1887–1963], one box; minister to the Finns of Canada.

JAMES HUGHESON [1871–1938], one box and one reel; minister in Manitoba.

ALEXANDER IRWIN [1867–1957], three boxes; professor at Wesley College between 1914 and 1918.

WILLIAM IVENS, one box, correspondence concerning his dismissal from McDougall Church, Winnipeg.

ELGIE E. JOBLIN [1909–   ], four reels and 4 boxes; especially concerned with native peoples between 1946 and 1978.

FREDERICK W. KERR [1881–1925], twenty boxes, papers; professor at Manitoba College.

GEORGE B. KING [1879–1956], one box; professor at United College.

JOHN M. KING [1830–1899], one reel, correspondence; principal of Manitoba College.

JOHN E. LANE [1874–1955], one box; minister in Manitoba.

ERNEST AND DOROTHY LONG [1901–   ], twenty-nine boxes combined, papers; secretary of General Council between 1955 and 1972.

JOSEPH LOUSELEY [1870–1962], one box, memoirs of his life as a minister at Norway House.

EDWARD LUND [1878–1939], one reel; minister in Manitoba.

THOMAS McCORD [1872–1957], one reel; sometime minister in Manitoba.

JOHN MACKAY, three reels; principal of Manitoba and United College.

DONALD McKERRACHER [–1881], two boxes; minister at Fort William and Prince Arthur.

JOHN MACLEAN [1858–1928], eighty boxes, papers and manuscript histories; missionary and historian.

ALEXANDER MATHESON [1827–1911], one box, sermons and study notes; minister in Manitoba.

T. ALBERT MOORE [1860–1940], one box; secretary of General Council.

JAMES MUTCHMOR [1892–1980], sixteen boxes, papers; associated with the Board of Evangelism and Social Service.

JAMES NISBET [1823–1874], one box, correspondence between 1861 and 1874; missionary in Manitoba and Saskatchewan.

HUGH PEDLEY [1852–1923], one box, sermons; minister in Winnipeg.

JOHN H. RIDDELL [1863–1952], one box; principal of Wesley College.

JAMES ROBERTSON [1839–1902], three reels; superintendent of Western Missions for the Presbyterian Church in Canada.

DONALD ROSS, one reel; associated with Hudson's Bay Company and Western missions.

ROBERT RUNDLE [1811–1886], one box, typescript of journals.

JOHN SEMMENS [1850–1921], one box, personal history and biography.

ALBERT E. SMITH, one box and one reel; leading Canadian socialist.

ROBERT STEINHAUER [1820–1884], one box, copies of records from Alberta Archives.

FREDERICK STEVENS [1869–1946], one box (includes memoirs of Mrs. Stevens on the life of a missionary); missionary in Manitoba.

ALEXANDER SUTHERLAND [1833–1910], one box; secretary of the Board of Foreign Missions of the Methodist Church.

PERIODICALS

Most of the periodicals in the Central Archives contain information scattered through their pages on Manitoba and northwestern Ontario. The Central Archives has the following relevant periodicals:

Methodist
The Christian Guardian (1829–1925), *The Wesleyan* (1840–43) (Ontario), *British North American Wesleyan Methodist Magazine* (1840–46), *Canada Christian Advocate* (1845–84), *The Wesleyan* (1838–1884) (Halifax), *The Christian Journal* (1860–83), *The Observer* (1867–84) (Bible Christian), *Evangelical Witness* (1873–74), *Canadian Methodist Magazine* (1875–1906), *The Missionary Outlook* (1881–1925), *Canadian Methodist Quarterly* (1889–95), *Wesleyan Methodist Missionary Notices* (1854–78), *Missionary Leaflet of the Woman's Missionary Society* (1890–1925), *Onward* (1891–1938), *Vox Wesleyana* (1897–1925) (Wesley College, Winnipeg), *Canadian Epworth Era* (1899–1916), *Western Methodist Recorder* (1899–1925), *The Missionary Bulletin* (1903–21), *Youth and Service* (1916–20). British Methodist periodicals relating to Manitoba and northwestern Ontario are: *The Wesleyan Magazine* or *Arminian Magazine* (1778–1913), *The Primitive Methodist Magazine* (1818–86) and the *Wesleyan Methodist Missionary Notices* (1816–92).

Presbyterian
The Presbyterian Witness (1848–1925), *The Canadian United Presbyterian Magazine* (1854–61), *The Presbyterian* (1848–75), *The Canadian Presbyterian Magazine* (1851–54), *The Ecclesiastical and Missionary Record* (1844–61), *The Home and Foreign Record,*

Canada Presbyterian Church (1861–75), *British American Presbyterian* (1872–77), *The Presbyterian Record* (1876–1925), *The Canada Presbyterian* (1877–88), *Monthly Leaflet*, Woman's Foreign Missionary Society (1884–97), *Foreign Mission Tidings* (1897–1914), *The Missionary Messenger* (1914–25), *Dominion Presbyterian* (1898–1910), *Presbyterian Review* (1886–98), *East and West* (1902–1922), *The Westminster* (1896–1916), *The Presbyterian* (1902–16), *The Presbyterian and Westminster* (1917–20).

Congregational
The Canadian Independent (1854–94), *The Canadian Advance* (1887–90), *The Congregationalist and Canadian Independent* (1894–98), *The Canadian Congregationalist* (1899–1925).

The United Church of Canada
Missionary Monthly (1925–61), *The New Outlook* (1925–39), *The United Church Observer* (1939–83), *United Churchman* (1925–74), *United Church Record* (1925–39), *Western Recorder* (1925–37), *Canadian Viesti* (1930–78) (Finnish), *Canadian Ranok* (1932–58) (Ukrainian), *Spiritual Light* (1932–66) (Norway House).

Other Periodicals
Montreal Witness (1845–67), *The New Dominion* (1867–79), *Woman's Journal* (1885–1903) (WCTU), *Canadian White Ribbon Tidings* (1904–79) (WCTU), *The Canadian Evangel* (1917–69), *The Church* (1837–1856).

THESES

The United Church Central Archives contains several theses which relate, at least partially, to the work in Manitoba and northwestern Ontario. William H. Brooks, "Methodism in the Canadian West in the Nineteenth Century" (University of Manitoba, Ph.D., 1972) and George Emery, "Methodism on the Canadian Prairies: 1896–1914" (University of British Columbia, Ph.D., 1970) are the best treatments available. Neil Semple, "The Impact of Urbanization on the Methodist Church in Central Canada, 1854–1884" (University of Toronto, Ph.D., 1979) touches on the expansion into the West and on the institutional framework that develops there.

George Dowker, "Life and Letters in Red River, 1812–1863" (University of Manitoba, M.A., 1923) and John C. Walker, "The Early History of the Presbyterian Church in Western Canada from the Earliest Times to the Year 1881" (University of Edinburgh, Ph.D, 1928) represent dated work in the field.

John S. Murdoch, "Syllabics: A Successful Educational Innovation" (University of Manitoba, M.Ed., 1981); Douglas F. Pratt, "William Ivens and the Winnipeg Labour Church" (St. Andrew's College, B.D., 1962); and William Sherwin, "The History of the Methodist Church in Northern Ontario during the Nineteenth Century" (Victoria University, M.Th., 1961) represent more limited approaches to narrow historical topics.

SPECIAL COLLECTIONS

Photographs
The photographic collection at the Central Archives covers the work of the United Church and its antecedent denominations in Canada and overseas where mission

operations were conducted. Photographs of most ministers, missionaries, and many churches and church institutions are included in the collection. Furthermore, the collection contains photographs of native peoples and immigrants; and photographs depicting industry, farming, settlement and urban life.

Biographical Files
Specific files are maintained for most of the ministers, missionaries and commissioned deaconesses of the United Church and its antecedents. The files include general biographical information and obituaries, and sometimes miscellaneous correspondence and short sketches.

Church History Files
The Central Archives retains files containing unpublished material, newspaper clippings, service folders and related historical information, as well as small published histories pertaining to Manitoba and northwestern Ontario.

Notes

ABBREVIATIONS

CMS	Colonial Missionary Society of the Congregational Church of England and Wales
CMSL	Church Missionary Society, London, England
HBC	Hudson's Bay Company
HBCA	Hudson's Bay Company Archives, Winnipeg, Manitoba
PABC	Provincial Archives of British Columbia, Victoria, B.C.
PAC	Public Archives of Canada, Ottawa, Ontario
PAM	Provincial Archives of Manitoba, Winnipeg, Manitoba
PWMS	Presbyterian Women's Missionary Society
UCA	United Church Archives, Toronto, Ontario
UCA-MNO	United Church Archives, Conference of Manitoba and Northwestern Ontario, Winnipeg, Manitoba
UMA	University of Manitoba Archives, Winnipeg, Manitoba
UWA	University of Winnipeg Archives, Winnipeg, Manitoba
UWO	University of Western Ontario, London, Ontario
WFMS(WD)	Presbyterian Woman's Foreign Missionary Society (Western Division)
WMS	Wesleyan Missionary Society Archives, London, England

BRITISH METHODISTS

1 HBC Governor George Simpson to Dr. Robert Alder, secretary of Wesleyan Missionary Society, 22 January 1840, HBCA, A 1/60.

2 John McLean, *James Evans: Inventor of the Syllabic System of the Cree Language* (Toronto: William Briggs, 1890); Egerton R. Young, *Rev. James Evans: Apostle of the North* (Toronto: William Briggs, 1900); Nan Shipley, *The James Evans Story* (Toronto: Ryerson Press, 1966).

3 HBC Governor George Simpson to Bishop of Juliopolis, 17 February 1840, HBCA, A 1/60.

4 George G. Findlay and W.W. Holdsworth, *The History of Wesleyan Methodist Missionary Society*, vol. 1 (London: Epworth Press, 1921), 466.

5 Hugh A. Dempsey, *The Rundle Journals*, introduction and notes by Gerald M. Hutchinson (Historical Society of Alberta and Glenbow-Alberta Institute, 1977), 16.

6 T.C.B. Boon, *The Anglican Church from the Bay to the Rockies* (Toronto: Ryerson Press, 1962), 75.
7 Dempsey, *Rundle Journals*, 30.
8 Rev. Ephraim Evans to Rev. J. Carroll, 1865, UWO, London, Ontario, James Evans papers, #243.
9 Correspondence between George Simpson and Donald Ross, PABC, Donald Ross papers, AE R73.
10 Rev. James Evans to Chief Factor Donald Ross, 19 May 1845, HBCA, D 5/14.
11 Sir George Simpson to Dr. Robert Alder, 16 June 1845, HBCA, A 12/2.
12 Sir George Simpson to Chief Factor Donald Ross, 29 December 1845, PABC, Donald Ross papers, AE R73 La5.
13 Margaret Arnett Macleod, ed., *The Letters of Letitia Mactavish Hargrave* (Toronto: The Champlain Society, 1947), 207.
14 WMS, School of Oriental and Asiatic Studies, University of London, private file, no date.
15 Dr. Robert Alder to Sir George Simpson, 1 December 1846, HBCA, D 5/13.
16 Statement by William Mason to Wesleyan secretaries, 23 December 1853, WMS, box 106, item 12.
17 Boon, *Anglican Church*, 79n.
18 Ibid.
19 The primary documentation for the work of Mason as printer at Rossville and the materials produced by the Rossville Mission Press is to be found in the archives of the Wesleyan Missionary Society, London, England. Extensive letters and reports to the Wesleyan Missionary Society covering the years between 1846 and 1854 were written by Mason to the society. This material has been summarized and supplemented by Dr. Bruce Peel, librarian emeritus, University of Alberta, in a publication entitled *The Rossville Mission Press* (Montreal: Osiris, 1974).
20 UCA, 30 December 1886, doc. E99, C88m.
21 Boon, *Anglican Church*, 79–80.
22 Ibid., 463.
23 Ibid., 94.
24 Wallace L. Chafe, *The World of the North American Indian* (Washington, D.C.: National Geographic Society, 1974), 154.
25 "Annual Conference, June 1854," in J.E. Sanderson, *Methodism in Canada*, vol. 2, 1840–83 (Toronto: Briggs, 1910), 96.

AS OTHERS SAW US

1 See Christopher Vecsey, *Traditional Ojibwa Religion and its Historical Changes* (Philadelphia: American Philosophical Society, 1983), especially pp. 45–58.
2 The James Evans papers, the library, UWO. See the entry in his journal for 18 May 1829.
3 Hugh Dempsey, ed., *The Rundle Journals, 1840–1858* (Calgary: Glenbow-Alberta Institute, 1977), 116.
4 The Rev. A.G. Morice, O.M.I., *History of the Catholic Church in Western Canada*, vol. 1 (Toronto: Musson, 1910), 190.
5 See: Morice, *History of the Catholic Church in Western Canada*, from Lake Superior to the Pacific, 200; Pierre J.B. Duchaussois, *Mid Snow and Ice: the Apostles of the North-West* (London: Burns Oats and Washbourne, 1923), 82. It was on the 1844 journey, when Evans was racing Thibault to Ile a la Crosse, that the accidental shooting death of native teacher Thomas Hassel occurred, aborting the journey.

6 Joseph E. Champagne, *Les missions catholique dans l'Ouest canadien: 1818–1875* (Ottawa: Editions des Etudes Oblates, 1949), 190.

7 Ibid., 191. The translation of these two passages is my own.

8 Dempsey, *Rundle Journals*, 192.

9 Ibid., 193–95.

10 The archives of the CMS, 8 August 1840.

11 CMSL, 3 August 1840.

12 *Letterbook*, 1821–46, p. 202, CMSL.

13 The Journal of John Smithurst, 5 January 1842, CMSL.

14 Ibid., 6 October 1840.

15 Smithurst to the Secretaries, 5 August 1847, CMSL.

16 *Church Missionary Intelligencer* (London), vol. 1, no. 8 (December 1849), 177.

17 Ibid., vol. 4, no. 3 (March 1853), 64.

18 UWO, no. 105.

19 WMS, box 109, file 19g, Woolsey to the WMS, 23 June 1864.

20 Smithurst to the Secretaries, 29 December 1845, CMSL.

21 The Journal of John Smithurst, 8 July 1848, CMSL.

22 Committee Minutes, box 549, bk. J., p. 144 (15 January 1840), WMS.

23 Ibid., p. 117 (12 February 1840).

24 For a detailed discussion, see my article, "Irony and Liberation," in the *Annual* of the Society of Christian Ethics, 1983.

25 HBCA, D.4/25 f. 75d-76, 1 March 1840.

26 James Evans to Ephriam Evans, 15 October 1838, UWO, no. 71.

27 HBCA, B.154/b/1, 30 December 1840.

28 HBCA, D.5/6, 10 April 1841.

29 James Hargrave, *The Hargrave Correspondence, 1821–1843*, ed. G.P. deT. Glazebrook (Toronto: The Champlain Society, 1938), 171.

30 George Simpson to James Evans, 24 July 1841, WMS, box 105, file 12.

31 Letitia Hargrave, *The Letters of Letitia Hargrave*, ed. Margaret A. Macleod (Toronto: The Champlain Society, 1947), 96.

32 HBCA, B.154/c/1, 3 August 1840.

33 James Evans to George Simpson, 28 July 1843, HBCA, D.5/8.

34 HBCA, D.4/29, 29 June 1843.

35 HBCA, D.5/8, 28 July 1843.

36 Ibid., 17 August 1843.

37 HBCA, D.4/66 f. 67, 2 December 1844.

38 HBCA, D.5/14, 19 May 1845.

39 WMS, box 103, file 13g, 19 May 1845.

40 HBCA, D.5/14, 19 May 1845.

41 Ibid., 21 May 1845.

42 Ibid., 10 June 1845.

43 WMS, box 103, file 13g, 20 June 1845.

44 HBCA, D.4/33, 16 June 1845.

45 For the clearest account of this exceptionally complicated affair, see Gerald M. Hutchinson, "James Evans' Last Year," in *Journal of the Canadian Church Historical Society*, vol. 19, nos. 1 and 2 (March/June 1977), 42–56.

46 The Journal of Thomas Hassal, 7 March 1844, UWO, no. 261.

47 James Evans died suddenly of "apoplexy" on 23 November 1846, while on a speaking tour in England.

48 George Steinhauer to the WMS, 26 August 1850, WMS, box 105, file 15g.
49 HBCA, D.4/68 f. 125, 7 July 1846.
50 For a painfully clear account of how this process continues in Canada today, see Paul Driben and Robert S. Trudeau, *When Freedon is Lost* (Toronto: University of Toronto Press, 1983).
51 The Journal of William Mason, 2 October 1840, WMS, box 101, file 11g.
52 Dempsey, *Rundle Journals*. The entry is for 14 September 1846.
53 Ibid., 29 November 1840.
54 UWO, no. 259, 23 October 1841.
55 For a carefully reasoned discussion of the overall effect of Christian missions on Amerindians in Canada see John Webster Grant, *Moon of Wintertime* (Toronto: University of Toronto Press, 1984). See especially chap. 11, "A Yes that Means No?"
56 James Evans to Ephriam Evans, 6 November 1841. The James Evans papers of the E.J. Pratt Library, Victoria College, University of Toronto.
57 UWO, no. 261, 8 March 1844.
58 On this indigenous religious movement, see the following: Jennifer S.H. Brown, "The Track to Heaven: The Hudson Bay Cree Religious Movement of 1842–1843," in *Papers of the Thirteenth Algonquian Conference*, ed. William Cowan (Ottawa: Carleton University, 1982); John Webster Grant, "Missionaries and Messiahs in the Northwest," in *Studies in Religion /Sciences Religieuses*, vol. 9, no. 2 (1980); and Norman J. Williamson, "Abishabis the Cree," in *Studies in Religion/Sciences Religieuses*, vol. 9, no. 2 (1980).
59 See Hutchinson, "James Evans' Last Year."
60 WMS, box 101, file 11g, 11 March 1840.
61 Robert Burns, "To a Louse," in *The Penguin Book of Scottish Verse*, ed. Tom Scott (London: Penguin Books Ltd., 1970).

JOHN BLACK

1 George Bryce, *John Black, the Apostle of the Red River* (Toronto: William Briggs, 1898), 49.
2 Ibid., 49.
3 Ibid., 49.
4 John Black to James Black, 11 January 1849, UWA, John Black letters, #7.
5 Bryce, *John Black*, 51.
6 Robert Burns to James Ballenden, 8 May 1851, PAM, Alexander Ross papers, MG2 C141.
7 Bryce, *John Black*, 31, 32.
8 UCA-MNO, Black letters, #7.
9 John Black to James Black, 30 May 1851, UWA, Black letters, #8.
10 John Black to James Black, 16 July 1851, UWA, Black letters, #9.
11 John Black to James Black, 31 July 1851, UWA, Black letters, #10.
12 John Black to James Black, 15 August 1851, UWA, Black letters, #11.
13 Bryce, *John Black*, 70.
14 John Black to James Black, 14 December 1851, UWA, Black letters, #12.
15 George Simpson to Alexander Ross, 16 September 1853, PAM, Ross papers.
16 James Ross to Alexander Ross, 16 September 1853, PAM, Ross papers.
17 William Ross to James Ross, 4 November 1853, PAM, Ross papers.
18 John Black to William Black, 15 November 1853, UWA, Black letters, #14.
19 William Ross to James Ross, 11 September 1852, PAM, Ross papers.
20 John Black to James Ross, 7 February 1855, PAM, Ross papers.
21 John Black to James Black, 13 April 1877, UWA, Black letters, #41.

22 John Black to James Black, 21 September 1854, UWA, Black letters, #15.
23 John Black to James Black, 8 August 1878, UWA, Black letters, #44.
24 John Black to James Black, 8 August 1857, UWA, Black letters, #22.
25 Instructions to J. Ross, 12 October 1869, PAM, Ross papers, #317.
26 John Black to James Black, 12 February 1872, UWA, Black letters, #35.
27 John Black to James Black, 8 November 1856, UWA, Black letters, #18.
28 John Black to J. Ross, 9 February 1854, PAM, Ross papers, #72.
29 D.C. Hill, "The Alexander Ross Story," unpublished sermon, Kildonan Church, 1965.
30 Bryce, *John Black*, 152.

PRESBYTERIAN CHURCH EXTENSION

1 The controversy known as the "Manitoba school question" broke out in August 1889 when the Liberal administration of Premier Thomas Greenway announced that the dual system of Protestant and Catholic schools would be replaced by one non-sectarian public school system. At the same time, the government announced that the official use of the French language in Manitoba's legislature and judiciary would be discontinued. Both the right of Catholics to maintain separate schools and the official use of French had been guaranteed in the Manitoba Act of 1870. A bitter argument ensued over the rightness and constitutionality of the government's action.
2 M.C. Urquhart, ed., *Historical Statistics of Canada* (Toronto: MacMillan, 1965), 18. As early as 1881, Presbyterians had made significant numerical gains in Manitoba (see *Census of Canada*, 1881, vol. 4, table B, pp. 6–7). See John Webster Grant, *The Church in the Canadian Era* (Toronto: McGraw-Hill-Ryerson, 1972), 52. Grant advanced the hypothesis that Presbyterian strength in the West was due to a higher level of Presbyterian immigration compared to that of other denominations. This theory deserves to be properly examined through demographic studies. Unfortunately, such a task is beyond the scope of this paper.
3 The Canada Presbyterian Church was formed by a union of the Presbyterian Church of Canada (Free Church) and the United Presbyterian Church in 1861. In 1875 all the Canadian Presbyterian Churches united to form the Presbyterian Church in Canada.
4 Canada Presbyterian Church, *Proceedings of the General Assembly* (Toronto: Canada Presbyterian Church, 1865), liii.
5 George Bryce, *The Mound Builders*, Historical and Scientific Society of Manitoba Transaction no. 18, (Winnipeg: Free Press, 1885), 20.
6 John C. Walker, "The Early History of the Presbyterian Church in Western Canada from the Earliest Days to the Year 1881" (Ph.D dissertation, University of Edinburgh, 1928). While outdated in other respects, this thesis remains a very accurate factual outline of Presbyterian church extension in western Canada between 1851 and 1881.
7 Presbyterian Church in Canada, *Proceedings of the General Assembly* (Toronto: Presbyterian Church in Canada, 1875), 17.
8 C.W. Gordon papers, UMA, box 7, folio 3A.
9 W. Stewart Wallace, ed., *The Macmillan Dictionary of Canadian Biography*, 3rd. ed. (London: Macmillan, 1963), 635.
10 *Report of the Church and Manse Building Fund*, UCA (Toronto: Presbyterian Church in Canada, 1886), 8.
11 Minutes of the Home Missions Committee of the Presbyterian Church in Canada (Western Section), vol. 1, UCA.
12 *Toronto Daily Mail* (23 March 1883), p. 2.

13 Minutes of the Church and Manse Building Fund of the Presbyterian Church in Canada for Manitoba and the North West, vol. 1, 5 December 1882, UCA.

14 Minutes of the Church and Manse Building Fund, vol. 1, Annual Report, 1883, UCA.

15 *Report of the Church and Manse Building Fund*, 1886, p. 9.

16 C.W. Gordon [Ralph Connor], *The Life of James Robertson* (Toronto: Westminster Co., 1908).

17 See Gordon papers, boxes 7 and 8, UMA. (These letters are transcriptions of the originals.) See also Andrew Baird papers, UCA-MNO and James Robertson papers, UCA.

18 James Ballentyne to Baird, 8 January 1885, Andrew Baird papers, box A, file 643–696, UCA-MNO.

19 Gordon, *Life of James Robertson*, 235.

20 *Birtle United Church Jubilee Booklet*, n.p., n.d., unpaginated, UCA-MNO.

21 Pierre Savard, *Aspects du Catholicisme Canadien-Francais au XIXe siecle* (Montreal: Fides, 1980), 19.

22 Canada Presbyterian Church, *Proceedings of the General Assembly* (Toronto: Canada Presbyterian Church, 1871), xcii.

23 Minutes of the Presbytery of Manitoba and the North West, vol. 1, p. 16, Canada Presbyterian Church, UCA-MNO.

24 James Robertson to Thomas Hart, 17 January 1884, Gordon papers, box 7, folio 3A, UMA.

25 W. Kristjanson, *The Icelandic People in Manitoba* (Winnipeg: Wallingford Press, 1963), 235–36.

26 Minutes of the Home Missions Committee (Western Section), vol. 2, Presbyterian Church in Canada, UCA.

THE WOODSWORTHS

1 James Woodsworth, *Thirty Years in the Canadian North West* (Toronto: McClelland, Goodchild and Stewart, 1917), vii.

2 Kenneth McNaught, *A Prophet in Politics* (Toronto: University of Toronto Press, 1959, 1967), 2.

3 Herbert Marcuse, *One-Dimensional Man* (Boston: Beacon Press, 1968), 257; R.B.Y. Scott, *The Relevance of the Prophets* (New York: MacMillan, 1953), 3. "The Great Refusal" is a term used by Marcuse to stress the importance of living out a constant "no" to the one-dimensional life of contemporary society that smothers dissent in assuming our society lives by consensus. This consensus, Marcuse suggests, never consults the marginalized, the poor, the women and those with no access to power. This principle of negativity takes over from the German philosopher Hegel, and remains the main theme of the biblical prophets. R.B.Y. Scott gives an important clue to the central message of the biblical prophets. He describes them as "forthtellers" rather than "foretellers."

4 James Woodsworth, *Thirty Years*, 36. (Emphasis mine.)

5 Ibid., 93.

6 Ibid., 79.

7 Ibid., 46.

8 Ibid., 98.

9 Ibid., 47.

10 Ibid., 201.

11 Ibid., 67–68.

12 Ibid., 98. He did not give sources for the figures he used.

13 Ibid., xiii–xiv.
14 Ibid., xvi.
15 Ibid., 108.
16 Grace MacInnis, *J.S. Woodsworth: A Man to Remember* (Toronto: MacMillan, 1953), 11; B.G. Smillie interview with Grace MacInnis, Vancouver, 4 June 1983, at the home of Mrs. MacInnis.
17 J.S. Woodsworth, "A Son's Tribute to his Father" (unpublished monograph, 21 September 1930, London, Ontario).
18 MacInnis, *Man to Remember*, 49; B.G. Smillie, *J.S. Woodsworth, Civic Pedagogue, 1874–1942* (Ed.D. thesis, Columbia University, 1970), 34fn, 57.
19 J.S. Woodsworth to Edith, 15 December 1899, PAC.
20 Ibid.
21 J.S. Woodsworth to his mother, 27 March 1900, p. 407, PAC.
22 J.S. Woodsworth, *Grain Growers Guide*, Winnipeg, 30 June 1915.
23 J.S. Woodsworth, "Eventide on the Prairie," *Hours That Stand Apart* (unpublished pamphlet), 5.
24 J.S. Woodsworth, "Son's Tribute."
25 A.R.M. Lower, *Colony to Nation* (Toronto: Longman's Green, 1946), 417–21.
26 Ibid., 428.
27 Vernon Fowke, *The National Policy and the Wheat Economy* (Toronto: University of Toronto Press, 1957), 14–17, 22.
28 Ibid., 74, 75; table 11, "Production of Wheat in the Prairie Provinces and Canada."
29 There is no date provided for James Woodsworth's birth in books published. Grace MacInnis recalls that her grandfather was 72 when he died in 1917.
30 MacInnis, *Man to Remember*, 11.
31 H.H. Walsh, *The Christian Church in Canada* (Toronto: Ryerson, 1956), 177.
32 James Woodsworth, *Thirty Years*, 1.
33 Ibid., 12; Carl Wittke, *A History of Canada* (Toronto: McClelland and Stewart, 1935), 228. Louis Riel led uprisings of the Métis against the encroachment of the Canadian government on the Métis land holdings. The first rebellion broke out in Manitoba on the Red River in 1869. Riel, who had fled to the United States, returned in 1885 to lead the Métis in another revolt. Again the issue was land grants. What the Métis demanded was individual land grants of 240 acres in accordance with the terms offered to the natives of Manitoba. In a land of millions of acres, the total demand would not have exceeded 50,000 acres. Riel was captured and hanged in Regina in 1885.
34 Ibid., 124.
35 Ibid., 230.
36 Ibid., 218.
37 J.S. Woodsworth, "Son's Tribute."
38 James Woodsworth, *Thirty Years*, 226.
39 Ibid., 225.
40 Ibid., 108, 109.
41 J.S. Woodsworth, "Son's Tribute."
42 The King versus J.S. Woodsworth, Court of King's Bench, Fall Assizes, 1919.
43 John Porter, *The Vertical Mosaic* (Toronto: University of Toronto Press, 1965; 1970), 288–89.
44 J.S. Woodsworth to C.B. Sissons, 17 June 1902, *Sissons Letters* (Toronto: UCA), 85. Sissons was a student friend at Victoria College, University of Toronto. He became professor of classics at Victoria College.

45 MacInnis, *Man to Remember*, 51.
46 J.S. Woodsworth to C.B. Sissons, 14 February 1901. Quoted by McNaught, *Prophet in Politics*, 24.
47 Ibid., 25.
48 Ibid.
49 J.S. Woodsworth to C.B. Sissons, 19 June 1907, 250–68, UCA.
50 J.S. Woodsworth, "Rural Social Problems," *Christian Guardian*, Toronto, 14 February 1912.
51 J.S. Woodsworth, letter to the editor, *Manitoba Free Press*, Winnipeg, 22 December 1916; J.S. Woodsworth's daughter, Grace MacInnis, said that her father's dismissal caused the Woodsworth family to be ostracized by friends in Winnipeg (B.G. Smillie interview with Grace MacInnis, 28 May 1969, House of Commons, Ottawa).
52 McNaught, *Prophet in Politics*, 75–76.
53 J.S. Woodsworth, *B.C. Federationist* (a labour paper), Vancouver, 2 January 1919.
54 "The Winnipeg General Strike," *Information*, Toronto, United Steelworkers of America, vol. 17, no. 1 (May 1969): 5.
55 J.S. Riddell, *Methodism in the Middle West* (Toronto: University of Toronto, 1950), 108.
56 Ibid.
57 J.S. Woodsworth, "In Christian Canada in the Twentieth Century: What are we doing about it?" *Christian Guardian*, 16 November 1909.
58 J.S. Woodsworth, "Convictions and Freedom of Speech," *Christian Guardian*, 18 February 1914.
59 Ibid.
60 Ibid.
61 J.S. Woodsworth to C.B. Sissons, 6 March 1919, 406, UCA.
62 J.S. Woodsworth, "If I Don't Someone Else Will," *On the Waterfront*, n.p., n.d., 25.
63 Ibid., 26.
64 Ibid., 27.
65 Ibid.
66 J.S. Woodsworth, to Rev. Bert Howard, Delisle, Saskatchewan, 20 February 1928, PAC, vol. 2.
67 Ernest Marshall Howse, A Prayer offered by Dr. Ernest Marshall Howse at the Memorial Service of Mr. J.S. Woodsworth, Westminster United Church, Winnipeg, 29 March 1942.
68 The King Versus J.S. Woodsworth, Fall Assizes, 4 November 1919, 10.
69 J.S. Woodsworth, *Western Labor News*, Winnipeg Special Strike Edition, no. 23, 12 June 1919.
70 Hansard, Fifth Special War Session, 8 September 1939, 24.
71 Bruce Hutchinson, J.S. Woodsworth's obituary in the *Vancouver Sun*, quoted in MacInnis, *Man to Remember*, 32.
72 Goldwin French, "The People Called Methodists in Canada," *The Churches and the Canadian Experience*, ed. John Webster Grant (Toronto: Ryerson, 1963), 81.
73 James Woodsworth, *Thirty Years*, 61.
74 Ibid., 65.
75 Ibid., 77.
76 Ibid., 232.
77 Ibid., 85.
78 Ibid., 186.
79 Ibid.
80 MacInnis, *Man to Remember*, 231.

81 J.S. Woodsworth, "Solidarity, The Week Day Sermons by Pastor Newbottle," *The Voice*, vol. 28 (Winnipeg, 20 May 1919), PAC.

82 Ibid.

83 Ibid.

84 J.S. Woodsworth, "Let the Church Banish Poverty as Science Does Malaria," *The Winnipeg Tribune*, vol. 30 (12 June 1919), PAC.

85 J.S. Woodsworth, "Following the Gleam" (unpublished monograph), 5–7.

86 J.S. Woodsworth, "The Training of Ministers," *Christian Guardian*, 25 May 1916.

87 J.S. Woodsworth, "A Sabbath Day's Meditation," *On the Waterfront*, n.d., n.p., p. 21.

88 Ibid.

89 Ibid.

90 D. Summers, "The Labor Church and Allied Movements of the Late Nineteenth Century and early Twentieth Century" (Ph.D. dissertation, microfilm, Edinburgh University, 1958), 298.

91 J.S. Woodsworth, "Following the Gleam," 19.

92 Ibid., 16.

93 Ibid.

94 Ibid., 17.

95 J.S. Woodsworth, *The First Story of the Labor Church*, 10–11.

96 James Woodsworth, *Thirty Years*, viii.

97 Ibid., x.

98 Dorothea Soëlle, *The Arms Race Kills* (Philadelphia: Fortress Press, 1983), 45.

99 Paul Lehmann, *Ethics in a Christian Context* (New York: Harper and Row, 1963), 124.

CONGREGATIONALISM IN MANITOBA

1 *CMS Annual Report*, 1874, 8, UCA.

2 *The Canadian Independent* (12 June 1879), 3, UCA.

3 Ibid., 21 July 1879, 5.

4 Ibid., 28 August 1879; *CMS Annual Report*, 1882, 13.

5 *The Canadian Independent* (4 September 1879), 4.

6 Ibid.

7 "Interview with J.B. Silcox" (1930), p. 1, in Central Congregational Church, Winnipeg parish file, UCA.

8 Ibid., 2.

9 Ibid., 2–3.

10 It is not surprising to find that Silcox was an ardent supporter of church union after the turn of the century.

11 "Interview with J.B. Silcox," 3.

12 Strictly speaking, the new congregation was not liable for the debts of First Congregational Church.

13 General Meetings *Minute Book* (1887–1891), 4 January 1888, in Central Congregational Collection, PAM.

14 J.S.L. MacKinnon, "The Browns of Floral, The Campbells of Wood Bay, Rev. John MacKinnon and Wood Bay Early Church History," *Echoes of the Past*, ed. Mrs. C. Gosnell (Rural Municipality of Louise, 1968), 441.

15 Mrs. T.A. Cohoe, "History of our Church," *Pilot Mound United Church, 1888–1958* (mimeograph, 1958), 5.

16 *CMS Annual Report*, 1884, 12.

17 "Interview with J.B. Silcox," 3.

18 The second of these was J.L. Brown of Wood Bay.

19 *The Canadian Independent* (September 1888), 278.

20 Clipping from the *Manitoba Free Press* (30 May 1902), in the All Peoples' Mission parish file, UCA-MNO.

21 Now Pilgrim Baptist Church.

22 The mission later became part of St. Paul's Church.

23 An article signed "Criticus" and entitled "The Man and His Message – Dr. J.L. Gordon at Central Congregational Church," *Manitoba Free Press* (2 November 1912), reprinted with Gordon's sermon, "Is It Wrong?," in the Rev. James L. Gordon papers UCA-MNO.

24 Ibid.

25 Cybel (Mrs. J.F.) Stewart, the author, 10 May 1983.

26 Rev. James L. Gordon papers, UCA-MNO.

27 *The Canadian Congregationalist* ("Special Winnipeg Number"), 1 April 1909, 8, PAM.

28 "Congregational Church Extension Society of Western Canada: Letters Patent of Incorporation," Central Congregational collection PAM.

29 Woman's Missionary Society *Minute Book*, 18 May 1908 in Central Congregational Church parish file, UCA-MNO.

30 General Meetings *Minute Book* (1906–1928), April 1910, Central Congregational collection, PAM.

31 *CES Minute Book* (1909–1938), January 1912, 119, Central Congregational collection, PAM.

32 Ibid., May 1912 and April 1913.

33 Marguerite (Mrs. A.) Williams and Cybel (Mrs. J.G.) Stewart in separate interviews with the author, 1983.

34 General Meetings *Minute Book* (1906–1928), 29 December 1916, Central Congregational collection, PAM.

35 Now called Home Street Christian Church. Another structure was eventually built on the site of the old church.

36 The Church of the Nazarene is now located on the site.

37 The building is still standing at 418 Aberdeen Avenue. It is now occupied by the Ukrainian Catholic Centre.

38 "Interview with J.B. Silcox," 5.

39 In 1927, this anti-Union party, concerned in part about the ultimate disposition of the CES's funds, sought a legal opinion on the withdrawal of Central from the United Church. The opinion of C.P. Wilson, K.C. was that Central's property remained unaltered until a church meeting held under the terms of the church's constitution decided to pass it to the United Church; and that, because Central had been incorporated by an act of the legislature (1887), the Congregational Union of Canada could not vote it into the United Church. This could only be effected by an amendment to Central's own constitution. The annual meeting of 1928 carried a motion that the church revert to Congregational order and practice. Neither the legal opinion nor the motion seems to have produced further action.

40 General Meetings *Minute Book* (1906–1928), January 1926, Central Congregational collection, PAM.

41 Winnipeg Presbytery Minutes, vol. 1, 4 February 1930, UCA-MNO.

42 Ibid.

43 A.L. Maclean to the Chairman and Executive Members of Winnipeg Presbytery, 20 November 1930, Rev. P. Campbell Morgan biography file, UCA-MNO.

44 Winnipeg Presbytery Minutes, vol. 1, 29 March 1932.
45 Clipping from the *Manitoba Free Press* (19 January 1918), Crescent–Fort Rouge Church parish file, UCA-MNO.
46 Susan Mann Trofimenkoff, *Stanley Knowles, the Man from Winnipeg North Centre* (Saskatoon: Western Producer Books, 1982), 42.
47 Now the "old" Calvary Temple Building.
48 Trofimenkoff, *Stanley Knowles*, 47.
49 "The Man and His Message," *Manitoba Free Press* (2 November 1912).

HEAD, HEART AND PURSE

1 Minnie Campbell, "The Model Auxiliary," holograph manuscript, 1896, PWMS collection, UCA-MNO.
2 Sheilagh Parsons, "Women and Power in the United Church of Canada," *Women Work and Worship*, project coordinated by Shirley Davy (Toronto: United Church of Canada, 1983), 176.
3 United Church of Canada, *General Council Proceedings 1926* (Toronto: United Church of Canada, 1926), 349.
4 The Thirtieth General Council of the United Church of Canada acted to establish in December 1984 a standing committee of General Council to address the changing roles of women and men in the Church. This standing committee replaced the Interdivisional Task Force on the Changing Roles of Women and Men in Church and Society.
5 *Our Jubilee Story: 1864–1924* (Women's Missionary Society, Presbyterian Church in Canada, WD, 1924), 25.
6 Ann Douglas, *The Feminization of American Culture* (New York: Avon Books, 1977), 133.
7 Ibid.
8 Barbara Brown Zikmund, "The Feminist Thrust of Sectarian Christianity," *Women of Spirit: Female Leadership in the Jewish and Christian Traditions*, ed. Rosemary Reuther and Eleanor McLaughlin (New York: Simon and Schuster, 1979), 206–22. Zikmund describes the Shakers as egalitarian and as holding a bi-sexual view of God and human life. Christian Science also brought female images into theology and supported women's rights. Zikmund claims, "Sectarian religious commitment in the nineteenth century was far more than a set of beliefs or concepts, it was a new way of life. Those women who left traditional Christianity to join radical groups changed their way of living" (p. 212).
9 Dorothy C. Bass, "Their Prodigious Influence: Women, Religion and Reform in Antibellum America," *Women of Spirit*, ed. Reuther and McLaughlin, 281.
10 Ibid.
11 Rosemary Skinner Keller, "Lay Women in the Protestant Tradition," *Women and Religion in America*, vol. 1, ed. Rosemary Radford Reuther and Rosemary Skinner Keller (San Francisco: Harper and Row, 1981), 242.
12 *Our Jubilee Story*, 39.
13 Ibid., addendum.
14 WD (Western Division) defines the geographical area from Quebec to British Columbia. The maritime women in mission work functioned through the Eastern Division (ED).
15 *Our Jubilee Story*, 16.
16 Ibid., 71.
17 Ibid., 38.
18 Ibid.
19 Ibid., 42.

20 Amanda MacKay, "A Historical Sketch of the Work of the Women's Missionary Society in the Presbyterian Church in Canada in the Province of Manitoba," holograph manuscript, 1926, PWMS collection, UCA-MNO.

21 Minnie Campbell, First Annual Report of the Winnipeg Auxiliary, holograph manuscript, undated, PWMS collection, UCA-MNO.

22 Ibid.

23 Fanny Russell, "Second Annual Report of the Winnipeg Auxiliary," holograph manuscript, 8 February 1887, PWMS collection, UCA-MNO.

24 Grant MacEwan, "The Lady of Tullichewen," *And Mighty Women Too* (Saskatoon: Western Producer Prairie Books, 1975), 63.

25 Memorandum, author unknown, undated, PWMS collection, UCA-MNO.

26 MacKay, "A Historical Sketch."

27 *Our Jubilee Story*, 50.

28 Minnie Campbell, Annual Report of the Winnipeg Presbyterial, Presbyterian Woman's Foreign Missionary Society, holograph manuscript, 1896, PWMS collection, UCA-MNO.

29 *Fourteenth Annual Report of the WFMS(WD) of the Presbyterian Church in Canada, 1889–1890* (Toronto: Presbyterian Review Print, 1890), 16.

30 Miscellaneous papers, author unknown, undated, PWMS collection, UCA-MNO.

31 MacKay, "A Historical Sketch."

32 *Our Jubilee Story*, 44.

33 *Fifteenth Annual Report of the WFMS(WD) of the Presbyterian Church in Canada, 1890–1891* (Toronto: Presbyterian Review Print, 1891), 171.

34 Ibid., 50.

35 *Our Jubilee Story*, 43.

36 Amanda MacKay, address to Brandon Presbyterial, 1936, PWMS collection, UCA-MNO.

37 Reuther and Keller, *Women and Religion in America*, 264.

38 *Our Jubilee Story*, 44.

39 Ibid., 48.

40 Ibid., 49.

41 *Fifteenth Annual Report of the WFMS(WD), 1890–1891*, 43.

42 *Our Jubilee Story*, 48.

43 WFMS, *Twenty-fifth Annual Report of the WFMS, 1900–1901* (Toronto: Murray Printing Co., 1901), 18.

44 Ibid.

45 The PWMS secretary, "The First Auxiliary of the WFMS, undated, PWMS collection, UCA-MNO.

46 *Fourteenth Annual Report of the WFMS, 1889–1890*, 16.

47 Ibid.

48 *Our Jubilee Story*, 66.

49 Ibid., 68.

50 Ibid., 70.

51 Ibid., 71.

52 Ibid., 72.

53 Ibid., 73.

54 Ibid., 55.

55 Ibid.

56 Ibid., 93.

57 *The Woman's Missionary Society in Manitoba, 1884–1959*, Introduction by Jean Spice (no publishing data), 19.

58 Ibid., 24.

59 *Fifteenth Annual Report of the* WFMS, *1890–1891*, 16.

60 Helen King Gordon, address to a gathering, holograph manuscript, undated, PWMS collection, UCA-MNO.

61 Amanda MacKay's birth record was obtained from the certificate of her death (Winnipeg: Department of Vital Statistics, Province of Manitoba).

62 Information on the Norris family courtesy of Joan Nelson and Harvey Curtis of Nova Scotia.

63 Memorial editorial by K.M.H., "A Great Manitoban," *Winnipeg Free Press* (9 January 1943).

64 Nova Scotia Teachers' College Records (Truro: Nova Scotia Teachers' College), photocopy of the November First 1876 Ladies List.

65 Marriage notice, *Presbyterian Witness* (6 December 1879), Nova Scotia Archives, Halifax.

66 Lillian Gibbons, "An Album of Winnipeg Women," *Winnipeg Tribune* (1937) PWMS collection, UCA-MNO.

67 *Presbyterian Church in Canada Year Book 1884* (Toronto: Presbyterian Church in Canada), appendix 232.

68 Gibbons, "An Album of Winnipeg Women."

69 Amanda MacKay, "Notes on the Early History of the Indian Residential School, Portage la Prairie," holograph manuscript, undated, PWMS collection, UCA-MNO.

70 Ibid.

71 Ibid.

72 Ibid.

73 Ibid.

74 Gibbons, "An Album of Winnipeg Women."

75 *Annual Reports of the* WFMS *of the Presbyterian Church in Canada,* WD. The record of Amanda MacKay's activity in the WFMS and the PWMS was obtained by tracing the officers of the organization over the span of years of her active involvement.

76 Amanda MacKay, "History of the Presbyterian Women's Union," holograph manuscript, undated, PWMS collection, UCA-MNO.

77 Memorial Editorial, "A Great Manitoban."

78 MacKay, "History of the Presbyterian Women's Union," 2.

79 Ibid.

80 Ibid.

81 Ibid.

82 Richard Allen, ed., *The Social Gospel in Canada*, National Museum of Man Series History Division Paper 9 (Ottawa: 1975), 193.

83 Memorial Editorial, "A Great Manitoban."

84 MacKay, "History of the Presbyterian Women's Union," 3.

85 Ibid., 5.

86 Obituary, *Winnipeg Free Press*, 1943.

87 Amanda MacKay to her niece, Margaret MacKay, in Nova Scotia, 30 October 1941, courtesy of Margaret MacKay, New Glasgow, Nova Scotia.

88 Amanda MacKay to Margaret MacKay, 30 June 1942.

89 Helen MacKay to Margaret MacKay, 1943.

90 Amanda MacKay to Margaret MacKay, 18 July 1934.

91 Gibbons, "An Album of Winnipeg Women."

92 Rosemary Skinner Keller, "Creating a Sphere for Women," *Women in New Worlds: Historical Perspectives on the Wesleyan Tradition*, ed. Hilah F. Thomas and Rosemary Skinner Keller (Nashville: Abingdon, 1981), 258.

93 Douglas, *The Feminization of American Culture*, 7.

94 Reuther and Keller, *Women and Religion in America*, xiii.

95 Campbell, Annual Report of the Winnipeg Auxiliary 1896.

96 William L. O'Neill, *The Woman Movement: Feminism in the United States and England* (London: George Allen and Unwin Ltd., 1969), 33.

97 Wendy Mitchinson, "Canadian Women and Church Missionary Societies in the Nineteenth Century: A Step Towards Independence," *Atlantis*, vol. 2 (Spring 1977), 73.

98 Barbara Welter, "She Hath Done What She Could: Protestant Women's Missionary Careers in Nineteenth-Century America," *American Quarterly*, vol. 30, no. 5 (Winter 1978), 624.

99 Ibid., 634.

100 Mitchinson, "Canadian Women and Church Missionary Societies in the Nineteenth Century," 73.

101 *Twenty-fifth Annual Report of the wfms 1900–1901*, 17.

JOHN MARK KING

In doing the research for this article, the author had access to the John Mark King papers, a collection of letters, sermons, lectures and notebooks retained by the Gordon family. Letters or notebooks cited here are from this collection. The author wishes to express his gratitude to Ruth Gordon and other members of the family for making these sources available to him.

1 Minutes of the meeting for 17 November 1899, *Records of the Synod of Manitoba and N.W.T.* (1884–1899) p. 597f, uca-mno.

2 There is some uncertainty concerning the precise date of King's birth. The twenty-ninth of May 1829 is the date given by Sir Thomas W. Taylor in *The Manitoba College Journal*, Memorial Number, 174; by C.W. Gordon in *The Manitoba College Journal*, vol. 23, no. 2 (1907): 1; in F.H. Schofield's *The Story of Manitoba*, 3 vols. (Chicago: S.J. Clarke Publishing Co., 1913), vol. 2, 615; and by A.G. Bedford in *The University of Winnipeg: A History of the Founding Colleges* (Toronto: University of Toronto Press, 1976), 17. The twenty-fifth of May 1829 has also a strong claim. It is the date given in *The MacMillan Dictionary of Canadian Biography*; it is also the date provided in a brief biographical sketch that appeared following an article by King in *The Manitoba College Journal*, vol. 8, no. 6 (July 1893): 134; it is the date on the tombstone. There is also a letter written to King by his daughter Helen from Scotland in 1897 which is dated 25 May which has for its opening words, "This is your birthday. . . ." The official date provided by the General Register Office of Scotland is, however, 26 May 1829.

3 John M. King, "Edinburgh Ministers of Many Years Ago," *Manitoba College Journal* (January 1890): 41.

4 Among his closest Scottish friends were Henry Calderwood, David Cairns, David Pirret, William Scott and James Parlane. The spiritual earnestness of this group is discussed in *The Life of Henry Calderwood*, By His Son and the Rev. David Woodside, B.D. (London: Hodder and Stoughton, 1900), 38–41.

5 For the story of this Church and King's ministry in it, see Sir Thomas Wardlaw Taylor, *Historical Sketch of Saint James Square Presbyterian Congregation, Toronto, 1853–1903* (Toronto: Brown-Searle Printing Company, 1903).

6 King discusses the illness and operation in a letter dated 16 June 1882 to his great friend Rev. James Parlane in Hawick, Scotland. Henry Calderwood, professor of moral philosophy in Edinburgh and King's lifelong friend, wrote a letter dated 17 July 1883, weighing the

conflicting claims. On the one hand, he remarked, "the pastoral charge you now hold is one of such vast importance, that it is hardly possible to overrate it," but on the other, "the immense importance of the position to which you have been called is obvious. To stand on the line of advancing civilization, to be a central [power?] in the midst of people arriving in great numbers from Scotland, to train students to minister to them, and to guide the Church in overtaking the immense demands of such a country as the far west is to be, are features of usefulness which must be regarded as having a strong claim on one."

7 King to Mrs. King, 24 November and 27 November 1883.
8 King to Mrs. King, 17 November [1883].
9 King to Mrs. King, 8 December 1883.
10 King to Mrs. King, 7 December 1883.
11 King to Mrs. King, 8 December 1883.
12 King to Mrs. King, 11 December 1883.
13 King to Mrs. King, 20 December 1883.
14 A number of letters from King to his wife covering these two periods of canvassing are extant. From them his journeys from place to place can be traced.
15 "As Financial Administrator," *Manitoba College Journal*, Memorial Number, 161.
16 James Robertson to King, Woodstock, 28 February 1888.
17 Rev. Prof. Hart, "Personal Reminiscences," *Manitoba College Journal*, Memorial Number, 181.
18 Alice Hamilton has a discussion of the work of Henry Holiday and specifically this window in her article, "King's Queen," *The Uniter*, The 100th Anniversary Issue, University of Winnipeg Press (October 1971). There are six brief letters or notes from Holiday to King regarding work on the window. Another window of like design by Holiday is in Drew University, Madison, New Jersey. It seems clear that the design for the Manitoba College window was originally made for the one in Drew. Holiday discussed the design of the window in a letter addressed to someone at Drew Theological Seminary dated 20 April 1888. The letter is in Drew University Archives. Holiday also discusses the window in his book, *Stained Glass as an Art* (London and New York: The MacMillan Co., 1896), 51–54.
19 John Mark King, "Notes of a Visit to the University of Berlin," *The Manitoba College Journal* (January 1892): 68, 71.
20 John Mark King, *A Critical Study of "In Memoriam"* (Toronto: George N. Morang, 1898).
21 James Robertson, "His Place in the Church," *Manitoba College Journal*, Memorial Number, p. 172.
22 "The Pastor in his Study, Lecture 1 on Pastoral Theology, contained in a black notebook.
23 *Winnipeg Daily Tribune*, 6 and 7 March 1899.
24 King, *A Critical Study of "In Memoriam"*; John Mark King, *The Theology of Christ's Teaching* (Toronto: Westminster Company Limited, 1903).
25 John Mark King, "The Spirit in Which Theological Enquiry should be Prosecuted," *The Manitoba College Journal*, vol. 8, no. 6 (July 1893):127–28.
26 Ibid., 128–30.
27 Ibid.
28 The Rev. Principal King, *The Atonement* (Winnipeg, The Stovel Co., Printers and Stationers, 1895), 4, 5.
29 Ibid., 12ff.
30 Ibid., 16ff.
31 Ibid., 7.
32 Ibid., 38.

33 W.E. Dodge to King, 4 August 1895.

34 The Rev. Principal King, *The Purely Ethical Gospel* (Winnipeg: The Stovel Co., Printers and Stationers, 1897), 14.

35 Ibid., 24.

36 Ibid., 23.

37 Ibid., 25.

38 Ibid., 34.

39 Ibid., 37.

40 George Adam Smith to John Mark King, "on the train," 29 June (no year).

41 King, *The Atonement*, 7.

42 *The Winnipeg Daily Tribune* (7 March 1899), p. 5.

PRESBYTERIAN SCHOOL-HOMES

This paper was presented originally to the Canadian History of Education Association meetings, Vancouver, B.C., in October 1983. The author is grateful for the patience and suggestions of Drs. J.S. Moir, Hesh Troper, Alison Prentice and Katherine Ridout. The limitations of the research and presentation of the conclusion remain the author's.

1 John S. Moir, *Enduring Witness: A History of the Presbyterian Church in Canada* (Don Mills: Presbyterian Church in Canada, 1975), xi.

2 This paper is largely drawn from the writing of WHMS members, missionaries and supporters in these publications.

3 See: Rev. J.D. Byrnes, "The New Home Missions," *Missionary Messenger* (September 1918):242–43 (hereinafter cited as *MM*); Rev. J.D. Byrnes, "God's Word at Work in Our School-Homes, Canada," *MM* (February 1918):54–55; Margaret Jamieson, "Keeping Canada God's Country," *The Message* (September 1914):13–14.

4 N.K. Clifford, " 'His Dominion': A Vision in Crisis," in *Religion and Culture in Canada/ Religion et Culture au Canada* (Waterloo: Canadian Corporation for Studies in Religion, 1977), 24.

5 John Webster Grant, "The Reaction of WASP Churches to Non-WASP Immigrants," Presidential Address to the Canadian Society of Church History, 1968; John Webster Grant, "Religion and the Quest for a National Identity: The Background in Canadian History," in *Religion and Culture*, 7–21; Clifford, " 'His Dominion,' " 23–41; Marilyn Barber, "Nationalism, Nativism and the Social Gospel," in *The Social Gospel in Canada*, ed. Richard Allen (Ottawa: National Museum of Man, 1975). 186–225; Howard Palmer, *Patterns of Prejudice: A History of Nativism in Alberta* (Toronto: McClelland and Stewart, 1982), 11–47; *Acts and Proceedings of the General Assembly of the Presbyterian Church in Canada*, 1913, Appendices, "Report of the Board on Social Service and Evangelism," 28–91; *Acts and Proceedings*, 1914, Appendices, "Report of the Board on Social Service and Evangelism," 317–19.

6 *The Presbyterian Record* (April 1900):98 (hereinafter cited as *PR*).

7 *Acts and Proceedings*, 1904, Appendices, "Report of the Home Mission Committee, Western Section, 1903–04," 5.

8 Rev. Malcolm McGregor, "The Canadian Storm Centre," *The Presbyterian* (19 July 1902); "Round About Winnipeg," *The Presbyterian* (19 July 1902).

9 *PR* (April 1900).

10 *Acts and Proceedings*, 1904, Appendices, "Report of the Home Mission Committee, Western Section, 1903–04, 5, 11, 13, 27; *PR* (April 1901).

11 Rev. J.D. Byrnes, "Immigration and Emigration," *PR* (August 1912); "New Ontario," *PR* (August 1912).

12 R. Craig Brown and Ramsay Cook, *Canada, 1896–1921: A Nation Transformed* (Toronto: McClelland and Stewart, 1974), 54–74.

13 Stephen Steinberg, *The Ethnic Myth: Race, Ethnicity and Class in America* (New York: Atheneum, 1981), 47–48, 67–69. Also see Robert Crunden's argument that progressivism was essentially a secularized national religion, in *Ministers of Reform: The Progressive's Achievement in American Civilization, 1890–1920* (New York: Basic Books, 1982), 51.

14 Rev. C.W. Gordon, "A Suggestion for New Work," *The Home Mission Pioneer* (April 1910) (hereinafter cited as *HMP*). Gordon worried that intermarriage between Canadian males and immigrant females would lead to the bastardization of the Canadian race: "Our young men surrounding these [foreign] colonies are even now marrying the daughters of these foreigners, and unless these girls are educated and toned up in their moral standards, they will certainly tone down our national life." A contrasting perspective is offered by the June 1910 editorial in *The Home Mission Pioneer*: "Already there is intermarriage with the strangers within our gates. We hear of the Galician man marrying the Scotch girl. Will she be brought down to the level of his idea of women – a wife who becomes his property whom he may abuse and beat as he sees fit." Apparently Presbyterian women believed that the Anglo-Saxon female would be downgraded through marriage with the non-Anglo-Saxon male and not have a strong positive influence on her mate.

15 Grant, "Reaction of the WASP Churches" 3; Grant, "Religion and the Quest for a National Identity," 16–17.

16 Hospitals and educational stations were located at Teulon, Manitoba (1904) with Rev. A.J. Hunter, M.D., as superintendent; Wakaw, Saskatchewan, Rev. R.Y. Scott, M.D., as superintendent; Sifton and Elthelbert, Manitoba, with Dr. R. Gilbert as superintendent; Vegreville, Alberta, with Rev. George Arthur as superintendent; and Canora, Saskatchewan.

17 See "A Visit to Pointe-aux-Trembles," *MM* (July-August 1915):209–11; Madame W. Bieler, "Two New Home-schools of Quebec Province," *MM* (January 1916):9–11; *MM* (September 1914):35; W.H. Pike, "The Flame," manuscript, UCA.

18 It would seem that most of the children who resided in the school-homes were placed there by their parents so that they might attend the public school at a time when public schools did not reach all settlements in the Canadian West. Other children were patients in the hospitals, where they were instructed in "Christian" principles by the staff and, perhaps, encouraged to remain on as students.

19 Brian Fraser, "Education for Neighborhood and Nation: The Educational Work of St. Christopher House, Toronto, 1912–1918" (Master's thesis, University of Toronto, 1975), 8.

20 Grant, "Reaction of WASP Churches," 7.

21 Palmer, *Patterns of Prejudice*, 42–43.

22 Ibid., 40–41.

23 William Simon, home mission superintendent for northern Saskatchewan, cautioned that the assimilation process, occurring without the oversight of the church, already had created severe social problems in the country. Also see *Acts and Proceedings*, 1915, Appendices, "Report of the Board of Home Missions (Western Section), 1914," 34–42; Rev. J. Cameron, "Canada's Greatest Problem," *MM* (June 1915):1169; Rev. A.J. Hunter, "Our Mission Work in Western Canada," *MM* (July-August 1915):200–02; Mrs. Elizabeth Bayley, "Hospitality," *MM* (September 1914):40–44; and H.A. Pearson, "Immigration," *MM* (July-August 1914):22–23.

24 *Acts and Proceedings*, 1915, Appendices, "Report of the Board of Home Missions, 1914," 41.

25 Rev. W.D. Reid, "Home Mission Work in Alberta," *HMP* (January 1911):156; Rev. W.D. Reid, "Presbyterial Notes," *HMP* (September 1911):89; J.S. Woodsworth, "Our Citizens of Foreign Birth," *HMP* (January 1913):151–52; W.W. Lee, "The Reflex Action of Home Missions," *HMP* (January 1913):149–50; J.S. Woodsworth, *Strangers Within Our Gates* (Toronto: University of Toronto Press, 1972), 206–07; Gordon, "A Suggestion for New Work," *HMP* (April 1910):21; "Presidential Address," *HMP* (June 1910):11.

26 "Editorial Notes," *MM* (June 1915):24 and *MM* (January 1916):4.

27 Mrs. Edward Cockburn, "Our Educational Work," *HMP* (May 1913):37.

28 Ibid., 36; Mrs. H.M. Kipp, "With Our Indian and Foreign Children," *MM* (October 1914):76–77; "Mission Notes," *MM* (October 1915):3; Margaret Jamieson, "Who and What We Are," *The Message* (August 1913):13; "Home Mission Letters," *The Message* (February 1913):4; *HMP* (January 1911):163.

29 See *HMP* (June 1910):11; Dr. F.O. Gilbart, "A Missionary Doctor in Foreign Colonies in Canada," *MM* (March 1915):75–77; Mary McNab, "Strangers at Our Gates, *HMP* (September 1910):115; Mrs. McClelland, "Work in the North End of Winnipeg," *HMP* (March 1912):4; Rev. D.G. McQueen, "Canada – A World Highway," *HMP* (May 1912):39.

30 Rev. W.D. Reid, "The Non-Anglo-Saxons in Canada – Their Christianization and Nationalization," *Pre-Assembly Congress of the Presbyterian Church in Canada* (Toronto: Board of Foreign Missions of the Presbyterian Church in Canada, 1913), 123.

31 "Program for January Meetings," *HMP* (January 1911):159–60; George Arthur, "Reaching Forth Unto Those Things Which Are Before Us," *HMP* (January 1911):156; A.J. Hunter, "Appeal for a Residence for Children at Teulon," *HMP* (February 1911):171; Cameron, "Canada's Greatest Problem," 167.

32 John Higham, *Strangers in the Land: Patterns of American Nativism, 1860–1925* (New York: Atheneum, 1978), 237, 131–39.

33 *Acts and Proceedings*, 1904, Appendices, "Report of the Home Mission Committee, Western Section, 1903–04," 5; *PR* (April 1901).

34 Rev. W.G. Brown, "Along the Frontier," *PR* (October 1909):437–38.

35 Ibid.; "Alberta Synodical Report," *HMP* (July 1910):62; "37th Annual Meeting," *The Message* (July 1913):17; Hunter, "Our Mission Work in Western Canada," 200–02; "Concerning Children," *The Message* (July 1913):3–6.

36 Arthur, "Reaching Forth Unto Those Things Before us," 156; "Editorial," *MM* (November 1914):67; F.O. Gilbart, "Education – A Factor in Mission Enterprise," *MM* (October 1914):80–81. For contemporary accounts of the efficiency of the public school system in the North-West, especially the teacher training facilities, see Cornelius Jaenen, "Ruthenian Schools in Western Canada, 1897–1919," *Pedagogica Historica*, vol. 10, no. 3 (1970):517–41; Cornelius J. Jaenen, "Minority Group Schooling and Canadian National Unity," *Journal of Educational Thought*, vol. 7, no. 2, 81–93; Josaphat Skwarok, o.s.b.m., "The Ukrainian Settlers in Canada and their schools with Reference to Government, French Canadian and Ukrainian Missionary Influences, 1891–1921" (Master's thesis, University of Alberta, 1959); Jessie M. Deverall, "The Ukrainian Teacher as an Agent of Cultural Assimilation" (Master's thesis, University of Toronto, 1941); M.P. Toombs, "A Saskatchewan Experiment in Teacher Training, 1907–1917: The Training School for Teachers for Foreign Speaking Communities," *Saskatchewan History*, vol. 17, no. 1 (1964):1–11.

37 A.J. Hunter, "Galacians in the Northwest," *PR* (November 1905):436–37.

38 For an excellent discussion of the problems of rural education on the prairies and efforts to overcome the difficulties (including church boarding homes), see Marilyn J. Barber, "The Assimilation of Immigration in the Canadian Prairie Provinces" (Ph.D. dissertation, University of London, 1975), 72–207.

39 E.E. Sprague, "To The Children of Old Ontario," *HMP* (December 1909):133–34; M. Goforth, "The Needs of the Children of the Foreigners," *HMP* (December 1909):134.

40 F.O. Gilbart, "Pioneer Hospitals in Western Canada," *MM* (July–August 1914):13–14; Goforth, "The Needs of the Children of the Foreigners," 134.

41 Sprague, "To The Children of Old Ontario," 133.

42 A.J. Hunter, "The Education of the Foreigner," *MM* (October 1916):237–40.

43 "Superstition Among the Foreigners," *MM* (January 1915):12–13.

44 Kipp, "With Our Indian and Foreign Children," 76; "Home Mission Secretary's Notes," *The Message* (May 1915):9; Reid, "Home Mission Work in Alberta," 156; *MM* (November 1914):100.

45 "Editorial," *HMP* (October 1911):102–03; Rev. John Somerville, "The Responsibility of Mothers," *HMP* (October 1911):98–99. These were the first of many articles which studied the function and idealogy of "motherhood" in different cultures.

46 George Arthur, "The Needs and Your Opportunity," *HMP* (May 1912):36.

47 Gilbart, "A Missionary Doctor in the Foreign Colonies in Canada," 75–77.

48 "Alberta Synodical Report," *HMP* (July 1910):162.

49 Rev. R.B. Arthur, "The Boys' Home," *HMP* (January 1911):157.

50 Kipp, "With Our Indian and Foreign Children," 76.

51 Mrs. Arthur, "The Child a Factor in Future Work," *HMP* (May 1912):36; Rev. A.J. Hunter, "The Boys' Residence at Teulon," *HMP* (March 1912):2; Hunter "Education of the Foreigner," 237.

52 Mrs. H. Johnson, "Ruthenian Pupils Note Degrading Customs," *MM* (May 1916):150–51; Lena Kuryk, "Customs in Her Country as Told by A Vegreville Pupil," *MM* (June 1916):192; "Superstitions Among the Foreigners," *MM* (January 1915):237.

53 Miss Beveridge, "A Glimpse of the Work at Teulon," *HMP* (May 1912):37–38; Miss Lawrence, "A Boys' Darning Bee at Vegreville," *MM* (April 1915):118.

54 "Seventh Annual Report," *HMP* (June 1910):24.

55 Cockburn, "Our Educational Work," 37; "Brief Review of Our Work in Canada," *MM* (May 1916):137–38; Mrs. S.W. Dyde, "A Link Towards Assimilation, *MM* (May 1916):148; George Arthur, "Appeal for a Residence," *HMP* (February 1911):171; Gilbart, "A Missionary Doctor in the Foreign Colonies in Canada," 75–77; Rev. Peter Strang, "Southern Saskatchewan," *PR* (August 1914):342. Most Presbyterian medical missionaries conducted their preaching in the Ruthenian language, when they had acquired facility in the language. Ability to converse in Ruthenian and English was deemed important as a means to evangelize the non-Anglo-Saxon immigrant.

56 See Miss Harriet Johnson, "A Ruthenian Conference," *MM* (September 1915):239–40; Z [Rev. M. Zalizniak], "A Ministry of Love," *MM* (October 1916):278; Rev. S.C. Murray, "A Red Letter Day at Ethelbert, Man.," *MM* (February 1916):42–44.

57 Z, "A Ministry of Love," 279; Miss Smith, "Hugh Waddell Hospital, Canora, Saskatchewan," *MM* (April 1916):100; Rev. Maxim Zalizniak-Khizhniaksff, "The Ruthenians of Western Canada," *HMP* (March 1913):2–4; Cockburn, "Our Educational Work," 36; *MM* (February 1918):35–36; Dyde, "A Link Towards Assimilation," 148.

58 See "Notes," *HMP* (January 1911):160; Beveridge, "A Glimpse of the Work at Teulon," 37.

59 R.B. Arthur, "The Boys' Home," 157.

60 Arthur, "The Needs and Your Opportunity," 36. Arthur's sentiment was reaffirmed many times in the pages of *The Home Mission Pioneer*. See "President's Address," *HMP* (June 1910):12–16.

61 *HMP* (January 1911):163.

62 "A progressive School Boy, Teulon," *MM* (March 1915):89.

63 *Home Mission Work in the Loggers' Mission, Indian Missions, New Canadian Fields, All Peoples' Missions, School-Homes, Social Settlements* (Toronto: Presbyterian Church in Canada, Board of Home Missions and Social Service, 1922), n.p. Also see, "A Foreign 'Boy Teacher' in a Foreign Colony," *MM* (February 1917):55; "Efficiency and Zeal in the Work at Teulon," *MM* (February 1918):45; "Editorial," *MM* (June 1915):163; *Our Near Field* (Toronto: Presbyterian Church in Canada, Women's Missionary Society, 1917), 4–5.

64 *MM* (January 1918):3.

65 Kipp, "With Our Indian and Foreign Children," 76.

66 *MM* (January 1918):3.

67 Rev. E.H. Edmison, "European Immigration," *MM* (October 1918):275–76.

68 *Home Mission Work in the Loggers' Mission*, n.p.; W.H. Pike, "The Flame," manuscript, UCA, 28–29.

69 See: Paul Yuzyk, *The Ukrainian Greek Orthodox Church of Canada, 1918–1951* (Ottawa: University of Ottawa Press, 1981), chaps. 2–4; and, especially, *Acts and Proceedings*, 1913–1919, Reports of the Board of Home Missions and the Board of Home Missions and Social Service.

70 Palmer, *Patterns of Prejudice*, 176–78.

71 See: Yuzyk, *The Ukrainian Greek Orthodox Church of Canada*, 49–53; Jaroslaw Petryshyn, "Canadian Perceptions of the North-West and the East Europeans, 1891–1914: The Case of the Ukrainians," Journal of Ukrainian Studies, vol. 6, no. 2 (Fall 1981):43–65; Grant, "Reaction of WASP Churches," 7–8; *Acts and Proceedings*, 1905, Appendices, 10–11; *Acts and Proceedings*, 1906, Appendices, 13–14; *Acts and Proceedings*, 1915, Appendices, 41. Throughout the reports on Western Canadian Presbyterian missions in *The Home Mission Pioneer* and *The Missionary Messenger*, intelligence of the Independent Greek Church and its successor was provided. For a participant's view of the inception of the Independent Greek Church, the role of the Presbyterian Church and the problems experienced by the Ruthenian ministers, see John Bodrug, *The Independent Greek Church* (Toronto: Ukrainian Canadian Research Foundation, 1980) and Edward Bodrug, "John Bodrug: Ukrainian Pioneer, Preacher, Educator, Editor in the Canadian West, 1897–1913," manuscript, UCA. Also see Charles Grosvenor Ross, "A Visit to Wakaw," *MM* (May 1915):142; and Rev. E.H. Oliver, "The Ruthenians of Saskatchewan," *MM* (May 1916):144.

NELLIE L. MCCLUNG

The Nellie L. McClung papers are held by the Provincial Archives of British Columbia.

1 W.A. Dunbar, typescript of poem found in McClung papers, vol. 22.

2 Wm. Arthur Deacon, "A Western Woman," *Mail and Empire*, Toronto (9 November 1935), McClung papers.

3 Nellie L. McClung, *The Stream Runs Fast* (Toronto: Thomas Allen Limited, 1945), x.

4 Nellie L. McClung, *Clearing In The West* (Toronto: Thomas Allan Limited, 1935), 281–82.

5 McClung, *The Stream Runs Fast*, 16.

6 Ibid., 75.

7 Ibid., 61.

8 Nellie L. McClung, "An Insistent Call," undated pamphlet published by Woman's Missionary Society, the Methodist Church in Canada, p. 5, UCA.

9 *Free Press News Bulletin*, Winnipeg, undated clipping, McClung papers.

10 The account is fully told in McClung, *The Stream Runs Fast*, 101–06.

11 Quoted by C. Savage in *Our Nell* (Saskatoon: Western Producer Prairie Books), 87, from clipping in McClung papers from Carman Handard, 11 June 1914.

12 McClung, *The Stream Runs Fast*, 115.

13 Ibid., 125.

14 *Portage la Prairie Graph* (14 May 1914), clipping, McClung papers, vol. 35.

15 McClung speech, "The Social Responsibilities of Women," McClung papers, vol. 23, folder 3, 35–41.

16 Ibid., 36.

17 Ibid.

18 Ibid., 37.

19 Nellie L. McClung, "Before They Call" (Toronto: Board of Home Missions, United Church of Canada, 1937), 32.

20 Nellie L. McClung, "The Religion of Labour."

21 Nellie L. McClung, *In Times Like These* (Toronto: McLeod and Allen, 1915), 20, 21.

22 Ibid., 108.

23 Ibid., 109.

24 Ibid., 112, 113.

25 *The Acts and Proceedings of the Forty-Eighth General Assembly of the Presbyterian Church in Canada*, 1922, 279, 280.

26 *The Acts and Proceedings of the Forty-Ninth General Assembly of the Presbyterian Church in Canada (Port Arthur)*, 1923, 620.

27 *Proceedings of the Fifth Ecumenical Methodist Conference* (Toronto: The Methodist Book and Publishing House), 1921, 257, 258.

28 Ibid., 259.

29 "Ordination of Women to Ministry Left Undecided," undated clipping, McClung papers, vol. 17. The date, judging from the content of the article, was probably Friday, 14 September 1928. Of the title of the newspaper, all that is visible is "Free Press Eve."

30 Nellie L. McClung, "Shall Women Preach," *Chatelaine* (September 1934), 15.

31 Nellie L. McClung, *More Leaves From Lantern Lane* (Toronto: Thomas Allen Publishers, 1937), 184, 186.

32 In 1927, McClung was a co-appellant of Emily Murphy's historic question to the Supreme Court of Canada: "Does the word Persons in Section 24 of the British North America Act, 1867, which details the eligibility of persons to the Senate include female persons?" When the case was heard in March 1928, the ruling was that it did not. Murphy and her co-appellants appealed the decision before the Privy Council in London, England, and on 18 October 1929 the decision was reversed and women were declared to be persons!

33 McClung, *The Stream Runs Fast*, 212.

SALEM BLAND

1 It is quite understandable, of course, that he is treated so in such works as: David Jay Bercuson, *Confrontation at Winnipeg* (Montreal: McGill-Queen's University Press, 1974), 5–7; Ramsay Cook, "Introduction," Catherine Cleverdon, *The Woman Suffrage Movement in Canada* (Toronto: University of Toronto Press Reprint, 1974), 47–48. A Ross McCormack, *Reformers, Rebels and Revolutionaries: The Western Canadian Radical Movement, 1899–1919* (Toronto: University of Toronto Press, 1977), 87, 134; John Herd Thompson, *The Harvest of War: The Prairie West, 1914–1916* (Toronto: McClelland and Stewart, 1978), 31, 38, 105, 126, 135.

2 *Manitoba Free Press* (hereinafter cited as *MFP*) (17 September 1903), 3.
3 See Salem Bland papers, no. 428, "Echoes of the Conference of 1903," UCA.
4 Educational address, 14 March 1903, Bland papers, no. 23, UCA.
5 *Methodist Magazine and Review*, 56 (July–December 1902):377.
6 *MFP* (29 September 1903), 16; *MFP* (30 September 1903), 16.
7 See Irene Spry, "The Great Transformation: The Disappearance of the Commons in Western Canada," in Richard Allen, ed., *Man and Nature on the Prairies* (Regina: Canadian Plains Research Center, 1976).
8 *Canadian Men and Women of the Time*, 1912.
9 See W.L. Morton, *Manitoba, A History* (Toronto: University of Toronto Press, 1957), chap. 9.
10 *MFP* (14 June 1904), 8; *MFP* (31 October 1904), 6.
11 *MFP* (29 June 1904) 10; *Vox Wesleyana* 8 (November 1903):34–35.
12 *Telegram* (5 October 1903). See also *MFP* (21 November 1903), 5.
13 *Vox Wesleyana*, vol. 2, no. 6 (1898), 178.
14 "The Needfulness of Fellowship," 1 August 1896, Bland papers, no. 342.
15 *Vox Wesleyana* 8 (November 1903):35.
16 *MFP* (10 October 1903), 5; *Vox Wesleyana*, vol. 7, no. 6 (1903):106; vol. 16, no. 6 (1912):1–5; "Thoughts on Art," 7 December 1907, Bland papers no. 43; "Talk on Reading," November 1906, Bland papers, no. 37.
17 "Paul's Greatest Prayer," 15 June 1903, Bland papers, no. 417; *Vox Wesleyana* 10 (November 1905):10–12.
18 Ibid.
19 "Christian Perfection," 4 December 1880, Bland papers, no. 243. See also Richard Allen, "Salem Bland: The Young Preacher," *The Bulletin* (United Church Archives), no. 26 (1977):82
20 See the citations in Morton Paterson, "The Mind of a Methodist: The Personalist Philosophy of George John Blewett in its Historical Context" (paper presented to the World Methodist Historical Society, Toronto, 1977).
21 Minutes of Methodist Ministerial Association, 1903–1913, UCA-MNO.
22 Ibid., 14 October 1907.
23 *Western Methodist Bulletin* [later *Western Methodist Times*], December 1904. Thirteen issues of the paper exist spanning December 1904 to July 1906, all in the Salem Goldworth Bland collection, UCA.
24 *MFP* (28 June 1904), 4.
25 These views of Bland's are scattered through such frequently delivered addresses and sermons as numbers 1, 2, 10, 381 in the Salem Bland collection, UCA.
26 "The Saints for the Age," Bland papers, no. 16; "Four Steps and a Vision," Bland papers, no. 18.
27 "The Social Ideal," 13 February 1905, Bland papers, no. 28.
28 Journal of Manitoba Conference, 9 June 1905, 21; 13 June 1905, 38–9; Minutes of Manitoba Conference, 1905, 66–67, UCA-MNO.
29 *MFP* (4 December 1905), 13; *MFP* (9 December 1905), 13; "Winnipeg Politics," 3 December 1905, Bland papers, no. 33.
30 *The Voice* (1 December 1905), 6.
31 Journal of Manitoba Conference, 9 June 1905, p. 23; 13 June 1905, p. 36; 11 June 1906, p. 62; 12 June 1906, p. 65; 16 June 1908, p. 129, UCA-MNO.
32 See reading lists, Bland collection, UCA.

33 "The Place of the Kingdom of God in the Preaching of Today," 12 February 1906. For some reason, this address, which I used in my Master's thesis, "Salem Bland and the Social Gospel in Canada" (University of Saskatchewan, 1916), is not listed in the finding aid for the Bland papers compiled later by Mary Vipond.

34 See title page with date of delivery, "Four Steps and a Vision," Bland papers, no. 18.

35 The upshot for Bland was probably more a radicalizing and historicizing of idealism than a full turn to empiricism as laid out in S.E.D. Shortt, *The Search for an Ideal* (Toronto: University of Toronto Press, 1976).

36 Adolf Harnack, *What is Christianity?*, 4th ed., trans. Thomas B. Saunders (New York: Williams and Norgate, 1923); "The Place of the Kingdom of God in the Preaching of Today," 12 February 1906.

37 Ibid.

38 *MFP* (9 March 1907), 3.

39 Lane to Bland, 3 May 1907, Bland papers, no. 885, miscellaneous correspondence.

40 Ibid., Whittaker to Bland, 13 February 1907.

41 William H. Brooks, "Methodism in the Canadian West in the Nineteenth Century" (Ph.D. dissertation, University of Manitoba, 1972), 327, 340.

42 See such sermons and addresses as: "The Contribution of the College Man to the National Life," 24 April 1904, Bland papers, no. 431; "The Spell of Jesus," 11 December 1904, Bland papers, no. 436; "Christianity a Spirit rather than a Creed," June 1907, Bland papers, no. 441; "Study of Comparative Religion," 27 November 1907, Bland papers, no. 442; and "The Duty and Difficulty of Preserving Unity in the Church," 20 March 1896, Bland papers, no. 339.

43 *Selkirk Weekly Record* (21 October 1910), 1; see also: *Crystal City Carrier* (24 December 1903), 1; *The Western Prairie*, Cypress River (4 March 1904), 4; *The Neepawa Press* (13 November 1906), 1; *The Holland Observer* (1 November 1907), 1; *Carberry News* (21 January 1910), 1; *The Stonewall Argus* (4 May 1910).

44 *The Killarney Guide* (19 November 1914), 1; and (25 November 1914), 5.

45 *Grain Growers' Guide* (26 February 1913), 7, 10.

46 *Christian Guardian* (8 July 1908), 9–10.

47 G.N. Emery, "The Methodist Church and the 'European Foreigners' of Winnipeg, the All Peoples' Mission, 1889–1914," paper read before the Historical and Scientific Society of Manitoba, series 3, no. 28, 1971–72, pp. 85–100; *Vox Wesleyana* (December 1908):62–63; Faculty minutes, 15 January 1919, p. 304.

48 *The Voice* (2 May 1910).

49 14 January 1911, Bland papers, no. 449.

50 "Signs of the Times," 26 February 1911, Bland papers, no. 450.

51 *MFP* (21 November 1903), 5.

52 Winston Churchill, *The Inside of the Cup* (New York: Macmillan Co., 1914); "Winston Churchill's *The Inside of the Cup* or Religion no substitute for Justice," 3 August 1914, Bland papers, no. 455. It is instructive to compare the Rev. Frederick DuVal's treatment of the same book as reported in the *Manitoba Free Press* (4 August 1913). DuVal holds the issue at arm's length and gives the congregation an easy out. See also *Grain Growers' Guide* (6 August 1913), 847.

THE LABOR CHURCH IN WINNIPEG

In this volume, the British spelling is used for such words as *honour* and *labour*. The founders of the Labor Church used the American spelling. We respect their usage and use "Labor Church" throughout this article.

1 J.S. Woodsworth, *The First Story of the Labor Church* (Winnipeg: Labor Church Publication, 1920), 14.

2 Richard Allen, in *The Social Passion: Religion and Social Reform in Canada, 1914–1928* (Toronto: University of Toronto Press, 1971), chap. 1, gives a well-documented account for the basis of the social gospel in Canada.

3 See B.G. Smillie, "The Social Gospel in Canada: A Theological critique" in Richard Allen, ed., *The Social Gospel in Canada* (Ottawa: National Museum of Canada, 1975), 320ff.

4 The writings of Charles Kingsley, George Eliot, William Morris, and the preaching of Hugh Price Hughes and Mark Pearse were also important.

5 Allen, *Social Passion*, 4.

6 Ibid., 17f, to which this section is indebted.

7 Ibid., 17.

8 "He could not accept the interpretation put by his church upon baptism and the Lord's Supper, he did not believe in the doctrine of the atonement; he had difficulties about the religious experience of conversion and about many other things. . . ." (Frank H. Underhill, "James Shaver Woodsworth: Untypical Canadian" [Ontario Woodsworth Memorial Foundation, 1944], 11).

9 J.S. Woodsworth, *Strangers Within Our Gates* (Toronto: 1909 and 1972), 129.

10 J.S. Woodsworth, *My Neighbour* (Toronto: The Missionary Society of the Methodist Church, 1911), 327–28. While he was a student at Mansfield College, Oxford, Woodsworth spent some months at Mansfield House, London, and from this experience modelled his People's Forum.

11 Ibid., 328.

12 See Dennis Butcher, "Rev. Dr. Salem G. Bland" (unpublished honours paper, University of Manitoba, 1970). Note especially Bland's earlier efforts (1911) with Dr. C.W. Gordon in the Great West Saddlery dispute where conditions were particularly discouraging for the workers.

13 A.E. Smith, *All My Life* (Toronto: Progress Books, 1949), 42.

14 Ibid., 43.

15 Allen, *Social Passion*, 84.

16 See J.M. Bliss, "The Methodist Church and World War I," *Canadian Historical Review* 49 (September 1968). It should be noted that pacifist sympathies were not dead within the Church and revived again strongly in the 1920s and 1930s.

17 Richard Allen, "The Crest and Crisis of the Social Gospel in Canada: 1916–1927," (Ph.D. dissertation, Duke University, 1966), 31.

18 David Summers, "The Labor Church and Allied Movements of the Late 19th and 20th Centuries" (Ph.d. dissertation, Edinburgh University, 1958), 6. There were also other efforts, among them those of S.S. Craig in Toronto, Herbert Cassion in Lynn, Massachusetts, and several others in Canada, all of which are beyond the scope of this paper.

19 Grace MacInnis, Summers and Allen all posit a British-influenced church, but F.L. Paulley believes that "similar conditions simply gave birth to similar institutions."

20 Summers, "Labour Church," 83.

21 Woodsworth, *First Story*, 8.

22 Ibid.

23 Found among the Woodsworth papers in the Provincial Archives of Manitoba, PAM.

24 Woodsworth, *First Story*, 8.

25 D.C. Masters, *The Winnipeg General Strike*, (Toronto: University of Toronto Press, 1950), 50.

26 *The People's Church Hymn Book*, n.p., n.d., p. 45.

27 A.E. Smith, Dr. Bland, S.J. Farmer and F.L. Paulley, John Queen, A.A. Heaps and a host of others spoke frequently, while R.E. Bray and R.B. Russell also appeared (*Western Labor News* [hereinafter cited as *WLN*], 18 July 1919).

28 *WLN* (17 January 1919).

29 W. Irvine, "The Labor Church in Canada," *The Nation*, vol. 110, no. 2861, (May 1929):584.

30 Allen, "Crest and Crisis," 108.

31 William Ivens's personal papers, PAM, no author, no date. Also quoted in D. Pratt, "William Ivens and the Winnipeg Labor Church," (B.D. thesis, St. Andrews College, Saskatoon, 1962).

32 Woodsworth, *First Story*, 15–16.

33 Pratt, "William Ivens," 64–66.

34 *WLN* (23 July 1919).

35 Woodsworth, *First Story*, 11.

36 Ibid., 12.

37 R. McNaught, *A Prophet in Politics* (Toronto: University of Toronto Press, 1967), 100–02, lists some of the various interpretations: "to establish a Canadian Soviet Government"; "merely to improve wages, working conditions, labour's bargaining position"; "part of a grand revolutionary plan." See also A. Ross McCormack, *Reformers, Rebels, and Revolutionaries: The Western Canadian Radical Movement 1899–1918* (Toronto: University of Toronto Press, 1979), 165ff.

38 Allen, "Crest and Crisis," 88.

39 McNaught, *Prophet in Politics*, 177.

40 The exceptions would be Armstrong and Johns, although R.B. Russell is recorded as having addressed the Labor Church only after his arrest, and then only a few times (*WLN*, 18 July 1921; *One Big Union Bulletin* [hereinafter cited as *OBU Bulletin*], 5 November 1921).

41 McNaught, *Prophet in Politics*, 129.

42 *WLN* (11 July 1919). Also reproduced in part in Woodsworth, *First Story*.

43 The Canadian census of 1921 was the only time the Labor Church was listed as a separate sect.

44 This has a peculiarly scriptural ring, as when Jesus said to the "they" of his day, "When I was with you day after day in the temple [the Methodist Church?] you did not lay hands on me" Luke 22:53.

45 *The King* vs. *Ivens*.

46 Allen describes the Walker Theatre incident, in which there were three cheers for the Soviet Union and similar unacceptable behaviour.

47 *The King* vs. *Ivens et al.* Also recorded in Pratt, "William Ivens," 45.

48 Masters writes that "Ivens was near collapse after addressing the jury for 14 hours" (Masters, *Winnipeg General Strike*, 122). Pratt maintains, "Ivens began speaking on Thursday afternoon, continued all day Friday until 10 p.m., and concluded Monday morning, a total of 20 hours" (Pratt, "William Ivens," 47).

49 *The King* vs. *Ivens*; Pratt, "William Ivens," 45.

50 Grace MacInnis, *J.S. Woodsworth: A Man to Remember* (Toronto: The Macmillan Co. of Canada Ltd., 1953), 155.

51 See "Information Respecting the Russian Soviet System and Its Propaganda in North America," p. 14. Pratt says that "apparently" Robertson wrote and published a pamphlet attacking the Labor Church, but a search of the Dominion of Canada Archives and of the Parliamentary Library, kindly instituted by Mr. Stanley Knowles, revealed only the article referred to.

52 Allen, "Crest and Crisis," 221.

53 See the statements issued by the Committee on Social Service and Evangelism of the Methodist Church, 1918; see also the editorial comments and articles in the *Christian Guardian* during the Winnipeg Strike.

54 Allen, "Crest and Crisis," 221.

55 "Notes on the Labor Churches," quoted in Allen, "Crest and Crisis," 200. See Allen, *Social Passion*, 169–73, for an account of the Hamilton-Moore correspondence and its results.

56 Allen, "Crest and Crisis," 217.

57 Ibid., 220.

58 D. Butcher, "Salem G. Bland," 32.

59 Pratt, "William Ivens," 70. Summers says about the British Labor Church, "The majority [of lecturers] were more concerned with electioneering and with political problems." (Summers, "Labor Church," 94).

60 Allen, *Social Passion*, 169.

61 For example, P.F. Lawson declared in Edmonton that "anyone who believed in a God helping the workers accomplish their emancipation was a traitor to the working class" Allen, *Social Passion*, p. 163.

62 *OBU Bulletin* (13 January 1927): "Comrade Miller of Ft. Rouge, who has had considerable experience in the Labor Sunday School, led the class in singing." *OBU Bulletin* (3 February 1927): "The Weston Labor S.S. has loaned its song books. . . . They have also offered us the children's library."

63 For example, *OBU Bulletin* (5 January 1928): "West End Forum" with F.J. Dixon, same address as the Labor Church. Woodsworth was another popular speaker, presumably between sessions in Ottawa.

64 Interview with the writer, April 1974.

65 Interview with the writer, February 1974.

66 Pratt, "William Ivens," 113.

67 Summers, "Labour Church," 602.

PRINCIPAL J.H. RIDDELL

1 John H. Riddell, "Gateways to a Life of Service: An Autobiography," (unpublished manuscript, n.d., ca. 1941–43). Further details on his career can be obtained in: David Owen, "Dr. J.H. Riddell," *Winnipeg Free Press* (13 November 1952); Minutes, Alberta College Board of Directors Minutes, Provincial Archives of Alberta; "Obituary by George B. King," biography file, UCA. A study which contains some revealing parallels is Michael Bliss, *A Canadian Millionaire: The Life and Business Times of Sir Joseph Flavelle, Bart., 1858–1939* (Toronto: Macmillan, 1978). The Wesley College years are best examined in A.G. Bedford, *The University of Winnipeg: A History of the Founding Colleges* (Toronto: University of Toronto, 1976).

2 Riddell, "Gateways to a Life of Service," 234.

3 Ibid., 239.

4 Executive Minutes, 23 December 1919, Wesley College (hereinafter cited as wc) Board of Directors, WC-5-5, uwa.

5 Minutes of Proceedings of Manitoba Conference, 1918, Methodist Church.

6 "Residence Life" by W.M.S., March 1931, *Vox Wesleyana*, 42–43; Minutes of wc Students' Representative Council (hereinafter cited as src), WC-5-26, uwa.

7 Executive Minutes, 30 May 1925, wc Board of Directors, WC-5-6, uwa.

8 They wished that "a higher type of life" be pursued at the College; Minutes, 19 October 1921, wc Faculty Committee, WC-5-12, uwa.

9 Executive Minutes, 5 May 1922, wc Board of Directors, WC-5-12, uwa.

10 Minutes, 20 April, 20 April (evening) and 27 April 1922, wc Faculty Committee, WC-5-12, uwa.

11 Executive Minutes, 27 April 1932, 6 February 1933, 23 February 1934, wc Board of Directors; Minutes, WC-5-6, 21 February 1934, Faculty Committee, WC-5-15, uwa.

12 Minutes, 6 February 1930, wc Faculty Committee, WC-5-14, uwa.

13 Minutes, 11 March 1926, wc Faculty Committee, WC-5-13, uwa.

14 The issue can be followed in the Minutes, 11 March 1926, 16 May 1928, 30 October 1928, 6 February 1930, 31 December 1930, 19 January 1931 and 28 April 1932 of the wc Faculty Committee, WC-5-13 and WC-5-14, uwa.

15 Minutes, October 1919, 5 January 1923, 19 January 1923, WC-5-12; 6 March 1925, WC-5-13; 12 January 1933, WC-5-16, wc Faculty Committee; Executive Minutes, 6 February 1933, 23 February 1934, WC-5-6, wc Board of Directors.

16 Executive Minutes, Riddell to Rev. J.N. Anderson, History Department appointee, 11 June 1927, WC-5-6, wc Board of Directors.

17 The debate is joined in the Minutes of 28 February 1919 and 10 March 1919 of wc, src (WC-5-26). It is noted in the Minutes of 14 March 1919 of the wc Faculty Committee, (WC-5-12) and the above "solution" was drafted and passed at the 15 April 1924 faculty meeting.

18 Executive Minutes, 12 May 1924, WC-5-7, wc Board of Directors.

19 *Vox Wesleyana* (March 1930); Minutes, 1928, WC-5-13, wc Faculty Committee; Minutes, 17 February 1933, WC-5-15, wc Faculty Committee, which note that "Hebrew" students will be given a copy of "their own scriptures."

20 Minutes of Proceedings of Manitoba Conference, 1921, Methodist Church, uca-mno.

21 W.L. Morton, *One University: A History of the University of Manitoba 1877–1952* (Toronto: McClelland and Stewart, 1957); Riddell, "Gateways to a Life of Service"; Bedford, *University of Winnipeg*.

22 Riddell, "Gateways to a Life of Service"; Methodist Church, Minutes of Manitoba Conference, 1918, Methodist Church, uca-mno.

23 Minutes, 19 October 1921, WC-5-12, wc Faculty Committee.

24 Executive Minutes, 10 June 1927, 11 July 1927, WC-5-6, wc Board of Directors.

25 *A Synopsis of the Report of the Royal Commission Appointed to inquire into and report upon the Penal System of Canada*, prepared by J.H. Riddell (Winnipeg:[n.p.,]); *The Eldership: A Study in Official and Individual Privilege and Responsibility in the Christian Church* (Toronto: United Church of Canada, 1940); "Gateways to a Life of Service: An Autobiography"; "Living Together: A Study in the Social Life of Canada" (unpublished manuscript, n.d., ca. 1946); *Methodism in the Middle West* (Toronto: Ryerson, 1946).

26 Executive Minutes, 1917, WC-5-4, wc Board of Directors; Bland-Irwin file, uwa; Minutes, 1917, 1918, 1919, Manitoba and Saskatchewan Conferences, Methodist Church. A conditional bequest by J.T. Gordon was said to have been involved (Riddell, "Gateways to a Life

of Service," 275–76). The context is discussed in Richard Allen, *The Social Passion: Religion and Social Reform in Canada, 1914–28* (Toronto: University of Toronto Press, 1971) and Richard Allen, "Children of Prophecy: Wesley College Students in an Age of Reform," *Red River Valley Historian* (1975), 15–20.

27 Smith Case Correspondence, Riddell-Smith letters, January to May 1921, and Smith Case Miscellaneous File, WC-10-1, UWA.

28 Arnup to Riddell, 7 February 1921, Creighton to Riddell, 3 February 1921, T.W. Neal to Riddell, 16 February 1921, all Smith Case Correspondence, WC-10-1, UWA.

29 Riddell to Smith, 14 March 1921, Smith Case Correspondence, WC-10-1, UWA.

30 Undated Riddell memorandum outlining his view of the issues, Smith Case miscellaneous file, WC-10-1, UWA; Smith Case, Examination of Plaintiff for Discovery, 7 February 1923, and Examination of Dr. Riddell for Discovery, 17 February 1923, Court of King's Bench.

31 The trials are discussed in Vera Fast, "Smith, Riddell and Wesley College" (unpublished essay, 1976).

32 Ashdown to Smith, 24 March 1922, Smith Case Correspondence, WC-10-1, UWA.

33 J.L. Granatstein *The Ottawa Men: The Civil Service Mandarins, 1935–1957* (Toronto: Oxford University Press, 1982), 208–12. Lower's memoirs provide an interesting perspective upon Wesley College but do not mention this episode; Arthur R.M. Lower, *My First Seventy-Five Years* (Toronto: 1967). A different view on the College is given by Watson Kirkconnell in *A Slice of Canada: Memoirs* (Toronto: University of Toronto Press, 1967).

34 Riddell, "Gateways to a Life of Service," 457.

35 A.E. Vrooman memorandum, Smith Case miscellaneous file WC-10-1, UWA; Committee and Church Reports, Board Committee re Principal, 10 January 1923, Smith Case miscellaneous file, WC-10-1, UWA.

36 J.H. Riddell, "The Student and World Problems," *Vox Wesleyana* (December 1922).

37 J.H. Riddell, "Popularity," *Vox Wesleyana* (November 1923).

38 Riddell statement at funeral of T.A. Burrows, *Vox Wesleyana* (March 1929).

39 "Wesley College Portraits: The Principal," *Winnipeg Tribune* (30 April 1935).

A HERITAGE OF HEALING

1 Hospital Reports, Elizabeth M. Crowe Memorial Hospital, Eriksdale, Manitoba, p. 65, UCA.

2 *Home Mission Pioneer* (May 1912), published monthly by the Women's Home Missionary Society of the Presbyterian Church in Canada, from a report by Mrs. H.M. Kipp, secretary of the society.

3 Hospital Committee Report, Board of Home Missions/Womens' Missionary Society, the United Church of Canada (1929), p. 5.

4 *The History of the Woman's Missionary Society in Manitoba 1884–1959, The United Church of Canada* [Jean Spence, historian, Manitoba Conference Branch].

5 Hospital Committee Report, Board of Home Missions/Women's Missionary Society, the United Church of Canada (1929), p. 5.

6 *Home Mission Pioneer* (March 1914), 183, a report to the Women's Home Missionary Society by Dr. A.J. Hunter, missionary doctor at Teulon.

7 Ibid., July/August, 1908, report by Mrs. H.M. Kipp.

8 Ibid., vol. 3, 1906, report by Rev. Campbell Munro, missionary at Ethelbert.

9 Mary Quartarone McElroy, "United Church Hospital, Ethelbert, Manitoba, 1927–1929," notes compiled in 1982 from a consultation with her grandmother, Lenore Kirk (nee Shaldemose), who was a nurse at Ethelbert between 1927 and 1929.

10 Margaret J. (Mustard) Crookes, *Built by a Woman*, autobiographical account of her work at Gypsumville, pages not numbered, UCA-MNO.

11 *Home Mission Pioneer* (March 1914), 184.

12 Minutes, Vita Hospital Board, 15 April 1924, Vita Hospital collection, UCA-MNO.

13 Edward Shillito, "What Medical Missions are Not," *The United Church Record and Missionary Review* (February 1934):4.

14 A.J. Hunter, *A Friendly Adventure* (Toronto: Committee on Literature, General Publicity and Missionary Education of the United Church of Canada, 1929), 11–14.

15 *Home Mission Pioneer*, vol. 3, 1906, excerpt from a letter by Dr. A.J. Hunter to Mrs. H.M. Kipp, 6 February 1906.

16 Ibid. (December 1913), 139, report by Dr. A.J. Hunter.

17 Hospital Reports, Ethelbert, Manitoba, p. 15.

18 Crookes, *Built by a Woman*.

19 Minutes, Vita Hospital Board, 3 December 1923, clipping from the *Christian Guardian*, Vita Hospital collection, UCA-MNO.

20 *The History of the Woman's Missionary Society in Manitoba 1884–1959, The United Church of Canada*, p. 96.

21 Lucy Lindell, *Memory Opens the Door*, history of the Eriksdale community (Altona: published privately, n.d.), 114.

22 Bible, Nehemiah 4:6.

23 *The Planting of the Faith* (Toronto: Women's Missionary Society of Presbyterian Church in Canada, 1921), 256.

24 *17th General Council Record of Proceedings* (Toronto: United Church of Canada, 1956), Commission on Church Hospitals, p. 156.

25 *Missionary Monthly*, vol. 3, no. 2 (February 1928), publication of Woman's Missionary Society of the United Church of Canada.

26 *Year Book* (Toronto: The United Church of Canada, 1927) 121.

27 Crookes, *Built by a Woman*.

28 Hospital Reports, Ethelbert General Hospital, no page number.

29 *Home Mission Pioneer* (May 1912), 141.

30 *The United Church Record and Missionary Review* (February 1934):7.

31 Crookes, *Built by a Woman*.

32 Hunter, *A Friendly Adventure*, 25–26.

33 Bible, Hebrews 11:32.

34 Hunter, *A Friendly Adventure*, 132.

35 Minutes, Vita Hospital Board, 30 June 1943, 29, Vita Hospital collection, UCA-MNO.

36 Lindell, *Memory Opens the Door*, 114.

37 *Winnipeg Tribune* (19 May 1947).

38 *Stories From Vita* Manitoba Conference files.

39 Hunter, *A Friendly Adventure*, 59–61.

40 *Missionary Monthly*, vol. 5, no. 2 (October 1932):462.

41 *17th General Council Record of Proceedings* (Toronto: United Church of Canada, 1956), Commission on Church Hospitals, p. 156.

42 Minutes, Board of Home Missions, The United Church of Canada, 1952–53, 14–16 April 1953, pp. 72–73, UCA.

43 Malcolm C. Macdonald, *From Lakes to Northern Lights*, review of mission enterprises in Canada, (Toronto: the Committee on Missionary Education, the United Church of Canada, 1951) 111.

44 *The United Church Record and Missionary Review* (January 1929):19.

45 Bible, 2 Timothy 4:7.

CHURCH UNION AND WESTERN CANADA

1 E.H. Oliver, *The Winning of the Frontier* (Toronto: United Church Publishing House, 1930), vi, 252.

2 See the pamphlet, *Address by Rev. Edmund H. Oliver, Ph.D., Principal of Presbyterian Theological College, Saskatoon, Sask., at a Complimentary Banquet given by Sir James Wood, K.C.M.G., January 9, 1923* (Toronto: Presbyterian Church Union Movement Committee, 1923).

3 Ibid.

4 Ibid.; and Thomas Bengough, "Stenographic Report of the Proccedings before the Private Bills Committee of the House of Commons, concerning the United Church of Canada Act," 2 vols., UCA. The idea that the Methodists and Presbyterian churches alternate stations down the various prairie railroad lines is Oliver's. The idea that this begin in 1899 was also Oliver's. While discussions were held in 1899, the plan did not materialize in the West until 1911. See the pamphlet, *Agreement for Co-operation in Home Mission Work Between the Presbyterian, Methodist and Congregational Churches in Canada*, 1911, UCA, Co-operation and Local Union, box 2, file 23.

5 Ibid.

6 W.G. Brown, "The Alberta Plan for Co-operation in the Home Mission Fields," *Presbyterian* (2 February 1911), 139–40.

7 *Address by Rev. Edmund H. Oliver, 1923.*

8 Ibid.

9 *Record of Proceedings 1925*, 5–6, 15.

10 See R.D. Tannahill to George Dorey, 6 March 1961, UCA, Co-operation and Local Union, box 1, file 18. In this letter, Tannahill states: "The record of Local Union Churches has disappeared. It was in the hands of Rev. John Reid of the Bible Society, who was secretary of the council, and on his death, his widow, who was a stranger to it all, disposed of the records, how and where we have been unable to discover." In the same file see also James G. Gardiner to George Dorey, 26 June 1961. Gardiner also indicates that he cannot find any records, although he was on the executive of the Union Churches of Canada. He states that he sent his materials to the Rev. W.H. Hughes, his minister at Lemberg, Saskatchewan, who was the field and financial secretary of the Council.

11 *Acts and Proceedings 1924*, 380–82, 384–85, 388–91, 394–99.

12 Oliver circulated four maps: (a) Halifax Presbytery; (b) Northern Ontario; (c) Manitoba; and (d) Saskatchewan. See Bengough, "Stenographic Report."

13 Bengough, "Stenographic Report."

14 W.A. Cameron to J.W. MacNamara, 5 February 1923, Presbyterian Church Association Papers, case 1, file 4.P.C., Archives, Knox College, Toronto.

15 Bengough, "Stenographic Report."

16 Cameron to MacNamara, 5 February 1923.

17 Ibid.

18 C.E. Silcox, *Church Union in Canada* (New York: Institute for Social and Religious Research, 1933), 216–30.

19 *Address by Rev. Edmund H. Oliver, 1923.*

20 *Acts and Proceedings 1925 (Part II)*. "A Summary of Non-Concurring Congregations to June 10, 1925" appears in the appendix, 17–36. [United Church readers should note that Part II is the *Acts and Proceedings of the 1925 General Assembly of the Continuing Presbyterian Church in Canada* which is rarely available in United Church libraries.]

21 McConnell to J.W. MacNamara, 8 February 1924, Presbyterian Church Association Papers, case 3, file 39.P.C.A., Toronto. This letter contains a full report of the meeting at Norwood Church. See also the *Winnipeg Free Press* (6 February 1924), 6.

22 *Winnipeg Free Press* (8 February 1924), 2.

23 In 1924 there were eight presbyteries in the Synod of Manitoba. The opponents of union secured churches in all but two of these presbyteries: Glenboro and Dauphin. Their largest gains were in the presbyteries of Winnipeg, Portage la Prairie and Brandon. There is nothing in the existing literature, however, which would explain why there was more opposition in some presbyteries than in others.

24 Peter Strang, *History of Missions in Southern Saskatchewan* (Regina: published by the author, 1929).

25 *Acts and Proceedings 1924*, 444–45.

26 *Winnipeg Free Press* (15 February 1924), 4.

27 *Edmonton Journal* (7 March 1924), 8.

28 *Edmonton Journal* (13 March 1924), 18.

THE CHINESE UNITED CHURCH OF WINNIPEG

1 Malcolm C. Macdonald, *From Lakes to Northern Lights* (Toronto: United Church of Canada, 1951), 92.

2 S.S. Osterhout, "Orientals in Canada," 106.

3 Files of Chinese United Church, Winnipeg, Conference office.

4 Ibid.

5 Ibid.

6 Ibid.

7 Ibid.

8 Minutes, Board of Home Mission, April 1962.

9 Paper prepared by Dr. Alexander Pan in observance of the 66th Anniversary of the Chinese United Church of Winnipeg, 1983.

GEORGE RODDICK

1 History of the Brandon Hills Church from the program for the centennial celebration of Cornwallis Municipality, Manitoba, 8 July 1984.

2 Rev. George Roddick, "Reminiscenses of the Very Early Years," *The Brandon Sun* (Brandon, Manitoba: 1898) reproduced 1 March 1910.

3 Interview with Mrs. Ethel Nimmo, a niece of Elizabeth Roddick at Durham, Nova Scotia, August 1883.

4 Record of the Roddick and Johnson families compiled by Harriet and Dorothy Roddick at Carthage, Texas, 1980.

5 Martin Kavanagh, *The Assiniboine Basin* (Brandon, Manitoba: 1946), 117.

6 Record of the Roddick and Johnson families by H. and D. Roddick.

7 Last will and testament of James Roddick of West River, Nova Scotia, 26 May 1870.

8 Record of Roddick and Johnson families by H. and D. Roddick, p. 2.

9 Ibid.

10 T. Cummings, Presbytery Clerk, Presbytery of Pictou, Presbyterian Church of Canada, Minutes, 16 January 1879.

11 *Eastern Chronicle*, New Glasgow, N.S., 27 March 1879 (Halifax: Nova Scotia Archives), recorded 2 August 1983.

12 Beecham Trotter, *The Horseman of the West* (Toronto: The MacMillan Company of Canada, 1925), 56.

13 "Blue Hills of Brandon Settled by Pictonians," *The Brandon Daily Sun*, (1 March 1910).

14 Presbytery of Manitoba, Presbyterian Church of Canada, Minutes 17 September 1879.

15 Ibid.

16 Roddick, "Reminiscences of the Very Early Years," records the marriage of John Barron at Pine Creek, near Austin, Manitoba.

17 The Big Plain area is now known as "Beautiful Plains" and includes the communities of Carberry, Neepawa and Gladstone in Manitoba.

18 Presbytery of Manitoba, Minutes, 20 May 1880.

19 Charles W. Gordon, *The Life of James Robertson* (Toronto: The Westminster Company, 1908), 203.

20 Ibid.

21 Ibid.

22 Ibid., 204.

23 Methodist Conference, Minutes, August 1883, p. 5.

24 Minutes of the Assembly, Presbyterian Church of Canada, 1884–1896.

25 *The Brandon Hills Story* (Winnipeg: Murray McPherson, 1979), 13.

26 Ibid.

27 Ibid.

28 Ibid.

29 Ibid.

30 *Municipal Memories* (Brandon: Cornwallis Centennial Committee, 1984), 67.

31 Ibid.

32 Ibid., 328.

DAND UNITED CHURCH

The writer is grateful for the work done by Marguerite Miller and Jack Whetter and for the assistance of Bill Whetter and Eva Cassils (nee Godfrey) in the preparation of this article.

1 Even in recent years, some people in the area have been baptized as adults, no baptism having been available in the Quaker church of their youth.

2 Minutes of the Hartney Monthly Meeting of Friends, quoted in "Chain Lakes Quaker Church," *Golden Memories: A History of the Dand Community* (Dand Women's Institute, 1967), 3.

3 Ibid.

4 Ibid.

5 Ibid., 7 July 1908, 5.

BLEST BE THE TIE

The following resources were used in the writing of this piece: minutes and records of Sioux Narrows United Church, including various letters; *Nestor Falls, A Collection of Memories* (not dated, but clearly published since 1980); the personal recollections of Doug and Sue Obee. The author wishes to acknowledge the contribution of Howard Groom in writing this article.

A LONG GOODBYE TO MOTHER CHURCH

Howard and Louise Albright's relationship was characterized by warmth and strength, and they were devoted to the life of Grace Church. Louise died in 1948, but Howard was a vital and active part of Grace's story to the very end. The author feels that Louise's presence in the unfolding action of the play as a living character in the final chapters of the story of Grace is essential in order to emphasize the significance of their contribution to the Church.

1 Minutes of Winnipeg Presbytery, 10 May 1955, UCA-MNO. Presbytery refused to specify an amount or percentage to which Grace congregation would be entitled from the proceeds of the sale of Grace Church.

2 "Dr. Best [Superintendent of Home Missions] made this statement years ago: 'There is a barrel of money in Grace Church property; let it be sold and the congregation scatter to other churches' " (H.H. Albright to Dr. George Dorey, 15 July 1955, UCA-MNO, Grace Church collection.)

3 "I had thought of an appeal to yourself and the sub-executive but – why – You were asking the guidance of Presbytery – Presbytery claimed the right of disposition [of the monies realized in the sale] so I cancelled that thought as useless. I appreciate your sympathies as was expressed in a letter some time ago but the members of our board feel it very strange that neither yourself nor Dr. Long contacted us or Dr. Martin while at Conference in Brandon or while in Winnipeg" (Ibid.)

4 "Sunday School Union," *Manitoba Daily Free Press* (3 January 1890), 4. This article contains an account of the first gathering of all the teachers and officers of the Methodist Sunday Schools. These statistics from that article indicate the dedication to temperance of the Methodist movement and Grace Church, in particular.

	Teachers	Scholars	Temperance Pledges
Grace	42	544	315
Zion	40	308	110
Wesley	29	190	109
McDougall	21	268	43
Ft. Rouge	18	94	
	150	1,378	542

5 Grace Church Collection, letter, H.H. Albright to Gordon Sisco, Secretary, General Council of the United Church of Canada, 20 June 1953. "We are the headquarters of the Salvation Army Tag Day Appeal; the Mount Carmel Sanatorium (Jewish) Tag Day; The Manitoba Wheelchair Organization; The Arthritic Association monthly meeting. To all this may be added the use of the hall for educational, medical and religious conferences and conventions. Particular mention should be made of the Templeton Crusade. All the noon meetings were

held at Grace where a record attendance was established (2,200). . . . The after-church
Fireside hour is the finest institution in the west . . . with its average attendance of 250"
(H.H. Albright to Gordon Sisco, secretary, General Council of the United Church of
Canada, 20 June 1953, Grace Church collection.

6 *Manitoba Daily Free Press*, Evening Bulletin (15 October 1921), 31.

7 George Young, *Manitoba Memories: Leaves From My Life in the Prairie Provinces 1868–1884*
(Toronto: William Briggs, 1897), 187–93.

8 "The Retiring Pastor of Grace Church Takes Leave of His Congregation," *Manitoba Daily
Free Press* (23 June 1890), 5. The quote is from Rutledge's farewell sermon based on Acts
4:8–12 as reported in the article. The character of W.L. Rutledge, as portrayed in this play,
owes more to dramatic license and a knowledge of how fashions change in the church than to
historical research.

9 W.L. Rutledge served Grace Church for three years as the sixth minister of the new Grace
Church built on the corner of Notre Dame and Ellice in 1883. He returned to the east in 1890
at the end of his term at Grace.

10 "Retiring Pastor," *Manitoba Daily Free Press* (23 June 1890).

11 Information on the sewing machine from Grace Church collection, service leaflet, 5 January
1913.

12 *Grace Church Bulletin*, vol. 1, no. 6 (February 1911):1, Grace Church collection.

13 *Winnipeg Tribune* (14 March 1939), 8.

14 C.L. McIrvine, *A Short History of Grace Church* (Winnipeg: Grace Church, 1920).

15 Minutes of the Executive Committee, Grace Church Collection. These minutes record the
several discussions, hopes and fears related to the properties and the mounting debt
repayment problems, including a plan to appeal for funds from the Forward Movement.

16 The 203 Battalion, called the Hard and Dry Batallion, contained a platoon recruited from
the Young Men's Club of Grace Church. This Club had frequently enjoyed sessions with J.S.
Woodsworth, a former assistant pastor at Grace (1902 to 1906) and a devout pacifist.

17 McIrvine, *Short History*, 2.

18 James A. Richardson, Isaac Pitblado and Gordon H. Aikins. Aikins was a member of
Grace, and a son of Sir James Aikins, K.C., a former lieutenant-governor of the province.
Sir James had provided much of the original support to McIrvine's fund-raising campaign
and vowed to continue the leadership of that drive upon McIrvine's death. Unfortunately,
his own death in 1929 intervened. Pitblado was a widely respected lawyer and businessman
whose faith and curiosity often led him to explore issues others would have rejected out of
hand. Richardson was a highly innovative businessman who preferred to maintain a low
profile in his support of a wide range of church and community affairs. Together these three
discharged the mortgage and held the property in trust for the benefit of the United Church
of Canada in Winnipeg and Manitoba.

19 "At the very commencement of J. Richmond Craig's ministry in Sept. 1929, the late Mr. R.T.
Riley announced from the pulpit on a Sunday morning that arrangements had been made for
the congregation of Grace Church to have the use of the plant at the nominal rent of $1.00
per year on the understanding that they would enthusiastically promote the downtown cause
and develop it." Other than this, the congregation did not seem to have been involved either
in setting the direction of ministry or in choosing the new minister. (E.R. Tennant to
Commission, entered as testimony, 14 June 1948, Grace Church collection, file 1, General
Council Commission on Grace Church, Winnipeg, 1948).

20 Craig's report was presented to the Trustees and the Presbytery representatives at the
Manitoba Club. The term *institutional social engineer* comes from the enthusiasm of that

report. His vision for Grace can be seen in this exerpt: "Grace occupies the most strategic center of all and immediately presents a challenge to the institutional social engineer. The location is the best of the three [Knox, Central and Grace churches] . . . In connection therewith there is sufficient land upon which to erect a modern downtown structure that would be revenue producing as well as ideal for the carrying on of church and associated institutional programs. The only danger in this idea is to guard against the tail wagging the dog" (Grace Church collection, file 1, report of J. Richmond Craig to the trustees of Grace Church, May 1929, p. 2.)

21 A former Minister of Education in the provincial government of Ontario, W.G. Martin was a skillful orator, a popular after-dinner speaker, a lecturer on his many travels, a weekly fixture on radio with his Children's Radio Broadcasts, and, according to the *Winnipeg Tribune* (2 January 1939, p. 3), he held the "marrying parson title" for a second year in a row, beating Dr. Duckworth of St. Andrew's and Rev. J.W. Clarke of Knox. He conducted 148 marriages to claim the honour.

22 The congregation of Grace fought the transfer of the title of the property to the General Council on the floor of General Council (*Proceedings of the General Council*, 21 September, 1948, pp. 66, 117–19) opposed the terms of the trustee relationship before a special General Council commission, opposed the sale of the property in 1950 because they thought the price ($100,000) too low, and opposed the right of Winnipeg Presbytery to determine the disposition of the capital realized from the sale of the property (Minutes of Winnipeg Presbytery, 9 March 1955). All the way, they fought for what they believed in but could never achieve – a viable Grace Church. They fought for the right to "serve the truly downtown areas of Winnipeg . . . at the core of hotels, office buildings, and business houses, etc. where we believe God has a right to be represented" ("Grace Church, A Statement," *Winnipeg Free Press*, 21 May 1955). (Thomas Hill to Alexander Robertson, 11 April 1955, Grace Church collection.)

23 The Winnipeg firm of Osler, Hammond and Nanton were busy soliciting tenants for the "new ten-storey, four million dollar Manitoba Merchandise Mart," the building to be ready for June 1956. Office space was promised at the rate of four dollars per square foot but the mart never saw the light of day. Thomas W. Hill of New York (originally a Portage la Prairie native) re-sold the property to a local group whose plans to build a five-decker parkade on the old Grace site made new headlines. This venture, too, failed and no further development has ever taken place. The site is now a paved parking lot.

Editors and contributors

RICHARD ALLEN, professor of Canadian history at McMaster University, is the author of *The Social Passion: Religion and Social Reform in Canada, 1914–1928* and other studies of the social gospel in Canada. A former professor at the University of Regina, he was founder of the Canadian Plains Research Center. He is currently a member of the Ontario legislature and has for some time been working on a biography of Salem Bland.

JOHN BADERTSCHER, a United Church layman, is associate professor of religious studies at the University of Winnipeg. He received a Ph.D. from the Divinity School of the University of Chicago. His publications have been in the area of ethics in contemporary civilization.

DENNIS BUTCHER, minister of Atlantic–Garden City United Church in Winnipeg, has served on the Conference Archives Committee since 1976 and the national United Church Committee on Archives and History since 1980. He was ordained in 1973, and is a graduate in history from the University of Manitoba and in church history from Princeton Theological Seminary.

N. KEITH CLIFFORD is professor in the Department of Religious Studies at the University of British Columbia. He is a past-president of the Canadian Society for Church History and is currently a member of the editorial board of *Studies in Religion*. His publications include *The Resistance to Church Union in Canada 1904–1939* and numerous articles and reviews.

VERA FAST has recently completed her doctoral studies in history at the University of Manitoba and is currently a research fellow in St. John's College at the same University. Her publications include *Missionary on Wheels* and *God's Galloping Girl: The Diaries of Monica Storrs* with W.L. Morton.

GERALD FRIESEN teaches history at the University of Manitoba. He is a native of Prince Albert, Saskatchewan. His publications include *A Guide to the Study of Manitoba Local History* with Barry Potyondi, and the recently published *The Canadian Prairies: A History*.

CAROL L. HANCOCK is completing her work for a master's degree with a thesis on Nellie L. McClung. After being ordained in 1977, she served two United Church parishes in Saskatchewan. She currently lives in Armstrong, British Columbia, with her husband, the Rev. F. Stephen Willey, and their daughter Kate.

GORDON HARLAND is head of the Department of Religion of the University of Manitoba. He is the author of *The Thought of Reinhold Niebuhr* and several articles on American and Canadian religious history. An ordained minister of the United Church of Canada, he has lectured and preached widely across Canada and the United States.

HARTLEY J. HARLAND is a retired minister of the United Church of Canada, having served the Church for many years, chiefly in Birtle Presbytery. He was statistical secretary of Manitoba Conference for many years and is a member of the Archives Committee of the Conference.

GERALD M. HUTCHINSON, born in Alberta of Quaker and Presbyterian origins, was drawn into Methodist historical study through an interest in Robert Rundle. He is a retired minister of the United Church, having served the Student Christian Movement, several rural churches in Alberta and as executive-secretary of Alberta Conference.

CATHERINE MACDONALD has been archivist of the United Church Archives, Conference of Manitoba and Northwestern Ontario, since 1975. In 1983 she completed an M.A. in Canadian history at the University of Manitoba with the thesis entitled "George Bryce: Manitoba Scientist, Churchman and Historian, 1844–1931."

IAN MACDONALD was ordained in 1971 and has been a member of the ministry team at Augustine United Church, Winnipeg, since 1979. Most of his writing efforts culminate in weekly puppet skits performed during worship at Augustine.

JAMES D. MARNOCH is a retired Presbyterian minister who has served pastorates in Manitoba and Ontario. A former moderator of the Synod of Manitoba and Northwestern Ontario, he is currently writing a history of the Synod.

MARGARET MCPHERSON is assistant archivist, United Church Archives, Conference of Manitoba and Northwestern Ontario. She is a graduate in science and education from the University of Manitoba. Actively involved in the United Church at the presbytery and conference levels, she has a special interest in the role of women in the church.

MURRAY MCPHERSON is a professor in the Faculty of Education at the University of Manitoba. Born and raised in the Brandon Hills district of Manitoba, he edited *The Brandon Hills Story*. An active layman in the United Church, he serves on conference and national church committees as well as in the church men's organization, AOTS (As One That Serves).

SUE OBEE lived for ten years at Sioux Narrows, Ontario, where she served on various committees of the United Church. Currently she and her husband, Doug, and their daughter, Anne, divide their time between Winnipeg and Sioux Narrows where they operate a summer business.

MICHAEL OWEN has recently completed doctoral studies at the Ontario Institute for Studies in Education. He holds an M.A. in education from the University of Alberta and has actively pursued his interest in social, educational and religious history as a researcher for the Jackman History of Canadian Methodism Project.

DONALD ROSS served congregations in Thunder Bay, Pinawa and Hamilton before becoming minister of Crestview United Church, Winnipeg, in 1975. He has received training in church music and has special interests in liturgy and church architecture.

J. CLARK SAUNDERS is minister at Charleswood United Church, Winnipeg. He holds an M.A. in modern history from the University of Toronto and has done post-graduate work in liturgy at Cambridge University. Two of his articles on worship in nineteenth-century Scotland have been published by the *Liturgical Review*, Edinburgh.

NEIL SEMPLE received his Ph.D. in Canadian history from the University of Toronto and has worked as assistant archivist at the Central Archives of the United Church. He has edited the *Papers* of the Canadian Methodist Historical Society and has published several articles on the transformation of nineteenth-century Canadian Methodism, the changing status of "childhood," and revivalism in English Canada.

BENJAMIN G. SMILLIE is professor of church and society at St. Andrew's College, Saskatoon. His doctoral thesis at Columbia University was done on J.S. Woodsworth. His publications include *Keep Awake With Me* (Lenten Book), *Political Theology in the Canadian Context*, and *Visions of the New Jerusalem: Religious Settlement on the Prairie*.

RAYMOND R. SMITH, currently convenor of the Archives Committee, Conference of Manitoba and Northwestern Ontario, is a retired minister who has served pastorates in Saskatchewan and Alberta and administrative offices in Manitoba. He has written several articles on mission and stewardship concerns of the United Church and was editor of the conference newsletter called "Cross Currents."

A. McKIBBIN WATTS, dean of the Faculty of Theology at the University of Winnipeg, received his Ph.D. from the University of Edinburgh. A United Church minister, he has served in rural congregations and for twelve years was chaplain at the University of Manitoba. He is editor of the journal, *Touchstone: Heritage and Theology In a New Age*.